National Security for a New Era

Globalization and Geopolitics

Donald M. Snow

University of Alabama and University of South Carolina, Beaufort

PEARSON
Longman

New York   San Francisco   Boston
London   Toronto   Sydney   Tokyo   Singapore   Madrid
Mexico City   Munich   Paris   Cape Town   Hong Kong   Montreal

Vice President and Publisher: Priscilla McGeehon
Executive Editor: Eric Stano
Senior Marketing Manager: Megan Galvin-Fak
Managing Editor: Valerie Zaborski
Project Coordination and Electronic Page Makeup: Stratford Publishing Services, Inc.
Cover Designer/Manager: Nancy Danahy
Cover Images (clockwise from left): Photodisc Inc./Getty Images; © AP/Wide World; background montage: © digitalvision/Getty Images.
Manufacturing Buyer: Alfred C. Dorsey
Printer and Binder: R. R. Donnelley and Sons Company-Crawfordville
Cover Printer: Coral Graphic Services

Library of Congress Cataloging-in-Publication Data

Snow, Donald M.
    National security for a new era : globalization and geopolitics / Donald M. Snow.—1st. ed.
        p.   cm.
    Includes bibliographical references and index.
    ISBN 0-321-08881-6
        1. National security—United States.   2. United States—Military policy.   3. World Politics—
1995–2005.   I. Title.

UA23.S5253 2004
355'.033073—dc22   2003024464

Copyright © 2004 by Pearson Education, Inc.

Please visit our website at http://www.ablongman.com

ISBN 0-321-08881-6

3 4 5 6 7 8 9 10—DOC—06 05 04

Contents

PART II   THE CHANGING WORLD   153

CHAPTER 6 Security, Interests, and Power   155

CHAPTER 7 The Foreign and Domestic Environments   181

Preface

Between 1985 and 1998, I published four editions of *National Security*. During that period, the environment in which national security matters are considered changed radically with the collapse of Soviet communism and the consequent artifice of the Cold War that had provided the framework for national security. The end of the Cold War provided a traumatic event, what I call a *fault line* in the pages that follow. The perfidious attacks on the World Trade Center and the Pentagon on September 11, 2001 represented the second great trauma for national security analysis.

The times have changed sufficiently that the old ways of looking at things contained in my earlier book and its various editions seem woefully inadequate to understand current and future realities. It seemed to me that it was time to construct a new, fresh way to look at "national security for a new era." The pages that follow represent my attempt to provide such a fresh look.

Things have changed in many ways reflected in this new effort. One way in which change is manifest is in thinking about basic paradigms of how the international system works. As the subtitle suggests, the alternative models are the globalization of the 1990s and the geopolitics of the Cold War and, arguably, the period since 2001. The question is which will be dominant in a national security environment that has elements of both. Another way in which the environment is different is that national security concerns have broadened from a strictly military base to include elements that are semi-military (terrorism) and non-military (economic security). The three pictures on the cover are designed to depict this distiction between military, semi-military, and non-military problems.

This new text is, in some sense, a lineal descendent of my previous work on national security. Readers familiar with that work will find some familiar materials here—the chapter on the American military experience, for instance. At the same time, there is a great deal of change. Reflecting the changed American place in the world, there is considerable emphasis on problems that were much more muted during the Cold War—asymmetrical warfare, terrorism, and the extension of the campaign against terrorism to places like Afghanistan and Iraq. There is even a chapter on peacekeeping and state building that might have been handy to those designing the post-war phase of the Iraqi campaign. Recognizing that many of the students who will read this book lack much historical perspective on the material, I have tried wherever possible to point directly to the relevance of material to the present, both in the text and the accompanying feature boxes (*Amplifications* and *Challenge!*).

No work of this magnitude is accomplished alone. During the drafting and redrafting of the text, I have benefited from the useful comments and suggestions of a number of reviewers whose suggestions have strengthened the effort. They include: Valentine J. Belfiglio, Texas Woman's University; Patrick J. Haney, Miami University; Christopher M. Jones, Northern Illinois University; Richard J. Kilroy, Jr., Regent University; Edward G. Moore, University of Texas at Brownsville; Linda L. Petrou, High Point University; and Chris Van Aller, Winthrop University. Any remaining errors are, of course, my own.

Donald M. Snow
Tuscaloosa, Alabama

INTRODUCTION

Framing the Problem of National Security

Since the tragic events of September 11, 2001, American concern for national security has been almost totally focused, some might argue transfixed, by the problem of international terrorism and its likely recurrence on American soil. In the immediate wake of the airplane hijackings that ended with those airplanes being used as missiles against highly visible and symbolic American economic (the World Trade Center towers) and military (the Pentagon) targets, the astonished reaction was of a world fundamentally transformed by the acts of Usama bin Laden and his terrorist organization, Al Qaeda. We launched a military campaign against Afghanistan to overthrow the government there, which had provided the terrorists sanctuary, and began a manhunt for the elusive bin Laden and his cohorts that continues to this day. The national security establishment reoriented itself to a primary emphasis on suppressing terrorism and preventing its recurrence. The invasion and conquest of Iraq in 2003 by the United States and its coalition partners was partly justified as part of the terrorist campaign as well.

The transition has been difficult, partly because of the nature of the new challenge, terrorism. Although actions that most observers would call *terrorism* are certainly not very new, their application by foreigners on American soil *is* novel. Domestic acts that might be labeled terrorist have certainly occurred sporadically throughout American history—the assassination of American presidents, for instance, or the bombing of the Murrah Federal Building in Oklahoma City in 1995. At times, Americans overseas have been the victims of terrorist attacks; during the 1990s, for example, the same Al Qaeda network that committed the September 11 acts was implicated in attacks against the American embassies in Dar es Salaam, Tanzania, and Nairobi, Kenya, in 1998 and against an American warship, the USS *Cole*, moored in a Yemeni port. The September 11 attacks dwarfed these previous actions physically and conceptually: thousands of people were killed in the shocking events, which were committed by foreigners on our own soil.

Part of the ensuing confusion was conceptual as well. Although a small community of analysts has studied the problem and likelihood of terrorist activity for years, the subject of terrorism had not previously caught the public attention. There is, for instance, a great deal of disagreement about what exactly constitutes terrorism. After

September 11, definitions became expansive, with more and more phenomena defined as acts of terrorism. Part of the problem was that there is little agreement on what is or is not terrorism. Although it is not an unassailable definition, we will define terrorism for our purposes as the use of unpredictable violence to achieve political ends. Thus, actions must possess two basic characteristics to qualify as terror: they must employ violence in ways that are hard to anticipate in advance, and they must be linked to some political objective.

Although we will analyze the problem of terrorism later in this volume, our basic interest is broader. Our primary problem and focus is the national security situation that faces the United States and the policies the United States has or should adopt to confront that situation. Clearly, international terrorism is an element in that equation—arguably the predominant influence in the contemporary environment—but it is not the entire problem.

To look at the national security problem—to begin thinking about national security—I will introduce and outline two primary emphases that will recur in the chapters that follow. One of these emphases is the theme of change, which has two aspects in light of the September 11 events: (1) the extent and depth of change that the terrorist attacks introduce into the calculus of national security; and (2) the changed dynamics of the environment in light of critical events in the past decade or more—chiefly, the changing nature and profundity of threat. The second emphasis is on the basic nature of the national security environment, and I will introduce and examine two fundamental depictions: an environment dominated by international economic growth and expansion (globalization) and one dominated by military threats and plans for what to do about them (geopolitics). The geopolitical viewpoint predominated during the Cold War, which is the backdrop of the current period, and although it has returned to dominance since September 11, 2001, the roots of that return entered the White House with George W. Bush in the form of a series of advisers known as the "neo-conservatives." The globalization viewpoint dominated the decade between the two most traumatic, environment-altering experiences in recent history—the end of the Cold War and September 11.

THE NATURE OF CHANGE

As noted, the question of change is really two questions: how much the environment has truly been altered by events such as those of September 11 and what dominant characteristics of the national security environment have resulted from the changes that have occurred. Because of the proximity of some of the events, there is not consensus on either of these matters. In these introductory pages, we will introduce perspectives that will be elaborated in the body of the text.

How Much Has Changed?

Immediately after the trauma of September 11, the almost universal reaction of Americans and many people overseas was that the change wreaked by the suicide air bombers was profound—that *everything* (at least figuratively) had changed. With the benefit of some elapsed time since, a second, more muted interpretation has emerged, which argues that the roots of change were present before the bombers struck and that those influences remain as prominent aspects of the national security environment. From this perspective, the underlying dynamics have not changed so much as have the vivid demonstrations of some of the most dramatic, traumatic implications of those dynamics. Each perspective deserves at least brief elaboration.

The popular view of the impact of September 11 on the national security environment is that it represents a fundamental, encompassing alteration of the problems facing the United States in the world and the way in which these problems must be confronted. Partially born of the sheer magnitude and audacity of the events and their vivid, relentless depiction on television (notably, the second airliner crashing into the north tower of the World Trade Center), the initial reaction was that everything had changed—a perception largely reinforced by the volume and emphasis of the news media and by political figures. The terrorist acts were so atrocious and so alien to the conceptualizations of most Americans that it was easy to view this as a "new kind of war," which Americans had difficulty understanding.

Two related elements stand out from the initial shock. The first was the realization of physical vulnerability facing Americans. As pointed out in Chapter 3, one of the unique and favorable parts of the American historical experience has been the virtual invulnerability of American soil to foreign attack. The last time there was an organized physical assault on American soil was during the War of 1812. Although Soviet nuclear forces were capable of destroying the United States physically during the Cold War (see Chapter 4), American soil has seldom been threatened, and the integrity of the American homeland has rarely been a source of major concern. The terrorist breach of American invulnerability was thus particularly shocking. Although international terrorists did not (and do not) threaten American existence in the way that Soviet rockets did, our vulnerability to harm (if not extinction) was established.

The second, related aspect was the continuing nature of vulnerability and the realization that the problem would not dissipate soon. This "new kind of war" would not be climactically decided on some major battlefield, where the perpetrators would be decisively vanquished. Rather, the "war on terrorism" would be a long and difficult *campaign* (to borrow the description of French President Jacques Chirac) that would take considerable time and vigilance.

Were these perceptions accurate reflections of the panorama of change caused by the visitation of international terrorism on American soil? Or were the perceptions hysterical and distorting, even to the point of overemphasizing elements of change and underestimating continuity? The answer is probably a little bit of both.

A contending interpretation suggests that less has really changed than was presumed immediately after the tragedy. This assertion that not a great deal has changed emphasizes continuities in the pre– and post–September 11 environments. It suggests, for instance, that the basic sources of instability in the international system before the events came from the most unstable countries of the developing world— and that they still do. During the 1990s, the manifestations of this instability were largely chaotic civil conflicts that I call new internal wars (discussed in some depth in Chapter 11), for which the policy question was whether they were important enough for our involvement. Contemporary conflicts continue in some of these states, and they are the same kinds of places that provide the apparent breeding grounds for terrorism, the eradication of which is the current underlying policy rationale. In the 1990s, the United States joined an international humanitarian effort in Kosovo; in 2001, the United States assisted in the overthrow of the Taliban government on the grounds of denying sanctuary for terrorists, followed by "regime change" in Iraq in 2003. For these efforts ultimately to succeed, we will have to engage in state-building activities so that the target countries will emerge as stable places that eschew violence and terrorists (also discussed in Chapter 11). Is that a sign of change?

At the same time, terrorism was a problem before 9/11, and it continues to be a problem. Usama bin Laden had attacked Americans before his most spectacular foray, and he remains a potential menace. The anti-terrorism community had been warning of possible terrorist attacks directly against the United Sates for years, but their warnings had largely gone unheeded (at least partially because previous warnings had proven false). While it is true that essentially no one had predicted the scale, exact nature, or audacity of the attacks that did occur, it is equally true that terrorism did not come into existence on September 11. At the same time, the notion that this represents some novel method of war also does not stand up on any vigorous assessment of the history of warfare.

New Dynamics in the Environment?

The last fifteen years have been an especially dynamic period in the evolution of American national security. As argued primarily in Chapter 3, the first two hundred years of the republic witnessed two major periods in national security terms. The first of these was what I will call the *formative period*, lasting from the birth of the Republic to World War II. This period was distinguished by a relatively low order of priority for national security concerns and relatively low commitments to defense matters, with "spikes" of concern when the country was thrust into war situations, followed by a return to the normalcy of peacetime. The second period was the Cold War, from the late 1940s until the implosion of Soviet communism in 1991 (the subject matter of Chapter 4). This period was distinguished from its predecessor because it was the first sustained American involvement in national security affairs, when the United States developed and maintained large standing armed forces in peacetime, and when the prevailing paradigm was the national security state (the situation in which preserving the integrity of the state is a major defining purpose of government). It was also the first time the very existence of the United States became a matter of concern, as Soviet nuclear weapons could physically destroy the United States as a functioning society—although admittedly with likely terrible consequences for the Soviet Union as well.

The period from the downfall of Communist regimes in Europe in 1989 through the terrorist events of 2001 produced large changes in American national security problems. Two major events—which we will call "fault lines"—have largely defined those perceived changes. As a result of September 11 in particular, there has also been a growing belief that the nature of warfare itself may be changing.

Fault Lines.   What is a *fault line*, as I am using the term? The main idea of the analogy is that fault lines represent traumatic events that alter the environment and require an adjustment in the post-traumatic period—akin to the ruptures of physical fault lines on the earth's surface that create earthquakes. The notion is fundamentally compatible with the concept of "tectonic shifts," which Graham Allison introduced over a decade ago to describe the impact of the implosion of Communist rule.

Two of these fault lines have emerged since 1989 and have altered the national security environment in fundamental ways. Both are discussed extensively in Chapter 1 and elsewhere throughout the text, but I will introduce them here. The first fault line was the end of the Cold War, symbolized by the peaceful implosion of the Soviet Union and the fall, in most cases peacefully, of Communist regimes there and elsewhere. The net result has been the end of both the military and ideological competition between the Communist states led by the Soviet Union (and to some extent China) and the West, led by the United States. Only four states in the world remain technically Communist today, and two of those—China and Vietnam— have renounced Marxist economics, a major underpinning of the ideology. (Only North Korea and Cuba remain staunchly Communist.) In systemic terms, this fault line is the more consequential of the two, because it affects the very nature of the operation of the international system and the basic threats to that system's existence

The second fault line is the emergence of international terrorism through the events of September 11, 2001. As noted, those events and their aftermath have had their main impact on the United States (many other states had already experienced this phenomenon and made whatever adjustments they could to it). The impact of this traumatic event has been to raise awareness of a vulnerability not previously acknowledged and to mobilize government and society to try to reduce that vulnerability.

A comparison of the two fault lines is not without irony, particularly when the measure is the impact of the two on *threats*, which are the major concern of national security planning. Threats (promises to do harm in the absence of compliance with some demand) can be usefully analyzed on two criteria: the likelihood of their being carried out and the consequences of their actualization. Likelihood can range from virtually zero (when threats are false—bluffs—or the threatener cannot carry them out) to virtual certainty. Consequences, on the other hand, range from the ability of a threatening party to do great *harm* by carrying out a threat to the ability to imperil the *physical existence* of the state by carrying out the threat.

National security environments and the impact of lacerations of the fault lines can usefully be categorized in these terms. During the Cold War, the stakes were exceedingly high—certainly much higher than they are now—because the potential consequences of war between the superpowers and their allies (planning for which was the central national security problem of the era) included an all-out nuclear exchange. That the Cold War could escalate to a nuclear hot war was plausible in an environment of ideological and political competition for predominance in the world.

As the Cold War evolved, however, those very consequences contributed to a gradually lowering likelihood of war. As time passed and arsenal sizes and deadliness increased, both sides increasingly realized that a hot war could effectively destroy them both, leaving no winner. The result was what I call a *necessary peace*, a situation in which both sides avoid war not because of any mutual empathy but because of fear of the consequences of war. As argued in Chapter 4, that realization contributed to the perceptions leading to the end of the Cold War.

Exposure of the first fault line—the end of the Cold War—obviously changed the nature of the threat environment. Russia, as the major successor state of the defunct Soviet Union, maintained the nuclear power to destroy the United States, but the death of Communism left it without any plausible ideological reason to use such weapons against a former adversary that was gradually becoming a friend and even an ally. Although the arsenal sizes remain formidable, arms control agreements, culminating in 2002, have reduced their size on both sides, as noted in Chapter 8. Thus, the period ushered in by the end of the Cold War (roughly the 1990s) saw both a reduction in the likelihood of major threats being carried out and a gradual lowering of the consequences.

Exposure of the second fault line further changes the threat calculus in different ways. Al Qaeda, and probably other groups in the future, show a very high level of willingness to carry out threats that, as argued in Chapter 10, probably cannot all be prevented: Some will succeed. Thus, the likelihood of threats being carried out, in this case by international terrorists, has increased from the Cold War and post–Cold War periods, though it is impossible to specify in quantitative terms. While the drama and scope of the 9/11 attacks serve as stark testimony to the willingness to do as much harm as possible, the consequences of terrorist threats are considerably less than would have been the case had the Soviet Union launched a nuclear strike during the Cold War. The threat posed by terrorists, in other words, is to do harm, not to threaten the basic integrity of the American state. Should terrorists come into possession of some of the so-called weapons of mass destruction (WMD—including nuclear, biological, and chemical weapons)—as many fear and predict, the amount of harm they could do would increase; it is hard to imagine their development of a capability that would threaten the integrity of the United States.

The quality of the threat environment has thus evolved. The Cold War—the memory of which is slipping from our consciousness—was a very deadly environment (enormous potential consequences of war) but one that became less dangerous (lower likelihood that threats would be carried out) as time passed. The end of the Cold War gradually reduced the deadliness of threats both psychologically (reduction of motivation) and physically (arms control reductions of arsenal sizes) and reduced the dangerousness of threats as well, since they gradually dissipated.

The exception to the absence of plausible threats came from international terrorism, specifically the threats of Usama bin Laden and his adherents. As I have chronicled elsewhere (see Chapter 16 of *Cases in International Relations*), bin Laden's threats to do harm to the United States were pronounced publicly in a series of statements beginning in 1996, and he has shown a willingness to carry out those threats. Unless his capacity to do physical harm increases dramatically, however, such threats will remain at a much lower level of deadliness than was the case during the Cold War.

The Changing Nature of War?   Reaction to the terrorist attacks and subsequent analyses that include the ongoing American campaigns in Afghanistan and in Iraq have given rise to a popular notion that warfare may be changing, both in the sense that the terrorists are practicing a "new kind" of war and that, in the future, traditional, conventional forms of warfare may have to be altered or may become obsolete. These arguments are treated in some detail elsewhere: traditional forms of warfare in Chapter 8, the "new kind of war" in Chapter 9, and the Afghan experience in Chapter 11 (terrorism is discussed in Chapter 10). They are introduced here as part of the general introduction of the themes of this book.

The term to describe this phenomenon, somewhat popularized by Defense Secretary Donald Rumsfeld, is *asymmetrical warfare*. The term itself, which has previously been used as one of a number of more or less interchangeable ways to describe irregular warfare, is newer than the dynamic it purports to capture. In fact, the term refers to a form and approach to warfare as old as war itself.

At its base, asymmetrical warfare is defined as the situation in which both (or all) sides do not accept or practice the same methods of warfare. Asymmetry can extend both to the methods opposing sides use to conduct military operations and to the rules of warfare to which they adhere. Guerrilla warfare, which the United States encountered in Vietnam through the use of irregular enemy soldiers engaging in tactics such as ambushes, is one form of asymmetrical warfare. Terrorism is another. Those fighting asymmetrically may also reject the rules of war favored by their opponents—for example, consciously targeting civilians.

The concept of asymmetrical warfare implies its opposite: symmetrical warfare. Symmetrical warfare occurs when both sides fight in the same basic ways and follow the same basic rules. In the contemporary environment, symmetrical warfare generally refers to fighting between traditional, European-style armed forces (armies, navies, air forces) where both sides agree to be bound by the same rules of engagement, basically as specified in the various Geneva Conventions on war. A synonym for *symmetrical warfare* is *traditional war*. World War II was the epitome of symmetrical warfare (even if some isolated combatants fought asymmetrically). In the American and European tradition, it is the acceptable, "honorable" way of war.

Why would someone in effect break the accepted conventions and rules on war and fight asymmetrically (a synonym for which is *dishonorably*)? The historical answer is clear: What we now call asymmetrical warfare is the approach of a weaker foe trying to overcome the advantages of a force that is superior in whatever the accepted, conventional forms of warfare of the time prescribe. If you know that you will lose if you play by the opponents' rules, then it only makes sense to reject those rules in ways that may turn your weakness into strength and negate your opponents' strengths. There is certainly nothing new or novel about this; in fact, it may be the only thing that makes sense for a weaker party.

Those who are stronger by conventional standards will always decry the resort to asymmetrical means. The U.S. Army would always prefer that its opponents face it in massed formations on conventional battlefields where overwhelming American firepower can be brought to bear to destroy the opponents. Inferior opponents would be foolhardy to cooperate in their own destruction by fighting the way the Americans prefer to fight. Therefore, they adopt other means.

Those who argue that asymmetrical warfare is becoming the norm may have a point, although they seldom recognize the irony of why they are correct. Since the end of the Cold War, the gap between American conventional (symmetrical) military capability and that of any conceivable foes has progressively widened. This gap was first demonstrated in the Persian Gulf War of 1990–91, and it has increased since. In 2002, for instance, the defense budget of the United States stood at about $350 billion, out of a worldwide total of about $800 billion. American military expenditures for 2002 were greater than the expenditures of the next fourteen largest spending states combined. The budget increases for 2003 pushed the U.S. total to over half the global total, meaning the United States spent more on defense than the rest of the world combined.

The result is a conventional, symmetrical military situation in which, effectively, *no state or probable combination of states can successfully confront and fight the United States symmetrically*, using conventional methods and rules. The very success of the American military machine is to negate its own advantage. Any potential adversaries contemplating fighting the Americans can only conclude that their only chance is to change the rules to negate the American advantage. In an act that amounts to an unconscious self-fulfilling prophecy, the United States has created the situation in which its future warfare will almost certainly be against opponents fighting asymmetrically.

The Afghanistan experience illustrates both this gap and how opponents can seek to reduce it. In essence, we will likely look back upon our experience in Afghanistan as having consisted of three fairly discrete parts—one completed and successful, one ongoing and inconclusive as of the middle of 2003, and one hardly yet begun. When the Afghan campaign is viewed this way, as it is in more detail in Chapter 11, both the distinction between symmetrical and asymmetrical warfare and the complexity of modern situations are illustrated.

Very briefly, the first phase consisted of American assistance in the overthrow of the Taliban. The United States used both traditional air forces and less conventional special operations forces (SOFs) in this campaign, the purpose of which was to aid the various anti-Taliban forces in their defeat of the terrorist-supporting government. For the most part, the campaign was basically conventional and symmetrical. The Taliban and the Northern Alliance were engaged in a conventional civil war, in which each side occupied territory and operated from defined, static lines. With the help of SOF spotters, American air forces were able to locate Taliban forces and subject them to overwhelming firepower, the American symmetrical preference. The Taliban could not take asymmetrical action, such as dispersal and hiding, because doing so would mean quitting the field in the face of their Afghan opponents. As a result, American assistance was effective, and the mutual objective of the Americans and the anti-Taliban forces was achieved.

The second phase, which has consisted of attempts to "wipe up" remaining Taliban and Al Qaeda forces, illustrates the difficulty of defeating an opposition that will not play by the established rules. After the Taliban were thrown from office, the remnants reverted to asymmetrical methods, retreating to and hiding in the mountains of Afghanistan and Pakistan to avoid annihilation. Initial American and Afghan ground attempts to locate and destroy them (e.g., Operation Anaconda) failed miserably, and the United States reverted to air attacks as the primary method. As of July 2002, these attacks had killed an estimated 800 Afghan civilians and an unknown number of Al Qaeda and Taliban. The original goal of capturing and killing bin Laden had been officially abandoned as unnecessary. It is not clear when, how, or if this phase will be concluded successfully.

The third phase, producing a stable Afghanistan that will resist future terrorist appeals (what I call *state building* in Chapter 11), has hardly begun. The purpose of this phase is to "drain the swamp" of those living conditions that make societies susceptible to the appeals of religious and terrorist fanaticism. The major emphasis of this phase will be on political and economic development and, to be effective, will require massive influxes of capital and expertise to transform the war-torn Afghan infrastructure. As of mid-2003, much more help had been promised than delivered.

The early assessment of Iraq offers a variation. American overwhelming strength caused both Iraqi conventional *and* nonconventional forces to collapse. Predictions of an urban guerrilla campaign did not materialize as the Americans swept into Baghdad. Instead, the opposition waited for the American forces to settle into occupation and then began attacking them in an apparently low-level, persistent manner.

GLOBALIZATION AND GEOPOLITICS

The other major theme of this book is the competition between the two conceptualizations of the international system: globalization and geopolitics. Which of these basic dynamics has dominated across time? Which is the paradigm that most accurately depicts the national security situation?

Raising the distinction in this manner is a reflection of the odyssey that international politics has traveled over the last fifteen years. Geopolitics, the perspective that views military conflict (or its potential) in a hostile environment against which national security preparations are largely defined militarily as the centerpiece of concern, is the historically dominant perspective. That perspective, captured in some detail in Chapter 2 in the form of the realist paradigm, was clearly the central perspective during the Cold War, and it has returned to a position of central importance since September 11, 2001 with the rise of the neo-conservatives. During the Cold War, of course, the overarching national security concern was confronting and containing an expansionist Communism in a competition primarily defined in military terms. This perspective emphasizes hostilities in the environment as a primary feature, in which the forces of "godless Communism" or the "axis of evil" and international terrorism may provide the hostile opposition.

The 1990s represented an interlude between geopolitical ascendancies. During the period between the end of the Cold War and September 11, the forces of economic globalization—the spread of market democracies and a gradually expanding economic prosperity globally—began to take hold and spread as the major dynamic of international life. This period coincided with a receding threat environment for the major powers, especially the United States. The implosion of Communism meant there was no major challenger to Western-style market democracy ideologically or physically. The violence in the system, as already mentioned, was concentrated in the poorest parts of the developing world, and while it was often ghastly and gruesome, it did not threaten the integrity of the international system nor compel military action. In this environment, the so-called American model of development reigned supreme.

The reason for casting a major thrust of our discussion in terms of these two forces is to help understand the direction of the present national security environment. It is not an either/or question, since both dynamics coexisted before and continue to operate. The threat environment that is the central concern of geopolitics was present during the 1990s in the form of forces such as those led by bin Laden, but they were less prominent and compelling. Similarly, the machinations of globalization continue in the post–September 11 atmosphere, but at a lower level of visibility. For example, the meetings of the Group of Eight (G-8) economic world leaders (which used to be the G-7 but admitted Russia in 2000 as a kind of honorary member) continue to be held and receive much public attention. The meetings of such organizations as the Asia-Pacific Economic Cooperation (APEC), which President Clinton attended annually with much ado, have faded from center stage, however.

The two dynamics also contradict one another, reflecting different worldviews on the parts of adherents of one force or the other. Globalization represents a highly internationalist approach to the world, placing global concerns and the reconciliation of international differences through international efforts at the center of national concerns. It raises idealist concerns with improving the human condition through international actions to a high priority and tends to view geopolitics through a more cooperative, multilateralist lens than does traditional geopolitics.

The geopolitical perspective is inherently more conservative and suspicious of the environment. Reflecting its grounding in traditional realism and its skeptical view of human nature, the geopolitical perspective emphasizes *national* security as its central value (as opposed to international security), and thus is more inward looking and prone to unilateral as opposed to multilateral solutions to problems. The neo-conservative philosophy represents the new thrust of geopolitics.

Which of these competing worldviews will dominate the early twenty-first century? In the immediate aftermath of the September 11, 2001, terrorist events, geopolitics enjoyed a renaissance as the United States responded to the activation of real threats that had been festering outside the spotlight of the 1990s. Support for globalization was eroding at the time, as the world economy slowed and was further buffeted by revelations of corporate malfeasance in the United States and the subsequent downturn of the world's stock markets. The Bush administration's "war on terrorism" was a clear expression of a geopolitical direction from a president who had campaigned in 2000 as a free trade advocate (one of the central values of globalization). Whether there will be a resurgence of economic globalization in the near and mid-term future is a possibility that we will explore.

CONCLUSION: QUO VADIS?

This brief introduction featuring the two emphases of the nature of change and the conceptual competition between globalization and geopolitics are intended to help frame the material that will follow. Because this book is intended as a core text for national security courses (although hopefully with an appeal beyond that core), the text will contain additional material necessary for a comprehensive overview of the field that does not neatly and directly tie into either theme. The discussion of nuclear weapons in Chapter 8, a part of the Cold War national security architecture but not clearly so central to the present, illustrates this situation.

Having said that, the text will proceed within the context of the two themes. Chapter 1 will elaborate on some of the themes cited in this Introduction and will add other organizing concepts, notably the division of the international system into two distinct categories (or tiers) of states and some preliminary assessment of how the United States fits into the system. As the Part I heading suggests, the following four chapters will deal with the context in which the current debate over themes exists: Chapter 2 explores the roots and content of the realist paradigm that is the conceptual base of geopolitics; Chapter 3 views the basic underlying forces that have colored the American worldview on national security matters; Chapter 4 concentrates on that part of the geopolitical past represented by the Cold War; and Chapter 5 ends the part with a discussion of the rise and content of globalization.

Part II deals more directly with the issue of change. It begins with Chapter 6, on the basic underlying concepts with which national security must deal—notably the idea of instruments of power—and how these have changed across time. In Chapter 7, we then review the contemporary environment through the dual lenses of depictions of that environment and institutional American responses to the environment. The part concludes in Chapter 8 with an assessment of how so-called traditional defense problems—the stuff of symmetrical approaches to war—have survived the end of the Cold War and into the future.

Part III looks at contemporary challenges to national security, emphasizing both the dynamics of change and the competition between geopolitics and globalization. Chapters 9 and 10 deal primarily with the assertions of change cited in this Introduction that represent changes in traditional geopolitical perspectives. Thus, Chapter 9 elaborates the discussion of whether there is a "new kind of war," and Chapter 10 surveys current geopolitical threats in areas such as regional conflicts, terrorism, and drugs. Chapter 11 reintroduces the emphasis on global conflict resolution through the ideas of peacekeeping and state building, the latter being a bridge concept between globalization and geopolitics by injecting non-military elements into geopolitical situations. Chapter 12 raises and probes the relationship between the two core concepts and their relationship to change in a dynamic environment. This relationship is further projected into the future in the single chapter of Part IV, which also suggests some ways in which the two concepts may be compatible and reconcilable.

SELECTED BIBLIOGRAPHY

Allison, Graham T. Jr. "Testing Gorbachev." *Foreign Affairs* 67, 1 (Fall 1988), 18–32.

Byford, Grenville. "The Wrong War." *Foreign Affairs* 81, 4 (July/August 2002), 34–43.

Campbell, Kurt M. "Globalization's First War?" *Washington Quarterly* 25, 1 (Winter 2002), 7–14.

Delpech, Therese. "The Imbalance of Terror." *Washington Quarterly* 25, 1 (Winter 2002), 31–41.

Doran, Michael Scott. "Somebody Else's Civil War." *Foreign Affairs* 81, 1 (January/February 2002), 22–42.

Hoffmann, Stanley. "Clash of Globalizations." *Foreign Affairs* 81, 4 (July/August 2002), 104–15.

Howard, Michael. "What's in a Name?" *Foreign Affairs* 81, 1 (January/February 2002), 8–13.

Kagan, Robert, and William Kristol (eds.). *Present Dangers: Crisis and Opportunities in American Foreign and Defense Policy.* San Francisco, CA: Encounter Books, 2000.

Miller, Steven E. "The End of Unilateralism or Unilateralism Redux?" *Washington Quarterly* 25, 1 (Winter 2002), 15–30.

O'Hanlon, Michael. "A Flawed Masterpiece." *Foreign Affairs* 81, 3 (May/June 2002), 47–63.

Rotberg, Robert I. "The New Nature of Nation-State Failure." *Washington Quarterly* 25, 3 (Summer 2002), 85–96.

Snow, Donald M. *September 11, 2001: The New Face of War?* New York: Longman, 2002 (reprinted and revised as Chapter 16 of Donald M. Snow, *Cases in International Relations: Portraits of the Future.* New York: Longman, 2003).

Wallerstein, Immanuel. "The Eagle Has Crash Landed." *Foreign Policy,* July/August 2002, 60–69.

PART I

THE CONTEXT

This part of the book consists of five chapters, each of which has the purpose of providing some perspective, or context, for understanding the national security situation in the 2000s. In Chapter 1, we will look at some basic dynamics of the system, including elaboration of the idea of fault lines and their impact on change, as well as dividing the system into two types of states (tiers) and discussing the American role in a new world system. We then turn, in Chapter 2, to the operating rules of international politics since the peace of Westphalia, the so-called realist paradigm that defines the geopolitical approach. That paradigm was under some fire during the 1990s as an adequate description of a globalizing world; it has been revived with the campaign against terrorism and thus must be assessed as the primary tool for a new reality. The United States has had a unique historical experience in matters of national security, and the evolution of that experience is the chief topic of Chapter 3. Among the elements of that experience has been a feeling of security based in the impregnability of the country that has now been effectively deflated.

The Cold War was the major element in the environment in which much of current American national security policy was developed. Because of the holdover effect that Cold War thinking has on the present, Chapter 4 looks at the dynamics of how the Cold War works and how it ended. The Cold War shares characteristics with September 11, in that both were almost entirely unanticipated and both created the need for adjustment. The other thread in the ongoing debate about the nature of national security is globalization, the dominant theme of the 1990s. Because its relevance remains, Chapter 5 is devoted to the other important approach to the evolution of the post–World War II, contemporary international economic globalization.

Fault Lines: World Politics in a New Millennium

This chapter begins to elaborate the themes laid out in the Introduction by examining the impact of the two fault lines on American security. Because the fault lines largely cleave the developed and developing worlds, that cleavage is presented through the concept of a world of tiers and a discussion of how those tiers relate to the central debate about globalization and geopolitics. This discussion is then applied to the central role of the United States in the evolving international system. The chapter concludes with some initial speculation about the continuing role of force in the national security system of the early twenty-first century.

Our interest in and concentration on matters of national security varies, driven largely by the ebb and flow of events in the world and our reactions to them. In relatively tranquil times, when the United States feels unthreatened by forces that might do us harm, our level of interest and concern tends to be low. Most of American history between the end of the American Revolution and World War II was of this nature; only the self-infliction of the Civil War seriously interrupted our national tranquility and made a concern and commitment to the most obvious form of national security—military force—seem particularly important. We languidly reestablished the "normalcy" of nonconcern between the world wars. We will almost certainly look back on the period between the end of the Cold War and the terrorist attacks of 2001 as a time of similar tranquility.

Times have not always been so tranquil, of course, and when they have not been, our level of concern with national security concerns—with geopolitics—has been heightened. The Japanese surprise attack on Pearl Harbor—delivered an hour before the Japanese ambassador to Washington presented the American government with an ultimatum tantamount to a declaration of war (which was part of the plan)—rocked the American psyche, ended the appeal of isolationism, and propelled us into a patriotic war to crush fascism. Japanese Admiral Isoroku Yamamato, after learning of the failure to deliver the ultimatum before the attack began, stated "We have awakened a sleeping giant and filled him with a terrible resolve." That resolve carried over to the Cold War that followed World War II. The terrorist attacks of September 11, 2001, were similar in form and in effect to Pearl Harbor; once again, our attention is refocused on matters of geopolitics and national security.

As the discussion in the Introduction suggests, we have undergone two profound events in the past decade and a half. The distinguished Harvard political scientist Graham T. Allison Jr. analogized the first event, the end of the Cold War, to an earthquake, a "tectonic shift" in the structure of international relations and our place in them. Put another way, 1989 and 2001 revealed major fault lines in the evolution of the international environment. Before the fault lines were revealed, the world looked one way; afterward, it looked very different.

The largest scale manifestation of this change is suggested in the title of this book. Before the end of the Cold War, geopolitics was the large concern in a hostile world environment, and that emphasis and perception returned after New York and Washington were victims of commercial airliners turned into lethal missiles. The period between the two major events witnessed a major ascendancy of the emphasis on economic globalization and interdependence.

These alternate emphases are not mutually exclusive, of course. The seeds of the globalization of the 1990s were sown in the last decades of the Cold War, and the contemporary system is struggling with how globalization is affected and must adapt in an environment where dealing with the geopolitical reality of international terrorism occupies center stage. Similarly, our concern with geopolitics did not disappear in the geopolitical tranquility of the 1990s; it was just not as pronounced a concern as before and after the globalization decade.

The first fault line was revealed between 1989 and 1991. No matter how one counts or from what point one begins the count of when the Cold War ended, it is now well over a decade removed. Whether one dates the beginning of that change to Poland's defiant election of a non-Communist president in 1989, the breaching of the Berlin Wall on November 9, 1989, or the official demise of the Soviet Union at the last click of the clock in 1991 in Moscow's Red Square, the Cold War structure that dominated international politics for forty-plus years after the end of World War II has crumbled. We were still adjusting to those changes when the airplanes slammed into the World Trade Center and the Pentagon.

The end of the Cold War traumatized policy makers mostly because it was so unanticipated. Certainly a few observers saw it coming—George F. Kennan prophesied in 1948 that vigilant containment could cause Communism's implosion, and New York Senator Daniel Patrick Moynihan consistently suggested its demise—but they were beacons whose message was largely not believed and ignored. The Soviet Union crumbled as Soviet republics declared their withdrawal from the union throughout 1991, but the policy of the American administration of George H.W. Bush continued to be to try to keep our mortal enemy of forty years intact nearly to the end, fearful and suspicious of the alternatives to a known enemy.

Had we anticipated what was going to happen, we might have been better prepared for it. World War II had hardly begun, for instance, when planning for the postwar world after the Axis defeat was instituted. As a result, the institution of a new structure for the international system could be implemented quickly after the guns were stilled. Unfortunately, so few believed in the end of the Cold War—and those who did were ridiculed for their "naivete"—that no real planning was done to accommodate the possibility. We were caught nearly entirely off guard.

The result was to leave the large contours of foreign policy adrift, and no place was that drift more apparent than in thinking about and planning for national security. In some ways, the trauma was natural because of the nature and impact of change. The Cold War was, after all, a quintessentially geopolitical competition, and the centerpiece of that confrontation was the military might that both sides possessed and projected against one another. Two great land masses were locked into a deadly dance, and keeping the competition below the level of mutual incineration was a time-consuming and energy-draining enterprise. With the stakes so high and the possibilities so grim, it is not surprising that those committed to the process would find the peaceful alternatives to Cold War the stuff of mere dreams.

But the Cold War ended, and we struggled for a decade, conceptually and practically, to describe and understand how the world is different. During the 1990s, the forces of economic globalization slowly overshadowed the forces of geopolitics within the American administration and raised questions about something like a paradigm shift from geopolitics to globalization. When George W. Bush entered the White House in 2001, he brought with him a foreign and national security team of "cold warriors" (people who had gained much of their knowledge and expertise in global affairs during the Cold War). Like the Clinton administration that preceded them, they struggled during their early months in office for a basis on which to reorient national security policy. The fact that Bush was an avowed free trader (the heart of globalization) added to the indeterminacy about the appropriate paradigm. Response to the terrorist attacks provided that focus, which largely defines the Bush administration.

We are still struggling to describe the new international system and appropriate policies and strategies with which to cope with it. The purpose of this book is to examine the ensuing debate and its impact on national security policy. The two lenses through which we will view the question, as already noted, are those of traditional geopolitics and more contemporary globalization, including permutations and combinations of the two, along with the theme of change.

This chapter will begin to examine the problem. In the first section, we will take a first, tentative look at what changed after the end of the Cold War and then again on September 11, introducing themes that will be amplified and elaborated upon in the remainder of the chapter and subsequent chapters. One of those themes will be the depiction of the contemporary international system as consisting of two distinct subsystems—what I will call "tiers"—each with its own dynamics and implications for thinking about security. This depiction will lead to the introduction of the central theme and debate of the book: the extent to which old-fashioned, national security–based geopolitics or economic globalization is the central dynamic of the international system and the implications of that distinction for security concerns. Because the United States has such a prominent place in the debate and in the system generally, we will look at what it means to describe the United States as the "remaining superpower." The chapter will conclude with a first look at the continuing relevance of force in contemporary international relations, particularly since 2001.

THE FIRST FAULT LINE: THE WORLD A DECADE AFTER THE COLD WAR

We entered the new century in a very different atmosphere and with very different perspectives and expectations than we had in the 1990s. In 1990 and 1991, breathtaking political change was virtually the norm. The central feature of that change, of course, was the death of Communism, as country after country peacefully (except in isolated cases like Romania) eschewed Marxism-Leninism and the Soviet Union, the leader and enforcer of Communist orthodoxy worldwide, stood idly by. As noted, in 1991 constituent parts of the Soviet Union itself began the process of secession from the Union of Soviet Socialist Republics; ultimately the Soviet empire (and it was, in many important respects, the last European empire, since much of the territory had been acquired by force by Russia) broke into fifteen independent states, all of which officially disavowed Communism. By the time the dust had settled on the Marxist experiment, only four states in the world remained nominally Communist by the end of the decade. Two of those states, Cuba and North Korea, entered the twenty-first century professing a continued dedication to the principles of Communism, although most observers expect that façade to disappear when Fidel Castro leaves power in Cuba and North Korea reunifies with the South—both events likely to occur in the next decade. The other Communist states, China and Vietnam, retain the dictatorship of the Communist Party politically but openly reject Marxist economics and are enthusiastic participants in the globalizing economy. As a competitive political ideology, the belief system articulated by Karl Marx and Friedrich Engels has essentially been consigned to the dust pile of history.

The implosion of Communism was the most obvious, dramatic, and important change of the last decade of the twentieth century, and was arguably the most important international event since World War II. In some ways, it was a unique series of events, in the sense that a major global power source simply vacated the playing field without a shot being fired. The same Soviet Union that had, for the most part, brutally imposed Communist systems on most of what was known as the Second (or Socialist) World, simply watched those systems being toppled with scarcely a shrug of its national shoulders. The virtually peaceful implosion of the Soviet Union itself was an act of nonviolence without precedent. Large states and empires had, of course, disappeared before, but virtually all the other dismemberments were the direct result of major hot wars. To borrow an old phrase, the Cold War ended with a whimper, not a bang.

The end of "operational Communism" (Communism as the official political organizing system for a country) has had major systemic impacts to which the world is still adjusting. The Cold War international system was what is called by political scientists a *bipolar system*, which means a system dominated by two opposing states (the United States and the Soviet Union) around which other states congregated and sought or had imposed differing degrees of association. The nature of bipolarity had evolved during the Cold War period. In the first decade or so of the Cold War, the system was described as one of *tight* bipolarity, which meant the two dominant parties could influence or control the actions of their "client" states to a large degree. For a variety of reasons, this control was gradually relaxed, and the system evolved into one of *loose* bipolarity. The ultimate manifestation of loosening of control, of course, was the inability of the Soviet Union to keep the members of its bloc adherent to the political principle of Communism that was the source of their sameness.

The result has been a power vacuum. With one pole physically disappeared, the system can no longer be described as bipolar. There is only one pole left, as Russia, the successor to the Soviet Union, lacks the stature and resources to be a "superpower" in the Cold War sense beyond its continued possession of a large but (thanks to arms control agreements) shrinking arsenal of nuclear weapons (which was a major criterion for superpower status during the Cold War). No one is willing to designate the system as *unipolar*, because that would imply a level of American control that does not exist and that most other states would (and do) oppose. The United States remains the central power, but defining what that centrality means has been a critical part of defining the new system. It is probably of some symbolic importance that we have never formed a consensus on what to call the new system and that the most common name describes what it is not—the post–Cold War world.

As it evolved over time, the Cold War had the major physical and intellectual advantage of developing a very orderly set of rules of interaction. The competition for global power and influence between the Communist and non-Communist worlds was well defined, as were the rules by which that competition was carried out, both directly and indirectly in the developing world. It was conceptually a *zero-sum game*, in which the gains of one side were assumed to be the losses of the other, and the possibilities of *positive-sum* outcomes to situations (in which both sides gained) were infrequent and considered unlikely in any particular situation. The lingua franca of this competition ultimately was the maintenance of enormous military machines by each side, capped by the possession of enormous arsenals of thermonuclear weapons, which, if ever employed against one another, would probably have ended civilization as we know it.

Yet the system produced an orderliness within which the "cold warriors" could think about world problems and dynamics based in the competition and its management short of war. The end of the Cold War shattered that order. As Georgi Arbatov, director of the Soviet USA and Canada Institute and a member of the Central Committee of the Communist Party of the Soviet Union, put it to the Americans in mid-1991: "We have done a terrible thing. We have deprived you of an enemy."

Conceptually, it was indeed a terrible thing, in the sense that national security thinking—clearly grounded in the Soviet threat and deflecting and managing that threat—suddenly lost most, if not all, of its relevance. The result was both physical and intellectual disorder in how to think about the world, which has not yet been resolved. While the process was going on, in 1990, University of Chicago political scientist John Mearsheimer even lamented in the title of an *Atlantic Monthly* article, "Why we shall soon miss the Cold War." What we would miss, he contended, was the order and predictability of events and the ability to act appropriately within the bounds of that order. One of the problems facing the national security bureaucracy of the 1990s and 2000s has been to find analysts and policy makers who are not so grounded in the old realities that they can adapt to the new environment.

The demise of the international political system of bipolarity and the debate over what should replace it raged on inconclusively until the debate was suspended by the events of 2001. There are, however, clear benefits to the changes that hardly anyone could or would try to deny. At the same time, there are evolving systemic dynamics about which there is a considerable amount of disagreement within both the academic and policy communities that continue to enliven debates within those communities.

Undeniable Benefits

The most obvious and most dangerous manifestation of the Cold War was the military confrontation between the competing blocs led by the United States and the Soviet Union. Managing that confrontation—"preparing for and fighting the country's wars," in the military's parlance—was a serious consequence of the nature of international politics and one that, given the possible consequences of a misstep, had to be taken very seriously. The prospect of general war employing nuclear weapons even produced a fatalistic political culture about the future and resulted in the expenditure of large amounts of resources in its name. Keeping the Cold War cold was the preeminent international responsibility, beside which other priorities paled by comparison.

The post–Cold War world produced no equivalent of the East-West, Communist–anti-Communist military confrontation, and this fact had two obvious and overwhelming benefits for the citizenry of the 1990s that were not enjoyed by people in the 1980s and before. Both benefits condition how we thought and still think about the problem of national security in the contemporary world, even after the second fault line was revealed.

The first positive change, and the one most relieving for those who participated in the Cold War period, is the absence of any real concern about the possibility of a general systemic war that could threaten national and international survival. Within the context of the Cold War, the possibility—thought by some as a probability—of a global World War III in which nuclear weapons would be used massively was an ever-present prospect, a problem that never went away. The two sides were certainly politically opposed enough to find adequate cause for war between them, and managing the competition in such a way as to reduce the likelihood that such a war would begin was a major task. Trying to avoid a nuclear holocaust occupied the concerted efforts of scholars and strategists and spawned the pseudoscience of nuclear deterrence.

Since then, the situation is both radically different and the same. Physically, Russia and the United States have reduced the size of their nuclear arsenals and conventional forces, but they retain large enough nuclear forces to be able to do great damage to one another on a scale only slightly smaller than during the Cold War. The demise of Soviet Communism, however, has removed the political differences that could provide the rationale for war. As noted in the Introduction, we possessed both the physical means and the potential motivations for World War III. Today, we retain most of the means but lack the motives. The world is still deadly but less dangerous.

This changed dynamic enormously relaxed the security environment, because it removed the "worst case" planning problem. The United States and other countries still may face the possibility of going to war, as we did over Kuwait in the Persian Gulf area at the beginning of the 1990s and, in modified form, in Afghanistan a decade later. All of the realistic contingencies for the present and foreseeable future are more limited in conduct and potential for expansion to general war. It is virtually impossible to conjure a realistic scenario that would lead the world to war and cause the nuclear bombs to start being hurled in a general, systemic way. The signing of an arms control treaty between the United States and Russia in 2002, which will further shrink nuclear arsenals, and the increasing inclusion of Russia into the North Atlantic Treaty Organization (NATO) further reduce the plausibility of the worst case.

We had become basically unconcerned about this new reality before the terrorist attacks reminded us that the world could still be a dangerous place. During one of the televised debates during the 1992 presidential campaign, for instance, incumbent President George H. W. Bush proudly proclaimed that Americans no longer went to bed worrying about the possibility of awakening to nuclear war. Some older Americans could remember having such thoughts, but most younger Americans had *never* known the fear and wondered what the president was talking about.

The result was to take some of the urgency and fervor out of the national security debate. To borrow a distinction from one of my other books (*When America Fights*), the United States faced very few potential situations in which it would have to fight and, especially, use its total military might (employments of necessity); rather, Americans debated in which kinds of places we might use our forces, knowing the decision would not likely compromise American interests greatly one way or the other (employments of choice).

The second change flows from the first. During the Cold War confrontation, both potential adversaries and their major allies maintained large and expensive military machines that could be quickly inserted into the fray should war somehow break out. Given the destructiveness such a war could rapidly produce, it was assumed that it would be fought and completed with the forces on hand when it began—what was called the "force in being"—and both sides maintained large forces for that possibility.

It was a very expensive proposition. During the 1950s, the United States dedicated as much as half the federal budget to defense. After the spate of entitlement legislation was passed during the 1960s, that proportion fell to about 25 percent of the budget and into second place among categories of federal expenditures. Although reliable budget figures for the Soviet Union were always elusive, the estimates were that they spent between 15 and 25 percent of gross national product (GNP) on the military (with a much larger economic base, the spending equivalent for the United States never exceeded 6 percent of GNP).

The end of the Cold War was accompanied by a sizable demilitarization among the major players, especially the leaders of the Cold War coalitions. Troop strength for the United States went from 2.15 million active duty troops in 1988 to 1.4 million in 1998. The Russians have cut their forces down even more, although the ten-year comparison is distorted in that 1988 figures reflect the entire Soviet Union, whereas 1998 figures (which show an active force of 1.16 million) are all Russian. In any case, force sizes and expenditure levels are down substantially for all the major powers.

The cutbacks have been highly differential on a worldwide base, with the United States having reduced spending comparatively little compared to other countries. Using International Institute for Strategic Studies (London) figures for spending in 1998, the United States spent $265.9 billion on defense. By contrast, the next *seven* countries in descending order of defense spending (Russia, France, Japan, China, the United Kingdom, Germany, and Italy) cumulatively spent $259.2 billion; only when one adds the ninth-place spender (Brazil) does the total pass that of the United States, at 277.3 billion. As noted in the Introduction, that gap has increased steadily since then. At that, the American total was only slightly larger in actual dollars than the 1988 total, and as a proportion of the budget, it has slipped to below 20 percent and to third place (behind entitlements and service on the debt) among categories of expenditure. What the comparisons reveal is that other countries have cut their military spending in real terms (smaller amounts for defense), rather than slowing growth that would likely have been greater had the Cold War not ended, as has happened in the United States. That trend toward decline was reversed after 2001, as we noted in the Introduction and shall see in the next section.

Debatable Changes

Although the danger of global war and the need to prepare for it undeniably receded during the 1989–2001 period, there were other changes in the environment that had effects on which there was some level of disagreement. While making no pretense of inclusiveness or exhaustiveness, three interrelated changes with some impact on the security equation and the relevance of geopolitics and globalization are worth raising in this context.

One change, from which the others follow to an extent, is a greater emphasis on the developing world, or Second Tier. In one sense, this emphasis did not represent much of a change in national security terms. While the focus of national security during the Cold War was on the major power competition, virtually all actual fighting involving American forces occurred in the developing world. The United States, for instance, *deployed* forces worldwide, including in the developed world (Europe, Japan); it *employed* force exclusively in the developing world (Korea, Vietnam, Grenada, for example). The reasons for this state of affairs are complex, of course, but the fact that most of the violence and instability were in the developing world had something to do with this pattern of employment. In addition, in most instances violent confrontations between clients of the two sides could be waged without a real danger of escalation to direct superpower confrontation. Since many of the conflicts that occurred had Communists battling anti-Communists, the use of force could be argued to have been necessary to avoid shifting the geopolitical balance between the East and the West.

The situation after the Cold War had both similarities and differences. The Second Tier remains the part of the world where virtually all the violence resides, and most of it is still internal in nature (a point elaborated on in the next section). This emphasis has continued since 2001, because the developing world is also the seedbed for most of the international terrorism the combating of which has become the fulcrum of national security concern. Thus, most of the opportunities to employ force are where they always were.

What is utterly different, of course, is that developing world violence no longer has a Cold War overlay. That is both good and bad. It is beneficial in that internal grievances are no longer distorted by what were largely irrelevant Cold War concerns. It is malevolent in that old Cold War sponsors are no longer around to insist upon restraint in the conduct of these affairs, which are often particularly bloody and gruesome. At the same time, the absence of the Cold War patina eliminates ideological guidance about which of these to engage in and which to ignore, meaning that participation is almost exclusively in the form of employments of choice. As we shall see, the criteria for involvement in the post–Cold War world tended toward humanitarian grounds, but these have shifted to the campaign against terrorism.

The result of tranquility among the major powers is that much more of our attention can be directed at the Second Tier than it was before. In a direct national security sense, this fact is reflected in an ongoing debate over the nature and appropriate uses of force in the developing world. It is also reflected in disagreement about the extent to which the forces of globalization are having an impact on this part of the globe.

The point of contrast and continuity cannot be overstated, because it is so often erroneously suggested that potential involvements in things like peacekeeping operations in the developing world mark a radical departure for the United States and other major powers. To repeat, using military forces to influence internal wars in the developing world is not at all unique to the post–Cold War world. What is different is the rationale for putting American or other troops potentially in harm's way and the ways in which they are employed.

During the Cold War, the Second Tier uses of American armed forces were conventional in terms of purpose and methods of employment: The reason to use American military might was to thwart Communist takeovers that might occur in the absence of American assistance, a direct extension of the central geopolitical competition. Whether that force was warranted or wise in particular places, such as Vietnam, was a matter of debate, but the central purpose was not. In those circumstances, the way forces were used—strategically if not always tactically—was conventional: The idea was military victory over a well-defined enemy. That enemy might fight unconventionally (what we now call asymmetrically) and thus create the need for tactical adjustment to bring about enemy defeat, as was the case in Vietnam, but the goal was traditional—for example, preparing for and fighting the country's wars in support of traditional governments.

Contemporary opportunities to employ force are different on both counts. The disappearance of communism meant that involvement in a Second Tier internal conflict could no longer be justified in terms of the kinds of geopolitics that underlay Cold War actions. More typically, justifications became "softer," framed in terms of arresting and reversing humanitarian disasters in situations where clearly military conflict between defined military forces was not present. The purpose was more often framed in terms of reinstituting peace and protecting civilian populations from the return of atrocity. As a result, military victory in a traditional sense gave way to an open-ended commitment to imposing, enforcing, and keeping a fragile peace. That reorientation runs counter to traditional military ways of thinking about the use of force in the American experience, as we shall see in Chapter 3.

When the new Bush administration entered office in 2001, it clearly demonstrated the ambivalence created by this debate over how and when to use force. During the 2000 campaign, Bush had come out strongly in opposition to future uses of American force for peacekeeping where American interests were not clearly engaged. Dr. Condoleeza Rice, who became national security advisor, was the point person for this position, arguing that the United States should not act as the "world's 911," that it was an improper role for elite American troops like the 82nd Airborne to be used to escort children to kindergarten in places like Kosovo, and that endless deployments were eroding troop morale. The Bush team even suggested the desirability of terminating American involvement in Kosovo and Bosnia.

These positions did not long survive the oath of office. European allies quickly informed the new administration of the necessity of maintaining the missions in the Balkans and of the vitality of American presence in those missions. The rhetoric of noninvolvement was quietly cooled, and Secretary of Defense Donald Rumsfeld quickly announced a comprehensive review of American military strategy and missions, which presumably included involvement in peacekeeping operations. The events of September 11, 2001, and the subsequent reorientation of policy left this debate moot for the time being.

Globalization is the other trend with a significant Second Tier element and disagreement about what it does and how or whether it should be promoted. Bursting upon the scene and coinciding with or stimulating (there is disagreement about which) the worldwide economic expansion and prosperity of the global economy in the First Tier, globalization spread to selected parts of the Second Tier during the 1990s as well. During the first half of the decade and beyond, the results appeared overwhelmingly positive and formed the core of the Clinton administration's foreign policy of engagement and enlargement (engaging those countries most capable of joining the global economy and thereby enlarging what Clinton called the circle of market democracies). In its purest form, the expansion of the globalizing economy would be accompanied by political democratization and contribute to a spreading *democratic peace* around the globe. In this scenario, as democracies increasingly came into power, peace would follow, since it is well established (or at least well asserted) that political democracies do not fight one another. Moreover, as the global economy reached out and encompassed more and more countries, the motivation to fight would give way to economic interdependence.

In this happy scenario, a geopolitical perspective that seeks to minimize violence and instability in the world appears to coincide with and reinforce globalization, since they are both aimed at the same ends. Unfortunately, the rosy outlook of the 1990s began to fade as the twentieth century wound to an end. As the international system faced the new century, the desirability and contribution of globalization became more debatable.

At least three things contributed to the ambivalence about globalization. First, its proponents were too optimistic in their advocacies, and events proved their most expansive projections to be at least partially wrong, thereby casting doubt on the process of globalization. During the height of the "go-go" 1990s economy, some analysts predicted that globalization had fundamentally altered the nature of traditional economics; modern technology could make adjustments heretofore impossible in such areas as product mix and inventory control, meaning that the business cycle of boom and bust could effectively be surmounted, even eliminated.

These predictions proved overly optimistic, even wrong in some cases. Knowing they were producing too many automobiles did not keep the world's automakers from producing 80 million cars a year for a market that could only absorb 60 million in the late 1990s. The result was large excess inventories as the centuries changed, which resulted in layoffs, unprofitable discounting, and other phenomena familiar in the old economy. In 1997, a currency crisis broke out first in Thailand and spread rapidly to other East Asian states that were considered pillars of globalization (discussed more fully in Chapter 5). When the signs of economic weakness became evident even in Japan, the "economic miracle" that accompanied globalization seemed suspect.

The geopolitical consequences of globalization provided a second source of controversy. The argument to use economic globalization as a way to entangle and drag countries into the web of market democracies was no more vigorously pursued anywhere than it was in China. The prevailing idea was that by tying the Chinese to the global economy through such mechanisms as most favored nation (MFN) status and membership in the World Trade Organization (WTO), pressure could be brought to bear that would force the Chinese to improve their human rights record and to allow for increased political democracy in the country. The Communist regime's obdurate resistance to loosening its political monopoly or allowing greater political freedoms has made that strategy suspect and has rekindled a renewed debate on how to treat China, which will almost certainly be rekindled as China makes the transition to the fourth generation of Communist leaders, which began in late 2002. In places like Indonesia, embrace of globalization has apparently helped contribute to the political chaos that country is undergoing, or at least that is the conclusion of part of the Indonesian population.

The failure of globalization to produce all of its most optimistic (and probably unrealistic) outcomes has created a third problem, which is a backlash against the phenomenon of globalization—especially its most prominent institutional manifestations. The first overt demonstration of strident, organized opposition to globalization came in late November 1999 at the Seattle annual meeting of the WTO, where an estimated 20,000 demonstrators voiced their objections to the consequences of globalization (and engaged in considerable destructive vandalism in the "Emerald City"). Prominent participants included labor unions, fearful of the movement of jobs to cheap labor markets, and environmentalists, fearful that multinational corporations and other private firms would ignore environmental protection. Other groups with parallel concerns, such as those fearful of U.S. global domination and groups seeing globalization as an assault on sovereignty, added their voices to the dissent.

This backlash became a regular part of the institutionalization of globalization in its various aspects and the dialog on globalization. Attempts to disrupt organizations meeting to promote global values like free trade have become an apparently inevitable part of such meetings. The 2000 meeting of the International Bank for Reconstruction and Development (IBRD, or World Bank) in Washington, D.C., was interrupted by roughly the same coalition of rejectionists as those who had appeared in Seattle. This phenomenon was internationalized amid great worldwide television coverage as demonstrators battled teargas-wielding police at the third Summit of the Americas in Quebec City, Canada, in April 2001 to oppose progress toward forming a Free Trade Area of the Americas (FTAA) between the thirty-four democratically elected governments of the Western Hemisphere (all countries except Cuba) by 2005. The groups that have attracted demonstrators are diverse. The WTO has been in existence for less than a decade, with the purpose of promoting and monitoring the removal of trade barriers among its members (currently about 140 states); the World Bank is one of the original Bretton Woods institutions that came out of World War II to reorder the world economy principally by making loans to credit-worthy countries; and the FTAA is an unratified proposal originally announced at the first Summit of the Americas in Miami in 1994. The common thread among all three, however, is that they are a general part of the process of globalization.

THE SECOND FAULT LINE:
THE WORLD AFTER SEPTEMBER 11

It is difficult to specify the characteristics of the contemporary international environment. Like the post–Cold War world it supersedes, it does not have a universally accepted name: The closest we have come in the immediate wake of the traumatic events is to proclaim it as the "war on terrorism," but that sobriquet is unlikely to endure as a description of the era. For one thing, the response to the terrorist acts is not a war in any traditional, recognizable way (a point argued at length in the pages to follow); for another, it is not yet certain that we have witnessed a profound and *lasting* change in the way the system works. It is possible that international terrorism will be reduced to the status it had before the attacks (a peripheral place in the scheme of things) or eliminated, in which case we may view this period as an interlude in the post–Cold War world. Alternatively, terrorism may be an enduring problem with which we have to contend concertedly for some time. It is simply too early to tell.

Our perspective is further clouded by subjective factors. The fact that the traumatic events were so recent leaves us with minimal perspective on the events or their longer term impacts. The fact that powerful symbols of the United States were attacked makes the events more personal and emotional than they might otherwise have been. The obvious equation of the attacks with the Japanese attack at Pearl Harbor creates a sense of "infamy" around the events that seems to dictate a swift and decisive retribution; that this remained elusive in the months after the attacks adds to our frustration. The amorphous nature of a terrorist opponent that operates in the shadows makes it difficult to fashion effective ways to eradicate the "evil" that terrorism represents.

If it is difficult to specify the new environment in any detail, it is possible to discern differences on the post–September 11 side of the second fault line. Among other things, the balance between geopolitical and globalization concerns has clearly shifted from the latter to the former. Geopolitics has had a rebirth that is clear and undeniable even if we still are searching for new, adequate ways to describe the new geopolitical reality. One of the new forces that has clearly entered the public international calculus is the emergence of so-called nonstate actors in the form of international terrorists whose bases and loyalties do not coincide with any country. The debate between internationalism and unilateralism has also been affected, as the neo-conservatives have seized upon September 11 as a rallying cry for their militant unilateralist visions in places like Iraq. If globalization has receded, we are still trying to see exactly how far and in what direction.

The revealed vulnerability of American soil to attack has quickly revived an interest in the tool of geopolitics—military forces—in the American debate after a decade or more when they received much lesser attention. One of the most obvious beneficiaries has been military spending. In 1999, the United States spent $263.1 billion on defense, which was more than the next seven countries combined in descending order of spending. In 2002, the Bush administration proposed to spend over $350 billion, and some members of Congress argued that was not enough.

In the patriotic outpouring following the terrorist attacks, this shift to an almost obsessive sense of national security emphasis went virtually unchallenged. In the area of defense spending, for instance, the expected tough debate over modernization—which new systems to buy, which not—turned into a frenzy of trying to procure everything on the menu, despite the tenuousness of the arguments regarding how different capabilities would contribute to the central thrust on combating terrorism. President Bush's suggestion during the 2000 campaign that the United States might simply leapfrog a generation of new weapons fell rapidly off the table in the process.

The ascendancy of geopolitics has been accompanied by the assertion that we are locked in a "new kind of war," a theme raised shortly after September 11 by the Bush administration and picked up by the media. Although it was never quite clear what was new about combating terrorism, it was widely advertised that the new, and amorphous, enemy is engaged in what has been called *asymmetrical warfare*, by which is meant that the terrorist opponent does not employ conventional, Western-style methods of conducting warfare (at which it would certainly lose) but instead adopts unconventional methods to avoid annihilation and to maximize the likelihood of accomplishing its goals.

Calling such approaches "new" strains credulity to the breaking point. As noted in the Introduction, the adoption of methods to negate the advantages of a larger and superior force are as old as the first time a weaker foe outdid a superior enemy, and the United States confronted—unsuccessfully—what we now call an asymmetrical enemy in Vietnam a third of a century ago. There is certainly nothing new about the use of terrorism—only the instruments have changed. What is new in the contemporary context is the relative emphasis we are now placing on combating unconventional opponents. During the Cold War, most of our emphasis was on strategic nuclear and large-scale conventional war with the Soviet Union in Europe—a sort of grand-scale reprise of World War II. Some emphasis on asymmetrical warfare—in forms such as anti-terrorism or guerrilla warfare—was part of planning, but it was relegated to a lower order of priority. Special operations forces (SOFs) were the large repository of such concern, and because those missions were considered less important than the central conflict, the result was to help trivialize the importance of the SOFs. In a contemporary environment where there are few dangers of large-scale conventional warfare, priorities have been essentially inverted—witness the importance now attached to SOFs as the United States confronts Bush's "axis of evil" in places like Iraq.

A more prominent characteristic of the new geopolitical order is its increased emphasis on so-called *nonstate actors*, organizations that have neither a permanent territorial base nor loyalty to any particular country but engage in activities that cross state borders. In a generic sense, such actors are also nothing new; the most prominent examples of nonstate actors are nongovernmental organizations (NGOs)—nonstate-based international organizations that perform a variety of useful functions within the system, such as provision of humanitarian assistance (CARE, Doctors without Borders) or monitoring of human rights violations (Amnesty International, Human Rights Watch).

The terrorist attacks riveted our attention to a subcategory of nonstate actors who are violent in their actions. Once again, violent transnational groups are not a novel feature of the post–Cold War world and beyond. In contemporary terms, the international drug cartels have been a prototype of sorts, and international terrorist organizations have operated for years. What is different is that organizations such as Al Qaeda occupy a central position in our attention.

Dealing with nonstate actors in the form of international terrorist organizations poses some unique problems for national security policy makers (beyond the fact that they were not given high priority in the past). Our conventional and historical experience has been combating the agents of state-based governments who represented a conventional (or symmetrical) threat. Our armed forces, our doctrines for warfare, and the whole legal and ethical framework for warfare are geared to fighting such foes. International terrorism stands these concepts and rules on their heads in several ways.

One problem is how to depict efforts to combat international terrorists. The analogy of "war," which has its roots and designations in conventional interstate war and classic internal war over control of governments, does not clearly fit an opponent that has no territorial base or loyalty and is apparently uninterested in gaining and exercising authority over territory. Who does one attack in this war? Historically, acts of war are committed against states and their agencies. In the case of international terrorists, such distinctions are at best indirect—for example, the designation of the Taliban regime as an opponent because of its shielding of Al Qaeda. It is relatively easy to assign blame when actions can clearly be identified with a particular state (and especially when that state acts overtly); it is more difficult when dealing with a nonstate-based opponent.

This difficulty became particularly clear in the case of Taliban and Al Qaeda prisoners sent to Guantanamo Bay in Cuba in 2002 after the campaign to overthrow the Taliban in Afghanistan succeeded. Were these individuals prisoners of war (POWs), in which case they were subject to treatment as such under the Geneva codes of war (see Amplification 1.1)? Or were they "detainees," as the administration maintained? Had there been a literal, legal state of war, there would have been no question about POW status. Since there was not, their status was debatable and controversial. The compromise solution of treating Taliban prisoners as POWs because they were soldiers of the Taliban regime and Al Qaeda as something else was not legally or politically pleasing.

Nonstate actors such as international terrorists are difficult to combat in conventional, military terms, as the U.S. military has learned. These groups do indeed engage in asymmetrical forms of combat, in the process not honoring traditional rules of engagement or conventional laws of states. As we shall discuss in Chapter 10, terrorist acts invariably break laws and are considered criminal by the targets, just as they are considered acts of war by the terrorists.

A further characteristic of the changed environment is how the American role in the world is viewed. In particular, the question that has been raised frequently is how dealing with terrorism has predisposed the United States to act in concert with its allies and the international community (a position known as internationalism) or on its own with little regard for others but in what it believes to be its individual self-interest (unilateralism). Although this distinction is developed more fully later in the chapter, it is worth mentioning now.

In the immediate aftermath of September 11, 2001, there was great agreement on the perfidy of the attacks and on the need to combat them through concerted, international action; the Bush administration responded by calling for a response that would be broadly international. The rationale was that since international terrorism represented a threat that did not honor borders, the response to it must be international as well in areas such as intelligence gathering and sharing, detention of suspected terrorists, and the like. The internationalist instinct seemed to prevail.

By the beginning of 2002, that consensus had begun to erode as the campaign to capture and destroy Usama bin Laden and his associates proved more difficult than imagined. In that atmosphere, the U.S. government began proposing more militarily oriented actions, which met with cool receptions almost everywhere else. The first lightning rod of international concern was the detainees at Guantanamo and the stern refusal of the United States to listen to international entreaties about their treatment. When President Bush announced the "axis of evil" designation of Iraq,

Amplification 1.1

THE RULES OF WAR: WHO IS A POW?

One of the fallouts of American participation in the campaign to overthrow the Taliban government of Afghanistan was the question of the status of hostile prisoners captured by American and Afghan forces. It was a complicated problem in two ways. The first revolved around whether a state of war existed, since war was never declared formally either by the Afghan government, the coalition of forces seeking to overthrow the government, or the intervening United States. The other complication came from the fact that the prisoners included both soldiers supporting the Taliban regime and Al Qaeda terrorist members fighting alongside the Taliban. The first objection did not apply to international standards on treatment of prisoners; the second did.

The question of prisoner status was first raised when a number of captured Afghans were transported to detention at the U.S. naval base at Guantanamo Bay, Cuba. The explanation for the transfer was that the "detainees," as the Bush administration labeled them, were dangerous individuals who might escape if left in Afghanistan and cause havoc there. In addition, the United States wanted to isolate and interrogate suspected Al Qaeda members to aid in the campaign against terrorism.

The question became critical at this point. The Bush administration maintained that the detainees did not qualify for prisoner of war status under the Geneva Conventions of War (more specifically, Convention III: Relative to the Treatment of Prisoners of War, Geneva, August 1949), to which the United States is a signatory. After some discussion, it was conceded that the Taliban, as representatives of the government of Afghanistan, qualified under Article 4 of the convention but the Al Qaeda detainees did not. The administration, anxious to get as much information as possible from the detainees, initially resisted differentiating between members of the two groups. Article 5 of the convention, however, is quite clear on this matter: "Should any doubt arise as to whether persons, having committed a belligerent act and having fallen into the hands of the enemy, belong to any of the categories enumerated in Article 4, such persons *shall enjoy the protection of the present convention until such time as their status has been determined by a competent tribunal*" (emphasis added). Ten months after their arrival, no tribunals had been convened for that purpose.

Why was the administration so reluctant to afford prisoner of war status to the Afghans? The answer was straightforward: If the detainees were legal POWs, there were sharp limits on the American right to extract information from them. Part III, Section 1, Article 17 defines the problem: "Every prisoner of war, when questioned on the subject, is bound to give his surname, first names and rank, date of birth, and army, regimental, personal serial number, or failing this, equivalent information." Since that is *all* the information a POW is required to provide, granting that status would clearly have hamstrung the anti-terrorist effort. The question is whether the additional information was worth the price of the United States apparently violating a basic treaty obligation.

Source: Convention III: Relative to the Treatment of Prisoners of War. Geneva, Switzerland, August 1949. (Text available from the Society of Professional Journalists at *http://www.the-spa.com/ genevaconventions/convention3.html.*)

Iran, and North Korea in his 2002 State of the Union address and vaguely threatened the likelihood of military action to deal with their alleged transgressions without consulting American allies in advance, many in the international community saw a return to the unilateralism they had suspected before the attacks. Ignoring world opinion, the advice of some allies, and a UN Security Council certain to veto an authorizing resolution, the invasion of Iraq supported by a "coalition of willing" represented the ultimate triumph of unilateralism.

Finally, September 11 affected discussions and emphases on globalization. Some of the optimism about spreading globalization had already been dampened by economic events of the end of the 1990s. The shock of the terrorist events further removed the luster that had surrounded globalization, as the system reoriented its focus toward the problem of international terrorism. The more profound effects of the changed environment on globalization will be examined throughout this book. For present purposes, it is sufficient simply to suggest the contours of short- and long-term prospects.

In the immediate wake of the attacks, negative impacts tended to be emphasized. For example, one of the reasons the Al Qaeda terrorists were able to enter the United States is the relative ease with which people and products enter and leave the country. That penetrability is a distinct asset for increasing international economic activity such as trade, but it also makes monitoring and interception of terrorists more difficult than would be the case with greater restrictions on movement. As discussions turned to the prospects of terrorists moving weapons of mass destruction into the country (especially after the anthrax scare of November 2002), there were quite understandable calls for increased security on America's borders. The question was how this could be accomplished without unduly strangling trade and effectively undoing globalization.

In the longer term, it is possible to think of the emphases on geopolitics and globalization as being potentially reinforcing, part of a comprehensive policy toward the world. A reasonable consensus has emerged that a basic reason for terrorism is the abysmal living conditions in parts of the world that are breeding grounds for the hopelessness that makes terrorism an attractive option. Economic development—draining the so-called swamps in which terrorism thrives—thus becomes part of a longer-term means of eliminating the terrorist threat. Since a major component of alleviating human misery is improving living conditions through economic prosperity, the spread of the globalizing economy to places that have hitherto been those swamps can become part of overall geopolitical strategy.

THE NATURE OF THE SYSTEM: A WORLD OF TIERS

One of the clear intellectual victims of the implosion of Communism and the Cold War political system was the old way of describing and discussing the nature of the international system. Bipolarity, for instance, could not describe a world with only one remaining pole—but that was not all. One of the most common descriptions of the international system divided the world into three (or even four) worlds: a First World consisting of the most advanced countries, a Second World encompassing the

Socialist or Communist countries, and a Third World made up of the developing countries. (Some depictions included a Fourth World for those extremely poor and hopeless developing countries with little or no meaningful prospects for development.)

The disappearance of the Second World made that scheme inapplicable to describing post–Cold War reality. The world is still clearly differentiated in terms of economic and political development, so some more accurate means of differentiation was clearly needed. One way to accomplish this altered reality was to distinguish between the developed and the developing (or less-developed) worlds, but that distinction fell prey to criticisms based in political correctness and even condescension (it is clearly "better" to be more developed rather than less so, and thus it is pejorative to be referred to as less developed). While it is probably impossible to find distinctions to which someone will not find objection, my solution is to describe a world of tiers.

The fundamental distinction for and rationalization of this categorization comes from a seminal work by Max Singer and the late Aaron Wildawsky, first published in 1993. Arguing that hardly any generalization one could make about the world today would apply equally well to all countries, they proposed to talk about the world as divisible into two "zones": a *zone of peace* that includes the major developed market democracies (essentially the old First World) and a *zone of turmoil* that encompasses the rest of the world. It is possible, they argued, to make meaningful, if sometimes opposite, generalizations about conditions in the two zones that help us to understand the overall international system better.

The zones form the basis for my world of tiers, an analytical tool that the late Eugene Brown and I elaborated on most fully in *International Relations* (which, in an appendix, classifies all countries into one tier or another). The First Tier includes the major Western democracies and is, like Singer and Wildawsky's zone of peace, the equivalent of the old First World. The Second Tier, like the zone of turmoil, is made up of the rest of the countries of the world and is sufficiently diverse within itself as to create the need for further differentiation into subtiers. In order to begin more fully to map out the locus of violence and the sorts of places where the United States and other similar First Tier states are likely to find the occasions to engage in military activity, we will examine the two tiers and where they come together.

The First Tier

As noted, the First Tier and the old First World are essentially synonymous. The membership of the tier includes the twenty-five to thirty most developed market-based democracies in the world, including the major democracies of North America (the United States and Canada), the membership of the old European Economic Area (the European Union, European Free Trade Area, and neutral states), Japan, and the Antipodes (Australia and New Zealand). What these countries have in common is that they all have stable political democracies (that is, democracies that have endured over a period of time through such stressful events as peaceful governmental successions after free and fair elections) and advanced market-based economies (that is, economies that are part of the technology-driven globalization

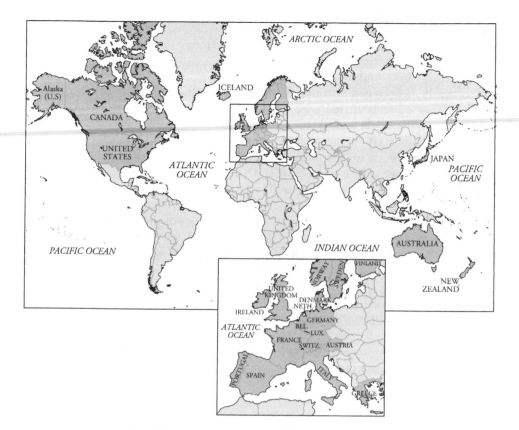

system and that are contributors to rather than primarily consumers of cutting-edge technology). Aspirants to the First Tier generally lack one or another of these attributes. The South Korean economy, for instance, qualifies, but its nascent democracy has not met the test of several peaceful successions (the same could be said of most members of the proposed FTAA).

Two behavioral characteristics define the members of the First Tier: homogeneity and peace in their relations among themselves. The two characteristics are, of course, related to one another. The basis of their homogeneity is that they basically have the same political and economic philosophy. All are political democracies, and although they have some marginal economic differences regarding the amount of government participation allowable in economic matters (why they are designated as *market-based* rather than simply *market* economies), these disagreements are not fundamental. The upshot of this ideological agreement is that they have nothing important enough to fight about physically, which contributes to their status as the heart and best example of the democratic peace discussed earlier as a benefit of the end of the Cold War.

Basic homogeneity does not mean that the members agree on everything and that there are no disputes among them. Although virtually all members are committed to the principle of free trade, for instance, there are periodic, even well-publicized differences in the terms of trade between them. The United States and Japan disagree about whether the Japanese discriminate against American imports on a wide range of products, from apples and citrus fruit to rice and automobiles. The Americans and French argue about limitations on the availability of American movies and music, which the French argue are culturally diluting, and the import of American meat products that have been fed supplements. Politically, they disagree on relative approaches to the world and, especially since 1989, the quality of American leadership in global affairs (the theme of internationalism or unilateralism).

What is uniformly true of these disagreements is that they are at the margins of relations among First Tier states rather than being central matters of concern. Because they agree on most things and disagree on relatively little, it is basically inconceivable to imagine the use of military force by any First Tier member against any other member. If one were to array all the countries of the First Tier on a wheel and then draw lines connecting all possible combinations (or "dyads," to borrow from political science jargon), it would be essentially impossible to imagine when or why any two of them might come to blows.

This realization has important implications for thinking about the national security problem, especially when two other factors are added. The first of these is the realization that the membership of the First Tier includes the most important and powerful countries in the world. Of the nine countries with the greatest expenditures on defense, discussed earlier, only two (China and Russia) are not members of the First Tier. Admittedly, countries like Russia and China (and also India) are not inconsequential countries, and part of Western policy is aimed at trying to boost them into the peaceful First Tier, but the most important countries are First Tier states.

The other factor regards the interests of the United States. During the Cold War, the most important (or vital) interests of the United States revolved around our major economic and political brethren, which meant Western Europe and Japan—roughly, the First Tier. If the United States were to fight in an engagement of necessity, it likely would have been in the defense of one (Japan) or more (NATO) First Tier states.

The end of the Cold War competition virtually ended that prospect. The assertion that the world is a much better place (at least prior to September 11, 2001), in which the threat of systemic war has largely disappeared, means, in these terms, two things. First, since most of the major states are part of the First Tier and do not threaten one another, major power conflict is essentially eliminated. Second, the demise of operational, evangelical Communism means nobody particularly threatens these core actors; instead, outsiders such as the Russians and Chinese see their interests in joining the greater prosperity of the First Tier, not in destroying it. Globalization and geopolitics both affect the system, and globalization turns out to be dominant within the First Tier states' patterns of interaction.

If the prospect of large-scale, systemic wars of necessity have faded into great unlikelihood, this should have an impact on the national security equation. At one level, it should affect the kinds of wars for which the military prepares to fight: Are there, for instance, any great mechanized, mobile wars between massed armies on something like the northern European plain for which to prepare? Early in the new Bush administration's tenure, Secretary of Defense Donald Rumsfeld apparently concluded there was not—canceling plans to increase the arsenal of the army's main battle tank (the MIA2) and axing altogether plans to deploy a long-range, self-propelled, heavy artillery platform. Both weapons were most clearly relevant for fighting a World War II–style war of mass armies; it was apparently not clear to Rumsfeld where, when, or especially against whom such a war was likely in the current or foreseeable future. This line of reasoning has largely been shelved in the post–September 11 frenzy of defense spending in the name of the war on terrorism.

The Second Tier

In some important ways, the Second Tier is the flip side of the First Tier. The Second Tier is as heterogeneous as the First Tier is homogeneous, and the general peacefulness of the First Tier stands in contrast to the instability and violence that marks parts of the Second Tier.

Because it is so diverse, it is almost as difficult to generalize about the Second Tier as it is to make meaningful generalizations about the entire international system. The Second Tier is generally less economically developed than the First Tier, but it encompasses a wide range of economic circumstances from countries whose economies are virtually as well developed as those of the First Tier (South Korea, Taiwan, and Israel, for example) to countries that are abjectly poor and have very poor prospects of becoming prosperous in the short to medium run (Bangladesh, Nepal, and a good deal of central Africa, for instance). Politically, the Second Tier includes political democracies (for example, India, the world's largest democracy), remaining devout Communist states (North Korea and Cuba), Cold War–era autocracies (Burma/Myanmar, for example), and anarchical "failed states" (Somalia and Haiti are prime examples). Geopolitically, the Second Tier runs the gamut from the highly consequential (such as China, Russia, and India) to the virtually inconsequential (most of Micronesia, for example).

Generalizing about the Second Tier is thus treacherous business. It helps somewhat to differentiate among subtypes, or subtiers, to make more meaningful distinctions. I have done this by dividing Second Tier countries into three categories, based on levels of economic and political development. At the top are members of the *developed subtier*: countries whose economies approximate but do not quite match those of the First Tier and who either have unproven democracies or who have not yet evolved democratic forms. Some meet First Tier standards on one criterion but not the other. South Korea, Singapore, South Africa, Brazil, and Israel fall into this category.

A step developmentally below this subtier is the *partially developed subtier*. As the name implies, countries in this category have a generally less well developed economy (for instance, specializing in the manufacture of products based on First Tier technology) or may not be uniformly developed (China's special economic zones versus the underdeveloped interior); politically, most have either nondemocratic or fledgling democratic forms. This category includes a wide range of states, from Russia to India and China to places such as Bolivia and Suriname.

At the bottom of the developmental hierarchy is the *developable subtier*. Numerically, this is the largest category, comprising about half the countries of the Second Tier. Countries in this category have generally not entered or are only beginning to enter the developmental process from subsistence societies to industrial to post-industrial status. This category ranges from countries that have developed primitive economic systems and may be poised for the partially developed world to very poor, destitute countries whose economies are based almost entirely in subsistence agriculture, extractive industry, fishing, lumbering, and the like. (In addition, the scheme includes a category called the *resource-rich subtier* to house the very rich oil producers whose economies are otherwise quite underdeveloped.)

This hierarchy has practical implications. On one hand, it helps to define the process and outcomes of globalization. One way to think about countries joining the globalizing economy is in terms of their progression through the developmental hierarchy represented by the subtiers. States in the developable subtier, for instance, are unlikely to be major participants because they have little to offer to a system that operates on the Ricardian principle of specialization and comparative advantage as the vehicle to become engaged in a system whose major dynamic is the efficient movement of goods and services across boundaries (free trade). Subsistence-based systems do not meet that kind of criterion, and until they can develop something at which they are competitive, they are of little interest to the system. If they do, of course, the nature of their economies (and possibly their political systems) would be transformed and they would move into the partially developed subtier. The same is true for partially developed countries as they become more broadly competitive and move up the hierarchy to the developed subtier. Assisted progression through the subtiers is a way to think about how geopolitics and globalization can be married to reduce the appeal of terrorism in terrorist-producing societies.

This movement and progression has tended to be geographically specific in the as yet brief history of globalization, and the areas that have become most deeply involved in the globalizing system have tended to be those where there are institutional devices to facilitate development and participation. Various forms of affiliation with the European Union (EU), for instance, provide a device for poorer European countries, such as those in the Balkans and the former Warsaw Pact countries, to join the general prosperity; and membership in the Asia-Pacific Economic Cooperation (APEC) has stimulated globalization around the Pacific Rim. If it reaches fruition, the Free Trade Area of the Americas (FTAA) provides similar tantalizing possibilities.

The areas of the world where these economic associations are active represents a good depiction of where the global economy is operating, and those areas that are not part of any of these associations are those most effectively excluded from the globalization process. The most obvious areas on the outside are Africa and a good deal of central and southern Asia.

Aside from the fact that the areas outside the associational network are generally poorer and more destitute than those inside (and thus more likely to be in the developable subtier), there is also a more strictly geopolitical consideration: The areas outside these associations are more prone to violence and instability than members of the globalizing economy. Examining the Project Ploughshares data on violent conflicts for 1998, for instance, I found that of violent conflicts going on in thirty-three countries that year, six were occurring in countries that are part of the globalizing economy (operationalized as members in EU, APEC, or FTAA), while twenty-seven were occurring in countries outside the system. Virtually all the states identified by the U.S. Department of State as sources or supporters of terrorism are also located outside the globalizing system.

Intersecting the Tiers

The analysis of the Second Tier suggests that the leading powers of the First Tier have been successful in engaging parts of the developing world into the globalizing system that they dominate, but they have not been successful universally. If one assumes that the dynamics of globalization take root and spread in an atmosphere of relative peace and stability, and that adoption of the values of political democracy and economic prosperity undergird the First Tier's homogeneity, it thus is in the First Tier's best interest to proselytize in those parts of the world currently excluded.

Reaching out to "engage and enlarge the circle of market democracies" (to borrow language used to describe foreign policy during the Clinton administration) has been selective, not universal. Part of the reason for this is that some countries have been better positioned physically and otherwise to be attractive and have followed strategies for inclusion (discussed more fully in Chapter 5). At the same time, however, parts of the world, such as most of Africa and parts of central Asia, have not been pursued because they rate low on the rankings of interests that the First Tier has in various parts of the world. Prior to the campaign to overthrow the Taliban and uproot Al Qaeda, Afghanistan was a primary example in central Asia.

DYNAMICS OF THE NEW SYSTEM: GLOBALIZATION AND/OR GEOPOLITICS

As the discussion of tiers fairly clearly suggests, the relationship between geopolitics and globalization is an intertwined, intimate, and evolving proposition, not an either/or matter. During the Cold War, geopolitical concerns were clearly and appropriately dominant given the nature of the international situation. Yet, while the geopolitics of East-West confrontation dominated the international agenda, the forces that would propel globalization were being set in place, ready to enter the calculus.

During the 1990s, two quite opposite forces seemed to be at play that changed the relative importance of globalization and geopolitics and ended up creating an exaggerated view of the post–Cold War world. One of these forces was the apparently receding importance of the most visible manifestation of geopolitics: military force. The demise of the military confrontation clearly devalued standard, traditional military force within the First Tier conglomerate of important countries, and this devaluation led many states sharply to reduce their forces. Following the apparent last hurrah of twentieth-century-style warfare in the Persian Gulf war, military concerns shrunk to smaller tasks, such as peacekeeping.

At the same time, the impact of globalization was making enormous headway as the leading edge of the great and spreading prosperity of the 1990s. During the first seven or so years of the decade, economic growth and prosperity seemed inexorable, at the very same time that major systemic instability and violence faded from the world stage. The result was a euphoria that would prove to be partially false with time. To enthusiasts like *New York Times* correspondent Thomas L. Friedman, however, we were entering the "age of globalization," a systematic transition from the old to the new.

At one level, the rise of globalization is nothing more than the latest conceptual and physical reaction to the realism represented by the geopolitically dominated Cold War period. Because it is discussed in detail in Chapter 2, we will not describe or critique realism here. Suffice it to say that realism and geopolitics represent the conflictual side of international relations—the dark side, or yin, in politics. Globalization, on the other hand, emphasizes the cooperative side of the international equation, the idealist assault on the worst outcomes of a realist-dominated world—war. This assault has known many names, from interwar idealism and its attachment to international organization to the functionalism of the early post–World War II emphasis on the UN system to make war functionally impossible. The more direct

---

Amplification 1.2

SYSTEM CHANGES AND
CONTINUITY: 1900 AND 2000

It was the turn of the century, and there was great anticipation in the air. There had not been a major war in thirty years to interrupt the basic peace, and there was great physical prosperity that reached nearly everywhere in the developed world. The result was an atmosphere of almost unbridled optimism for the new century. In the minds of most pundits, the major cause for joy came from an economic system that was spreading itself globally and entwining all members in a web of economic interdependence that made war between them unthinkable and possibly even physically impossible. Those who grumbled about overly euphoric projections of this situation into the future were deemed as grouchy doomsayers who were out of touch with the times.

The year, of course, was 1900, not 2000, and the pundits proved tragically wrong. The first round of globalization did not produce the general peace its enthusiasts projected; rather, it was the presage of the bloodiest, most war-torn century in recorded history. What does that say for the twenty-first century?

Mostly, it counsels restraint and modesty in our projections into the future. The simple fact is that we lack the scientific knowledge to make confident predictions about something as complex as the workings of the international system for anything but the shortest time periods. As we look at the kinds of forces in the contemporary environment, it is worthwhile to remember that almost all of them have been present before, but with very different outcomes. So, as we raise and try to answer questions about forces such as globalization and geopolitics, it is worthwhile to remember that our projections are no more than well-informed speculation. No one, after all, predicted the attacks of September 11, 2001. We could be right, we could be wrong, or, more likely, we will end up somewhere in between.

lineage attaches to the idea of complex interdependence popularized by Robert Keo-hane and Joseph S. Nye Jr. in the 1970s. Globalization emerges as the yang to the geopolitical yin.

The result is, as noted, a fast-moving and changing international dynamic. The seemingly inexorable ascent of globalization was delivered a sobering blow by the East Asian crisis that swept through the global economy in 1997 and 1998 and reminded us that the growing prosperity was neither automatic nor nonreversible. In turn, the ensuing turmoil brought geopolitical elements back to the fore in diverse places. In Indonesia, for example, the crash laid bare the last vestiges of corruption in the Suharto dictatorship, hastening his resignation from a presidency to which he had had himself appointed for life and setting in motion centrifugal forces in the archipelago that continue into the new century. In order to straighten out the eco-nomic mess revealed by the crisis, the old-fashioned economic instrument of power (although not called that) was invoked in the form of International Monetary Fund (IMF) sanctions in offending countries. At the same time, the carrot and stick of WTO membership and most favored nation status was waved under the noses of the Chinese in order to secure their adherence to other quite different standards, such as human rights. The dark side of geopolitics reasserted itself decisively as the commer-cial airliners slammed into the icons of geopolitics (the Pentagon) and globalization (the World Trade Center) on September 11, 2001.

What this reveals is that globalization and geopolitics have become intertwined in complicated ways, which we will explore in the pages that follow. In some ways, the economic aspects of globalization supplanted—at least part of the time and in some instances—the military aspects of geopolitics during the 1990s. Certainly this was true in relations within the First Tier, as already noted, and doubtless there are other instances. At the same time, globalization may be the servant of geopolitics, as in the complex motivations and debates about the use of economic incentives toward China to entangle that country in a spider-like web that will draw it toward the economic and political values of the First Tier–dominated system.

Globalization and geopolitics may thus be the yin and yang of modern geopoli-tics, sometimes competing with one another and other times complementing one another. Before beginning the journey to try to decide the direction, nature, and velocity of that relationship, it is necessary to introduce one other major characteris-tic of the contemporary environment: the central role of the United States.

THE AMERICAN ROLE IN THE NEW WORLD SYSTEM

As already suggested, one of the ways the new international order is different from the Cold War era is in the distribution of power and influence among states; and we continue to struggle for appropriate language to describe the new arrangement. The language of bipolarity and multipolarity is clearly no longer descriptively accurate, and the use of the term *unipolarity* has connotations of a level of control, even hege-mony, that the United States does not possess and to which most Americans, includ-ing their leaders, do not aspire.

It has become fashionable to describe the United States as the remaining super-power, but a new term has also entered the lexicon to describe how much more influ-ential the United States is than other states in the system. That term is *hyperpower,* which connotes the great qualitative advantage of the United States in addition to quantitative advantages, such as having the world's largest economy and most lethal military. It is a term sometimes used out of awe and respect, but it is also attached to what the late Arkansas Senator J. William Fulbright called "the arrogance of power."

What are the bases of American preeminence in the world? It is possible to use the traditional measures of national power to compose that advantage: the so-called political, economic, and military instruments of power. (As we shall see in subse-quent discussions, notably in Chapter 7, other elements may be added to this list, such as information possession.) During the Cold War, the United States had the advantage in employing each of these measures, but its advantage was challenged by different powers in each category. Marxism-Leninism posed a challenge (which turned out to be overestimated) to the political appeal of Western democracy; the economies of Japan and the European Common Market (now the EU) posed an eco-nomic challenge; and Soviet nuclear and massive conventional forces challenged American dominance on the military dimension.

During the 1990s, the United States clearly established its preeminence on all three measures of power. Part of the reason was that the United States outperformed its rivals, especially in the economic realm. At the same time, the demise of the Soviet Union meant that the source of challenge to both the political and military dimensions of power quit the field, leaving the United States as the sole possessor of significant amounts of all the instruments of power.

Politically, the United States emerged as "the indispensable nation," as former Secretary of State Madeleine Albright put it. The basis of American political advan-tage was at least twofold. On the one hand, the power and appeal of the American system and political ideals (Nye's "soft power") make the United States the model that many states and peoples worldwide seek to emulate. At the same time, the United States is the only country that has truly global interests. This means that whenever situations arise almost anywhere, the United States is affected and has an interest in influencing the outcome—a situation highlighted when the United States became the direct victim of international terrorism. Because of American power on the other dimensions, American preferences are consequential and sought out, regardless of the location.

The economic dimension is similar. After nearly two decades of economic dol-drums during the 1970s and 1980s, when it became popular in this country and abroad to talk about American decline, the American economy revived and led the expansion of the globalizing economy during the 1990s and into the 2000s. The United States had remained the world's largest economy even during the down years, but as expansion occurred and the globalization system became a trading sys-tem, the United States also blossomed as the world's great market, which everyone sought to enter. At the same time, America's economic rivals relatively declined. The German economic "miracle" was slowed by the greater than anticipated burden of absorbing the former German Democratic Republic (East Germany) into the Federal Republic in the early 1990s. Also, by the end of the 1990s, the Japanese economy was faced with a serious downturn; joining the American-inspired and American-led "circle of market democracies" added to the luster of its soft power.

American military advantage increased the most. The most obvious reason for this was the decline of America's military rivals. Russian forces are far inferior in size and quality to the old Soviet military machine, and the retention of a comparable nuclear arsenal to that of the United States is about the only way in which America's past rival poses any threat. Similarly, the People's Republic of China retains the world's largest army but has no way to project it far from its borders and, by official accounting, spends less than 10 percent the amount on defense that the United States does. As the adversaries have melted away, America's allies have also cut back their forces at a more rapid rate than the United States has, contributing to the substantial gap in military capability between the United States and everybody else.

The gap is qualitative as well as quantitative. As was first demonstrated convincingly in the Persian Gulf War, the results of the so-called revolution in military affairs (RMA) in adapting technologies such as electronics to the battlefield have given the United States (and its close allies) an enormous qualitative advantage militarily. The only other states that have undergone aspects of the RMA are First Tier allies like France and Great Britain. Second Tier states (like Iraq in 1991 and again in 2003) simply stand no realistic chance when confronted by a military machine such as that which can be fielded by the United States and its NATO allies.

The result of these military advantages is that the United States has the military reach to match its global interests, and it is the only country that can project military power globally. At the operational level, the United States is the only remaining power with a global blue-water (major ocean-going) navy, and it is the only country that has global air power projection capabilities. Not only does this mean that the United States has great advantage in projecting its own forces into faraway places; it also means that others must rely on American capabilities to get their own forces to distant battlefields or to deployments in the name of peacekeeping, for instance.

This position of preeminence is not always nor universally appreciated, and its implications are controversial. It is commonplace to hear objections to American global leadership on grounds such as American "arrogance" or some similar charge. At the same time, one of history's lessons would seem to be that nature abhors vacuums in all guises, including balances of power. Some argue that American singularity of power will create rivals to fill the vacuum left by the Soviets, and occasionally there is some mention of the possible formation of rival coalitions (such as Russia and China). These never seem to come to fruition, and American preeminence has remained unchallenged for a decade. In fact, following the Afghan campaign and the American-led campaign to bring down the government of Saddam Hussein unilaterally in the face of international opposition, there was speculation that American military prowess may have gotten too great—to the point that the United States no longer needs its allies to accomplish military goals and thus can ignore their advice. Using American military power to create and enforce an American vision of the world is the neo-conservative's evangelical dream that produces nightmares in many foreign capitals.

CONCLUSION: THE CONTINUING ROLE OF FORCE

There are two broad interpretations about the extent to which the recourse to force has changed in the post–Cold War world. If one begins from an emphasis on the potential applications of force, then the change has been dramatic, since the most notable potential use used to be the ultimate employment of necessity—a military confrontation with the Soviet Union. That contingency has obviously disappeared, and with it much of the potential use of force in conventional interstate warfare has faded in the general tranquility among those countries with conventional forces, notably the First Tier countries. It is still possible to conjure interstate wars on the peripheries (such as the war with Iraq or other members of the "axis of evil"—Iran and North Korea), but none of these has the immediacy and importance of the Cold War confrontation. Combating terrorism has replaced large-scale warfare at the pinnacle of national security priorities. This assessment has major implications, of course, for the kinds of forces the United States develops and the missions for which they are prepared.

The other way to look at the problem is to note how and where forces were actually employed in the past and how they are in the present or future. From this vantage point, the change is not very dramatic at all. As already noted, the United States employed force exclusively in the old Third World during the Cold War, and the current pattern emphasizes deployments in the Second Tier. In both periods, the conflicts were generally internal affairs—civil wars of one kind or another. The difference is in the motivation underlying involvement: During the Cold War we were primarily motivated by ideological, Cold War reasons, whereas now we are tempted to intervene either to relieve human-induced chaos and suffering, in effect to save countries from themselves, or to root out sources of international terrorism.

This distinction is not insignificant, for at least three reasons. One is the relative importance we attach to potential involvement. In the Cold War context, one could make the argument—admittedly sometimes a stretch—that we were impelled to act in the developing world because of the geopolitical implications of the outcome. Should our side lose, it would be yet one more instance of the "victory" of Communism in the global struggle. Thus, intervention could be arguably a matter of necessity. Such geopolitical motivations are generally missing in many contemporary situations, in which the goal often is to restore order after some humanitarian disaster. In any geopolitical sense, these are clearly employments of choice. The employments of necessity deal with terrorism; the elusive, secretive nature of the terrorist opponents, however, makes specification of where and how engagement might occur difficult.

What we do in internal wars has changed as well. During the Cold War, conflicts were usually clearly drawn competitions between a government and an insurgent group, each of which fielded an organized armed force and sought militarily to defeat the other. In these circumstances, the purpose of inserting American armed forces was to assist "our" side in defeating the enemy. American forces were sent "to fight and win" in familiar military terms. In the contemporary environment, this is not the case. Normally, the situation is one of more or less chaos, and the contending parties are shadowy organizations with inarticulate political goals, supported by armed bands that are barely military in composition. The purpose for using force in these situations is to suspend the fighting and, in effect, to impose peace on the area. This is best done by simply intimidating the warring parties with a show of force and then keeping them physically apart. Ideally, the soldiers do no fighting at all, since their simple presence accomplishes the goal. Force used in this manner is more difficult to understand than more traditional uses. The first phase of the Afghan campaign, where American force was used to help topple a regime, returned us to a more traditional reason for fighting, at least for a limited period of time.

Finally, the two different contexts require a rethinking of how we look at the international system and our place in it. During the Cold War, our thinking was dominated by geopolitics in the form of something called the *realist paradigm*, a construct that tied the use of force to the most important American interests and counseled that force not be used in less weighty circumstances. When the global balance between Communism and non-Communism was at stake, the paradigm provided guidance about when and when not to employ force. Applying the same standards to the humanitarian disasters of the 1990s and 2000s could paralyze the use of force in ways that might be undesirable, and it is not clear the neo-conservative-inspired assault on Iraq would have passed the traditional realist standard of worthiness. Whether the realist paradigm is an adequate device for dealing with the use of force is one of the most fundamental questions facing contemporary thinking about national security. Therefore, Chapter 2 begins with a description and critique of the concept.

SELECTED BIBLIOGRAPHY

Allison, Graham T. Jr., and Robert Blackwill. "America's Stake in the Soviet Future." *Foreign Affairs* 70, 3 (Summer 1991), 77–97.

Friedman, Thomas L. *The Lexus and the Olive Tree: Understanding Globalization.* New York: Farrar, Straus & Giroux, 1999.

Fukuyama, Francis. *The End of History and the Last Man.* New York: Free Press, 1992.

Fulbright, J. William. *The Arrogance of Power.* New York: Random House, 1966.

Gaddis, John Lewis. "Setting Right a Dangerous World." *The Chronicle of Higher Education: The Chronicle Review* 48, 18 (January 11, 2002), B7–B10.

Keohane, Robert O., and Joseph S. Nye Jr. *Power and Interdependence*, 2nd ed. Glenview, IL: Scott Foresman/Little Brown, 1989.

Mearsheimer, John J. "Why We Shall Soon Miss the Cold War." *Atlantic Monthly* 266, 2 (August 1990), 35–50.

Nye, Joseph S. Jr. *The Paradox of American Power: Why the World's Only Superpower Can't Go It Alone.* New York: Oxford University Press, 2002.

Project Ploughshares. *Armed Conflicts Report, 1999: Sixth Annual.* Waterloo, Ontario: Center for Peace and Conflict Studies, 1999.

Singer, Max, and the Estate of the Late Aaron Wildawsky. *The Real World Order: Zones of Peace, Zones of Turmoil,* rev. ed. Chatham, NJ: Chatham House, 1996.

Snow, Donald M., and Eugene Brown. *International Relations: The Changing Contours of Power.* New York: Longman, 2000.

———. *The Shape of the Future: World Politics in a New Century.* 3rd ed. Armonk, NY: M. E. Sharpe, 1999.

———. *When America Fights: The Uses of U.S. Military Force.* Washington, DC: CQ Press, 2000.

2

Geopolitics: America and the Realist Paradigm

Realism and the realist paradigm are central to the operation of the international system and American attitudes toward the world. Moreover, geopolitics, one of the two competing themes around which this book is organized, finds its philosophical and operational basis in realism and the paradigm. Because of these factors, this chapter lays out the realist argument and its implications in a geopolitical world to help in understanding the contemporary national security environment. Many opponents of realism, including some advocates of globalization, oppose the paradigm and its consequences, and their objections are also discussed. The chapter concludes with a discussion of the future relevance of the realist paradigm.

The United States has been a leading member of the international system at least since the end of World War II, which means that it has occupied a position as a major international force for the entire lifetime of most present Americans. Most of us have never known a time when the United States was not a major player on the world scene, regardless of whether we were born here or immigrated to this land. This fact has the potential to distort our perceptions about global geopolitics and our role within the national security arena in which geopolitics is acted out. As Americans look forward toward the new millennium, it is wise to place our experience in perspective, which is the purpose of this chapter and Chapter 3.

This American preeminence has not always been the case. The simple fact is that geopolitical participation—especially leadership—is the exception to rather than the rule for the United States historically. For most of our history, Americans sought to be above what was viewed as the corrupting influence of power politics, and the result has been an ambivalence about our role in international politics, including its more openly geopolitical aspects. As a result, we wonder where we fit into the system and what role we want to take in structuring and participating in the geopolitical game.

There are several reasons for this ambivalence, and although any list of these reasons will be subject to criticism for both what it includes and what it omits, we can identify at least three factors from what we might call the American strategic culture that capture the essence of typical American attitudes toward the world of geopolitics.

The first factor is what some analysts have called *American exceptionalism*. Rightly or wrongly, Americans have always thought of this country as a special place, one that is qualitatively better than other places. The United States was, after all, the first modern country in the world to adopt political democracy, and the United States has long provided a refuge from political tyranny elsewhere in the world: from Europe in the eighteenth and nineteenth centuries and from much of the rest of the world since. As a result, Americans think of themselves as a kind of chosen people and view intrusions from the outside as a potential source of taint. The fact of steady immigration into the country (contrasted by essentially no emigration) reinforces this preference, as captured in the Statue of Liberty's invitation to bring us "your huddled masses" seeking freedom. America is, in Ronald Reagan's phrase, "the shining house on the hill."

The perception of being exceptional leads to a second strain in America's historical view of itself: *isolationism*. Because contact with and participation in the international system entails a potentially tainting effect, there is a residual sentiment to limit the degree of American participation in an essentially corrupt enterprise. In its most extreme form between the world wars, this sentiment manifested itself in a virtual withdrawal from international politics (though not international economics) under the banner of so-called splendid isolation. In a more contemporary sense, *neoisolationism*, most clearly associated politically with presidential candidate Patrick Buchanan, argues for sharp limits on the degree of American interaction with and leadership in the world. This sentiment finds substantive voice in policy areas as disparate as American misgivings about participation in United Nations–sponsored peacekeeping missions and opposition to economic globalization. There is, quite simply, a strand in the American political experience that, like the late Swedish actress Greta Garbo, simply wants to be left alone. To many foreign and domestic critics of American policy, this tendency manifests itself as American *unilateralism*, the tendency to ignore the sentiments and advice of others and to act alone in international affairs, a charge leveled at the George W. Bush administration by many foreign detractors surrounding the Iraq war.

There is also another factor, which is what one might call American *ambivalence* about the effects of geopolitical participation. Very few Americans would describe themselves as isolationists or maintain that the United States has no leadership role in the world. Pure isolationism ended effectively with the Japanese attack on Pearl Harbor, and neoisolationism was badly crippled by September 11, 2001. Nonetheless, ambivalence remains. The consequence of involvement often is to ensnare the country in a web of international rules and regulations (what are sometimes called regimes) that limit American independence in ways about which many have second thoughts, because such involvement can preclude some actions the country might prefer to take.

American attitudes toward its sovereignty stand out as examples of our ambivalence. Sovereignty, which means supreme authority, is central to the realist paradigm and is discussed more fully in the next section of this chapter. For present purposes, suffice it to say that the United States is among the strongest defenders of state sovereignty among the world's countries (along with China), because strict sovereignty minimizes the extent to which the judgments or standards of outsiders can be imposed on the country or on individual Americans. Thus, for instance, the United States is one of only a handful of states that has refused to ratify the statute of the International Criminal Court (ICC), which has the jurisdiction to try people accused of committing war crimes. The reason for the U.S. government's refusal to accede to the statute is our reluctance to permit Americans to be tried by foreign judges if they are accused of committing war crimes. As an example, when an American soldier was accused of raping and killing a young girl in Kosovo shortly after the United States joined the Kosovo Force (KFOR) peacekeeping mission in 2000—an act deemed a crime against humanity and thus a war crime—he was whisked off to an American base in Germany and tried there by an American military tribunal rather than facing the ICC. (He was sentenced to life in prison, which is the most severe penalty he would have faced if he had been tried and convicted by the ICC.)

This reluctance to dilute authority puts the United States at odds with much of the international community on a number of matters, and our ambivalence toward participation results in anomalies and inconsistencies in our relations with the world. For instance, although American insistence on maintaining our sovereignty is not something to be challenged or violated, there have been situations when the United States has felt perfectly within our rights to violate other countries' sovereignty without seeing any inconsistency. American relations with Cuba illustrates this ambivalence and occasional incongruity.

Since 1960, the United States has imposed an economic boycott on dealings with the Communist government of Fidel Castro. This boycott is viewed by virtually the entire international community as anachronistic (a recent vote in the UN General Assembly condemned it by a vote of 143 to 3), and U.S. legislation to enforce it brings cries of violations of sovereignty from friends and allies "alike." For instance, provisions of the Cuban Democracy Act of 1992 and the Helms-Burton Act of 1995 impose sanctions against foreign governments and corporations for doing business with Cuba, in effect making it illegal in the United States for a British company to sell its products in Cuba. This is accomplished by imposing sanctions on doing business with the United States if one violates the provisions of the acts. According to critics of U.S. policy toward Cuba and foreign companies and governments, these are clear and obvious violations of the sovereignty of foreign governments and corporations that, if imposed on the United States, would be roundly condemned in this country.

These examples are simply illustrative of the tension, ambivalence, and complexity with which the United States fits itself into the geopolitics of the contemporary system, and these problems are likely to be accentuated as the United States adjusts its policies in response to international terrorism. Moreover, these issues broadly define the differences between a broadly internationalist emphasis on globalization and a narrower emphasis on geopolitics. To understand that position more fully, we will begin by looking at the geopolitical system we inherited from the Cold War, the so-called realist paradigm, and objections to it as the operating principle of international politics. With this foundation established, we will turn, in Chapter 3, to the American historical experience with national security and how that history contributes to current attitudes and perspectives.

REALISM AND THE REALIST PARADIGM

Realism is one of the leading theoretical approaches to the study of international relations and provides a useful way to organize our understanding of the world. In addition, realism serves as a practical guide for political leaders as they conduct foreign policy. Realism thus serves as both an intellectual tool and a set of guidelines for policy makers.

These dual functions are not coincidental. The academic basis of realism came from the study of international relations by scholars whose first interest was in physical observation of how world leaders, diplomats, soldiers, and the like, actually carried on their relations. Developed and ordered into a coherent explanation of international relations, the content of theoretical realism has roughly coincided with the actual conduct of international affairs. One of the reasons the approach is called realism is because it is said to reflect reality.

Realism is controversial, largely because many people—especially a number of international relations scholars—dislike the reality the realists portray and seek more or less actively to reform or reverse some of the basic dynamics that the realists portray. Among the phenomena that realists describe and reformers wish to change is the "normalization" of the recourse to force—in other words, war.

As a theoretical approach, realism is as old as observation about the relations between independent political units. Many believe that Thucydides' *History of the Peloponnesian Wars*, written in the fifth century B.C., is the original statement of the philosophy of realism, and many would add the sixteenth-century Italian diplomat and advisor Niccolo Machiavelli's *The Prince* to the roster of realist classics.

Realism became a dominant approach to understanding international relations in the period surrounding World War II. At the end of World War I, a group of scholars known as "idealists" came to dominate the study of the international system. Given the enormous carnage of the Great War, there was considerable sentiment to reform a system whose rules—based in realism—had allowed the first great conflagration of the twentieth century to occur. They based their reform on the institutionalization of peace around the League of Nations and grounded their scholarship in ways to improve the peace system by improving the effectiveness of the League in reinforcing and preserving the peace.

Unfortunately, their advocacy (what they sought to accomplish) colored their observation of the actual international politics of the interwar period (what was actually occurring). The idealists either did not see World War II coming or felt it could be avoided, but the institutional framework they had built to avoid war proved entirely inadequate to slow the rush to war in the 1930s. This failure was most dramatically stated by the English scholar E. H. Carr in his critique of idealism published in 1939, *The Twenty-Years Crisis, 1919–1939*.

Realism emerged from World War II as the dominant explanation and approach to international politics. In 1947, Hans Morgenthau published the first edition of his landmark exposition, *Politics Among Nations*, in which he laid out in detail the realist position. Emphasizing the roles of such concepts as power, conflict, and war, the resulting realist paradigm seemed particularly well suited for describing (in a scholarly sense) and organizing the policy response to the emerging Cold War competition between the Communist and non-Communist worlds.

Even at the height of the Cold War confrontation, realism never lacked for critics. Part of that criticism comes from the conjunction of the academic and practical aspects of realism: It is not only an academic theory for understanding the world, it is also a set of rules for conducting international affairs that includes at least a partial, implicit endorsement of its principles. The alternative to thinking about or acting outside the bounds of realism is, in a word, unrealistic. If one does not like the implications of a realist-run world, one probably does not like the academic approach either. In some cases, this intellectual objection is stated in terms of questioning the conceptual adequacy of the realist paradigm for describing and explaining international relations; in others, the objections are rooted in opposition to the effects of conceptualizing the world through the prism of the realist paradigm.

Resolving the theoretical debate about whether realism or some other theoretical framework better produces knowledge about international relations goes beyond our purpose here. As it relates to questions about the actual conduct of foreign and national security affairs, the basic concepts of realism form the framework within which national security decisions have been made since at least the 1940s. As a result, the pattern of historic and contemporary national security concerns cannot be adequately understood without understanding the realist paradigm. If the post–September 11 environment indeed represents a return to the ascendancy of geopolitics, then the contemporary world can be fully appreciated only by understanding realism. Similarly, criticisms of realism are important to us to the extent to which their implementation would alter those rules within which we think about national security and which are at least implicitly part of the rationale for the globalizing 1990s.

BASIC CONCEPTS AND RELATIONSHIPS

Although this runs some risk of oversimplification, we can reduce the realist paradigm to a series of six propositions about the international system that can be arranged deductively to produce a syllogistic order. Each individual statement contains one or more of the key concepts, and collectively they define the realist perspective. Although numerous observers object to the implications of some of the observations that make up the paradigm, hardly any student of national security would fundamentally question their accuracy in describing the operation of contemporary international politics.

The six propositions composing the realist paradigm are:

1. The international system is composed of sovereign states as the primary units in both a political and a legal sense.
2. Sovereign states possess vital interests and are the only units in the system entitled to vital interests.
3. Vital interests become matters of international concern when conditions of scarcity exist and are pressed by state actors.
4. When issues involving scarce resources are present in the relations between sovereign states, then power must be used to resolve the difference.
5. The exercise of power is the political means of conflict resolution in international relations.
6. One political instrument of power is military force, which is one option for resolving differences between states.

If one follows the syllogism from the first to the sixth proposition, the conclusion one must reach is that in a system of sovereign states, states must possess and, from time to time, use military force to resolve problems that arise for them in the system. Thus, the realist paradigm justifies a concern with national security defined, at least in part, in terms of military force. It should therefore not come as an enormous surprise that the realist paradigm finds considerably more intellectual favor among students and practitioners of military affairs and varying levels of disregard and disdain among people opposed to the use of military force as a "legitimate" tool for resolving differences among states.

As stated in terms of these propositions, the realist paradigm is only a skeleton of concepts and relationships. It gains meaning when the basic concepts that compose it are examined and put together in the logical sequence of their presentation, as depicted in that set of propositions.

Sovereignty

The most basic and critical principle of international relations is that of *state sovereignty*. The idea was originally articulated by a sixteenth-century Frenchman named Jean Bodin as a way to justify concentrating the authority of the French monarch by asserting his supreme authority over lesser French nobles. Sovereignty was enshrined as the basic operating principle of international relations through the series of agreements ending the Thirty Years War (1618–48), known as the *peace of Westphalia*. The Thirty Years War had been, in large measure, about whether the church or the state would be the principal holder of political authority in the future. Those supporting the notion of state authority prevailed, and they seized upon state sovereignty as the institutional and legal basis for institutionalizing their secular triumph over sectarian authority.

Sovereignty means *supreme authority*. Within a system in which sovereignty is the basic value, no entity can have authority superior to that of the sovereign. When

Bodin coined the term and it was adopted by others, such as the English philosopher Thomas Hobbes, sovereignty was thought to be a quality that primarily applied to the domestic relations among individuals and groups within states rather than the relations among states. In fact, Bodin never considered the effects on the relations between sovereign entities. In the early days of the modern state system, that domestic sovereignty was considered to rest with the monarch. The extension of the principle to the international arena occurred over the next century and has been the principal operating rule underlying international politics ever since.

Both the domestic and international ramifications of sovereignty remain in force, although with quite opposite effects. Domestic sovereignty remains the basis of the authority of the state over its territory, although we now think of sovereignty as residing with the people (who confer part of their sovereignty on the government), rather than with a person—the monarch. The result of sovereignty applied domestically is to create the legal and philosophical basis for political *order*, since authority to act rests with the state.

The effect of sovereignty on international politics is to create *anarchy* as the basis of the relations between states. In the international arena, state sovereignty means no state can have any jurisdiction over what goes on within another state. Thus, all relations among states are among equals, and no state has the authority to compel any other state to do anything, at least in a legal sense, which does not always conform to actual practice. There is no higher authority above those with supreme authority, which means that there is no basis for governance in international relations; thus, a formal state of anarchy exists in the international realm. Jurisdiction over disputes resides with the parties to the dispute, who must figure out how to decide their differences on their own, without recourse to an outside authority that can settle those differences. Although the inviolability of state sovereignty has never been as absolute as the definition implies (states violate other states' sovereignty routinely), it remains the major organizational tool for defining relationships within the international system.

On the face of it, this seems like an odd way for the international system to conduct its business, because the practical outcome is that there is no international equivalent of the judicial branch of government to settle disputes, and the parties are left to fend on their own when differences arise among them. The reason for this state of affairs lies, however, in the fact that states have matters of such importance to them that they are unwilling to have those matters left to the judgment of outsiders. As a consequence, states demand as total control over them as they can enforce. This leads us to the second major concept of the realist paradigm.

Vital Interests

The main reason states are generally unwilling to compromise on matters affecting their sovereignty is because states, unlike other entities in the Westphalian system, have what are called *vital interests*. Defined as properties and conditions on which states will not willingly compromise, vital interests are matters whose outcomes are too important to be submitted to any superior authority and which must be guarded to the full extent of the state's ability to do so. Some analysts would add that a vital interest is any interest that is sufficiently important that the state will use force to ensure its realization.

States normally rank their interests, formally or informally, in a hierarchical fashion that denotes how important a particular interest is and hence what measures the state will undertake to realize the condition or property in question. Donald Neuchterlein provides a useful way to categorize these interests in the form of the national interest matrix. (See Figure 2.1.) Both dimensions of the matrix are hierarchical. Clearly, the most intense interest a state has is its physical *survival*, followed by those interests on which the state will not willingly compromise (*vital* interests). *Major* interests are matters that would inconvenience or harm the state but which can be tolerated, and *peripheral* interests are, as the label implies, matters more of inconvenience than basic interest. Similarly, the most important basic interest a state has is in defending itself, followed by promoting its economic well being, its view of the world order, and its own values.

The critical point here as it relates to questions of national security is the boundary between vital and major interests, because it is generally agreed that vital interests are ones over which the state will use force to guarantee, and major interests fall below that threshold. The location of that boundary is a matter of disagreement within the national security debate when it is applied to individual situations.

In the early and middle 1980s, for instance, there were different assessments of the implications of a Marxist government in the Central American republic of Nicaragua. The the Sandinistas arguably threatened American interests in the area—notably, protection of access to the Panama Canal—and their existence had potential implications as a platform for the spread of Castroite Communism in the hemisphere. Some Americans—notably, the Republican administration of Ronald Reagan—found Sandinistas' rule intolerable, a threat to a vital American interest. Accordingly, they favored assisting an insurgent group, the so-called *Contras*, to overthrow the regime by force. Democrats in Congress disagreed with this assessment, downplaying the significance of the Sandinistas. They passed legislation (the so-called Boland Amendment, named after the Massachusetts House Democrat who sponsored it) prohibiting assistance to the Contras. Violation of those prohibitions by members of the Reagan staff helped trigger the Iran-Contra scandal toward the end of the second Reagan term. The disagreement boiled down to different conclusions about the level of U.S. interest involved in the situation.

The boundary between vital and less-than-vital interests is and will always be an important point of contention within the domestic and international security

Figure 2.1: National Interest Matrix

Basic Interest at Stake	Intensity of Interest			
	Survival	Vital	Major	Peripheral
Homeland Defense				
Economic Well-Being				
Favorable World Order				
Values Promotion				

debate. Looking at the basic interests at stake, for instance, there is little disagreement that defending the homeland is vital to the state, and hence challenges to that interest will be met by force. Responding to the September 11 attacks clearly follows from this interest. As one goes down the list of basic interests, however, the question of vitality becomes more debatable. In the Persian Gulf War, for instance, the American interests involved were clearly economic (access to petroleum energy that literally fuels the American economy). Then U.S. Secretary of State James Baker acknowledged this interest early in the conflict, when he replied to a reporter's question about why we were going to free Kuwait, "It's about jobs!" In contrast, promoting the American vision of the world, including our democratic and capitalistic values, is at a lower level of importance.

Amplification 2.1

FINDING THE BOUNDARY BETWEEN VITAL AND LESS-THAN-VITAL INTERESTS

One of the major alternatives to the definition we have used for vital interests is to say that vital interests are any interests worth fighting over. The danger of this definition is that, when reversed, it implies that any time a country is fighting, its vital interests must be engaged. This, of course, is a dubious proposition. But since people employ the distinction, it does mean that the boundary between vital and less-than-vital interests is an important one in the study of national security.

Unfortunately, the boundary does not actually exist, either in the abstract or regarding specific situations. The reason for this is psychological and subjective. What is an intolerable circumstance for some people may or may not be intolerable for someone else. The dictionary definition of *security*, for instance, is "safety or a feeling of safety." Beyond direct physical threats (e.g., a Russian missile or terrorist attack against the American homeland), most threats to security—or situations in which interests are at risk—fall within the psychological range of what makes one feel insecure and hence feel that one's interests are imperiled. Because people can and do honestly disagree on these matters, the location of the boundary between vital and less-than-vital interests becomes the benchmark in the national security debate over when to use force.

If we apply this abstract notion to the contemporary trouble spots in the world identified by the Bush administration as constituting the "axis of evil," for example, the question to ask in each case would be: "How intolerable would the worst possible outcome be to American interests; and thus, would I be willing to use force to ensure that the worst outcome does not occur?" If you compare your assessments with others, you will likely find that there are some instances of large-scale consensus: Most would endorse the use of force if Iraq invaded Kuwait again; there would probably be less support for military action against North Korea or Iran. How important are these countries—specifically, their alleged programs to gain weapons of mass destruction—to the United States? What actions are warranted against them? More specifically, was the invasion of Iraq justifiable on the grounds of vital interests?

The activation of concern over vital interests occurs in situations of scarcity, when more than one claimant to a scarce resource asserts that claim as an interest. Scarcity, for our purposes here, is the situation in which all claimants to a resource cannot simultaneously have all that they want (or feel that they need). The definition is drawn from economics, of course, and economic resources such as wealth are indeed one obvious arena where scarcity may occur. Scarcity may also be political (political power or office when more than one individual wants the position), social (everyone cannot, by definition, be part of the elite), or physical (possession of a piece of disputed territory or access to a natural resource like water). Conflicts over vital interests are activated when competing parties put forward incompatible claims to a scarce resource and insist on a quantity of the resource that does not allow the other party to have as much of the resource as it deems necessary.

An historical example may illustrate the point. In the 1850s, as the United States expanded west toward the Pacific Ocean, it came into direct conflict with Great Britain over where the northern boundary of the United States and the southern border of Canada should lie. The Americans claimed parts of what are now Canada (Vancouver Island, for instance), and the British claimed parts of what are now Washington and Oregon. Clearly, both countries could not simultaneously possess the disputed territories, which established their scarcity, and both sides deemed the outcome too important for compromise. At one point, there was even the threat of war—on the American side, under the slogan "Fifty-four Forty or Fight" (the latitude of the proposed American boundary). In the end, compromise prevailed. The United States dropped its claims to Vancouver, and Britain abandoned its claims to the American Pacific Northwest.

Two final notes should be included about vital interests and sovereignty, because the concepts are reinforcing. Because vital interests are so important, states are unwilling to accept contrary judgments about their interests when they can avoid them. As a result, a state is unwilling to submit disputes to a higher authority (a sovereign above the state), for fear such an authority might rule against the state in an unacceptable manner that would have to be disobeyed or ignored in order to ensure an acceptable outcome. Vital interests, in other words, are matters that are too important for the state to relinquish control over the outcomes. Having said that, the word *willingly* must be part of the definition of vital interests, because when vital interests come into conflict, normally the weaker party must *unwillingly* accept an unacceptable outcome. Thus, the interplay of vital interests in a realist world is, in fact, an exercise in power politics.

Power Politics

International relations is an inherently political enterprise in which the principal political actors are states seeking to maximize their advantage in an environment where all cannot be equally successful. Who gets what is the essence of the political process in this arena. For our purposes, we will use my variation of David Easton's definition of politics: *Politics is the ways in which conflicts of interest over scarce resources are resolved.*

Challenge!

Justifying the U.S. Invasion of Afghanistan

In response to the unwillingness of the Afghan Taliban regime to hand over Usama bin Laden and his associates living in Afghanistan after the September 11, 2001, terrorist events, the United States sent military forces into that country to work in cooperation with opposition elements to overthrow the Taliban regime. The opposition, notably the Northern Alliance, had been carrying on an unsuccessful war against the regime—making it a civil war situation. With the aid of U.S. Special Forces and the generous application of American airpower, the effort succeeded and the Taliban were removed from power.

The U.S. justification for intervention was based in the American interest in destroying the Al Qaeda terrorist network, clearly a vital American interest as part of the so-called war on terrorism. As long as the Taliban insisted on protecting bin Laden and his supporters from apprehension, Al Qaeda remained a threat to the United States. Thus, their removal was a necessary prerequisite to hunting down and extinguishing the threat.

But was it legal and justifiable? These are really two separate questions. In general terms, intervention in a civil war, even at the invitation of one of the parties, is illegal under international law, and there is no clear evidence such an invitation was issued anyway. Also, the United States never formally declared a state of war between itself and the Taliban—the term *war* was never used in its technical, legal sense.

The legality of the action under international law was thus open to question, and the Bush administration has done little to establish a legal position justifying its actions. But does that matter in the real world? The justification that was offered was geopolitical—entirely consistent with the realist paradigm. Are American national interests sufficient to warrant an act, regardless of its legality? Was the U.S. action against Iraq legal, or does that matter? What kind of justification is necessary in those cases? What if those actions are more or less universally condemned by other members of the world community? Do such objections matter?

This definition contains two related elements. The first is procedural, "the ways in which conflicts . . . are resolved." The second is substantive, what "scarce resources" have to be allocated and who gets those resources. The two dimensions are related because both the nature and the importance of the resource may determine the procedures that are employed to decide the outcome, and the procedures may influence or prejudice the substantive outcome. Generally, the less important the issue (in the interest terms discussed earlier, major or peripheral interests), the more likely a state will be to submit the matter to some authority to which it has given the ability to reach a judgment for an outcome. When a matter is of the highest importance to the state (a survival or vital interest), then the state is likely to invoke its own sovereign authority to maintain as much control over the outcome as it can.

The unique possession of vital interests by states produces a political structure in which state sovereignty is the central feature in determining political outcomes. As already noted, sovereignty within states provides the basis for producing a political order, including methods (legislation, adjudication, etc.) for resolving differences between individuals and between individuals or groups and the state. The interests of individuals and groups are ultimately subservient to those of the state to which sovereignty has been ceded for these purposes. Those same vital interests, however, preclude the formation of political processes that can authoritatively allocate values among states in areas deemed vital by the contending parties. The result, as noted earlier, is that the political form of international politics—at least in dealing with matters of interests vital to the state—is anarchical. As long as states retain vital interests, this essential anarchy will remain the central procedural aspect of international politics.

In the setting of anarchical international relations, states achieve their interests to the extent that they have the ability to do so—through a process sometimes known as *self-help*. Since the need to resolve important international political problems generally occurs when vital interests are involved and scarcity exists, the outcome is, by definition, likely to be that one or all parties must accept less of a condition or property than they had previously deemed vital. Determining outcomes is thus an exercise in the application of power.

Power is an elusive and highly controversial concept, but it is a central characteristic of the realist paradigm. Its elusiveness comes from trying to operationalize and measure power in order to predict who will prevail when states clash in the international arena. If the exercise of power is central to an understanding of international relations, then it clearly would be desirable to be able to observe the basis of power, so that one could predict in individual situations which party to a dispute could apply power to the other and thus prevail. This has led to a good deal of effort being expended on trying to develop ways to measure the power of states, none of which have proved entirely satisfactory in predicting political outcomes.

Power is also a controversial concept because one of the most obvious and prominent forms that power takes in the international arena (and within some states) is military force. Those who oppose the use of military force thus find themselves in opposition to a system in which power, including military power, is central, even normal, as a way to resolve differences. In their view, the key to a more tranquil, peaceful world lies in the abrogation of power as the basis of politics.

Part of the controversy is definitional as well. Although some analysts would say our definition really describes influence rather than power, we can adopt a common and straightforward definition of power: *the ability to get someone to do something he or she would not otherwise do*. The definition skirts the controversy over measurement of power by specifying not so much what power *is* as the *effects* of the application of power.

The definition highlights two major characteristics of a power situation. First, it says that power is not an attribute possessed by parties so much as it is a relationship between an entity seeking to exercise power and another seeking to resist the application of that power. The common form in which a power relationship is applied is through the issuance of a threat (a promise to do something harmful unless what is demanded is complied with) by one party against the other. The outcome depends

Amplification 2.2

MEASURING POWER

Although the concept of power is pervasive as a means to describe international relations, efforts to measure power have remained largely elusive. As noted in the text, finding ways adequately to measure and thus be able to compare the power that different states possess would be highly desirable, because it would make predictions of the outcomes of interactions between states much more accurate than they are in fact.

There are two difficulties involved. The first is finding physical measures that adequately describe the abilities of states to influence one another. A concerted effort has been made to find concrete, physical measures—such as the size or sophistication of countries' armed forces or the productivity of states' industrial bases—that could indicate which is the more powerful country in any head-to-head confrontation. The problem is that such measures work only part of the time. There is, for instance, no physical measurement to compare national capabilities that would have led to the conclusion that North Vietnam had any chance of defeating the United States in a war, but they certainly did.

The second problem is that measures have difficulty getting at the psychological dimension of the will and commitment that people may possess. How can an outside observer determine, for instance, when a clash of interests is clearly more important to one party to a dispute than it is to the other (at least before the fact)? Once again, the Vietnam War is illustrative. The outcome of that war—unification of the country—was clearly more important to the North Vietnamese and their southern allies than its avoidance was to the United States and the population of South Vietnam. This is clear in retrospect; it was not at all clear before and even during the hostilities. Being able to see clearly after the fact is of very little comfort to the policy maker. Having measures that accurately predict the future would be of far greater value.

on the action of the party threatened. If the threatened party believes the threatening party both can (has the capability to) and will (has credibility) carry out the threat in the face of noncompliance, the threatened party may comply. If, however, the threatened party doubts either the will or the ability of the threatening party to carry out the threat, it may conclude differently. At any rate, whether power is successfully applied is a mutual matter in the relationship between the parties, not something simple and concrete, like a comparison of the sizes of military machines or industrial capacity (although these are clearly relevant to deciding if the threatening party has the wherewithal to carry out the threat).

The other characteristic of a power relationship is that it is situation-specific. What this means is that the application of power does not occur in an abstract sense but within very specific situations. It is important to recognize this fact, because the vagaries and special circumstances surrounding any particular relationship may influence how a power relationship plays out, sometimes in unpredictable ways.

An example will help illustrate these characteristics. In the early 1970s, the African country of Uganda was ruled by a particularly objectionable ruler, Idi Amin

Dada. Amin, a sergeant in the British colonial force who declared himself a general when Uganda achieved independence in 1962, had seized power from the postcolonial government in 1971. His rule was harsh and objectionable. He had as many as 300,000 Ugandans of tribal origins other than his own killed, and in 1972, he had 45,000 Asian residents (who formed the backbone of the country's commercial system) expelled. As the country drifted toward chaos, the United States withdrew its diplomatic personnel from Uganda in 1973. Despite this, Amin continued to provide gratuitous advice to President Richard M. Nixon in a series of letters advising Nixon about how he should handle his Watergate difficulties.

The United States—and a number of other countries—wanted Amin removed from the Ugandan presidency. Since Amin was not amenable to leaving, this meant that power would have to be applied to get Amin to do something he clearly would not otherwise do. The problem was: What kind of power did the United States have over the dictator? By any objective measure, the United States was overwhelmingly more powerful than Uganda, but was that power relevant to the specific situation of overthrowing him? Was there some form of leverage the United States could apply to remove Amin? Was American power relevant in this case?

The answer turned out to be that it was not. To try to achieve its goal, the United States threatened and implemented an embargo on the importation of Ugandan coffee into the United States (a prohibition ignored by the U.S. firms that bought Ugandan coffee until they were caught violating the sanctions), but the embargo volume was not enough to cause Amin to step down. In the end, Ugandan rebels—assisted by the neighboring Tanzanian armed forces, which possessed far less absolute but much more relevant and believable power than the Americans—finally managed to drive Amin out of power and into exile in April 1979.

It is the combination of capability and will that make power effective in individual situations. In the Ugandan example, for instance, the United States clearly had the military capability to overthrow the Ugandan regime (or, for that matter, obliterate it with nuclear weapons). What it lacked was the credible will to apply that force in a situation that was at most annoying but clearly did not rise to the level of vital interests. There may be some parallel between this experience and the American effort to remove Iraq's Saddam Hussein from power before the war, a prospect explored in an Amplification later in this chapter.

In order to exercise power, the state must be capable of carrying out threats. Doing this requires possessing the so-called *instruments of power*. In conventional, traditional terms, these instruments are divided into three categories: diplomatic (or political), economic, and military. Diplomatic/political power refers to such characteristics as the persuasiveness of a country's diplomatic corps, the attractiveness of the country's political profile, and the country's ability to use the other implements to back up political rhetoric. Economic power refers to the use of economic rewards (carrots) and deprivations (sticks) for compliance with a country's demands. Military power refers to the threat or actual use of military threats or actual military applications to achieve the country's goals. As noted in Chapter 1, one of the reasons for designating the United States as the sole remaining superpower is that it is the only country with significant assets in each of these categories, although the characteristics of power noted earlier do not mean that its power is unchallengeable in individual situations.

Some authors, as suggested earlier, believe the list of instruments should be extended in the contemporary environment. A leading candidate for inclusion is informational power—the ability to control and manipulate the amount and quality of information an adversary has in a power situation. Elements of this power include information-gathering ability (intelligence) and manipulation (interrupting information sources and transmission or distorting that flow). An exotic form is so-called cyberwar—attempts to disrupt and control computer systems and their ability to collect, analyze, disseminate, or even retain information.

In an anarchic system, power and politics are intimately related to one another. Politics, after all, is about who gets what in terms of scarce resources; and by definition, scarcity means that some parties will have to do what they otherwise would prefer not to do. In the absence of authorities that can decide on allocations, the parties must help themselves through the application of power, including the use of military force on occasion.

PARADIGM SUMMARY

With these basic concepts and relationships established, we can summarize the "rules of the road" that define the realist paradigm and how international relations are conducted in a system whose rules are paramount. Although a growing number of people decry the paradigm and its implications, it remains the basis on which international relations are conducted today. Moreover, the paradigm is especially applicable to our thinking about matters of national security, and it is the virtually unanimous choice as a model among those charged with the development and conduct of national security policy practically everywhere in the world.

The realist paradigm begins with state sovereignty as its basic value, which means that there can ultimately be no higher authority than the state in determining what happens to the state. The absence of a higher authority is not coincidental; it is the direct result of the possession of vital interests by states (but not other political entities). These vital interests are matters of such importance to the state that it will not willingly compromise on them and will use all available means, up to and including military force, to ensure that they are honored. The two concepts, sovereignty and vital interests, require and reinforce one another. The prosecution of vital interests in an anarchical system precludes the possibility that a superior authority could—perhaps capriciously—compromise a vital interest of the state. Sovereignty provides the conceptual bedrock to deny that possibility, and it is not coincidental at all that the governments of countries are among the strongest and most consistent champions of sovereignty and resisters of any dilution of state sovereignty.

The government of the United States has been and continues to be among the world's staunchest defenders of state sovereignty, and at the bottom of almost all its defenses of the concept is the insistence that no outside power should be allowed to create conditions to which Americans do not want to be and should not be subjected. Although this insistence often puts the United States in awkward, even embarrassing international situations, it is the fear that a dilution of sovereignty will permit the violation of American vital interests that provides the politically inviolable base for U.S. policy in this area.

In a world of plenty, the state of international anarchy would not be a particular problem, since states would rarely come into direct conflict with one another over who gets what. In the real world, of course, scarcity, not abundance, is often the case, which means that political processes are necessary to determine outcomes of disagreements. Since these situations often involve the vital interests of states, those states are generally unwilling to submit them to bodies that could exercise jurisdiction and prefer, instead, to rely on more informal means of conflict resolution to settle differences. Settlements in conditions of scarcity mean that some or all of the parties to a given dispute find that they must accept less than they would have preferred or that they must do something they would prefer not to do. Because of this, international politics inevitably is power politics.

In a world of sovereign states interacting through power politics, the state succeeds to the extent that it can succeed through self-help. In order to get others to do what you want but the others do not, states must possess the ability, in specific situations, to convince or compel other states to act in ways that serve their national interests. In other words, states must possess power to succeed.

Power comes in a variety of guises. The most common (but not only) forms are political or diplomatic power, economic power, and military power. Although the applicability of any particular form of power will vary—depending on the situation and both the ability and the willingness of a state to use its power to gain compliance with its positions—generally, the more power a state has, the more successful it will be in achieving its ends. In the anarchical situation of international politics, among the forms of power that must be available is military force. Thus, the international system ultimately is an environment in which the threat or recourse to force is a "normal" activity some of the time and in which states that will succeed must possess armed forces "to prepare for and fight the country's wars," to borrow from common military parlance.

CRITIQUES AND ANOMALIES OF THE REALIST PARADIGM

Most observers would, in some cases grudgingly, accept my portrayal of the realist paradigm as accurate, but many analysts both decry the sets of conditions produced by the realist paradigm and point to anomalies that it produces in the interactions among states. Some of the objections are academic, in the sense that they are more likely to be heard in academic circles than in the general policy debate. Others, however, apply directly to the day-to-day debate about national security policy.

An exhaustive criticism of the realist paradigm goes beyond our present intent. For our purposes, the criticisms can be viewed from two perspectives. One of these argues that the principles underlying the realist paradigm, especially state sovereignty, have never been as strictly adhered to in fact as they are in principle—in other words, the paradigm is only partially accurate. The other perspective maintains that adherence to the paradigm produces a flawed international system—in other words, the paradigm's effects are pernicious. In both cases, the conclusion drawn by the critics is that the international system should be reformed on principles other than those on which the paradigm is based.

Critiques

Because state sovereignty lies at the heart of the Westphalian system, it is the realist concept that draws the greatest negative attention. The principle of state sovereignty creates an international institutional setting of purposive anarchy that necessitates a world of power politics and guarantees that international relations will emphasize conflict rather than cooperation. The critics maintain that state sovereignty has never been as absolute as its extreme representation would suggest. However, the more closely one hews to the practice of absolute sovereignty, the more pernicious the effects are within the international realm.

Although such early political theorists as Hobbes and Bodin favored something like the absolute sovereign powers of the state as a way to justify the power of monarchs, the suggestion that the principle of sovereignty creates an impenetrable state that is unaffected or unlimited by outside forces is not, and never has been, more than a fiction. States interfere in the political life of other states all the time, and the behavior of states is limited by international regulations (usually ones that they have explicitly agreed to be limited by) on a regular basis. Moreover, contemporary forces such as economic globalization and the impact of the telecommunications revolution are making state boundaries increasingly porous and a state's control over what happens within its jurisdiction increasingly difficult to maintain. Critics of sovereignty argue that it is pure fiction to maintain otherwise. Moreover, important trends in international relations suggest that sovereignty will continue to erode in fact, if not in principle. The staunch defense of sovereignty is, in other words, a losing battle.

As sovereignty erodes, so does the salience of some of the operating principles of the paradigm, and this is nowhere truer than in areas related to national security and the use of force. It is not at all clear that some uses of military force to achieve national interests are not as acceptable today as they were a century, or even a decade, ago. Wars between states have virtually ceased. All members of the United Nations renounced their right to declare war as part of their conditions for joining the world body, and although that does not mean that force has disappeared, no state has formally declared war on another state since World War II. As the international response to Iraq's 1990 invasion and conquest of Kuwait clearly demonstrated, the aggressive use of force across borders is no longer acceptable behavior. The closest equivalent we have to interstate warfare is international terrorism initiated by nonstate actors, and hardly anyone would argue that such activity is either legitimate or consistent with the realist paradigm (although responses to terrorism may be).

The other manifestation of the realist paradigm that is under question is the use of vital interests as the benchmark against which to measure when force should and

Amplification 2.3

THE USES AND LIMITS OF POWER: DEALING WITH SADDAM

With the possible exception of Fidel Castro, there is no leader in recent memory that has vexed American policy and policy makers more than Saddam Hussein of Iraq. He became a major irritant when he invaded and annexed Kuwait in 1990, forcing the United States to take the leadership in forming the coalition that evicted the Iraqis from Kuwait in 1991. After the Persian Gulf War fighting ended, a series of demands were placed upon Mr. Hussein that, by and large, he refused to comply with—or did so very reluctantly. Ultimately his obstinacy was so great that the United States led a military campaign that removed him from power.

Under these circumstances, United States policy toward Iraq and Saddam Hussein had at least three goals, all of which the Iraqi leader refused to accept. The first and most obvious goal was his physical removal from power. The second was the abandonment of Iraq's program of developing weapons of mass destruction (WMD), including comprehensive inspection of suspected WMD production facilities. The third was to leave the Kurdish and Shiite minorities—who rose to overthrow Hussein with American encouragement in 1991—alone.

The problem was how to force Hussein to comply with these conditions that he resisted, which was a question of having the appropriate instruments of power in this particular situation. To try to bring Hussein down, the United States attempted to employ the diplomatic/political instrument of power, sponsoring international condemnation of the Iraqi regime in such international forums as the United Nations and supporting political alternatives to Hussein in Iraq (the Bush administration, for instance, spent $92 million in aid to political alternatives for 2001). Economically, the United States has been the mainstay behind economic sanctions designed to gain compliance with the WMD ban. Militarily, the United States and Britain (France previously participated but had dropped out) enforced the so-called no-fly zones over the Kurdish and Shiite regions of the country under the banner of Operations Northern and Southern Watch.

The difficulty was that, with the partial exception of the application of the military instrument of power, none of the attempts to apply power worked. International condemnations were ineffective, and there was growing opposition to continuing them. Hussein has had most of his opponents killed or chased into exile, making the identification and nurturing of "moderate" alternatives with any domestic support in Iraq difficult. The economic sanctions, as is often the case, caused well-publicized hardship to innocent women and children rather than to the leadership (the so-called "principle" of punishing the innocent), did not force compliance, and were increasingly opposed by the international community, which wanted them lifted. Moreover, the sanctions made smuggling into Iraq rampant. Operations Northern and Southern Watch kept the Kurds and Shiites reasonably safe, but they were open-ended commitments that would only be terminated by terminating the Saddam Hussein regime. Moreover, wider bombing campaigns such as Operation Desert Fox in 1999 failed to force Hussein to change his behavior.

The pre-invasion relationship between Saddam Hussein and the most powerful country in the world clearly demonstrated the limits of power. By any measure one might devise, the United States was clearly more powerful than Iraq, yet American power has proved inappropriate and ineffective in forcing the defiant Iraqi leader to do things he did not want to do but that the United States would have had him do. The frustration level this ineffectiveness created in Washington led to calls to consider more intense military efforts, up to and including the physical invasion of Iraq that ultimately occurred. Within the realist paradigm, the question that must be asked is whether Iraq's actions threatened vital American interests enough to justify those military actions.

should not be employed. This concern is largely the result of changes in the international threat environment since the end of the Cold War, and particularly the result of something I have called the *interest–threat mismatch*—the situation in which important interests and threats do not coincide.

During the Cold War, when the realist paradigm was clearly the dominant worldview of policy makers on both sides of the conflict, the benchmark clearly applied: Vital interests (national survival, for instance) were threatened, and thus the idea that force would be threatened or used in East–West confrontations provided clear guidance for the development, deployment, and potential employment of force. Interests, and threats to those interests, were clearly aligned and coincided with one another.

The situation changed radically after the implosion of the Communist half of the Cold War. The important interests of the United States have remained what they were before: American homeland security and a free and democratic Western Europe and Japan, with which the United States can engage in commerce and political relations. What changed was that those vital interests were essentially no longer threatened. There is no Communist menace hanging over Western Europe, as the West Europeans move steadily to incorporate more and more of formerly Communist Europe into institutions such as the European Union. (There are plans to increase membership in the EU from fifteen to twenty-five states during the next two rounds of expansion; the first five new members are scheduled to be Hungary, Estonia, Latvia, Slovenia, and the Czech Republic, all formerly Communist states.) Thus, where there were American vital interests, there is no meaningful threat that would justify the use of force; important interests and threats were misaligned.

There were and are, however, situations in the world that are threatening to the United States or to the international system more generally. There are, for instance, many internal wars raging in parts of the developing world—notably, in Africa and parts of Asia. Indonesia, the world's fourth most populous country, has several ongoing conflicts, the basic purposes of which are secession from the Indonesian republic. In Africa, the HIV-AIDS pandemic has reached such enormous proportions that in 2000, then-President Clinton declared it to be a national security concern, an emphasis that the Bush administration has continued through the personal concern of Secretary of State Colin Powell and his commitment of funding and trip to Africa in 2003.

What these and other examples of world problems share is that essentially none of them reach the level of being vital interests that would activate the American security system within the realist framework. In terms of interests at stake, they are mostly favorable world order or value questions at the intensity levels of major or, in most cases, peripheral interest to the United States. The threats do not measure up to important interests.

The interest–threat mismatch takes form from this assessment of the post–Cold War environment: *The most important American interests in the world are hardly threatened, and the threats that do exist are largely tangential (are hardly interesting)*. In these circumstances, if the realist paradigm is used as the sole (or main) criterion to determine when or if the United States will employ force in the world, the result will be paralytic, because hardly any situation will meet the criterion of engaging vital interests and thus justifying force. During the Cold War, the realist paradigm was the hawk's standard, because it counseled large and robust forces to deal with real threats to vital interests. In the post–Cold War world, that same paradigm turned the hawks into doves, since the paradigm directs noninvolvement with military force. The post–September 11 response to international terrorism, of course, realigns interests and threats in that area of concern. Whether this produces a Cold War–like coincidence of interests and threats across the board or a narrower coincidence in a more general environment of mismatch remains to be seen. Moreover, it is not clear to what extent military power is the appropriate instrument to deal with this threat.

An example may demonstrate how a part of the changing environment affects the relevance of the realist paradigm. One of the major sources of violence and instability in the world is the series of very bloody internal (civil) wars occurring in parts of the developing world. A number of these conflicts (e.g., Somalia, Bosnia, Sierra Leone, East Timor, Liberia) have gone beyond the ability of the countries involved to resolve, resulting in great suffering to the affected civilian populations (casualty rates in these conflicts often approach 90 percent civilian). The gruesome nature of these conflicts has led to international pleas for involvement, with military forces designed to stop the fighting and suffering under the guise of something like *humanitarian intervention*. These conflicts generally occur in places where there are no important American interests, and the application of the realist paradigm would suggest that the United States should remain aloof. The only way to justify the employment of force is either to ignore or expand the paradigm or to try to rationalize that heretofore less-than-vital interests are now more important (e.g., Macedonia is important to the United States because it is important to the allies.). The Bush administration has been much more reluctant than its predecessor to engage in such actions, largely justifying it in traditional realist terms.

The salience of the realist paradigm in describing reality is not the only source of opposition by critics. To a large number of interested observers, the paradigm is objectionable because of both the activities it legitimizes and the kinds of viewpoints it deemphasizes. The most obvious objectionable activity is the acceptance, even promotion, of military force as a normal and acceptable form of state action; the most obvious example of what it does not emphasize is cooperative behavior among states.

The realist paradigm legitimizes the recourse to armed violence as a means to achieve state interests by acknowledging military force as one of the normal instruments of power. In addition, the approach's emphasis on the observation of "reality" (actual behavior of states) notes that states (and groups within states) do, in fact, occasionally resort to the use of force to achieve their ends and that, in some cases, they succeed in achieving their ends by doing so—the ends justifying the means. Many realists would contend, for instance, that the attempt to downplay and even ignore the role of military forces between the world wars by the idealists contributed to the destabilization of the 1930s that ended with World War II. Moreover, given the predatory nature of some states (Bush's "axis of evil," for instance), the absence of force is a virtual invitation for states to take advantage of the militarily disadvantaged.

Opponents of realism contend that it is the very structure of an international system based in the realist paradigm that creates—even promotes—an emphasis on military force and the recourse to war. The villain, of course, is sovereignty-induced anarchy, which leaves international politics a Hobbesian "war of all against all." In this view, the solution to the "problem" of war is institutional reform of the international system to create orderliness through institutions that can enforce the peace and remove the vigilantism of a realist order. In order to accomplish this, the conceptual victim must be state sovereignty, replaced with ultimate authority either in the hands of a superior entity (e.g., a world government) or returned to the people—popular sovereignty. At any rate, the object is the sovereign state, which the opponents of war argue must be fundamentally reformed before peace can be instituted and enforced.

In addition to its alleged warlike implications, other critics point out that the principle of state sovereignty also tends to emphasize noncooperative rather than cooperative behavior in the relations among states more generally by erecting barriers to interaction across state boundaries. For instance, the sovereign independence of states, it is argued, runs counter to the growing globalization of the world's economy by erecting physical barriers to the movement of people and goods across sovereign boundaries. This argument has particular salience in an age of terrorism, when the protection of boundaries is an important part of protecting citizens from attack—a proposition that we will investigate in terms of its national security implications.

This line of objection can be put in a more general and theoretical form. Realism as an approach tends to emphasize the conflictual elements of international relations and to downplay evidence of international cooperation. While conflict is clearly an element of international relations, so too is international cooperation. There are certainly aspects of international interactions that are zero-sum (one party loses what the other party gains), but there are equally positive-sum situations (where both parties can gain). Critics of realism argue that the realists dismiss the cooperative aspects too much, and that an approach placing great emphasis on cooperation not only results in a more accurate description of international relations, but also leads to the promotion of a greater level of cooperation and thus enhanced international tranquility.

In some ways, this difference goes back to the disagreement in the philosophies of Thomas Hobbes and John Locke (among others) about the nature of man and society. The realists portray a more Hobbesian world (indeed, some of the early realists explicitly included their assessment of man's basically flawed nature as part of the philosophical underpinning of their theorizing), whereas those who emphasize cooperation are manifesting a more Lockean philosophy (wherein people enter into society out of a positive desire for association with their fellows). In more contemporary terms, the debate can be couched in terms of which is the dominant international reality—globalization (cooperation) or geopolitics (conflict), or some combination—which of course is the underlying theme of this book.

The merits of these arguments and counterarguments are not our primary concern. Although it is entirely safe to say that the strictest interpretations of realism are overblown, there are no imminent challenges to the Westphalian order that will render it obsolete and unworkable in the short run. Rather, it is more likely that there will be minor, indirect assaults on the primacy of the order that will slowly erode and change that order to something else. The basis of the international order—like virtually everything else in the natural order—is evolving.

Anomalies

In the meantime, there are anomalies in an international system that is built on the basis of realism but in practice does not precisely conform to the realist mold. Two examples, one American and one Russian, illustrate both the paradigm and its inconsistencies and difficulties.

As noted earlier, the United States is one of the staunchest defenders of the principle of state sovereignty in the world (along with the People's Republic of China). The political and philosophical base of this strongly held position is the belief that Americans and their government should not be subject to imposition or control by foreigners and that, as a result, the United States should resist international attempts to place the United States under regimes that restrict the freedom of action of the country or its people.

Regardless of its merits, this position often forces the United States into a politically uncomfortable position in the world—often in opposition to the vast majority of states and in the company of states with which we do not particularly like to be associated. Invariably, these situations involve American resistance to or refusal to join international agreements that limit the right of signatories to engage in certain behavior (and are most ominous when the treaty includes provisions for international enforcement—a direct abrogation of sovereignty). Ironically, the agreements to which the United States government objects are often proposed by the U.S. government itself (either the permanent bureaucracy or a previous administration), indicating substantial disagreement within the United States itself on the sovereignty issue.

The Bush administration's withdrawal of support for the Kyoto treaty on global warming in 2001 is a contemporary example of this situation. The treaty had been negotiated and supported by the Clinton administration, which had announced its intention to join the international regime created by the accord. When he entered office, President Bush announced his administration's withdrawal from the agreement. Bush did not cite sovereignty directly, but argued instead against what he called unequal and unfair obligations the United States would be forced to bear under treaty provisions and its preference for voluntary rather than mandatory compliance, enforced internationally. The United States stood virtually alone among developed countries in its position and earned a good deal of international criticism for its unilateralist stance.

The anomaly extends to a number of other issues. During the late 1940s, the United States helped sponsor two important treaties establishing universal standards of human rights: the Universal Declaration on Human Rights and the Convention on Genocide. The Universal Declaration, in particular, was based largely on the American Bill of Rights, but the U.S. Senate refused to provide advice and consent on either document until the 1990s, on the ground that they infringed on the rights of the American government to behave in ways prohibited by the agreements. In more contemporary, national security–related areas, the United States is one of the few countries that refuses to sign the international treaty banning land mines (which was originally proposed by a private American citizen) and the statute establishing a permanent war crimes tribunal, the International Criminal Court (ICC). In the latter case, the United States joins a handful of generally rogue states, such as Myanmar and Iraq, as the only states that refuse to accept the jurisdiction of the ICC.

The United States is not alone in being party to anomalies in the current system. Russia, which has acceded to the ICC, is clearly waging a genocidal campaign in the renegade province of Chechnya, which has been actively attempting to secede from the Russian Federation since the middle 1990s. The Russians have brutally repressed this movement, and war crimes have clearly been committed under orders that possibly go all the way to the top of the Russian political leadership. Yet there have been no serious calls for an investigation of the situation by the international war crimes apparatus. Why? One reason is that Russia maintains that the situation in Chechnya is purely an internal matter within the sovereign jurisdiction of the Russian government (and thus beyond the purview of any other authority). Another reason is that Russia maintains its Muslim Chechen opponents are terrorists, since many of the "freedom fighters" waging the war come from the same system that produced Al Qaeda terrorists (thus giving the Russians status as participants in the war against terrorism). Finally, Russia is also a large and powerful country that no one wishes to antagonize unnecessarily, so the position goes officially unchallenged.

The staunch American defense of sovereignty and the ambivalence Americans display when anomalous issues arise from its defense often confuse and mystify other countries, including both U.S. friends and foes. Defying international norms in the name of defending American freedom of action is often equated with American unilateralism—a kind of disregard for the rest of the world. This was clearly the case in the early George W. Bush administration. In addition to its reaction to the Kyoto convention, this was evident in 2001 in the administration's obdurately defended intention to field a national missile defense in the face of essentially universal opposition from abroad, as well as its opposition to the International Criminal Court and the land mines convention.

Defense of sovereign prerogative is also a politically partisan position in the United States, adding to international confusion. Although there are exceptions, the strongest advocacies of protecting American sovereignty have tended to be conservative and Republican, whereas the willingness to subject the United States to sovereignty-restricting provisions of international agreements has tended to be more liberal and Democratic. On other than trade matters, the Democratic Party has been more internationalist than the Republicans, which means that there is a likelihood that the transition in control between the parties will continue to have a real impact on attitudes toward international issues, with ramifications for American state sovereignty across time.

CONCLUSION: THE REALIST PARADIGM TODAY

Despite its limitations and the mounting criticism of it, realism remains the dominant organizational device by which the governments of sovereign states organize their approach to dealing with the world. The criticisms are, without doubt, growing. During the Cold War, these criticisms tended to be isolated within groups outside national governments—for example, academics, liberal commentators, and members and advocates of nongovernmental organizations (NGOs). Given the gravity of the task of managing international affairs in a world where the Soviet opponent was thoroughly committed to realist power politics, advocacies of ideas like reducing the influence of sovereignty fell on mostly deaf ears, particularly among political decision makers responsible for protecting national interests in a dangerous world, where the Soviet opponents were the ultimate realists. According to the prevailing wisdom, Communism could only be opposed in kind.

A less threatening, apparently more globalizing environment in the 1990s saw critical, less realist views becoming more acceptable in practice and in principle. At one level, the series of interventions in peacekeeping roles by UN-deputized forces represented an indirect assault on the notion of total sovereign control of territory. International agreements such as the ban on land mines or the establishment of the permanent war crimes tribunal were more direct assaults, as they subjugated the rights of states to act unilaterally in the face of international norms. Some see this trend as a healthy maturing of international relations. Others see grave dangers in these erosions of state sovereignty and assaults on the structure of the Westphalian order. The Clinton administration was more receptive to change; the Bush administration seems less so, a predilection reinforced after the terrorist incident of 2001 and responses to it.

Does the realist paradigm fit the new, evolving international order? Any direct, categorical answer will, of course, oversimplify a more complicated world order, in which yes-no answers exclude the middle ground between them and result in a distortion of ongoing reality. Cold War realism may not be the perfect paradigm for a post–Cold War and post–September 11 world, but its basic structure has not disappeared. The fault line that began to emerge in 1989 raised questions about the continuing relevance of the paradigm; such criticism has been much less evident since 2001.

A remarkable example may illustrate the evolution of the realist paradigm. On June 29, 2001, Slobadan Milosevic, the former president of Yugoslavia, was extradited from Belgrade to The Hague, Netherlands, where he faced charges of crimes against humanity, as specified in the statute of the International Criminal Court (ICC), which had issued the indictment under which his extradition was carried out. (Since the ICC statute had not been ratified by enough states to come into permanent being at the time, the indictment came from the tribunal established specifically for Yugoslavia.)

The extradition was the remarkable aspect of the event. Milosevic had been indicted in 1999 for his alleged participation in crimes against humanity committed against Albanian Kosovars in Kosovo in 1999. Although Milosevic was defeated in 2000 in his bid for reelection, it was widely believed that the indictment was symbolic and that any trial of Milosevic would have to be carried out in his absence (in absentia). It was assumed that the Yugoslav government, which was not a signatory of the ICC statute, would protect him on the grounds that any attempt to arrest and extradite him would be a violation of Yugoslav sovereignty. This obstinacy flew in the face of widespread world opinion, which regarded Milosevic as a war criminal—or at least believed he should face the charges against him. International economic sanctions against the country were put in place in 2000 to pressure the government into honoring the indictment.

So what changed the mind of the successor Yugoslav government of Vojislav Kostunica and caused it to turn over the former dictator to international authorities? Several factors, two of which bear mention, were involved, and they demonstrate the continuity and change of the new order.

The first factor was domestic and had the effect of eroding resistance to international demands for his surrender to international authorities. While many ethnic Serbs had denied the early charges of atrocities against the Kosovars ordered by the Milosevic government, evidence emerged in 2001 that clearly showed that mass murders had been committed that could only be linked to the government in power at the time. Defense of Milosevic became much harder to sustain, and the defense of his freedom based in national sovereignty gradually eroded. In the end, fully 60 percent of the Serbian population of Yugoslavia favored extradition.

The other factor was international—the effect of the sanctions imposed by the international community because of the Yugoslav campaign in Kosovo. In a word, the people of Yugoslavia became more intolerant of the physical deprivation they were enduring as a result of the sanctions than they were committed to their sovereign control and protection of the former leader. The NATO allies promised the Kostunica government that economic penalties would be lifted as soon as Milosevic was turned over to authorities; it was hardly a day after he reached the Hague that economic assistance began to flow to Belgrade.

So which principle prevailed? Geopolitics or the new order of globalization? The answer is clearly both. The international norm was strengthened by the fact that Yugoslavia relented and allowed the dilution of some of its sovereign jurisdiction over a distinguished citizen, hardly a vindication of the realist paradigm. At the same time, what caused the international norm to succeed was the application of the economic instrument of power in a way that would make the most hardened realist proud.

Selected Bibliography

Bodin, Jean. *Six Books on the Commonwealth*. Oxford, UK: Basil Blackwell, 1955.

Brodie, Bernard. *War and Politics*. New York: Macmillan, 1973.

Carr, E. H. *The Twenty-Years Crisis, 1919–1939*. London: Macmillan, 1939.

Cusimano, Mary Ann (ed.). *Beyond Sovereignty*. New York: Bedford/St. Martins, 1999.

Fromkin, David. *The Independence of Nations*. New York: Praeger Special Studies, 1981.

Kegley, Charles W. Jr., and Gregory A. Raymond. *Exorcising the Ghost of Westphalia: Building World Order in the New Millennium*. Upper Saddle River, NJ: Prentice-Hall, 2002.

Machiavelli, Niccolo. *The Prince*. Irving, TX: University of Dallas Press, 1984.

Morgenthau, Hans. *Politics Among Nations*, 6th ed. Rev. Kenneth W. Thompson. New York: Alfred A. Knopf, 1985.

Nuechterlein, Donald E. *America Recommitted: United States National Interests in a Reconstructed World*. Lexington: University of Kentucky Press, 1991.

Schelling, Thomas C. *Arms and Influence*. New Haven: Yale University Press, 1966.

Snow, Donald M., and Eugene Brown. *International Relations: The Changing Contours of Power*. New York: Longman, 2000.

Thucydides. *The History of the Peloponnesian Wars*. New York: Penguin Books, 1954.

Waltz, Kenneth. *Man, the State, and War: A Theoretical Analysis*. New York: Columbia University Press, 1959.

CHAPTER 3

The American Experience

The choice of a geopolitical, realist orientation toward the world or some alternative, such as globalization, is influenced by the generalized historical experience of a country. For most of American history, that experience has been primarily positive, with low levels and low qualities of threat that make the current high-threat environment all the more distinctive. This chapter begins by identifying general influences on the American experience, then looks at the question historically, designating and describing three parts of the national security experience. The chapter concludes with some suggestions about how the past may influence the present and future.

In any country, the attitude toward national security is conditioned by the country's historical experience and the "lessons" that experience apparently has taught. For some countries, the experience has been harsh. It is impossible, for instance, for any country on the northern European plain not to have some historically based fear of a possible invasion against its territory from one direction or another and, as a result, to view matters of national security very seriously. At the other end of the spectrum, a country like Japan, which successfully isolated itself physically from the rest of the world for hundreds of years, has an equally distinctive worldview and concept of what constitutes security.

The United States is no exception to this effect of history. Although the American experience is shorter than that of the traditional European and Asian powers, it has been conditioned by a series of factors that are both historic and physical. The result of American history has been a generally positive view of the world and the security of the United States in it, which did not require a great deal of emphasis or continuing effort on matters of national security until World War II and its aftermath. Americans have felt secure for most of their history as a country.

We will divide the American experience with national security concerns into three basic periods. Following a discussion of the basic, underlying conditioning factors that help shape the American worldview, we will begin with the formative period, from the beginning of the Republic in the eighteenth century through World War II—a period of relatively low, episodic American involvement in international affairs, including national security. The second period encompasses the Cold War, when the United States was thrown literally into the middle of the geopolitical fray as one of the two major actors and had to learn to act in that environment. We will conclude the chapter with a discussion of the third period, the contemporary system, and the impact of the two major fault lines on the ongoing period. Our discussion will include consideration of how the current situation resembles aspects of the formative period or the Cold War system.

CONDITIONING FACTORS
IN THE AMERICAN TRADITION

At least three factors stand out as important influences on the way Americans have come to view questions of defense and national security: the essential American lack of a sense of history, particularly shared history; the unique American geographical endowment, that has both isolated the United States from hostile others and provided the country with abundant resources to permit and nurture its isolation; and the country's Anglo-Saxon heritage, which affected its earliest attitudes.

American Ahistoricism

It is not unfair to typify the American people as basically ahistorical in their general attitude. This ahistoricism has several bases. One is that the American experience is fairly brief compared to the historical experience of our major European and Asian counterparts. Although the territory that the United States occupies was inhabited for thousands of years by Native Americans, most of the Indian nations did not keep a systematic history, and most Americans do not share a sense of ethnicity or history with these natives. Rather, American history, as most Americans perceive it, is a little less than 400 years old—and it is not even a history shared by most Americans. The pattern of American population settlement has been in immigrant waves, which means that relatively few Americans can trace their own roots back to the beginnings of the American experience. It is no coincidence, for instance, that no Vietnamese Americans are members of the Daughters of the American Revolution, and the same can be said for many other Americans whose ancestors had not yet immigrated to these shores when the "shots heard around the world" were fired in Massachusetts in April 1775.

This lack of historical experience has not been an altogether bad thing. Most Americans came to the United States either to escape some form of tyranny or calamity in their native lands or with the hope of becoming part of the greater prosperity that the United States appeared to offer. As a result, there has been a greater sense of optimism in this country than is present in many more-established cultures where the historical record offers a greater balance of positive and negative legacies.

More pointedly, with the exception of some aspects of the Civil War, the United States has had no national tragedy to mar the national consciousness and temper our optimism in the way, for instance, that the Battle of Kosovo in 1389 tainted Serbian history. (After losing the battle to the Ottoman Turks, Serbia fell under foreign control until the early twentieth century.)

American ahistoricism contributes to the American sense of exceptionalism and thus to American attitudes toward national security in a couple of ways. When combined with the fact and perception of American physical isolation from the world (discussed later), the result has been a positive self-image about the United States and its military experience. This perception of success also extends to the American attitude toward war and matters of national security more generally. Americans have historically viewed themselves as winners both at war and at peace. The revival of interest in America's most successful—and cherished—military experience, World War II, is emblematic of this attitude. The general ahistoricism also allows Americans to ignore less glorious aspects of the military experience, such as our performance in the War of 1812 (in which the United States decisively won exactly one land battle, at New Orleans—fought two weeks after the peace treaty was signed). This general attitude of success has made acceptance of the outcome of the Vietnam conflict all the more difficult, just as the territorial attacks by the September 11 terrorists have assaulted our sense of isolation and invulnerability.

Americans have also liked to portray themselves as an essentially pacific people, slow to anger but capable of vanquishing any foe once aroused. The premise underlying this belief is the idea that peace is the normal and preferred condition and war is an abnormality that is thrust upon us and that we must dispatch. The Japanese sneak attack at Pearl Harbor that dragged a reluctant United States into World War II is emblematic of this conviction, as has been the introduction of terrorism to our shores. When we are victimized, we become Yamamoto's "sleeping giant" (mentioned in Chapter 1).

Many outsiders, as well as Native Americans, would, of course, contest both the notion of American passivity and the American need to be provoked into violence. It is hard, for instance, to argue that most of the wars against the Indians of the Plains and the American West were "thrust" upon the United States; and the Spanish, who had already agreed to all of our terms when we declared war on them in 1898, would certainly question the "reactive" nature of the Americans in that situation. During the course of American history, the United States has fought six major wars (the Revolution, the Civil War, World Wars I and II, Korea, and Vietnam) and four minor wars (the War of 1812, the Mexican War, the Spanish-American War, and the Persian Gulf War). When one adds more minor engagements that do not qualify as wars (it is hard to know how to classify the campaign against Iraq in 2003), the number of times Americans have taken up arms in anger rises to around 200, hardly the clearest evidence of peacefulness, unless one is prepared to argue that each instance was a response to an injustice.

Accident of Geography

Geography has blessed the United States in at least two distinctly benign ways. First, the physical location of the United States between two of the world's great oceans has made it virtually an island, at least as far as potential foreign incursions from Europe or Asia are concerned. When combined with comparatively weak or friendly countries on the northern and southern borders of the country, the result has been a condition of virtual physical invulnerability for much of American history. With the exception of Pancho Villa's raids into the Southwest in the second decade of the twentieth century and a few submarine incursions during World War II, the forty-eight contiguous states of the United States (the continental United States, or CONUS) were safe from the danger of physical harm from 1814, when the British left at the end of the War of 1812, until 1957, when the successful testing of a Soviet intercontinental ballistic missile (ICBM) made the United States vulnerable to nuclear missile attacks. The only other sources of American physical vulnerability have come when the United States has expanded beyond the continental mass (e.g., Hawaii) or has added foreign colonies (e.g., the Philippines).

The other part of the geographic legacy is resource abundance. The American continental land mass is blessed in two ways. First, the central part of the United States has some of the best farmland in the world, allowing the United States to produce enough food for itself (and surpluses for export) without any necessary recourse to foreign sources. Second, the United States also possessed adequate supplies of both mineral wealth (e.g., iron ore, copper) and energy sources (e.g., coal, petroleum, natural gas) to allow the United States to proceed through most of the industrialization process without the need to rely on foreign supplies of natural resources.

The result of both of these geographic factors was to produce, as part of the American worldview, an essential independence and sense of invulnerability that set the country apart from most other countries of the world, which were physically vulnerable, foreign-resource dependent, or both. The United States thus had to spend little time or effort framing its needs in national security terms. Spared of the need to have to defend American territory from invading enemies, most uses of American force were expeditionary, sending forces overseas either to defend some American interest (e.g., U.S. colonies) or to come to the aid of a besieged country somewhere in the world. At the same time, there was no need to prepare to protect access to natural resources or food supplies from vulnerable foreign sources. Effectively, the result was that the United States had, for most of its history, no compelling need to form a national security strategy to protect it from the vagaries of a world that it could largely ignore if it chose to do so.

These unique geographic advantages began to diminish by the middle of the twentieth century. The Pearl Harbor attack and the Japanese conquest of the Philippines demonstrated that an extended United States was no longer physically invulnerable. Soviet missile capability made that vulnerability more dramatic, and advances in telecommunications and transportation have produced arguable American vulnerabilities to situations such as terrorist attacks or cyberwar, vulnerabilities dramatically brought home in 2001 and a continuing source of concern.

American resource independence has also been eroded. Increased demand for energy resources such as petroleum at low prices has made the United States dependent on foreign supplies, with strong and controversial national security consequences in places such as the Persian Gulf (as discussed in Amplification 3.1). At

---

Amplification 3.1

DEALING WITH DEPENDENCE
ON PERSIAN GULF OIL

The Persian Gulf littoral, under which two-thirds of the world's known reserves of petroleum are located, has been a major concern and problem for the United States since 1979. Prior to 1979, American interests in the region—almost exclusively based in uninterrupted access to reasonably priced oil—were ensured by America's closest ally, and the strongest power in the region, Shah Reza Pahlevi's Iran. In 1979, the Shah was overthrown by a violently anti-American revolution that catapulted Ayatollah Ruhollah Khomeini into power and resulted in a takeover of the American embassy in Teheran and the holding of its personnel for the duration of the Iran hostage crisis. It also removed the enforcer of U.S. policy in the region from power, thus calling into question the continuing security of American access to the region's oil.

The Persian Gulf has been a source of major foreign and national security concern ever since. In 1980, President Jimmy Carter issued the so-called Carter Doctrine, declaring access to Gulf oil to be a vital American interest. In 1990 and 1991, the United States led the coalition that evicted Iraq from Kuwait, followed by American leadership in trying to keep Iraq's Saddam Hussein from obtaining weapons of mass destruction. Usama bin Laden's ordered terrorist attack on the United States in 2001 was, by his profession, carried out to help convince the United States to leave Saudi soil. The result has been continuing U.S. presence in Afghanistan and war against Iraq. Most Persian Gulf states also oppose Israel in its struggle with the Palestinians, thereby complicating American policy in that part of the Middle East.

American policy in the Persian Gulf derives directly from U.S. dependence on petroleum from the region. There are alternative sources of oil, but they are either inadequate, inaccessible, or more expensive than Persian Gulf oil. In the case of Russian reserves, there is the ongoing question of political stability as well. Assuming that the United States would prefer to be less dependent on oil from the Persian Gulf region—and thus more independent in its policy options—what are the alternatives?

As framed in the partisan American debates on the subject, there are two alternatives. One, largely associated with Democrats, calls for an emphasis on conservation, thereby reducing the amount of Persian Gulf and other foreign oil needed, by such actions as attaining better fuel economy in transportation, moving toward alternative sources of energy, and the like. The other policy alternative, favored by the Bush administration and many other Republicans, features the development of alternative sources of petroleum, such as opening the Caspian Sea reserves or other sources in such places as the Alaska Wildlife Refuge. Until one or both of these approaches is adopted, it seems inevitable that the United States will be inextricably bound to the politics of the Persian Gulf region, including its violence.

the same time, the development and use of more exotic materials that are unavailable in the United States, such as titanium for jet engines, has reduced resource independence as well. The desire for exotic foodstuffs, such as year-round access to fresh fruits and vegetables, has made the United States an agricultural importer as well. The reversal of long-time American isolation has made this exposure to vulnerabilities more traumatic than it might otherwise have been.

The Anglo-Saxon Heritage

Although this country has greatly diversified ethnically and nationally, and much of the original American culture has changed as a result, the United States was originally a British colony, most of the original settlers in the United States were of British extraction, and they brought with them many of the customs and predilections of the mother country.

The Anglo-Saxon heritage affected the early American experience in some obvious and enduring ways. First, it created an aversion to, and suspicion of, the military—more specifically, the army—in peacetime. This aversion is largely the result of the British experience during the seventeenth century. During the Cromwellian period in the 1640s and beyond, the Commonwealth's armies were used to suppress political opposition to the regime. When the monarchy was restored in 1688, one of the provisions of the settlement of the Glorious Revolution was to forbid a standing army on British soil during peacetime to avoid a recurrence of military intrusion into civilian life. The British insistence on stationing elements of the British Army in the American colonies after the French and Indian Wars became a serious issue that helped produce the American Revolution. (Americans resented being subjected to a condition that citizens of the mother country would have found intolerable.) This aversion manifested itself throughout the formative period of the American national security experience (see the next section) in the tendency to essentially disarm after major wars and to rely disproportionately on part-time citizen-soldiers for the country's defense. The prohibition on the use of American forces in a law enforcement role on American soil (known as *posse comitatus*) further reflects the fear of military abuse that was invoked when some officials proposed an expanded military role in the "war" on terrorism.

The other Anglo-Saxon legacy is a strong commitment to constitutional rule, especially to the guarantee of individual rights and liberties. Since military service, especially when it is the result of conscription, is a clear intrusion on individual liberty, there has always been a political reluctance to compel Americans into service. The only exceptions to this have been American involvement in major conflicts such as in the world wars, which required the raising of large forces, and during the Cold War, when it was accepted that a large "force in being" (standing active-duty armed force) was necessary to deter the menace of expansionist Communism. This aversion reappeared when American opinion turned decisively against the war in Vietnam, which, in its latter stages, was fought mostly by draftees. The fact that no American has been involuntarily inducted into service since the end of 1972 partially reflects attitudes that go back to the formation of the Republic.

EVOLUTION OF THE AMERICAN EXPERIENCE

What can be viewed as the American military tradition has evolved over time and with the different experiences the country has endured. As noted earlier, that experience can be divided into three historical periods: a formative period from the beginning of the Republic to the end of World War II, the Cold War experience, and the contemporary, ongoing period. The two historical periods were distinct from one another in two clear ways. In terms of the levels of threats posed to the United States and the American role in the world, the longer, formative period was one of low threats and commitments, whereas the Cold War featured high threats and commitments. As we look at the contemporary environment, however, neither historic combination fits perfectly. On one hand, the level of American involvement in the world since 1989 has never been higher. At the same time, the degree of threat to the United States was greatly reduced during the period between the fault lines (1989–2001), but threats appeared to intensify greatly after September 11, 2001. A question that we will address in the conclusion of this chapter is which of the historic parts of the past may best inform our grasp of the present and future.

THE FORMATIVE PERIOD, 1789–1945

The period following the birth of the American Republic was obviously critical in developing what would become the American military tradition and the American concept of military force. The period was heavily influenced by the events surrounding the Revolution itself and the reasons it had come about. In retrospect (and certainly in comparison to the nature of modern revolutions), the American Revolution was a rather low-key affair, in terms of both its motivations and its conduct. As Dennis Drew and I have argued elsewhere, it might not have occurred at all had the British government acceded to the American demands to be treated not as colonial subjects but as British citizens, including not stationing British forces on American territory. When the fighting began more or less accidentally at Lexington and Concord in April 1775, it took the colonials almost fifteen months to declare they were, in fact, revolting by issuing the Declaration of Independence on July 4, 1776. The war itself was, by current standards, a low-key affair, fought between relatively small armed forces mostly when the weather was good. Although the style of linear warfare fought at the time could produce sizable casualties in pitched battle, bloodshed was also modest by contemporary standards.

A series of "lessons" about military force arose from the revolutionary experience and were reinforced, by and large, during the next century and a half before the United States was thrust into World War II and could no longer remain aloof from the power politics of the world. Five elements of the American military tradition were born during this formative period. The first four—an anti-military bias, the belief in the efficacy of the citizen-soldier, the myth of invincibility, and the preference for rapid mobilization and demobilization—can be directly attributed to the revolutionary experience. The fifth, a preference for total war, was more a product of the Civil War and the events that followed that conflict in the international system generally. All of these elements collectively reinforce a general sort of disdain for things military that manifested itself, until the Korean War, in an American military establishment that was, except during wartime, small, physically isolated, and generally held in low regard.

Antimilitary Bias

Although it may sound strange today—when public opinion polls regularly rate military service as one of the more prestigious professions—prior to the Cold War, military service was not held in high regard in the United States. The peacetime military was generally a small, skeletal body whose purpose was to be ready to train a civilian force for military duty when the need arose. For the most part, the professional military (especially the army) was consigned to military posts in remote areas of the country, where the general population's day-to-day exposure to it was fairly limited. Moreover, outside the ranks of the professional military itself, soldiering was not thought of as a particularly prestigious occupation. One can still occasionally find bar signs in New England antique stores declaring "No dogs or soldiers allowed," which captured the sentiment held by many Americans historically.

Much of this sentiment has its origins in the Anglo-Saxon tradition and the issue of British military presence in the colonies prior to the Revolution. After the French and Indian wars that coincided with the Seven Years War in Europe between 1756 and 1763, the Redcoats were stationed on colonial soil to provide a protection against frontier Indians. The colonists thought they could contain the Indians themselves, and they knew that the presence of the Redcoats would not have been tolerated in England itself. Moreover, the colonists were expected to subsidize this unwanted element by paying taxes that were levied without their permission. In addition, the soldiers were a potential menace politically, and when they were used to aid in tax collection, they became overtly political actors as well. This revulsion and suspicion were most highly developed in New England, where most of the soldiers were assigned and their negative consequences suffered.

In addition to creating a predilection toward keeping the military as small—and thus nonthreatening—as possible, this antimilitary bias also helped keep the military as apolitical—and hence politically nonthreatening—as possible. The U.S. Military Academy at West Point, for instance, was designed essentially as an engineering school to teach the science of war but not the reasons for going to war (a precedent essentially followed in the other service academies). The leading work detailing the relationship between war and its political purposes, Carl von Clausewitz's On War, was originally published in 1832 but was not translated into English and entered into the West Point curriculum until 1876. Moreover, professional members of the military were effectively disenfranchised until 1944, when legislation permitting absentee balloting was enacted. Prior to that, military personnel could vote only if they happened to be physically in their hometowns on election day, which rarely happened. Keeping the military apolitical was thought to be important enough not to remedy this situation until the heat of World War II.

The Citizen-Soldier

How could disdain and distrust for the military be reconciled with the occasional need for military forces to prosecute the wars foisted on the United States? Part of the answer, of course, was to keep the military as small and unthreatening as possible during peacetime. Since much of the distrust was based on the fear of military intrusion into politics, another goal was to make the military as apolitical as possible. In addition, another element was to develop a part-time military whose members were also integral parts of the civilian society from which they came. The result was to reinforce and glorify the militia tradition that was part of the colonial experience.

Militia members were part-time soldiers. As the lineal forefathers of the National Guard and reserves, they served in the militia for fixed terms and with limited commitments as members. Just as contemporary Guard and reserve units serve for limited periods each year (e.g., a weekend a month, two weeks of summer camp), militia units would drill periodically, often for short periods (some as little as a few days per year). The idea was that such limited commitment would not "infect" these citizen-soldiers with military values to the point that they would lose their primary attachment to the civilian community. The citizen-soldiers would, in other words, remain more citizens than soldiers.

This arrangement was satisfactory if one could assume that the militias were competent to carry out the country's military needs. From the revolutionary period, the myth was developed that this was indeed the case. To some measure, this was little more than wishful thinking, but militia units were involved in enough successful operations (Lexington and Concord, Breed's Hill, Saratoga) that one could embellish their performance and ignore instances in which militia units dissolved and ran when confronted with regular British Army opponents. When the country was not at war, the question was largely moot, since militias were rarely called upon to demonstrate their strictly military competence.

The argument over the efficacy of the militia has never disappeared and remains an active part of the debate over current and future forces. Reserve and Guard units remain an integral part of the U.S. armed forces, although they are assigned generally noncombatant roles. Their virtues are that they are less expensive than active-duty soldiers, and their attachment to their communities makes them popular politically, especially with members of Congress in the districts where they are located. The regular armed forces have a generally lower opinion of these successors of the militia men, emphasizing that the citizen component makes them less effective soldiers and thus of lesser value in military operations than full-time, active-duty forces.

The Myth of Invincibility

The myth of invincibility is the product of a selective reading of American military history. Its core is the idea that regardless of the circumstances, when the United States is forced to fight, it prevails. The general truth value of this belief is, of course, questionable. Although it is true that the United States has generally been successful when it has gone to war, American triumphs are liberally interspersed with episodes in which the country has been less than successful. A more precise statement of the myth would probably be that when the United States becomes involved in long, total wars—in which superior American physical resources can be brought to bear to wear out an opponent fighting according to prevailing rules and American preferences (in other words, symmetrically)—it generally prevails. But even that generalization must be tempered; in Vietnam, the opponent refused to wear out or to fight according to established norms (it fought asymmetrically), and the result was certainly not victory.

This generally positive assessment of the American military experience has two corollaries. The first is the "can do" syndrome—the idea that no military task is too difficult to overcome if Americans truly apply themselves to surmounting it. Conjuring the image of a John Wayne World War II movie, this syndrome can be a major impediment to objective assessment of potential missions for which American military forces might be employed. There is, for instance, little on the public record to suggest that any appropriate military officials considered in advance the prospects that the United States might not be able to prevail in Vietnam; no one in the appropriate position to do so effectively said *"can't do"*—a more accurate assessment and one held by many mid-level professional military and civilian analysts at the time.

The other corollary is that Americans prevail because of the brilliance and skill with which they fight. The facts fly largely in the face of such an assertion. The United States has produced no major strategist of land warfare, for instance, although it has produced exceptional battlefield generals like George S. Patton and strategists who have contributed in other media (sea and air). Moreover, although American fighting forces have acquitted themselves well, the United States entered all its wars prior to Vietnam almost unprepared to fight them, which meant that in the early going of those wars, American forces did not excel.

Mobilization and Demobilization

Through most of American history, the pattern of mobilization and demobilization has dominated the American military experience: When war seemed imminent or was thrust upon us, we would raise and train a force to fight it, but as soon as the fighting ended, we would decommission that force and return it to the normalcy of civilian life. This preference reflected numerous elements of the American culture, from a belief in the abnormality of war to the fear of a standing military in peacetime. It also meant that after every major war until Korea, the United States returned its armed forces to the skeletal form that had existed before the war.

The tradition was sustainable throughout the formative period, because the United States was never confronted with an enemy that could pose a direct and imminent threat to American territory; the accident of American geography prevented that occurrence. The luxury of forming a force after the fact was always available as a policy option. The experience in World War II, and the Cold War that followed, changed that conclusion. Following the attack on Pearl Harbor, American forces in the Pacific were nearly overrun and defeated to the extent that it could have been difficult to regain the initiative; only the heroic efforts of Americans at places such as the Battle of Midway and Guadalcanal allowed the United States to recover while it rapidly mobilized an adequate force to meet the emergency. The absence of

Amplification 3.2

READINESS AND PEARL HARBOR

The Japanese air attack on U.S. naval and other military facilities at Pearl Harbor was one of the most traumatic events in American military history. Despite a variety of warning signs (e.g., intercepted intelligence reports, suspicious ship movements, increasing strains in relations between the two countries), the United States was totally unprepared for the attack when it came early in the morning of Sunday, December 7, 1941. None of the bases on Oahu were on alert status—in fact, most of the personnel at Pearl Harbor had been out at social events the night before and had not yet reported for duty when the Japanese arrived. Virtually no one was even looking for evidence of an imminent attack, which added to the tragedy and destruction when it occurred.

It was partly the fault of the American military tradition that the attack came as such a complete surprise. To most Americans, nearly a century and a third of virtual invincibility had left them complacent, not mindful of the fact that such an attack *could* occur. Despite a war that had been raging for over two years in Europe and the growing expansion of the Japanese Empire into the South Pacific and East Asia, where it would inevitably collide with American interests, there had not yet been anything resembling a mobilization of the military by the United States. Some prominent Americans, such as Charles Lindbergh and his fellow members of America First, argued that the war was none of America's business and should be avoided at all costs. Isolationism, a prominent part of the American tradition in the formative stage, was still in full bloom before Pearl Harbor.

The elements of the American tradition that allowed the country to be so unprepared at Pearl Harbor suffered a humiliating discrediting when the Japanese attacked and destroyed much of the American Pacific fleet, which, ironically, had been moved from San Diego to the much more militarily vulnerable base at Pearl Harbor to be closer to the theater should war occur. But the lesson was partially lost in the war itself. When the Japanese surrendered aboard the USS *Missouri* (which is moored permanently at Pearl Harbor) to end hostilities, the United States promptly demobilized again, only to be shocked back to reality five years later by the North Korean invasion of South Korea.

preparedness had been the problem then, and when a similar circumstance nearly prevailed in Korea (only the ability to rapidly call up World War II veterans in the Reserves prevented the allies from being pushed off the Korean peninsula), the luxury of not having forces in existence was revealed as unacceptable.

Total War Preference

Whereas the first four elements of the American tradition are largely negative in their impact on thinking about the use of military force, a preference developed during the formative period for involvement in total wars, which at first glance appears paradoxical in light of the rest of the tradition. At one level, this development reflected changes in the international environment between the eighteenth and the middle of the twentieth centuries regarding the purposes of war. At the same time, it also was the result of an American perception that if we were to go to war, it should be for grand, righteous purposes that made it worthwhile.

The period beginning in the middle nineteenth century and ending in 1945 witnessed an expansion both in the means and the purposes for which war was conducted. The expansion of means was largely the result of the progressive application of the innovations of the Industrial Revolution to warfare. Gradually, it became possible to expand the extent of warfare by increasing the deadly effects of weapons and by increasing the media in which war could be fought. In 1789, warfare had been largely limited to ground combat wherever armies could march and organize their linear formations (essentially large, open fields) and on the surface of the ocean; by 1945, the only place war could *not* be conducted was in space (a deficiency since overcome). War became larger in terms of where and to what effect it could be fought.

This expansion in means coincided with and reinforced an expansion in the reasons for fighting. The triggering events in the expansion of purposes were the American and (especially) French Revolutions, which reintroduced political ideology into the causes of war. In the period after the end of the Thirty Years War in 1648, the system had been dominated by more or less absolutist monarchies who did not disagree on political matters and generally limited their fighting to small purposes. The French Revolution's evangelical period, when it spread its ideas across Europe, changed that, and as the means to conduct war expanded, so too did the reasons for fighting.

The purpose of war became the overthrow of enemy governments, which is the definition of total war. Although it was scarcely realized as such at the time, the prototype was probably the latter stages of the American Civil War, when the destruction of the Confederate Army and the overthrow of the government of the Confederacy were accepted as the necessary preconditions for reunion. The overthrow of the German government became the ultimate goal in World War I, and the epitome of total war was reached in the commitment to the unconditional surrender of Germany and Japan in World War II.

Total war fit the American worldview. American exceptionalism has always had an evangelical component that suggests the virtue of sharing the American ideal with others, and that evangelism could be extended to provide an adequate moral justification to breach the normalcy of peace and go to war. The epitome of this zeal is captured in Woodrow Wilson's address to Congress proposing an American declaration of war in 1917: "The day has come when America is privileged to spend her blood and her might for the principles that gave her birth and happiness. God helping her, she can do no other."

For anyone whose experience is totally restricted to the period since the end of World War II, or even the end of the Cold War, the discussion of these elements of the American tradition may seem odd, even anomalous, because they seem so far from our present experience. The anti-military bias of the revolutionary period is behind us; we no longer rely heavily on citizen-soldiers for our main-line defense (although the Reserves are more highly integrated with active-duty forces than ever during emergencies); and we recognize the limits of military power and accept the ongoing necessity of permanent standing forces. So what is the point of this historical excursion?

The answer is that these elements represent an experience accumulated over the majority of American history, and they are not entirely missing from the ongoing debate. Although they are largely the product of a different environment, when America's role in the world was much more restricted, nonetheless they still pop up from time to time. As we complete the transition from the end of the Cold War to a consensus on the contemporary environment, more of these elements may reenter the debate.

THE COLD WAR, 1945–89

The end of World War II radically changed America's place in the world and the way in which the United States had to consider matters of national security. As the wartime collaboration with the Soviet Union gradually deteriorated into the confrontation that would be the key reality in the Cold War, the question of national security moved from the peripheries to center stage in the political constellation. When North Korea invaded South Korea on June 25, 1950, and the United States responded (through the United Nations) by coming to the aid of the southerners, any doubt about the changed nature of international politics and the American role in it disappeared.

The Cold War made military affairs—national security defined in largely military terms—a central reality of American peacetime life for the first time in the country's history. Geopolitics was clearly dominant for the first time in U.S. history. Realizing from the Korean experience that a demobilized United States could not compete with a heavily armed Soviet opponent, the traditional practices of the formative period could no longer be afforded.

The Cold War presented the United States an apparently permanent military enemy for the first time since the rivalry with Great Britain was resolved after the War of 1812. Since the Soviets posed primarily a military threat through the challenge of expansionist Communism, American policy had to respond militarily. The result was the emergence of a *national security state*, in which matters of national defense took on a coequal footing with other foreign policy considerations and a large, permanent military establishment became a permanent part of the landscape.

The military culture changed because of several new conditioning factors in the environment, especially after the Korean conflict. Each factor represented a direct change—even, in some cases, a contradiction—with the previous American experience, yet the nature of the Cold War challenge caused these changes to be accepted without fundamental challenges from most Americans.

First, the Korean war created the recognition that the Cold War would require that the United States maintain a large active-duty force at all times. Part of the reason for this was the nearly disastrous Korean experience. Moreover, the Soviets did not demobilize after World War II, and they and their allies maintained large, offensive forces. Should the Soviets decide to invade Western Europe, as was widely feared, there would be no time to mobilize, train, and transport a force to the war zone. Instead, what became known as the "force in being" would have to be available on the scene at all times.

Second, this prospect of large standing forces meant that the United States would be in a permanent state of mobilization. During peacetime, this size force could only be sustained by the existence of a national conscription system, the first time an involuntary draft system had been used in peacetime in American history. As well, this state of perpetual mobilization meant that defense budgets would have to be greatly expanded to support the defense effort. During the middle 1950s (before the entitlement programs of Lyndon Johnson's Great Society inflated the overall government budget), the defense budget was fully half the overall federal budget; between the end of the Vietnam conflict and the end of the Cold War, defense spending hovered between 20 and 25 percent of government outlays.

Third, this expanded role and prominence of the military resulted in much greater prestige being bestowed on members of the military profession. With a constant threat against which to protect, the work of the military now seemed more vital than it had previously. The respect that Americans had bestowed on the World War II military was transferred to the "cold warriors" as well. Military service, and even a military career, now became attractive to growing numbers of Americans who probably would not have considered such a career before—a fortuitous phenomenon given the need for more military members.

Fourth, the growing lethality of the military balance created an urgency and vitality to national security that it had never had bestowed upon it before. The major agent of this change was the advent and expansion of thermonuclear weapons and the development and deployment of intercontinental range missiles by both sides. At the height of the Cold War competition, the two sides faced one another with arsenals of between 10,000 and 12,000 thermonuclear warheads that were capable of attacking targets in the other country and against which there were no defenses. An all-out nuclear war between the two countries would clearly destroy both as functioning societies and would have unknown but possibly catastrophic consequences for the rest of the world. In those circumstances, the successful management of the nuclear balance in such a way that nuclear war was avoided—nuclear deterrence— was our country's most crucial business (a literal survival interest). This life-and-death struggle added to the prestige and importance of the national security establishment that designed, deployed, and developed strategies for deterrence. The Cold War was a potentially very deadly place.

Fifth, there was also general acceptance that the Cold War confrontation was a protracted competition for which no one could project a peaceful ending. In the minds of almost all analysts, the only alternatives were Cold War and hot war, and since the latter would probably be nuclear, it had to be avoided at virtually all costs. This added a sense of grim vigilance to the entire national security enterprise. It also contributed to the absolute surprise of nearly all observers when the Communist world began to disintegrate in 1989. The possibility that one side or the other would simply collapse and that the competition would end with a whimper rather than a bang had not even been considered by most students of the Cold War, nearly all of whom would have dismissed the possibility as fuzzy-headed idealism.

Two things are notable about all these factors. The first and most obvious is that they represent circumstances that directly contradict the American experience to that point. The idea of permanent mobilization of large standing forces, for instance, would have absolutely appalled the Founding Fathers. A world of perpetual and potentially disastrous military conflict requiring constant vigilance and extensive preparation and spending was entirely foreign to a country whose broad oceans had provided a barrier that permitted the leisure and luxury of a general mobilization. The idea that a military career would bring great prestige would never have occurred to most of the champions of the militia tradition.

The second remarkable thing about these changed conditions is how readily they were accepted. Americans who had never been willing (or had the need) to allow themselves to be taxed to support a large standing military and who previously would have been fundamentally opposed to the existence of a draft during peacetime accepted both with virtually no complaint. The main reason for this changed acceptance, of course, was a threat that was real and ominous enough to justify greater sacrifices than had been necessary during the formative period of the American experience.

During the Cold War period, two additional elements of the American military tradition rose in prominence to become permanent parts of the military environment. Both the news media and democratic institutions had, of course, been present throughout American history. But particularly in the period surrounding the Vietnam conflict, their roles became more defined and influential.

The Role of the Media

The relationship between the media and the military has also changed over time. It has always been a complex and contentious relationship, with the two institutions eyeing one another with some distrust and occasional disdain, which was worsened by the very sour experience of the Vietnam conflict and its coverage. The relationship has arguably become even worse since the end of the Cold War.

There have always been two major concerns about the relationship of the media to national security matters. The first has to do with what is reported, a concern that centers especially but not exclusively on combat operations. The positions are diametrically opposed. From the vantage point of the press, coverage should be as complete and unfettered as possible. The press should have access to combat operations (whether they have a right to protection in combat zones is another controversial matter) and should be allowed to report what they observe. The media's underlying value is the public's right to know what its government's representatives (in this case, its military) are doing.

This viewpoint creates two problems for the military. The first is whether unfettered coverage will provide too much information, including material that, in the hands of the enemy, could compromise the integrity of military operations and even put soldiers at additional risk. Reporting the locations and outcomes of battles and the directions of troop movements are examples of cases in which reportage could aid the enemy and jeopardize our own forces. The other concern is that reportage, particularly of less than successful military actions, could have a negative impact on public morale, in effect undercutting our own morale and giving solace to an enemy. As an example, pictures of American Marines raising the flag on Mount Surabachi at Iwo Jima during World War II were a morale booster that has become an important symbol for the Marines. Photographs of the bodies of Americans floating in the surf where they were killed assaulting the beaches at Iwo Jima (which were not published at the time) would have had quite a different impact.

The solution to this dilemma historically has been military censorship. Reporters at the front could get their stories to their media outlets only by using military means of communications, thereby allowing the military to inspect outgoing material and remove anything it viewed as objectionable. For this kind of arrangement to be workable depended on two underlying dynamics. The first was a relative degree of trust between the soldier-censor and the reporter. The reporter had to believe that the censor was acting out of legitimate security concerns and not trying to hide evidence of military ineptitude; the censor basically had to believe the reporter was acting out of good faith in the stories he or she filed. Although that relationship always had some adversarial content, it worked adequately until the Vietnam conflict. The other dynamic was the dependence of the media on government means of transmission of their stories from the battleground home. That dependence has been broken by the invention of the video camcorder and the telecommunications satellite. In combination, these two technologies allow the reporter to witness, record, and transmit material without any assistance (or interference) from military censors.

The interaction between the media and the military in Vietnam transformed the relationship to one of nearly total animosity. Early in the war, the relationship was tranquil because reportage was passive: The military would tell the press their version of what happened in the fighting, and the press would dutifully report that information. The picture portrayed was uniformly positive and suggested not only that progress toward winning the war was occurring, but that victory was imminent.

That tranquility was destroyed by the Tet offensive by the North Vietnamese and Viet Cong in January 1968. The enemy launched a general attack throughout the country, especially against the cities, including the South Vietnamese capital of Saigon. The press was outraged and dismayed as they watched Viet Cong racing around the grounds of the American embassy. When the first footage of Tet reached New York, Walter Cronkite, the most revered and trusted figure in American journalism at the time, replied, "What the hell is going on here?" The basis of his question was the fact that the adversary could not possibly have mounted such an extensive action if the numbers of enemy killed that had been reported to the media in the months and years before Tet were true. The conclusion was that the military had systematically lied about enemy casualties and that the media had been duped into accepting inflated figures that, if true, would have left the North Vietnamese army and the Viet Cong with too few remaining effective forces for such an attack. As a result, the media lost trust in the military and refused to report successes—even when they were quite genuine. The military, in turn, blamed the media for undermining morale by refusing to report success after Tet. The relationship had become more adversarial than ever before.

It was in that atmosphere that the ability of the media to bypass military censorship electronically became a major factor. The military's response to the inability to edit coverage before its release has been to restrict media access to military operations. The intended effect is to restrict what the media can report (or misreport). This approach, predictably condemned by the media, was demonstrated in the Persian Gulf War, when only a few press members were allowed to accompany military forays, and then only carefully selected actions. Although media criticism of the military was muted by patriotic concerns in the Afghan campaign, reporters were rarely allow to witness military operations in that theater either. The further evolution of this relationship in Iraq is discussed in Amplification 3.3.

Amplification 3.3

THE MEDIA AND THE IRAQ WAR

Coverage of the Iraq War illustrates vividly the ever-changing relationship between the media and the U.S. military. As noted, that relationship had become highly adversarial during the Vietnam conflict. After Vietnam, the media remained suspicious of anything the military told them that they had not witnessed themselves, and many in the military continued to believe that the "liberal" media were out to get them. The fact that American journalists were not allowed to accompany the first combat forces that invaded Grenada in 1983 further soured relations, the fact that the first coverage of that event reached the United States via Radio Havana added fuel to the fire.

When Operation Desert Storm began in 1991, the major issue between the media and the military was, as it always has been, whether the military had the right to exclude reporters from the battlefield or whether it has an obligation to assist reporters in informing the population of the military campaign. Unable to censor news stories in the traditional manner because of the media's ability to file stories electronically without intermediation, the question of access to military operations became critical to any efforts either to restrict or to promote coverage. Predictably, the media argued for unrestricted access to the Kuwait Theater of Operation (KTO), and the military sought to restrict who witnessed what. The debate extended to the Iraq War.

The military's solution to this problem in Iraq was to "imbed" reporters with individual units. Under this arrangement, a select few reporters would be allowed to accompany military operations in Iraq, and they were restricted in what they would be allowed to observe and what they could report. The military argued that the restrictions were necessary to avoid reporting things that might compromise military operations and for the physical safety of the reporters. The media generally accepted this arrangement because it allowed them to be part of the "action" more than had been the case in Desert Storm, and many more reporters were allowed that access than twelve years earlier. The major criticism of the arrangement was that it fostered narrow, myopic reporting.

The military had learned, however, in the period since Vietnam and Desert Storm, how to use the media to dramatize the side of the war they wanted to dramatize. It was certainly no coincidence, for instance, that the American bombing campaign against Baghdad in Desert Storm began at precisely 6:55 P.M. Eastern Standard Time on January 16, 1991—during the evening news on the major American broadcast networks. In addition, the military made available highly selective but dramatic film footage of the bombing campaign against Baghdad to impress imbedded reporters and to dramatize the largely unopposed progress of American forces. The result was a public relations bonanza for the armed forces.

The other concern, especially since Vietnam, has been the supposed role of the media as agenda setters. Vietnam was the stimulus, because many veterans who were in the military during Vietnam were convinced that adverse coverage of the war effort after the Tet offensive was decisive in forcing an unsuccessful termination of U.S. participation in the conflict. It is a matter of major disagreement whether the United States could have prevailed in the Vietnam conflict under any circumstances, and the argument that the media helped force the American withdrawal—thus preventing victory—has served to obscure that argument for many critics.

This perception was also affected by the electronic technology that broadened both cable television and worldwide television. One of the outgrowths of the telecommunications revolution has been the development of 24-hour-a-day news networks, the prototypes of which are the Cable News Network (CNN) and the British Independent Television Network (ITN). These outlets, and others that followed the 1981 birth of CNN, have voracious news needs, and they have greatly internationalized news coverage, especially in combat zones.

The result is something known as the "CNN effect," which is the core of the concern for those who argue that the media serves as agenda setter. Critics allege (and the media itself generally denies) that policy makers tend to emphasize those international events that CNN and the others publicize, and that the news items they bring to light are often those involving war and other forms of human suffering for which military force may be viewed as an appropriate response. Thus, the emphasis of policy becomes the handmaiden of the media's attention on some matters (and inattention on others). General John Shalikashvili, chairman of the Joint Chiefs of Staff under Clinton, somewhat cynically captured the CNN effect on military operations: "We don't win until CNN says we win."

The public certainly first becomes aware of many events through television. The first public images of Somalia in 1992 were pictures of rail-thin Somali children with their distended stomachs; and Bosnia became public knowledge that same year through the haunting pictures of prisoners of war that look disturbingly like pictures from the Nazi death camps. Whether such reportage sets the public agenda or reflects simple coverage of what is occurring in the world is a matter of disagreement between the military and the media. It is aided, however, by anecdotal evidence. Early in the Clinton presidency, National Security Advisor Anthony Lake was asked by reporters as he headed into the White House what the day's agenda was. He replied, "I don't know. CNN hasn't told me yet."

The Impact of Democratic Institutions

Within a political democracy, popular will is always a matter of concern in the making of policy, especially in an area such as national security, when the ultimate expression of that policy can be war and can place citizens at physical risk. Nevertheless, the "democratization" of national security affairs is largely a post–World War II phenomenon that, like so many other influences on contemporary affairs, was accentuated by American participation in Vietnam. During most of the formative period of the American Republic, national security affairs were either of lesser importance or were more consensual in nature. During peacetime, there was little concern with military affairs, and most wars were either highly popular (the world wars, the Spanish-American War) or affected relatively few Americans directly by compelling them into service for unpopular causes (the Indian Wars). A partial exception to this depiction was Northern resistance to the Union cause in the American Civil War, in which some northerners refused to be drafted to serve.

The Cold War placed national security concerns into the spotlight. Suddenly, matters of national security quite literally became matters of potential life and death, and how well those matters were conducted became very serious and very personal business for the entire population—especially for those young Americans who might be involuntarily conscripted into military service. This first became a concern in 1950, when thousands of World War II veterans had to be recalled to active duty and an army of draftees was assembled to defend a Korea that many of them were unaware of before they were called into the service. It particularly became a concern as the Vietnam conflict dragged on and the American conscript force fought a war the public, including many of those inducted, opposed.

The sour taste left to many Americans by the Vietnam experience helped elevate the role of popular control over the democratic institutions that make decisions about war and peace. In the wake of Vietnam, the military itself engaged in a good deal of self-examination of what went wrong, and their major conclusion was that the war effort was undermined by the public support and opinion that evaporated around them as the war dragged on. (Vietnam was the longest war in American history.) To the military, the war violated the Clausewitzian trinity, which posited that war can be successfully waged only when there is a bond among the people, the military, and the government. Reasoning that the political authority had never explicitly solicited popular support for the Vietnam conflict (for a discussion, see Snow and Drew, Chapter 7), the armed forces (especially the army) vowed that this would not happen again.

The concern over popular support of military actions can be seen in a couple of ways in the contemporary environment. One of the victims of the Vietnam experience was the Selective Service system, which has periodically conscripted young Americans into service. The draft was suspended at the end of 1972, no American has been involuntarily forced into service since, and the whole question of conscription has effectively disappeared from the national agenda. Another concern is with the placement of American forces at risk. This has resulted in a level of concern—which some argue borders on hysteria—about casualties in American deployments in faraway places; this has carried through into the 1990s and beyond.

CONCLUSION: THE CONTEMPORARY PERIOD, 1989–PRESENT

The end of the Cold War represented a change in the environment in which Americans think about matters of national security of the same order of magnitude as had the onset of the adversarial environment it replaced. This change was not immediately recognized, nor was there a great initial effort to test the nature and implications of the collapse of the Soviet empire. The response to September 11, 2001, has further stimulated changes in thinking.

The reasons for a slow intellectual adjustment during the 1990s are numerous, and I have discussed them in some detail elsewhere (see *When America Fights*, Chapter 1). One reason was that the national security and foreign policy community was caught off guard by the sea change represented by the collapse of Communism. Planners had four years of combat to plan for the post–World War II international order and devoted considerable effort to the task. There was no equivalent adjustment period when Communism imploded.

Our thinking about and adjusting to change was also retarded by the fact that the national security bureaucracy was dominated by veteran observers of the Cold War, who were both very conservative and very suspicious of the changes they were observing. The tendency was either to disbelieve how fundamental the change was or to hedge against the possibility that the confrontation might soon reappear. Moreover, the Cold War mindset was a comfortable intellectual construct that, once mastered, many were unwilling to shed for the greater uncertainty apparent in the unfolding post–Cold War environment. At the same time, this new environment was clearly less threatening than the Cold War had been, and even if it contained new and annoying problems such as terrorism, the urgency of adaptation was clearly not as great.

With over a decade of the new environment behind us and the second fault line of terrorism revealed, how will the American tradition adapt to and be shaped by the contemporary situation? Key elements in the past two situations have included the role of the United States in the international system and the level of threat the environment provided, as noted earlier. The American experience reveals a contrast on these two variables, as shown in Figure 3.1. As the figure reveals, the two historic periods show that the United States has experienced both the "pure" combinations: high threat and a large international role during the Cold War and a low threat and small role during most of the formative period.

The contemporary period represents a hybrid of these circumstances. Clearly, the American role in the world is large, and with the collapse of the Cold War opposition, it is arguably relatively larger than it has ever been before. The question then becomes which part of the American tradition will dominate the contemporary view of the world? In some manner, the neo-isolationists, who would reduce America's aggressive presence and role, represented the legacy of the formative period's basic preference to be left alone. The cutback in active-duty troop strength and the disappearance of conscription as part of the potential political agenda suggested that all the elements from the formative period had not disappeared and might reassert

Figure 3.1   **American Roles and Threats**

Role	Threats	
	High	Low
Large	Cold War	?
Small	?	Formative

themselves as the United States returned from the "abnormality" of the Cold War to a more comfortable past.

The role of the United States, however, did not recede to where it was in the formative period; it has remained at least as prominent as it was during the Cold War. Does this mean that the internationalism that dominated the Cold War approach of the United States toward the world has become such a permanent part of the landscape as to be inescapable? The Bush administration entered office with the stated intention of trimming back America's commitments in areas such as peacekeeping and brokering the Middle Eastern peace, but it was mere months before the terrorist attack caused it to quietly jettison that rhetoric and adopt an aggressive military posture favored by the neo-conservatives to the international environment. In 2003, it reactivated the Middle East process as well (discussed in Chapter 10) and invaded Iraq.

Challenge!

How Much Has Changed?

Do the terrorist attacks on New York and Washington and the subsequent worldwide campaign against international terrorism fundamentally change the threat and role of the United States in a security sense? Prior to the attacks, one could argue that the United States was in the new situation of having a large role in an international milieu that posed few meaningful threats—a kind of hybrid of the formative and Cold War experiences. But what is the situation now?

This question requires an assessment of how fundamental the threat posed by international terrorism really is—a concern raised in the Introduction to this book. In the immediate wake of the 2001 incidents, the initial response of both the administration and the public was to portray the problem as global, pervasive, and extremely highly threatening. The Bush administration's pronouncements and actions seemed to reinforce, even to inflame, this perception. Troops were sent to Afghanistan in 2001 and the Philippines in early 2002 to fight the "war" on terrorism, and deployments were contemplated in numerous other places. The president's labeling of Iran, Iraq, and North Korea as the "axis of evil" extended the problem beyond a contest with nonstate actors to an interstate basis. Domestically, the Office of Homeland Security was created and began periodically issuing terrorist alerts, while an alternate government went underground to ensure governmental continuity in the event of a massive, crippling terrorist attack. The creation of the cabinet-level Department of Homeland Security (see Chapter 7) capped this effort.

Is all this activity warranted by the actual scale of the threat? Al Qaeda certainly does not have the capabilities to wreak havoc that a nuclear-armed Soviet Union had, but it *has* shown the ability to launch an operation that could kill three thousand Americans. Where does that place us in the matrix presented in the Conclusion to this chapter—in a high-threat environment, a low-threat environment, or somewhere in between? How we answer this question has, or should have, major implications for future national security considerations.

The past is never a perfect road map for the present or future, of course, but the past *is* the context within which the future comes to be. As suggested in the preceding pages, there have been two distinct historical influences on the evolution of the American military and how it has shaped the way Americans view the role of force in the world. Whether one of those influences will dominate the future or whether that future orientation will be a polyglot of those influences is an interesting question to ponder and to observe.

SELECTED BIBLIOGRAPHY

Brodie, Bernard. *War and Politics*. New York: Macmillan, 1973.

Clausewitz, Carl von. *On War*. Rev. ed. Trans. and ed. by Michael Howard and Peter Paret. Princeton: Princeton University Press, 1984.

Dupuy, D. Ernest, and Trevor N. Dupuy. *The Encyclopedia of Military History*. New York: Harper and Row, 1972.

Gaddis, John Lewis. *Strategies of Containment: A Critical Appraisal of Postwar American National Security Policy*. Oxford: Oxford University Press, 1982.

Hassler, Warren W. Jr. *With Shield and Sword: American Military Affairs, Colonial Times to the Present*. Ames: Iowa State University Press, 1984.

Leckie, Robert. *The Wars of America*. Rev. updated ed. edition. New York: Harper and Row, 1981.

Millett, Allan R., and Peter Maslowski. *For the Common Defense: A Military History of the United States of America*. New York: Free Press, 1984.

Snow, Donald M. *When America Fights: The Uses of U.S. Military Force*. Washington, DC: CQ Press, 2000.

———, and Dennis M. Drew. *From Lexington to Desert Storm and Beyond: War and Politics in the American Experience*. 2nd ed. Armonk, NY: M. E. Sharpe, 2000.

Weigley, Russell F. *The American Way of War*. New York: Macmillan, 1973.

Williams, T. Harry. *A History of American Wars: From Colonial Times to World War II*. New York: Alfred A. Knopf, 1981

The Nature and End of the Cold War

Although the Cold War has been over for more than a decade, its structures and the attitudes it produced continue to have an impact on the contemporary world. A distinctly American form of geopolitics was one product of the forty-year confrontation; many of today's national security leaders had their intellectual grounding during the Cold War; and the American military structure still predominantly reflects preparation to fight a World War III against a Soviet-style opponent. The Cold War is the dominating influence of the American experience as we face a changed environment. Thus, understanding how the Cold War occurred and evolved—especially in a military sense—and what residual problems remain is crucial to understanding how we are predisposed to respond to the future.

The contemporary international environment can fully be understood only in the context of the Cold War international system from which it has evolved and which helped form the world in which we live. These impacts of the Cold War on the present and future include the enormous effect of the Cold War on reforming the American attitude toward the world and its role in it; the influence of the Cold War on the worldview of the generations who presided over it, including much of the present leadership; and the traumatic effect of how and why the Cold War collapsed on our present and future.

The Cold War was a national baptism for the United States into the world arena. In the formative period, the country had not been a consistently major player in international relations. The accident of geography, disdain for what was viewed as a corrupt international system, and a general preference to be left alone to realize American manifest destiny had combined to keep the United States on the periphery of a European-centered international system. That system, in turn, had little need, most of the time, for American involvement in its affairs, except during systemic traumas such as the world wars.

The end of World War II made a return to isolation from the world impossible and thrust a reluctant, inexperienced United States onto the center stage of world events. When the last guns of the war were stilled, only two states, the United States and the Soviet Union, retained enough power to influence international events and to reorganize an international system laid prostrate by the war. The implications of this bipolar balance of power—especially its adversarial content—were not clear immediately but took shape in the five-year period that was climaxed by the Korean conflict. Events and circumstances of that period impelled the United States into the *realpolitik* of international relations for the first time.

Understanding and managing the Cold War became the central task for the generations of American policy makers, strategists, and scholars who had to manage and explain change as the world slid toward the Cold War between 1945 and 1950 and then adapt to the Cold War system for another forty years. Lurking constantly behind them was the shadow cast by the possibility that the Cold War could go very hot in a totally ruinous nuclear war.

The major organizing construct they built and managed was, of course, the realist paradigm discussed in Chapter 2. It was a harsh, confrontational relationship for most of its existence, and it became a very *conservative* construct in the pure sense of that term: It sought to conserve the system below the level of general war that both sides quite rightly feared. In the end, that construct and fear helped contribute to the end of the Cold War. While the Cold War lasted, however, it provided a virtually uncontested worldview, and those who challenged it were dismissed as dreamers and visionaries whose suggestions were too risky or foolhardy to be considered seriously. The realists were, after all, *realistic*.

It is important to emphasize the pervasive nature of the Cold War, because it still permeates the way people look at the world, especially in official circles. The people who have flag rank (generals or admirals) in the services today were educated in the 1950s and 1960s, by and large, and had their first personal experiences in the world in the 1960s and 1970s; and the same is true of the majority of civilians in the foreign and national security community. Many have sought to shed some of the inapplicable aspects of the Cold War mentality, with varying degrees of success, but they remain "cold warriors" nonetheless. The equation of the U.S. response to terrorism as a war between good and evil, for instance, has antecedents in the Cold War against "godless Communism." President Bush's "axis of evil" and President Reagan's "evil empire" come from the same intellectual cloth. Certainly, the "cold warriors" will eventually be replaced by a leadership cadre unencumbered by the Cold War worldview, but that group's ascendancy is sometime in the future.

The way the Cold War ended influences us as well. It was neither a planned nor an anticipated event. With the considerable benefit of hindsight, we have been able to find a series of signs of the impending doom of the Soviet Union that were not nearly so obvious at the time. The key player in the drama was clearly Mikhail S. Gorbachev, who became the Soviet leader in 1985 at the end of a succession crisis following the death of long-time strongman Leonid Brezhnev.

Gorbachev realized that there was a deadly malaise in the Soviet system, and he sought to reform the Soviet system and make it stronger and once again competitive with a West (especially the United States) that was clearly surpassing the Soviet Union by all measures of comparison. A lifelong, dedicated Communist, Gorbachev sought to strengthen his country and the Communist Party of the Soviet Union (CPSU). The actions he ended up taking contributed, first, to the demise of the dominance of the CPSU and eventually led to the breakup of the USSR itself. Had someone convincingly predicted for Gorbachev the effects his policies would have, he would almost certainly have resisted the changes he helped institute.

The Western leadership was equally at a loss to explain or understand events as the structures came falling down (literally, in the case of the most dramatic physical symbol of the competition, the Berlin Wall). Initial public and private reaction to the seismic changes ranged from disbelief to suspicion that it was all a ruse, some of the clever disinformation for which former Soviet leader Yuri Andropov (Gorbachev's mentor and the former head of the Committee for State Security, or KGB) had been famous. As late as the middle of 1991, with the Soviet state publicly disintegrating through the unopposed secession of its member states, the Bush administration debated whether the United States preferred a strong or a weak Soviet Union at the end of the process.

The Cold War and its demise is history, but it is important history that is relevant to us now. As a result, we will devote this chapter to the Cold War. We will begin by looking briefly at the essence of the Cold War relationship as a distinct international system. We will then turn to the distinctly military competition that was at the center of the U.S.–Soviet conflict. That military confrontation, in the end, helped contribute to the end of the Cold War, for reasons we will examine. Finally, some residues of the Cold War remain part of current reality; for instance, as the United States aligns itself with former Soviet states in the name of the war on terrorism, some of the Cold War concerns still affect the content of policy and its effects on our future.

THE COLD WAR SYSTEM

At the end of World War II, the international system was confronted with two fundamental questions, the consequences of which would evolve and dominate international relations for most of the rest of the twentieth century. One question centered on nuclear weapons. The use of atomic bombs against Hiroshima and Nagasaki, Japan, by the United States had helped to break Japan's will to continue the war; thus, these novel, and enormously deadly, weapons would be part of the calculation of future military affairs. Hence, a fundamental question facing planners was what difference these weapons would make, a matter we will take up in the next section of this chapter.

The other question was about the wartime collaboration between the United States and the Soviet Union. Would friendship continue in the postwar world, or would the deep ideological differences between them result in a future of conflict and confrontation? In retrospect, the answer seems stunningly obvious, and most observers at the time suspected that the collaboration could not be sustained. At the same time, if continued cooperation *could* be maintained, the result could be a much more tranquil international environment, and this hopeful possibility could not to be dismissed out of hand.

Planning for dealing with these postwar contingencies had gone on throughout the war in the United States, especially in the collaboration between the Americans and the British. Unlike the end of the Cold War, which caught everyone off guard, there was ample time to think about and plan for the post–World War II world. Uncertainty about what kind of relationship would exist among what became the superpowers of the Cold War system dominated the policy process. As a result, the planners devised a structure to accommodate either outcome—collaboration or confrontation.

The principal instrument for organizing the postwar world was the UN Charter. The primary purpose of the United Nations was to create a viable mechanism to organize the peace that would avoid a repetition of the slide to World War II. Critical to crafting a viable, working system was the question of whether the major powers, the United States and the Soviet Union, could agree upon a form of the peace they were willing to enforce.

Since the two powers had very opposing worldviews, the task of finding a mutually acceptable peace to defend was not going to be easy. Clearly, the United States preferred a world of Western-style political democracies and capitalism-based economies like its own, and the Soviets equally fervently wanted to promote the expansion of Communism in the world. Both sides were evangelical, and the secular "religions" they were promoting were incompatible. Thus, the prospects of peace and cooperation were prejudiced from the beginning.

What the UN Charter drafters sought to do was create a mechanism that would allow enforcement of the peace if the major powers could cooperate on a common vision but that would be disengaged if they could not. Cooperation would be accomplished institutionally through the UN Security Council, which the Charter empowers (through Chapters VI and VII) to take effective actions to squelch threats to or breaches of the peace. Each of the permanent members of the Council (the major victorious allies in the war—the United States, the USSR, Great Britain, France, and China) was given a veto over any action, thereby providing the disabling mechanism when the major powers disagreed in any given situation. In the event that disagreement became pervasive, the Charter, through Article 51, allowed the members the right to engage in "individual and collective self-defense," providing the basis for the opposing military alliances that institutionalized confrontation.

Collaboration was not sustainable, of course, because the two sides could not agree on the world they preferred. Thus, the mechanisms for organizing the peace through cooperation remained disabled and disengaged for the duration of the Cold War. The United Nations was able to act on Korea in 1950 because the Soviets were boycotting the organization in protest of the refusal to seat the new Communist government of China rather than the Nationalist government of Chiang Kai-shek in Taiwan and thus did not veto the action. After Korea, the mechanisms for enforcing the peace essentially went into a veto-induced hibernation for forty years. Then, a Russia that was no longer Communist did not have ideological grounds to veto potential UN actions, and the world body returned to life as promoter of the peace. Thus, the end of the Cold War produced an international environment more compatible with what the framers of the Charter had hoped would evolve in 1945, and the United Nations was reenergized.

The North Korean invasion of 1950 removed any lingering doubt that confrontation rather than collaboration would be the central feature of the Soviet–American relationship. After the Soviets exploded their first atomic bomb in 1949, the question of the role of nuclear weapons was added to the calculus of what became the Cold War international system. This system had several prominent characteristics that are worth considering. It also had within it the sources of future change.

Characteristics

First, the Cold War was a *pervasive political and military competition that dominated international politics*. Among the world's powers, only the United States and the Soviet Union emerged from World War II with enough residual power to organize and influence international events. The bases of American power were economic and military. The American industrial system was strengthened by the war and towered above everyone else. (For a period in the 1940s, the American economy accounted for nearly 40 percent of world productivity, as opposed to about half that today.) The military power of the United States was guaranteed through the sole possession of nuclear weapons. The much weaker Soviet economy had been virtually destroyed by the war, but the Soviets kept armed forces of close to twelve million under arms (the United States was demobilizing to around one million in 1946).

This distribution of power defined the international system as *bipolar* in nature: The United States and the USSR stood as the two remaining powers (or poles) around which other states congregated and could be controlled or influenced. The American lever of power was economic; everyone in the West needed American money and goods for recovery. The Red occupation army in Eastern Europe was able to impose regimes friendly to the Soviets in the countries that became reluctant parts of their orbit.

The Cold War and its pervasive nature took root first in a Europe divided by what British statesman Winston Churchill first called "the Iron Curtain" in a speech in Fulton, Missouri, in 1947. The relationship became formally militarized through the formation of the North Atlantic Treaty Organization (NATO) in 1949 and then its Communist counterpart, the Warsaw Treaty Organization (WTO or the Warsaw Pact), in 1955. The ideological struggle spread to the developing world as countries emerged from colonial rule, principally in Asia and Africa, during the 1950s and 1960s.

Nothing symbolized the fervor of the Cold War more dramatically than the nuclear competition between the two sides. At one level, the competition was incongruous, as both sides built arsenals for potential use against one another that were so large and excessive that a war between them would almost certainly destroy both. It became popular to depict the relationship as two scorpions in a bottle: Each scorpion was ready to kill the other and itself in a conflict that both feared the other might be tempted to initiate if they showed signs of weakness or vulnerability. Each came gradually to dread the prospect of that conflict enough that the issue of nuclear weapons helped to defuse the Cold War. The ultimate lunacy of the relationship did not prevent either side from spending lavishly, however, to ensure that the other did not gain what was sometimes described as an "exploitable advantage" in some measure of the weaponry.

Second, the conflict was viewed as *protracted*, a long-term competition for which only great patience would suffice and the management of which required great vigilance. The Cold War was a battle between two diametrically opposed systems of political belief that was enduring and that had an uncertain outcome. There was very little consideration of a possibly peaceful end of the relationship. It was broadly assumed that the only means by which closure could come was through a massive military clash, World War III, which would likely become nuclear and could destroy both sides. In that circumstance, the logic of avoiding war meant maintaining huge conventional and nuclear forces in Europe as a "rational" way to manage the relationship and keep the war *cold*.

The protracted nature of the competition became both a prediction of the future and a prime value, given its extremely destructive alternative. There was always something curious in this assessment, however. It was a matter of firm belief in the West that the Communist philosophy was inherently inferior to its capitalist economic and democratic political ideals. Somehow this belief was rarely translated into the idea that Communism might collapse on its own as those flaws became manifest (which, of course, is exactly what happened). Indeed, for a time it was even argued in some circles that Communism had a competitive edge in the developing world, where much of the competition played out, because Communist ideology laid out a concrete blueprint for development, whereas democracy offered only choices but little guidance. That the concrete blueprint was itself flawed and the choices it offered ultimately unpalatable never really entered the discussion.

The perceived basis of Communist strength—which was necessary to assume the protracted nature of the competition—was the totalitarian nature of Soviet rule. Soviet Communism, the argument went, could not fail because its coercive strength was so great that any opposition would be crushed mercilessly. Thus, even if the regime lacked broad popular support, as it did, its power could not be challenged effectively.

This was also a curious proposition, especially in retrospect. In the Western tradition, democratic theory argues that the basis of political stability is popular support for the government, or legitimacy; legitimacy is the source of strength in democracies. Arguments about the endurance of Communism implicitly maintained that legitimacy simply did not apply if a regime had enough guns and other forms of coercion to control the population. Coercion effectively trumped legitimacy. What this line of reasoning failed to consider was that the reason Communist governments needed to be totalitarian was because they were illegitimate. The monopoly on power was really an indirect indication of the weakness, not the strength, of the

Amplification 4.1

BETTER DEAD THAN RED?
BETTER RED THAN DEAD?

The 1950s was the decade when the Cold War was at its most intense and assessment of the future was most pessimistic. The Korean War, which had become intensely unpopular after it stalemated in 1951 but dragged on until 1953, was a recent memory of apparent failure. The liberation of North Korea had not been accomplished, and the Communist Viet Minh of Ho Chi Minh had prevailed in French Indochina—another victory for expanding Communism. When the Soviet Union beat the United States into space by launching *Sputnik* into the heavens first, and as Americans peered into the nighttime sky and saw it blink by overhead, there seemed some reason to be suspicious about who was prevailing in the competition. Nuclear war drills in schools and public buildings only added to the growing hysteria. The flaws of operational Communism had not become obvious to anyone.

In this atmosphere, a kind of despair emerged about how the Cold War might end. One possibility was that the Soviet Union might actually prevail, in which case the debate was whether it would be preferable to accept Soviet domination or to go down fighting in a cataclysmic nuclear war: better Red than dead? The second possibility was that war between the two systems was inevitable. It was not a question of *whether* there would be war, but *when*. The debate was turned around to ask if perishing in such a conflict was preferable to Communist overlordship: better dead than Red? In that atmosphere, hardly anyone could imagine the outcome that eventually prevailed: *neither dead nor Red*.

regimes. When populations throughout the Communist world shucked the system with no remorse or regret, starting in 1989, it proved that coercion can only artificially and temporarily substitute for legitimacy.

These intellectual blinders meant that there was much less consideration about ending the Cold War than if the participants had begun with the proposition that the competition was intellectually tilted in favor of the democracies. Over the years, a few observers had seen this, but their prophecies were largely ignored. George F. Kennan, the American diplomat who was the intellectual father of the U.S. foreign policy of containment, argued that a policy of diligence could contain Communism within the boundaries it had achieved. If containment was applied successfully, the inherent inferiority of the Communist system would eventually cause it to implode. He was, of course, proved correct.

A third characteristic of the Cold War system was that it became *global*. Originally, it was geographically limited to the boundary between Western and Eastern Europe and, after 1949, the area surrounding China. As independence movements produced new states in Asia and Africa during the 1950s, the 1960s, and into the early 1970s (decolonization was effectively over in 1975, when Portugal granted independence to the last members of its empire), both sides scrambled to gain favor, even allegiance, from newly installed governments in new states.

Because the new countries were gaining their independence from European states, most of them adopted nominally democratic systems based on the colonialist's form of government. Thus, the West initially was thought to have the advantage in this competition. Most of these new states were desperately poor, however, and in need of developmental assistance that was generally not available in adequate supply. Their new governments often proved to be inept or corrupt (or both), leading to a spiral of instability and violence. Those circumstances presented the Soviets with an opportunity to attempt to spread their influence by arguing that they advocated a superior alternative to the West.

This global spread of the competition universalized the Cold War, which meant that Cold War concerns permeated even the most remote parts of the globe. The American policy of containment was extended all along the Sino-Soviet periphery (over the objections of Kennan) and was manifested in a series of bilateral and multilateral collective defense arrangements (alliances) that globalized U.S. commitments and both justified and demanded robust forces capable of global projection. Although the competition generally remained below the level of direct military confrontation, American- and Soviet-supported forces did fight in areas where American interests consisted mainly of denying Soviet interests, and vice versa.

The Cold War competition did change over time. The presumption of an intractable, negative relationship in the 1950s softened with experience to the point that, at the time the Cold War ended, Soviet political leader Gorbachev was one of the most popular politicians in the West, adorning the cover of *Time* magazine as its Man of the Year.

Sources of Change

The Cold War system also had dynamics that led to change in two ways. The first occurred in the 1950s but was not widely recognized as such at the time: The two superpowers began to lose some control over their individual blocs. The early postwar system had been known as one of *tight* bipolarity, meaning that the major powers could control events within their blocs fairly closely. The system evolved, however, to one of *loose* bipolarity, wherein the ability to order events slipped for both powers.

Two events in 1956 started the change from tight to loose bipolarity. First, Great Britain joined France and Israel in an attack on Egypt, the purpose of which was to occupy the Suez Canal Zone (which Egyptian President Gamal Abdel Nasser had nationalized the previous year). The action was taken without prior consultation with the U.S. government (which almost certainly would have opposed it), and that was of symbolic value in and of itself. When the United States joined the Soviet Union in sponsoring a UN Security Council resolution condemning the invasion, the French concluded that the United States could no longer be trusted to support its closest allies and began the process of moving away from the United States to an independent position in international affairs. The American ability to control its bloc suffered a major setback.

The second event that started this change in control was the brutal suppression of the Hungarian rebellion by Soviet forces later in that same year. Initially seen as proof of the Soviets' ruthless effectiveness in controlling their bloc, there was a longer-term and quite opposite effect. The United States took the lead in an anti-Soviet publicity campaign, which included widely disseminating pictures of Soviet tanks rumbling through Budapest throughout the developing world, and the Soviets suffered an enormous propaganda black eye. They had portrayed themselves as the peace-loving champions of freedom and self-determination, and they clearly had been lying. The result was that the Soviets—and their client states—realized that they needed to avoid another embarrassment of that order. Eastern European countries learned that as long as they did not threaten Soviet security, they could act more independently than before—a sign of decay in the Soviet control of their bloc.

The second great change was in the nature of the competition, and the symbolic event was the Cuban Missile Crisis of 1962. In that confrontation over the Soviet attempt to deploy nuclear-tipped missiles in Cuba, aimed at the United States, there was a military standoff that almost all observers believed was the closest the two sides had come to nuclear war. That realization convinced both powers that their prior assessment that they had nothing in common was at least partly wrong. At a minimum, both sides realized a joint interest in avoiding destroying one another and possibly the world.

The Cuban crisis was the watershed in the confrontational nature of the Cold War. Prior to the crisis, the relationship was regularly marked by direct confrontations with at least some potential to spiral out of control—the Berlin blockade, Korea, and the Berlin Wall incident, to mention three. What these crises had in common was their escalatory potential to direct confrontation and even possibly war and the willingness of one or both sides to proceed to a potentially dangerous point of confrontation. After the Cuban missile crisis, that changed, and direct Cold War confrontations with obvious escalatory potential essentially disappeared.

The Cuban watershed changed the nature of the relationship in two ways, both of which reduced the likelihood that the two sides would again meet at the precipice of nuclear war. First, they began a process of nuclear arms control, signing a series of treaties aimed, first, at limiting where nuclear testing could occur and, later, at limiting the size and characteristics of the arsenals aimed at one another (a process that has continued to the present). Although avoiding the proliferation of nuclear weapons to states that did not already have them was part of the motivation, the shared realization of an interest in avoiding mutual incineration provided the compelling rationale for these efforts. After the missile crisis, direct confrontations with escalatory possibilities simply vanished from the international scene.

There is one apparent exception to this observation that actually proves the rule. During the Yom Kippur War of 1973, the Israelis pinned an Egyptian army in the Sinai Peninsula against the Suez Canal, with no way to retreat to Egyptian soil, and threatened to destroy that army "in detail." The Soviets reacted by threatening to airdrop Soviet paratroopers into the Egyptian lines to aid in their defense (a militarily ineffective act, since the lightly armed paratroopers would have been facing Israeli tanks). The United States responded by putting its forces on worldwide alert, and in the next 24 hours, there was a growing fear of escalation—with unknown consequences.

Frantic shuttle diplomacy by U.S. Secretary of State Henry Kissinger defused the crisis. Flying back and forth between Tel Aviv and Moscow, he convinced Israel to back down from its threat against the Egyptians and the Soviets to cancel plans to intervene. The rapidity with which both sides moved back from the brink demonstrated the understanding they had about the dynamics of the situation and their commitment to avoiding confrontation.

From a twenty-first-century perspective, much of this flavor of the Cold War may seem odd, even anachronistic and unreal. It was very serious business, however, to those who made and implemented policy, many of whom (to repeat) are still active in national security policy today. Nowhere is the furtiveness of the competition more evident than in the way the two sides prepared themselves for potential armed conflict.

FORMS OF MILITARY COMPETITION

The Cold War was both a military and a political competition, although the degree of emphasis on one aspect or the other varied across time and in different places. Originally, it was both. The communization of the occupied Eastern European countries was accomplished almost exclusively by the Red Army, rather than by the political interplay of Communist and non-Communist elements. At the same time, Communist parties competed politically in several Western European countries and even enjoyed some electoral success in France and Italy. By the end of the decade, however, the totalitarian nature of Communist regimes had been clearly demonstrated in such countries as Czechoslovakia (where a democratically elected government was overthrown by the Soviets and their Czech surrogates). The Communists ceased to compete seriously politically, instead becoming a fringe party in those countries that allowed them to operate openly (they were banned in West Germany, for instance). From 1950 until 1991, the Cold War in Europe was almost exclusively a military competition between NATO and the Warsaw Pact (after the WTO became operational in 1956).

The political dimension of the Cold War was thus limited to the peripheries—Africa, Asia, and, to a lesser extent, Latin America. The process of decolonization and the subsequent emergence of inexperienced postindependence governments created considerable political ferment into which both sides plunged, hoping either to gain influence or, more modestly, to deny influence to the other side. One of the means of currying favor was to provide military aid to various governments (or factions within countries). Occasionally, involvement would devolve into military intervention, as it did for the United States in 1965 in the Dominican Republic and Vietnam and for the Soviets in Afghanistan a decade and a half later. Nonetheless, the competition in the developing world had both a political and a military dimension.

The heart of the Cold War, however, was played out in Europe, along the so-called central front in Germany, which presumably would have been the focus of a Soviet invasion of Western Europe. That possibility formed the worst-case scenario against which NATO planners prepared. The rarely questioned presumption within

NATO was that the Soviet Union had serious designs on controlling Western Europe and that it might unleash the vast Red Army into NATO territory unless NATO could demonstrate sufficient military strength and resolve to convince the Soviets of the futility of such an attack.

How serious a threat the Soviets indeed posed to Western Europe is not the point here. Certainly, they maintained military forces far in excess of those needed for a purely defensive stance in Europe (as did NATO), and there was ample ideological antagonism between the two sides to place the worst possible interpretations on the intentions of the adversaries. Thus, it was not at all difficult for members of NATO to project a real and lively threat, against which vigilant defensive preparation was the only prudent recourse. The underlying point is that planners *believed* in the existence of the military threat and acted militarily on those beliefs.

The perceived nature of the military threat was colored by the time and place in which it occurred. The fact that the competition emerged in Europe on the heels of history's largest conventional war has affected the shape and purposes of military forces even to this day, when the military situation is quite different. Militarily, the Cold War began as an extension of a global conflict featuring conventional armed forces preparing to fight symmetrically. As a result, the military dimension of the Cold War had a distinctly World War II flavor, in terms of both how it would be fought and with what kinds of forces. Even though the weapons became more sophisticated and deadly across time and would have produced a much bloodier result, a war in Europe in which the United States and the Soviet Union were the principal adversaries would have been very much like World War II. Since the military and political leaders on both sides were, by and large, veterans of World War II, this was not an uncomfortable projection and basis for preparation for them. Hidden within the assumptions about preparing for World War III was the notion that the forces and doctrines would also be effective against smaller, unconventional (asymmetrical) foes. That assumption has proved to be dubious.

The wild card, of course, was nuclear weapons. The Cold War provided the first occasion when a war could be fought by two opponents that were both armed with these remarkably destructive weapons. Whether a war in Europe could be fought without releasing the nuclear genie was a hotly debated issue in military, political, and academic circles around which no real consensus ever emerged. A second lively question was whether the employment of nuclear weapons could be restricted to the immediate theater of operations (a possibility about which the Europeans who would experience a nuclear defense understandably had little enthusiasm) or whether their use would somehow inexorably spread more widely, beyond the battlefield. Whether conventional war in Europe would escalate into a general nuclear exchange engulfing the homelands of the superpowers was the ultimate concern for American, and presumably Soviet, planners.

These concerns have not entirely disappeared. The nuclear balance remains intact, though at reduced levels, even if Russia and the United States lack the realistic motivation to attack one another. American conventional armed forces are still largely structured basically as they were during the Cold War. The efforts of Secretary of Defense Donald Rumsfeld and others before him to reshape those forces continue to be resisted by military and civilian leaderships, who are at least implicitly clinging to Cold War roles and missions. Understanding those forces and why they are constructed the way they are is a necessary preface to dealing with contemporary forces for contemporary problems.

Conventional Forces

Militarily, the heart of the Cold War was a confrontation between conventional (nonnuclear) forces facing one another across the no-man's land that comprised the Iron Curtain—most especially the so-called inter-German border that divided East and West Germany and was widely expected to be the initial battleground in a NATO–Warsaw Pact war. For NATO planning purposes, a heavily armored Soviet breakout at the Fulda Gap in Germany seemed the most likely way that war would begin.

World War II and the military predilections of the leaders of the two coalitions heavily colored the way they conceptualized the problem. Everyone envisioned that the battlefield would be somewhere on the northern European plain, a relatively flat terrain that gave the advantage to mobile, yet heavily armed forces, such as the tank armies that leaders like General George S. Patton had popularized in World War II.

Both the Americans and the Soviets were oriented to this style of warfare, in which huge forces slug it out in an orgy of incredible violence until one side collapses. For the Americans, this had historically meant committing the superior U.S. productive system to building so much sophisticated equipment that the enemy eventually was beaten down by the sheer weight of arms. The Soviet experience on the Eastern Front had taught them that overwhelming numbers of troops could eventually carry the day, if at terrible human cost. The scenario of these two behemoths colliding on the battlefield produced a prospect of unprecedented carnage and destruction that, among other things, would leave the European landscape on which it was fought largely devastated. For this reason, Europeans dreaded the prospect of war much more than their superpower allies did.

The way the war would likely be fought affected the politics of war preparation. The focus of NATO preparation was to provide a sufficiently daunting prospect to the Soviets so that they would be deterred from starting a war. But politics got in the way. Since the Soviets always had a quantitatively much larger force than NATO and would have the advantage of choosing when and where to attack, how was NATO to provide such an inhibiting presence? The domestic politics of the NATO democracies made it politically suicidal to suggest conscripting a force that could match the Soviets soldier for soldier. Moreover, the longer war was avoided, the less belief there was in the need for the sacrifice of military service.

This left two major politico-military problems: where to fight and with what? In order to blunt a Soviet attack, NATO had three options of varying military and obverse political appeals. From a purely political viewpoint, the most desirable outcome would be to stop any Soviet assault dead in its tracks—before it penetrated Western Europe—and throw back the attackers. The problem was that this solution was not feasible militarily, since the boundary separating the Germanies was basically unfortified. The solution—erecting a Maginot Line–like structure to provide a barrier to invasion—would have required tearing up the richest farmland in West Germany, a political impossibility in Germany.

A second alternative was to allow the invasion to occur, but to slow it down gradually and bring it to a halt before it could achieve its presumed objective—conquering West Germany, at least to the Rhine River. This *defense in depth*, as it is known, would have had to be carried out in West Germany, where, for instance, one means of slowing the Soviet advance would have been at choke points in German villages, which almost certainly would have been leveled in the process. That solution was absolutely politically unacceptable in the German Federal Republic (West Germany). That left, as the only other alternative, carrying the war eastward in the direction of the Soviet Union. If it were physically possible, such a solution would avoid the military devastation in West Germany associated with the other approaches. The problem was that NATO explicitly fashioned itself as a defensive alliance; thus, it could not publicly endorse aggression into Eastern Europe.

The other concern was the weapons with which NATO could fight; and this concern was colored by perceptions of the conventional military balance that heavily favored the Communists. In 1985, for instance, the Red Army was nearly two-and-a-half times the size of its American counterpart; it had four times the number of tanks and armored vehicles and half again the number of combat aircraft. The United States had the advantage in helicopters and naval vessels, but their direct applicability to the central front in Germany was questionable. The numbers favored the Soviets.

Regardless of how one rated the relative quality of the two forces, these comparisons left the very real prospect that a Soviet-led assault in Germany might succeed *if the war remained strictly conventional*. What the NATO allies needed was so-called force multipliers—ways in which to enhance the comparative capability of the NATO forces (multiply their effectiveness). The most obvious candidates for this enhancement were battlefield and theater nuclear weapons, and analysts wondered aloud whether it would be better to accept conventional defeat on the battlefield or to escalate to nuclear exchange, with all the uncertainties that such a change would create for possible escalation to a general homeland exchange between the two superpowers.

How did the United States respond to these challenges? This question is germane because the blueprint for defending Europe is still largely in place as the rationale for current forces (despite efforts at change by Rumsfeld and others) and was the basis for the plan that defeated Saddam Hussein in 1991.

The plan for the defense of the central front represented a political and military compromise on the question of where to fight—in the guise of something known as *air-land battle*. The basic idea was to allow allied army corps commanders on the ground in Germany considerable latitude in how and where they would engage the invading Soviets. Armed with highly mobile armored assault weapons and supported by air force close air support, the army would engage in highly mobile warfare, similar to the final campaigns of World War II.

It was implicit that one of the places such maneuver warfare would take place was behind the enemy's front lines—in other words, in Eastern Europe. At the same time, the highly sophisticated NATO air forces would attack Soviet and Warsaw Pact relief columns, supplies, and the like, in eastern Europe in what were called *follow-forces attacks (FOFA)*. The idea was that the advanced thrust of the Soviet attack would be isolated, cut off from its supply and logistical base. So entrapped and isolated, it could be surrounded and forced to surrender.

These strategies were never implemented in Europe, of course, but they did produce a distinctive force structure and mindset for fighting that continues to this day. To many military planners, the plans were vindicated in the Persian Gulf War, where the basic land-based blueprint for engaging and defeating the Iraqis was the highly mobile air-land battle-style concept (a plan made easier to implement because there were no natural or man-made obstacles to rapid mobility in the Kuwaiti desert). That very success reinforced the continuing adherence in the army to a heavily armored concept and in the navy to forces based on aircraft carriers (which carried out a large part of the air mission in Desert Storm), despite the fact that some analysts maintain that both tanks and carriers are vulnerable and obsolete in an era dominated by missiles, an argument elaborated in Chapter 8.

Nuclear Forces

We should be grateful, of course, that the concepts adopted by the United States for fighting the Soviet Union were never tested, because, as already noted, there was considerable disagreement about whether they would have been effective and what their larger consequences might have been. Indeed, in some circles it was privately maintained that NATO's conventional role was simply to slow down a Soviet invasion enough so that one of two things could occur. Either the diplomats could arrange a truce wherein the Soviets could be convinced to settle for less than their total goals, or there would be time to make a rational decision between escalation to nuclear weapons or capitulation.

Nuclear weapons were the other legacy of World War II. A number of countries were studying nuclear physics on the eve of the war, and Albert Einstein convinced President Franklin D. Roosevelt of the need to engage in research on the weapons potential of nuclear power to hedge against the success of the German research program (which never reached fruition, in large part because a number of the critical German scientists were Jewish and fled the country). The American Manhattan Project succeeded in producing a bomb in early 1945, and the United States emerged from the war as the only nuclear power.

The U.S. nuclear monopoly did not last long. The Soviet Union exploded its first atomic (fission) device in 1949, and both countries successfully developed far deadlier nuclear explosives in the early 1950s. These thermonuclear (fission-fusion) devices replicate the energy production methods of the sun and produce explosions measurable in the equivalents of *millions of tons (megatons) of TNT*; by contrast, the atomic bombs of the 1940s produced explosions the equivalent of thousands of tons (kilotons) of TNT. (These dynamics are discussed in more detail in Chapter 8.)

Parallel research was going on in the area of delivering nuclear and other weapons to their targets. Advances in rocketry produced the first successful Soviet intercontinental ballistic missile (ICBM) in 1957, a feat rapidly duplicated by the United States. Combined with similar work on shorter range missiles, both sides had missile-borne nuclear bombs aimed at one another by the time of the Cuban crisis, and the weapons could be delivered against their targets with no reasonable expectation that they could be intercepted or neutralized. During the 1960s and 1970s, the arsenals grew enormously on both sides, with strategic inventories (those aimed at one another's homelands) numbering more than 10,000 apiece and shorter range missiles dedicated to the support of military forces in the European or other theaters numbering in the tens of thousands. Nuclear weapons thus served two distinct functions. The most dramatic and best publicized function was that assigned to the strategic nuclear forces (SNF), developed for potential use against the adversary's territory.

As the arsenal sizes grew and became impossible to defend against, the thrust in nuclear weapons thinking and planning shifted to *deterrence*: the development and maintenance of weaponry to convince the opponent not to use his weapons against you. Since neither side could defend itself against an attack that was launched against it by nuclear-tipped missiles, the threat had to be based in retaliation and punishment of a nuclear transgressor. The idea was that a potential aggressor would realize that the victim of the attack would retain such a large surviving force as to be able to launch a devastating retaliatory strike, making the initial attack, in effect, suicidal. One concept used to describe this dynamic and the strategy to implement it in the 1960s was *assured destruction*, to which a detractor added the prefix "mutual," thereby creating an acronym reflecting his assessment of the idea: MAD.

It required the mindset of the Cold War for this nuclear balance to make sense, especially as the arsenals grew to the point that an all-out attack would have enough destructive capacity to effectively immolate the enemy several times over—"make the rubble bounce," in Winston Churchill's phrase. Both sides continued aggressively to research and deploy yet more deadly weapons, out of the fear that failing to do so would create some advantage that the other side might feel it could exploit in a nuclear attack. Lamenting this aspect of the nuclear arms race, President Jimmy Carter's Secretary of Defense Harold Brown summarized it: "We build, they build; we stop, they build." That the result was a policy and effective strategy of genocide and counter-genocide (the effect if the arsenals were used) bothered mostly the nuclear disarmers.

The other role for nuclear weapons was in support for conventional operations, primarily in Europe. (The Soviets kept a large number of these weapons along their border with their Communist "brother," China.) The purpose of these "battlefield" or "theater" nuclear weapons was as a force multiplier. In American planning, for instance, a major mission for these theater nuclear forces (TNFs) was to help blunt the massive Soviet tank offensive that it was presumed would be the opening foray of World War III. When masses of Soviet tanks approached the border, they would be attacked with nuclear warheads, thereby breaking up the assault. A special form of nuclear explosive—the enhanced radiation warhead, or neutron bomb—was to be applied specifically to this purpose (see Amplification 4.2).

Amplification 4.2

THE CAPITALIST BOMB

A major objection to the contemplated use of nuclear weapons in Europe was the enormous devastation their use would create for the very territory they were designed to defend. Europe—especially Germany, where the bulk of the initial fighting would take place— would be a scarred and cratered radioactive moonscape, unlikely to sustain life for years to come. On the other hand, nuclear weapons seemed, militarily, an effective way to destroy the concentrated armored tank assault that would spearhead the Soviet attack and against which there were inadequate alternatives.

These two diametrically opposed priorities were partially reconciled by a new form of nuclear explosive, first tested in the early 1970s and proposed for deployment by the Carter administration during the late 1970s. The new technology was something called the enhanced radiation warhead (ERW), which quickly earned the popular name "neutron bomb." Its innovation was to rearrange the relative effects of nuclear explosives. Any nuclear explosive produces four effects: a fireball of heat; extremely high winds, known as blast overpressure; initial or prompt (beta and gamma ray) radiation; and residual radiation, also known as fallout. The chief culprits in a conventional nuclear explosion were blast overpressure, which knocks down structures and craters the landscape; the fireball, which causes fires; and fallout, which lingers in the physical environment for years to come. The fourth effect, prompt radiation, sends out deadly rays during the explosion itself, but once the explosion ends, it becomes relatively benign.

The neutron bomb rearranged nuclear effects so that 75 to 80 percent of the nuclear explosion involved the release of prompt radiation. This had two advantages, given the problem it sought to overcome. First, the other effects of the weapon were reduced greatly, thereby doing less environmental damage—the concern of the local citizenry. Second, it seemed ideal against the Soviet tank threat. If the weapons were detonated over advancing Soviet tank columns, the deadly gamma and beta rays would penetrate Soviet armor and incapacitate or kill the crews without destroying the tanks. The attacks would thus be halted; and one grisly plan was to have NATO troops remove the bodies and turn the tanks on the aggressors with NATO crews.

The Soviets howled at the proposal. They labeled it "the capitalist bomb," a weapon that killed people in a grotesquely cruel manner but did not destroy the productive system it sought to protect. They threatened to produce their own neutron bombs, and the Europeans could never quite bring themselves to support any nuclear defense of Europe. Deployment was delayed, and eventually the plan to deploy the capitalist bomb in Europe was scrapped with the signing of the Intermediate Nuclear Forces (INF) Treaty in 1988, which removed most nuclear weapons from Europe.

Theater nuclear weapons were always more controversial than their strategic counterparts, especially among the European allies who would be "defended" by them. There was deep suspicion in Europe that their use could not be controlled— that once the first nuclear weapons were used on the battlefield, the result would be escalation to broader use. Whether expansion would be limited to the theater or would expand to homeland exchanges between the superpowers could not be demonstrated. Since nuclear weapons had never been used in anger when both sides possessed them, there was absolutely no evidence to support or refute claims about whether or how escalation might occur.

Regardless of escalatory potential, most Europeans agreed that anywhere nuclear weapons were used would be a loser, an irradiated wasteland that would be uninhabitable until the radiation dissipated. Some Europeans even suspected that after decimating parts of Europe, the superpowers would pause, conclude that any further escalation placed their own territories at risk, and stop, arguing that they had done their duty to defend their allies.

The French took this argument a step further. They argued that no ally (in this case, the United States) would honor an alliance commitment in the future if doing so potentially threatened its physical existence. Since any defense of Europe could escalate to disastrous homeland nuclear exchange, the French concluded that, ultimately, the United States would not risk defending Europe. The United States vigorously denied these allegations, of course, but once again could offer no hard evidence to refute them. As a result, the French concluded that they needed their own independent nuclear strike force (the *force frappe*) with which to threaten the Soviets.

In retrospect, the logic and implications of the nuclear competition may seem bizarre. How could serious people embrace a policy and strategy that, if carried out, would amount to nothing less than genocide? Once arsenals grew to the point that they exceeded any rational purpose other than genocide, why did both sides continue to build more and more deadly weapons?

The answer lies in the enormous distrust and suspicion that engulfed the participants in the competition. It is hard to imagine that anyone would engage in the hideous calculations that underpin operational nuclear policy unless they assumed that their counterparts were planning for and willing to do the same thing. The American planning process, for instance, produced something called the Single Integrated Operational Plan (SIOP), a series of options for attacking various sets of targets in the Soviet Union, graded according to their importance. Their implementation would have resulted in the deaths of countless millions of Soviets. How could one justify taking part in such an inhuman enterprise? The answer is that one could do so by assuming that the other side was doing the same thing. If you were to ask the pilots who would drop the nuclear bombs or the missileers who would release the nuclear rockets whether they would hesitate to carry out their missions, their answers would uniformly be that they would not hesitate, because they would assume that they would be retaliating on behalf of and to avenge lost loved ones.

DEADLOCK OF THE COMPETITION

Even when the Cold War competition was proceeding most vigorously, the seeds of its demise were being sown. By the 1970s, two trends, unrecognized at the time, were beginning to emerge that would lead to the end of the Cold War. One trend was the weakening of the Soviet economy, both absolutely and in comparison to that of the

United States. The other was a growing recognition of a deadlock in the military competition between the superpower blocs. Although these factors were largely unacknowledged at the time, by the 1980s they coalesced to create the conditions that led to the end of the Cold War.

The Economic Dimension

The economic implosion that eventually engulfed the Soviet state had its roots in the 1970s. At that time, economic growth began to slow, and by the end of the decade, the Soviet Union had entered what Soviet economists would later call the "era of stagnation." By the early 1980s, the only economic growth in the Soviet Union was in the production of vodka; if vodka production was removed from measures of productivity, the Soviet economy was actually in absolute decline.

This problem was known to some Soviet academic economists, but they lacked access to the leadership cadre associated with Soviet leader Leonid Brezhnev (known as the *nomenklatua*), who benefited from the system and were uninterested in seeing change that might adversely affect their privilege. Therefore, the academic economists allied themselves with a rising star within the Communist Party, Mikhail S. Gorbachev, whose wife, Raisa, was their colleague at Moscow State University. When Gorbachev achieved power in 1985, this cadre was ready to roll out the mechanisms of reform. Unfortunately for them, their efforts were too little and too late.

A good bit of the Soviet decline was due to lagging behind in science and technology. The Soviets were largely excluded from the high-technology revolution in the West, which underlay the economic expansion of the 1980s and 1990s and the process of globalization of the world economy. Some of this exclusion was purposive on the Soviets' part—to shield a shaky economy from outside competition. At the same time, this progressive technological backwardness was also an unintended result of a conscious decision in the 1960s to concentrate Soviet scientific effort on weapons development rather than on basic science. Soviet scientists such as Andrei Sakharov had warned that this emphasis was shortsighted and would place Soviet science at a disadvantage in the future. Sakharov's prediction "won" him internal exile from the regime at the time; Gorbachev "rehabilitated" him.

This technological gap was exacerbated by two additional dynamics. First, the problem was progressive. The engine of technological growth was the development of more sophisticated generations of computers, which is a progressive process. The major tool for designing the next generation of computers is the current generation; thus, the computer's future health depends on its current competitiveness. Moreover, the developmental time between generations has grown shorter because of the greater power of newer machines. This means that the further behind a country is (the more generations removed from the cutting edge), the further it gets behind in the future. By the early 1980s, the Soviet Union was approximately three generations behind the United States, and the gap was widening.

The Soviets could not close the gap. The decision to concentrate on military development had closed the computer research section of the Soviet Academy of Scientists in the 1960s and distributed its personnel to military research. The Soviets even stole computers, tore them down, and put them back together again so that they could replicate the system (a process known as reverse engineering). The systems they stole represented current technology that was becoming obsolete, and reverse engineering took longer than the development of new generations.

The Soviets also could not collaborate with the West in computer development because of the second dynamic in the problem. Almost all of the technologies in which the Soviets were behind were *dual use*, meaning that they had both military and civilian applications. For instance, a computer designed for research in theoretical physics could be converted to applying physical principles to weapons design. As long as the Soviet Union was the avowed enemy, the United States and the rest of the West were not going to provide the Soviets with a capability to produce weapons with which to menace them.

Most of these dynamics went largely unnoticed in the West. Soviet economists were rarely allowed to communicate with their Western counterparts; the Soviet government doctored economic statistics that were notoriously inaccurate anyway (and thus disbelieved); and the military production system, on which attention was concentrated, seemed to be working well. In fact, when the Central Intelligence Agency produced an analysis of the Soviet economy in the mid 1970s suggesting the possibility of its decline, the report was condemned and an alternate panel was assembled to reassess the material. That second group produced a more ominous analysis, which was largely wrong. However, since its conclusions reinforced what officials believed to be the case, it was accepted.

The Military Dimension

By the end of the 1970s, the military competition was also undergoing change, to the ultimate disadvantage of the Soviet Union. The competition had essentially become locked into a very deadly but ritual confrontation in which neither side seemed to be able to purchase meaningful advantage. This competition was enormously burdensome to the Soviet economy, which was much smaller than that of the United States and which needed to divert the resources devoted to the military for economic purposes if the Soviets hoped to compete economically. The military competition, in a word, had become a millstone around the neck of the Soviet future. The weight became unbearable in the late 1980s, when the Soviets' ill-fated, expensive, and unpopular intervention in Afghanistan contributed to the demise of the Soviet state.

These developments were not without irony. The seeds for military deadlock can be traced back to the Cuban crisis, when both sides confronted the potential reality of nuclear war and did not like what they saw. Despite the recognition of a mutual interest in avoiding nuclear war, which was the major outgrowth of that crisis, the military competition expanded and intensified, if anything, in the following years. Many in the American national security community remained deeply suspicious of anything the Soviets did (and vice versa) and continued to build up stocks of arms, especially in the area of strategic nuclear forces, as if the Cuban experience had not changed anything.

As the potential deadliness of the nuclear balance expanded, the danger of nuclear war was declining, even if the latter dynamic was mostly unrealized as the buildup continued. The prospect of nuclear war with the levels of arms available in 1962 was sobering, but the prospect of such a war fought with the arsenals of 1980 was positively catastrophic. Leaders on both sides, going back as far as President Dwight D. Eisenhower in the 1950s and Soviet Premier Nikita Khrushchev in the early 1960s, had publicly proclaimed the unacceptability of nuclear war as a means to resolve East–West differences. These original pronouncements were made when arsenal sizes numbered in the hundreds; when both sides recognized what could happen if the 10,000 or more weapons both possessed were unleashed, avoiding such a war became imperative.

The necessary step to reduce the danger—or likelihood—of war between the two sides was the extension of the unacceptability of conventional war to the relationship. The key element in that extension was the uncertainty of the escalatory process. A conventional war was a nuclear war if escalation occurred, and there was no empirical basis on which to predict confidently whether escalation would occur. In that circumstance, the only certain way to avoid nuclear war between the superpowers was to avoid *any* war between them.

This "necessary peace," as I described it in a 1986 book with that as the title, reduced the Cold War military competition to ritual status. Both sides developed and deployed weapons and conducted war games with them for the precise reason of avoiding their use in war. The old military axiom of "preparing for and fighting the country's wars" became twisted to "preparing so as to avoid fighting the country's wars."

The recognition of military deadlock came at a propitious time in the history of the Soviet–American relationship. The burden of the arms race was clearly contributing to the crisis of the Soviet economy. As noted, the Soviets were plowing upward of one-quarter of gross national product (GNP) into defense spending from an economy that was probably only about one-third the size of the American economy. When their support for foreign adventures in places like Cuba and Mozambique and the direct expense of their war in Afghanistan were added to the Cold War bill for the Soviets, the burden became overwhelming.

The Americans were adding to the Soviet problem. In 1981, the administration of Ronald W. Reagan announced that one of its major priorities was to end what it called the "unilateral disarmament" policies of its predecessor. The result was the largest arms buildup in peacetime American history, and one of the explicit purposes of the increase in arms was to force the Soviets into an economically ruinous arms race by making them try to keep up with the American expansion.

Convergence

These two dimensions had come together by the time Gorbachev succeeded Konstantin Chernenko as the Soviet leader in 1985. Gorbachev seemed a new kind of Soviet leader. He was, for instance, the first leader of the Soviet Union with a college degree, and he was a lawyer by training. He was clearly more urbane and sophisticated than his predecessors, preferring well-tailored Italian silk suits to the baggy gray gabardine associated with earlier Soviet leaders. His professor wife, Raisa, was also a handsome, urbane, and very public figure—in contrast to the dowager images of her predecessors (some of whom were never seen in public). When Gorbachev went to London as one of his first acts and clearly charmed British Prime Minister Margaret Thatcher, it was clear that he was a different character from those he succeeded.

Gorbachev faced a daunting set of problems. He knew about the economic problems from the Soviet professors, and he sought to reform the economic system. As a believing Marxist, his approach was to fine-tune the existing system—to return it to economic health by making it work better. But the system was beyond repair, and he was slow to recognize that the system itself—and the assumptions on which it rested—was the problem.

He also realized that much of the economic problem was the result of the isolation of the Soviet economy. As noted, part of that isolation had been self-imposed in order to protect uncompetitive Soviet industries from outside competition and to shield the Soviet system from corrupting outside influences. Some of the isolation was imposed by a West that was suspicious of interacting with its enemies, especially in such areas as dual use technologies.

Gorbachev ultimately recognized that the only chance for economic redemption was to open his country to the West. Western technology was absolutely critical to any attempts at economic modernization and, hence, competitiveness, and an influx of Western capital was clearly necessary to fund improved economic performance. But how could the Soviets convince a suspicious West to engage itself with the Soviet economic system? How could they convince an even more suspicious American national security establishment that shared technology would not be turned into hostile tools of war?

The military problem was much the same. When Gorbachev entered office, the Soviets were engaged in their fifth year of a frustrating, unsuccessful war in Afghanistan, which was draining the treasury and corroding the society in ways not dissimilar to the effects of the Vietnam War on the United States. Eventually, Soviet forces would have to withdraw from Afghanistan in disgrace, which became a factor in the ultimate demise of the USSR. The effects of trying to match the Reagan arms buildup were adding to the strains, and pitiful client states like Cuba looked increasingly like an unaffordable luxury.

What was Gorbachev to do? The choices were not attractive. The status quo certainly could not be sustained, and trying to tinker with the system through the economic and political reforms known as *perestroika* was not working. The Soviet Union was sinking fast as a state and as a power. A radical solution was needed.

The answer was to sacrifice the Cold War competition. The logic of the Soviet situation dictated that decision. Economic stagnation was eroding the standing of the Soviet Union in the world and was progressively reducing the standard of living of Soviet citizens. The Soviet Union was becoming, as many critics described it, "a Third World country with nuclear weapons." To change that situation, they needed access to Western technology and capital, and their only hope was to cease being the enemy and to join the community of states as a normal, rather than a rogue, member.

The same logic held for the military dimension. Even though most of the Reagan buildup was completed by 1986, it had created a gap in capabilities that was appalling to the Soviet political and military leaderships. Until 1988, the Soviet military remained bogged down in Afghanistan, an adventure that was further eroding the prestige and morale of the military. At the same time, trying to sustain the competition meant diverting resources sorely needed in the civilian sector and continuing to prop up losers like Cuba's Castro. Canceling a losing game had an increasing appeal.

The world stood by in stunned silence as the Soviet leader began to unravel the forty-year-long confrontation. Gorbachev published a blueprint of the changes he proposed in a 1986 book, *Perestroika: New Thinking for Our Country and the World*. In it, he proposed a detailed internal reform plan. In the international realm, he detailed the transformation of the Soviet Union into a "normal" state by policy changes such as noninterference in the affairs of other states and renunciation of the so-called Brezhnev Doctrine, which had justified Soviet intervention in socialist states and had been used as the rationale for Soviet invasions of Hungary, Czechoslovakia, and Afghanistan.

Perestroika was initially greeted with skepticism in the West. Since Gorbachev was, after all, the protégé of the inventor of disinformation, many analysts presumed that the book was nothing more than an elaborate web of lies to lower the West's guard. But then Gorbachev began to act in accordance with the book's proposals. In 1988, the Soviet Union completed its military withdrawal from Afghanistan, despite having accomplished none of its goals there. In 1989, it stood idly by when the Polish parliament seated a non-Communist government, an act that opened the floodgates for the rapid decommunization of Eastern Europe and, in 1991, the formal dissolution of the Warsaw Pact. These inactions seemed to implement renunciation of the Brezhnev Doctrine and the principle of noninterference in the affairs of other states.

Domestic reform was neither dramatic nor attractive enough to avoid the breakup of the Soviet Union itself. Led by the Baltic states (Lithuania, Latvia, and Estonia), the constituent republics of the Soviet Union announced their intention to withdraw from the union and establish themselves as independent states. On the last tick of the clock of 1991, the red Soviet flag came down from the Kremlin for the last time, replaced the next day by the Russian tricolor of red, white, and blue.

The peaceful implosion of the Soviet state was—and is—an unprecedented political act in world history. Some states, including major powers, have from time to time ceased to exist—through Carthaginian peaces or partition at the ends of wars—but for one of the world's two most powerful countries simply to vote itself out of existence was something that had not happened before and that was entirely unanticipated both within and outside Russia. Ultimately, the reason we did not adequately consider the possibility of a peaceful end of the Cold War was because nothing like what happened had ever occurred before.

Certainly Gorbachev himself did not begin the odyssey of change with any premonition of the ultimate outcome. He came to power and adopted reform to create a stronger, more vibrant Communist state. He believed that "socialism with a human face" (the addition of democratic politics to socialist economics) would transform the Soviet Union and allow it to retain its place of greatness. He was wrong.

So why did Gorbachev end the Cold War? The short answer is that he had no choice. The old system was broken, even if not exactly the way he and his advisors thought at the time. Knowing that the system could not be revived without considerable outside assistance, Gorbachev also understood that the *sine qua non* for assistance was to end the Cold War and to remove its most obviously annoying symbols: the Iron Curtain, the Berlin Wall, and most important, the structure of military confrontation. He did not foresee that the cost would be the destruction of the edifice he had sought to strengthen.

Fascinating questions remain. Could the Cold War have been ended without the destruction of the Soviet Union? If so, what would world politics look like today? If Gorbachev had anticipated the real price of ending the Cold War, would he have gone through with it? In another vein, was the outcome foreordained regardless of who was in the Kremlin in the middle 1980s, or was it the unique contribution of Gorbachev to stimulate the destruction of the internal barriers to change and the Soviet state itself?

These questions are speculative, of course—counterfactual "what-ifs" that have no real answers. The end of the Cold War did not, of course, instantly erase all of the problems that had troubled the international system. There were residues of the competition that had to be dealt with, and though most of them have proved somewhat less troubling than the most dire predictions at the time, they remain areas of some current concern.

COLD WAR RESIDUES

Because the Cold War was primarily a competition over Europe, most remaining problems have focused on continental adjustments. The virtually worldwide demise of Communism has affected other parts of the world, of course, removing the patina of Communism–anti-Communism from many Second Tier conflicts, for instance. The ideological contest between Communism and the West has been decided. Communism lost decisively. The breakup of the Soviet Union and the fall of other Communist regimes have left their distinctive concerns behind them. The splintering of the Soviet Union into fifteen independent states has raised questions about the future of these states, but especially that of Russia, as the successor core of the Soviet empire. At the same time, the end of the Cold War and the decommunization of the formerly Communist states left a security void in the center of Europe, the resolution of which is ongoing.

Russia and the Successor States

When the Soviet Union dissolved, the largest single state that emerged was the Russian Federation, containing roughly half the population and three-quarters of the land mass of the old USSR. Russia also has maintained most of the military power of the old Soviet Union—notably, the thermonuclear arsenal. Although beset by enormous and debilitating political and economic problems that have unquestionably diminished its place in the world, Russia and its future remain an important international concern.

The Russian situation can be divided into political, economic, and military issues. The political and economic aspects focus on the transformation of the Russian system away from its totalitarian, socialist past under Communism to some more Western democratic and capitalist future. Its progress in these areas has been mixed. Militarily, Russia has been in a process of decline that began before the fall of Communism, but it remains a nuclear superpower.

The political and economic transformation of Russia has moved forward in interrelated fits and starts. In addition to replacing the whole set of Communist political actors, the political system has had to deal with the development of democratic support in a system where economic chaos and even free fall in the late 1990s have become virtually institutional features. Economically, there has been an attempt to institute market practices, but it is being done within an inherited institutional framework that is woefully inappropriate and inadequate for the market to take hold and prosper. For example, when the Soviet Union became Russia, the country had essentially no banking or other financial laws or institutions, making it virtually impossible to regulate financial dealings. It lacked mechanisms to collect taxes to run the government. The breakdown of the Communist levers of state coercion left the country with inadequate policing capacity, which has resulted in the violent actions of the "Russian mafia" and other forms of lawlessness. Pensioners who believed that the Communist state would support their old age have found themselves holding the bag, as the "social net" promised by the Communist state has been withdrawn from them.

Standards of living have declined precipitously within Russia, and there is little improvement in sight, despite a flow of assistance into the country from abroad. In these circumstances, it is somewhat amazing that the political process has remained intact. Russia has held three relatively free elections for president, and in the third one in 2000, power was peacefully passed from Boris Yeltsin to Vladimir Putin, a momentous occasion in Russian history. Critics point out that meaningful political democracy does not exist very far from major population centers, such as Moscow and St. Petersburg, but the fact that it has endured at all is an accomplishment.

Russia also has serious military and security problems. One of the major themes of Russian history has been a concern—some argue paranoia—with military security that has been reinforced by invaders as diverse as the Mongol hordes, Napoleon Bonaparte, and Adolf Hitler. After all, a major reason for constructing the Communist empire in Eastern Europe after World War II was to provide a *cordon sanitaire* (buffer zone) between Russia and future invaders. That buffer zone is gone.

The relative assurance of Russian physical security was a victim of both the end of the Cold War and the breakup of the Soviet Union. The demise of the Cold War meant that Russia lost its Warsaw Pact allies; the breakup of the Soviet Union meant that Ukrainians, Moldavians, and others were no longer part of the Russian security scheme and might even become part of the new security problem. Russian movement toward full NATO membership is meant to assuage these problems.

Russia has other military problems. Partly because of budgetary problems, the military itself has deteriorated markedly. Because they are unable to subsist on wages that often are not paid, it is not unusual to see Russian soldiers, in uniform, working second jobs or panhandling on the streets of Moscow. The backbone of the Russian army is first-term conscripts, many of whom desert at the first possible opportunity, with the implicit approval of the society. Even the prestigious Strategic Rocket Forces that control the Russian nuclear forces are leading advocates of arms control–dictated deep cuts in arsenal size, since they cannot maintain the current arsenal at any acceptable level of readiness and security. The army's efficiency has been reduced to the point that it has been unable to put down a ragtag Muslim rebellion in Chechnya and has resorted to atrocities and the virtual leveling of the province to maintain control.

Amplification 4.3

CHECHNYA AND THE PIPELINE

Russian security concerns and adaptation to a post–Cold War world have, in important ways, coalesced over the issue of Chechnya, a renegade republic in the Caucasus region of Russia that declared its independence from the Russian Federation in 1994 and has been fighting the Russians ever since to become an independent Muslim state. Like many other parts of the southern part of Russia, the citizens are not ethnic Russians and live in areas forcefully annexed to Russia.

Chechnya represents the Soviet dilemma of dealing with the post–Cold War period in at least three ways. One is clearly the precedent that would be set if Chechnya were allowed to secede from a Russia already diminished by the dissolution of the Soviet Union. Second, the ferocity—even barbarism—of the fighting is creating a public relations nightmare for the Russian government. The once-proud Russian army has largely been ineffective in putting down the rebellion and has been reduced to leveling Chechen cities such as Grozny to the ground, with pictorial documentation widely available worldwide. In the process, there have been widespread accusations by human rights groups of atrocities committed by the Russians, which have been embarrassing to the Russians and have slowed the flow of developmental assistance to Russia. Since September 11, 2001, the Russians have sought to portray the Chechens as part of the web of international terrorism operating out of Afghanistan and Pakistan. Some of the Chechen "freedom fighters" have been shown to have common roots with Al Qaeda and other terrorist groups, and this depiction by the Russians has stilled much of the criticism of their brutality toward Chechnya.

The real heart of the Russian problem in Chechnya, however, revolves around getting Caspian Sea oil from Azerbaijan to markets in the West. Because the pipelines that will carry the oil can be taxed, great potential wealth can be accrued to whatever country wins the competition to have the pipeline built across its territory. The possible routes are across Iran (not much of an alternative, since much of the reason for exploiting Caspian oil is to reduce dependence on the Persian Gulf), Turkey, and Russia. The Russians argue that the revenue is absolutely vital to Russian economic development, since it would greatly augment the central government's tax revenues. The problem, however, is that the only way to build a pipeline across Russia is to build it through Chechnya. As long as there is an embarrassing armed rebellion in that republic, Russia's chances are visibly diminished. (The pipeline problem is discussed in some detail in the author's *Cases in International Relations*, Chapter 14.)

Chechnya represents another important dimension of the Russian military security problem: relations with non-Russians, both within Russia and in the successor states. Even with the breakup of the Soviet Union, there remain parts of the Russian Federation that are not Russian, that consider themselves to be conquered territories, and that would prefer independence. This problem is particularly acute in the Caucasus region, of which Chechnya is a part, as well as in neighboring Dagestan. The Russians fear that the success of Chechen separatists would encourage outbreaks of similar sentiments elsewhere, although, as Amplification 4.3 points out, there are other dynamics at work in the Chechen situation. The Russians also worry about the fate of the Russians who are living as unwanted citizens in most of the successor states.

The ideal outcome to the Russian situation is the gradual emergence of Russia as a fully westernized political democracy, with a growing and prosperous market-based economy, that is a full participant in the international system. Some semblance of such an outcome is provided by the "honorary" membership of Russia in the G-8 deliberations of the world's most powerful economies and its increasing inclusion in NATO.

The direction and future of the poorer and more remote successor states, especially those in central Asia, have also become a source of concern. Most of these new countries are very poor, have few prospects for economic development or the emergence of democracy (generally lacking any democratic traditions), and have Muslim majorities or minorities that threaten to drag them into the instability of Muslim fundamentalism. In 2002, a number of these states were drawn into the campaign against international terrorism by the United States, with uncertain effects, as discussed in the *Challenge!* box.

The European Security Problem

The end of the Cold War disrupted the European security system, especially for the formerly Communist countries, including the new states that emerged from the former Soviet Union. There was some initial concern that NATO might atrophy and collapse without the military opposition that had provided its *raison d'être* for over four decades, but those concerns have faded. NATO has retained a vitality born of new roles, including extending membership to the formerly Communist world. The European security problem thus comes down to providing security to Eastern Europe and the former Soviet Union so that those countries do not threaten the security of the West. It is well under way.

In 1991, there was an initial fear that the toppling of Communist regimes would result in political instability in some of the poorer Eastern European countries (e.g., Albania, Bulgaria) and former Soviet states (e.g., the Central Asian republics). There was also concern about new interstate conflicts between such places as Romania and Hungary, which had a territorial dispute over Transylvania. The process, as it turns out, has been less traumatic than many analysts envisaged a decade ago.

Two reasons for this relative tranquility stand out. First, the people of Eastern Europe and the former Soviet Union both shucked Communist rule with ease and without regret and embraced Western values. They have tried to emulate and

Challenge!

The Former Soviet Union and the War On Terrorism

It is sometimes said that war makes strange bedfellows, and the attempt by the U.S. government to internationalize its warlike campaign against terrorism seems to provide some evidence for the truth of that proposition. Nowhere is that relationship more clearly demonstrated than in the extension of partnership in the war on terrorism to Central Asian states and Russia itself.

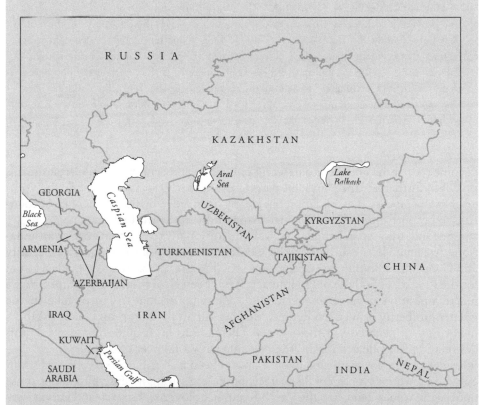

One of the chief problems the Bush administration encountered early in trying to mount military, especially ground, operations to clear out Al Qaeda and Taliban residues in Afghanistan was finding staging grounds for such efforts. For a variety of reasons, the territories of some American associates either were unavailable politically for such actions (Saudi Arabia and Pakistan, for instance) or were too remote for efficient use (Turkey). Therefore, the United States turned to contiguous states, former Soviet Central Asian republics that had gained their independence with the breakup of the Soviet

Union. To facilitate the military campaign, the United States signed basing agreements with some states, including Tajikistan, Kyrgyzstan, and Uzbekistan, and opened discussions with others.

These arrangements immediately brought the U.S. government into policy disagreement with itself—a problem that extended to Russian assistance in the effort as well. (After eight years of war in Afghanistan, the Russians are a major source of intelligence on that country.) The policy incompatibility pitted counterterrorism policy against human rights policy, because many of the new allies in the campaign against terrorism, including Russia, were also on the Department of State's list (as well as those of independent sources such as Amnesty International and Human Rights Watch) of states that violate the civil rights of their citizens and thus are to be sanctioned until those practices cease.

How is the dilemma to be resolved? Is the war on terrorism such an important priority that it overrides other concerns—in this case, human rights? Is there a parallel to the Cold War here? During the Cold War, the United States supported many corrupt right-wing regimes that regularly abused their citizens because their leaders professed staunch anti-Communism. Anti-Communism overrode other concerns. Is the profession of opposition to terrorism and willingness to aid in the campaign against terrorism the new anti-Communism of the contemporary age? Is it worth the price in the long run to be associated with regimes that abuse their citizens? Decide for yourself.

become part of the greater world system politically and economically. Certainly, this process is further advanced in some parts of the formerly Communist world than others, but the process of assimilation has clearly been aided by the desire of most countries to become "normal" states, participating fully in the world system.

Second, the system has adapted well institutionally to the challenge of assimilation. An umbrella organization, the Conference (now Organization) for Security and Cooperation in Europe (CSCE, now OSCE), already existed to provide a forum for the new states and the old to interact. It has been clear from the beginning that a major aspiration of most of the formerly Communist states is to partake in the greater prosperity of Western Europe. Membership in the European Union (EU) is a major goal of nearly all of these states. The EU has been quite responsive to this desire and has made economic arrangements with a number of the new states. The informal criteria for membership have always been a strong, market-oriented economy and a working political democracy, providing strong incentive to adopt those underlying values. Hungary, the Czech Republic, Slovenia, Estonia, and Latvia were scheduled to enter the EU in 2002, to be joined by Cyprus, Lithuania, Malta, Poland, and Slovakia by 2004.

The remaining obstacle was the extension of NATO into the formerly Communist world. The interim solution in the early 1990s was a Clinton administration initiative, the Partnership for Peace (PFP). Participation in the PFP, which was offered to the Eastern European states and the successor states to the Soviet Union, was a kind of partial membership in NATO, affording some benefits, such as nonvoting attendance at NATO functions and participation in some NATO military exercises, but not the guarantee that the full NATO membership will defend PFP countries in the event of hostilities. Most states became members of the PFP in what they saw as a first step toward full NATO membership.

Expansion into Eastern Europe began in 1999, when Hungary, Poland, and the Czech Republic were granted full membership in the organization, bringing the total to nineteen. In Prague in November 2002, the membership was increased to twenty-six states with the admission of seven former Communist territories: Bulgaria, Estonia, Latvia, Lithuania, Romania, Slovakia, and Slovenia. Russia has not yet become a full member but has negotiated a special status—the NATO-Russia Council—that allows it to participate in most NATO activities.

CONCLUSION: THE END OF THE COLD WAR IN PERSPECTIVE

If one views the Cold War strictly from the vantage point of the twenty-first century, it must seem an anomalous period—one that probably should be consigned to the history books. Although it is true that many of the problems and tensions associated with the second half of the twentieth century have proved to be less enduring than those of us who witnessed them thought they would be, such a view would be short-sighted and would miss the point of how the Cold War continues to influence us.

The Cold War remains the context from which the contemporary system is emerging. Among the overarching concerns of the new millennium are the integration of the formerly Marxist-Leninist states into the globalization system, a problem that clearly could not have existed had there not been a furtive competition between ideologically defined contenders in the first place. This process of integration is being stimulated by the enlistment of former enemies as allies in the campaign against terrorism. The consequences of this initiative are uncertain, but probably extend beyond the terrorism campaign itself. For better or for worse, many of the difficulties with which we grapple in the contemporary world have their origins in the Cold War and can be fully understood only in that light.

There is, I think, a more fundamental reason to understand the Cold War and its ending. For most of the people in important decision-making positions in the 1990s and 2000s—especially senior people in senior positions—the Cold War was their formative experience, and their thinking was and continues to be influenced by the very grim, determined worldview that "working" the Cold War produced. In the Bush administration, the list of foreign and national security policy insiders with Cold War credentials includes Secretary of Defense Rumsfeld, Secretary of State Powell, National Security Advisor Rice, and Deputy Secretary of Defense Paul Wolfowitz, to name the most prominent.

Some of the things that happen today make more sense in the light of the experience of the "cold warriors." A plan for the United States to spend as much as it is doing on defense and propose to spend even more on something like missile defense and antiterrorism makes much more sense coming from the minds of actors whose instincts tell them always to fear and prepare for the absolute worst. If, like Donald Rumsfeld, you were secretary of defense in 1976 and returned to that same position a quarter-century later, you could not avoid bringing some baggage with you. In the Cold War, the response to the threat was greater expenditure on conventional defense. Can it come as a great surprise that essentially the same actors who made those decisions then would respond similarly to the very different threat of terrorism now?

The same quality of response may not occur in ten or twenty years, when the world may have changed enough to remove the old residues and when the "cold warriors" have faded away and have been replaced by new decision makers for whom the Cold War is abstract history rather than personal experience. Until the system and its operators reach that point, however, the Cold War remains the context of the present.

SELECTED BIBLIOGRAPHY

Bialer, Seweryn, and Michael Mandelbaum, eds. *Gorbachev's Russia and American Foreign Policy.* Boulder, CO: Westview Press, 1988.

Brzezinski, Zbigniew. "The Cold War and Its Aftermath." *Foreign Affairs* 71, 4 (Fall 1992), 31–49.

Clark, Ronald W. *The Greatest Power on Earth: The International Race for Nuclear Supremacy from Earliest Theory to Three Mile Island.* New York: Harper and Row, 1980.

Claude, Inis L. *The Changing United Nations.* New York: Random House, 1967.

Fukuyama, Francis. *The End of History and the Last Man.* New York: Free Press, 1992.

Gaddis, John Lewis. *The United States and the End of the Cold War: Implications, Reconsiderations, Provocations.* New York: Oxford University Press, 1992.

Gorbachev, Mikhail S. *Perestroika: New Thinking for Our Country and the World.* New York: Harper and Row, 1987.

Mearsheimer, John J. "Why We Shall Soon Miss the Cold War." *Atlantic Monthly* 262, 2 (August 1990), 35–50.

Simes, Dmitri. "The Return of Russian History." *Foreign Affairs* 73, 1 (January/February 1992), 67–82.

Snow, Donald M. *The Necessary Peace: Nuclear Weapons and Superpower Relations.* Lexington, MA: Lexington Books, 1987.

———. *The Shape of the Future: The Post–Cold War World,* 3rd ed. Armonk, NY: M. E. Sharpe, 1999.

———. *Cases in International Relations: Portraits of the Future.* New York: Longman, 2002.

CHAPTER 5

The Rise of Globalization

This chapter introduces and traces the international dynamic competing with geopolitics: globalization. The concept of international economic phenomena as integral parts of the national security theme is of recent vintage, as is the idea of casting geopolitics and globalization as alternative national security paradigms. Therefore, the major thrust of this chapter is to introduce the international economic themes that culminated in globalization in a national security context. We will do this by means of an historical treatment of American participation in the post–World War II global economy, breaking the period into three distinct phases, including the present. The chapter will conclude with a preliminary discussion of the ongoing competition between geopolitics and globalization.

Globalization and the impact of the globalizing economy were the centerpiece of the 1990s, just as terrorism has become the lightning rod of the early 2000s. During the 1990s, the international system moved away from its Cold War emphasis on geopolitically based national security concerns to a different emphasis. After the global economic recession of 1991 faded in 1992 and 1993, a period of growing economic prosperity and expansion blossomed as a trade-driven global phenomenon, and the economies of participating countries expanded in nearly a decade of unprecedented economic growth. This phenomenon was felt in most of the developed world and parts of the developing world, but nowhere was it more evident than in the U.S. economy and for individual Americans. The U.S. economy emerged from a decade or more of relative economic listlessness to reclaim its position as the dominant economic force in the world.

This period of economic expansion induced an overreaction to the degree and depth of transformation that had occurred. Until the system endured a major shakeup in the form of the East Asian crisis of 1997 (discussed later), there was a near euphoria about the benefits and the endurance of globalization's seemingly inexorable advantages. Analysts suggested that this new phenomenon of globalization was fundamentally altering the world system. Globalization simultaneously changed and accelerated the product cycle and production system at a dizzying pace and allowed for unprecedented levels and speed of communication among governments, citizens, and firms worldwide. It seemed to its most vocal adherents that geopolitics was giving way to globalization as the dominant force in international relations.

The global slowdown of the world economy, the emergence of glaring economic weaknesses in places such as Japan, and the shift back toward geopolitics since September 11, 2001, has lessened the euphoria. The boom that marked most of the 1990s did not overcome the business cycle, as the most enthusiastic advocates had rhapsodically predicted, and geopolitics has not faded away. Thus, geopolitics and globalization have come to be recognized as existing side by side, sometimes complementing one another and at other times coming into conflict, with the ebb and flow of events influencing which system appears dominant at any given point in time.

This is not the first instance of an adjustment in the relative roles of economics and national security in international affairs. In some ways, the 1990s provide an eerie reminder of the first decade of the twentieth century. The 1900s, like the 1990s, was a decade of great economic prosperity, featuring increased commerce among countries, which was supposedly tying the developed world together in a web of interdependence that would make war—the ultimate expression of geopolitics— unthinkable. That decade was followed by the deadliest war in human history to that time, World War I. Although the 1990s showed little prospect of producing the germ for a war of that size or nature, the terrorist attacks of 2001 provided a similar reminder that the darker side of geopolitics has not disappeared from the scene.

The relative roles of geopolitics and globalization fit into the broader debate about America's place in the world, introduced earlier and to be developed throughout this book. The internationalist strain in America's view of the world has always been strongly represented in the economic debate, and the United States has been a leader in the promotion of increased world trade since it emerged as an industrial power after the American Civil War. Even when the country withdrew *politically* from international affairs between the world wars into "splendid isolationism," it remained a very active member of the international economic system. The same internationalism that manifests itself in a politically activist role and an expansive view of the country's military obligations is also part of the economic debate whose current focus is globalization. The so-called economic rejectionists, who have been active in disrupting proglobalization international economic meetings in recent years, can similarly be seen as the inheritors of the tradition of those who would prefer a more limited international role for the United States.

The purpose of this chapter is to create a foundation for thinking about the role of economic concerns in foreign and national security policy and their impact. We will proceed historically from the end of World War II, dividing the American experience into three distinct periods. We will begin by discussing the American-dominated economic system that emerged from World War II, the Bretton Woods system. We will then move to the transitional period between the American renunciation of the gold standard in 1971 and the emergence of globalism somewhere around the end of the 1980s. We will conclude with the contemporary period of globalization and a discussion of where it may be leading, particularly in light of the resurgence of terrorism-led geopolitics in 2001.

THE BRETTON WOODS SYSTEM, 1945–71

What became known as the Bretton Woods system had its roots in World War II. It reflected perceptions about how the interwar international economic system had helped precipitate the war and about the nature of the postwar international economic situation. The result was a series of international negotiations, dominated by the Americans and the British, that produced an institutional framework within which to organize the revised and rejuvenated economic order. The American position was crucial because of the overwhelming strength of the U.S. economy. When that preeminence began to erode, relatively, in the 1960s, the system (if not the institutions) eroded as well.

The Setting

Two overarching international economic facts dominated the international scene in 1945 and were the major concerns of postwar planners seeking to recreate an international system that would not slide back to instability and to yet another devastating war. The first fact was that the United States emerged from the war with the overwhelmingly largest and most robust economy in the world. It was thus the only country capable of leading a postwar reconstruction of the global economy. The second fact was that most economic observers believed that economic policies pursued between the world wars had contributed significantly to the slide toward war. Each of these facts had major implications for the restructuring of the global economy.

The American economy had been rescued and strengthened absolutely and relatively by World War II. The U.S. economy had been hard hit by the Great Depression (as had Germany's—and that impact was partially blamed for the rise of Hitler and thus the war). On the eve of World War II, the American industrial plant was working at only about a third of its capacity. When the United States entered the war, that unused capacity was activated to transform the country's industrial base into the "arsenal of democracy," producing the war materiel that would bring down the Axis powers. The unemployment that had been the most visible symbol of the depression evaporated in the economic and military mobilization. The American economy was thus revived by the war, and when the war was over, the economy was ready to turn its full strength to fulfilling consumer demand, which had been frustrated by the war effort. Moreover, the "accident of geography" identified in Chapter 3 was also at work. The United States was the only major participant whose economy was not damaged militarily; thus, the economy emerged unscathed by the ravages of war, a fate not shared by other countries, which had at least part of their economic capacity reduced to rubble and needing to be rebuilt.

The structural and financial damage to the various combatants was, of course, differential. The major defeated powers, Germany and Japan, had both been major industrial powers before the war and now lay in occupied ruin—the major result of the strategic bombardment campaigns that had destroyed the productive industries supporting their war machines. Physical occupation meant that their economic fate was at the mercy of the victorious Allies. Great Britain and France—especially Great Britain—suffered major physical and financial damage and emerged from the war political victors but economically diminished to the point that they would have to relinquish their colonial empires and assume the role of a regional rather than a global power.

The Soviet Union was a unique case. The Soviets had borne the brunt of Hitler's war machine in the fighting on the Eastern Front during the war. The Soviet economy, not very well developed before the war, was absolutely devastated: Two-thirds of Soviet towns and villages were leveled, and total casualties (civilian and military) were in the vicinity of twenty million (in addition to the estimated ten million killed by the Stalin regime in the 1930s purges). All the Soviet Union had left was a single symbol of power—a huge Red Army that formed the backbone of Soviet strength and power.

American economic preeminence meant that the United States was the only candidate to lead any global economic recovery. Because the United States possessed enormous leverage to structure that system with its own desires, it was very difficult for the other World War II participants to resist American preferences. The question was whether and how the Americans would lead the world economy to a stable new prosperity.

Answers about the direction of the global economy were worked out as part of the wartime allied collaboration that also produced the United Nations. The security problem during the interwar years had been the League of Nations, which was not strong enough to enforce policies that would maintain the peace. The economic realm was even worse. There, an international institutional void allowed states to pursue policies that created the economic crisis of the 1930s that many believed led to the war.

A major culprit in interwar economics had been the punitive nature of the Versailles peace treaty that ended World War I. In 1919, Germany was forced to accept total responsibility for starting the war through the War Guilt Clause, Article 231. This provision justified sizable reparations from Germany to pay for the destruction in France (where most of the physical fighting on the Western Front occurred) and in Great Britain. The reparations payments forced upon the democratic government of the Weimar Republic virtually ensured that Germany could not recover from the war economically. In the end, Germany was unable to meet the repayment schedules.

The effect was that the Great Depression hit Germany harder than any other country on the continent. Amid enormous depression-induced economic suffering in the early 1930s, the same Adolf Hitler who was laughed at and jailed when he first appeared on the political scene in the more prosperous 1920s was elected chancellor of Germany in 1932. Part of his appeal was his promise to restore economic prosperity.

The Great Depression also set off a wave of economic nationalism that worsened matters worldwide. As the effects of the depression spread throughout Europe and threatened the integrity of industries and businesses, governments responded with protective barriers in the form of very high tariffs and other devices designed to protect indigenous industries from foreign competition by making outside goods and services artificially more expensive than domestic counterparts. These barriers reduced trade to a trickle of its predepression levels and added to the general animosity between countries that was greasing the slide to world war.

These perceptions helped predispose those who would take the lead in fashioning the postwar economic system. The isolationism that had been a firm part of the economic nationalism of the 1930s—some called it economic warfare—was firmly rejected. So was the notion of a punitive peace, which had crippled the defeated Allies, ensured that they could not fully embrace the peace settlement, and ultimately encouraged another global war.

The Bretton Woods Institutions

Formal planning for the revised economic order was a wartime enterprise dominated by the Americans and the British. They had somewhat different perspectives on what should be done after the war ended, and each produced a different blueprint for the future.

The initial international conference to craft a new set of structures was held in July 1944 in the New Hampshire resort town of Bretton Woods at the magnificent Hotel Washington, nestled at the foot of Mt. Washington in the White Mountains. Attended by representatives of forty-four countries, the Bretton Woods conference was in an awe-inspiring physical setting, designed to maintain the concentration of the conferees (that the village was physically remote and not serviced by air or rail added to the physical enforcement of concentration).

The planners at Bretton Woods began by agreeing that the economic protectionism of the interwar years had contributed to the war and that protectionism had to be attacked if economic stability was to be reinstated. Specifically, they were concerned about international financial and economic practices: large fluctuations in exchange rates of currencies, chronic balance of payments problems experienced by some countries, and the high tariffs that had dominated the 1930s. All of these problems restricted the flow of international commerce, and there was a clear underlying preference for moving toward a system of considerably freer trade than had existed before the war. This free trade, internationalist position dominated the American delegation to Bretton Woods, although there remained significant protectionist sentiment within Congress and in some conservative American organizations, such as the U.S. Chamber of Commerce.

The conferees produced agreements that created two institutions to form the core of the Bretton Woods system. At the same time, they deferred consideration of the more politically divisive issue of institutionalizing free trade until after the war was over. The institutions created were the International Monetary Fund (IMF) and the International Bank for Reconstruction and Development (IBRD, or World Bank). Both had the initial purpose of dealing with the specific economic problems identified during the war. The IMF would deal with currency stabilization and balance-of-payments difficulties by authorizing what amounted to lines of credit to countries suffering difficulties in these areas. The World Bank, as its formal name implied, was authorized to grant loans for assisting in reconstructing war-torn economies and later developing less developed countries. Both organizations were funded by subscriptions from the members, with weighted voting privileges depending on the amount of initial subscription. Because the United States had the most money to subscribe, it received the largest bloc of votes (about one-third) in both organizations, thus providing an institutional basis for U.S. domination of the postwar economic order.

Both institutions were heavily American from the beginning. There was strong support for both the IMF and the IBRD in the United States, reflected by the votes authorizing participation in both by the U.S. Senate (61–16) and the House of Representatives (345–18). The permanent headquarters for the two organizations would be a city block in downtown Washington, D.C., that is a short walk from the White House and the old Executive Office Building, which houses most of the White House staff. The president of the World Bank has always been an American, and it is not infrequent for Americans to move freely between positions in the IMF or IBRD and such agencies of the federal government as the Treasury Department.

The fate of institutionalizing free trade was not so smooth, reflecting historic American debates about America's role in the world and questions about American economic and political independence in the world. The American impulse toward free trade reflects the internationalist approach to American policy, whereas protectionism (the opposite of free trade) is an extension of isolationism. Both positions have long been part of the American debate. The desirability of the United States being institutionally entwined in free trade regimes also raised questions among critics and opponents about impingement on state sovereignty. These opposing viewpoints were as present in 1945 as they are in 2003.

The attempt to institutionalize international free trade also began when the war ended, but it faced a much more perilous political course. Within the U.S. administration of Harry S. Truman, there was great support for an institutional commitment through an organization that would parallel the IMF and IBRD, thus making the Bretton Woods institutions a troika of international economic organizations. This idea had both domestic and international opponents, however, and they effectively blocked the idea.

The Truman administration's strategy for lowering trade barriers consisted of two parts, both of which have parallels in the contemporary debate over trade. One of these was to pursue bilateral and multilateral reductions in tariffs and quotas under the provisions of the Reciprocal Trade Agreements Act (RTAA) of 1934. The RTAA, which was passed in reaction to the extreme protectionism of the Smoot-Hawley Tariff Act of 1930, authorized the administration to reduce tariffs with other countries on specific items by up to 50 percent, but only if the reductions were reciprocal. It did not authorize the elimination of any trade barriers, and thus was only a modest first step toward the administration's goal of freeing trade. It was the precursor to so-called fast-track (or what the Bush administration calls trade promotion) authority.

The heart of the free trade initiative was to be an international organization, the International Trade Organization (ITO). The purposes of this organization were to

Amplification 5.1

THE ITO AND THE ANTI-FREE TRADERS

The noteworthy failure of the Bretton Woods process was the inability to bring the International Trade Organization (ITO) into existence. This result stymied the maximum promotion of free trade, which was one of the major objectives of the architects of the Bretton Woods system. Reflecting the long-standing American ambivalence about the proper role for the United States in the international economic order, the United States both proposed the ITO to the international community and brought about its defeat by failing to ratify the ITO treaty.

As a domestic political event, the scenario was familiar. The principal backers of the ITO were in the executive branch: The original impetus for the body came from State Department planners during World War II, and when Harry S. Truman succeeded the late Franklin D. Roosevelt, his administration took the lead in proposing a UN Conference on Trade and Development in 1946 to draft the statute for the ITO.

Major opposition congealed in the Congress. The major elements in the protectionist coalition were Republicans, who were influenced by major business and commercial interest groups that believed in protecting American products from foreign competition. Both manufacturing and farm elements were represented in this effort. At the other extreme, a number of liberal Democrats who believed that the ITO statute was too timid a document in promoting free trade joined the opposition, as did conservatives who opposed the ITO on the grounds that it represented a dangerous assault on American sovereignty. The opposition successfully blocked Senate advice and consent on the matter and provided a precedent for the kind of odd-bedfellows coalition that would emerge as rejectionists at the turn of the twenty-first century.

promote free trade among its members and to create an enforcement mechanism to investigate and punish those who violated trade agreements into which they had entered. In order to draft a statute for the ITO similar to the outcome of the Bretton Woods meetings, a preliminary meeting was held in 1947 in Geneva, Switzerland, to lay out trading principles under the title General Agreement on Tariffs and Trade (GATT). The GATT was intended as a temporary umbrella, an expedient device wherein general principles could be drafted to govern the permanent ITO.

The meeting at which the ITO was proposed was held in Havana later in November 1947. By the time it was convened, domestic and foreign opponents to the principle of universal free trade had organized themselves well enough to dilute the outcome. These early "rejectionists" argued *against* domestic and international impacts of loosening trading restrictions and *for* the protection of special arrangements, such as the British Imperial Preference System (which created special tariff status between Great Britain and members of the empire and Commonwealth). In addition, other national delegations refused to grant the United States the deference accorded it through weighted voting in the IMF and IBRD. Instead, they insisted that the United States would be given a single vote, like any other country.

The ITO never came into being. President Truman refused to submit the ITO treaty to the Senate in 1948. He feared that in an election year, free trade, with considerable opposition in Congress and the public, might become a campaign issue. In 1949, the administration's effort to gain ratification of the North Atlantic Treaty (the first peacetime military alliance in U.S. history) pushed the ITO off the agenda. By the time the president submitted the treaty to the Senate in April 1950, enthusiasm for international organizational solutions to problems had cooled, and the outbreak of the Korean War in June 1950 reinforced that sentiment. In November 1950, Truman withdrew the ITO proposal from Senate consideration, and the ITO idea was a dead horse until it was revived in 1993 as the World Trade Organization (WTO).

The GATT survived, however. Although protectionists did not like it much more than they liked the ITO, it was less threatening to their cause. The GATT was not an organization at all; it was a series of periodically convened negotiating sessions between sovereign states. This lack of structure meant that it would have no permanent investigating or enforcing staff that could enforce objectionable rules on countries and thereby infringe on their sovereignty. Also, because the GATT was a series of negotiations (that became known as "rounds"), the individual states retained maximum control over what they were willing or unwilling to accept in the free trade area by signing or not signing individual proposals.

The GATT thus became the banner around which the free traders could congregate until the time was right for them to assert their case for a permanent international organization. In the process, the GATT developed a set of four principles that defined its operation and remain important points of reference to this day (that are summarized in Rothgeb, p. 75). These include *nondiscrimination* (the promotion of most favored nation—MFN—status to all subscribing countries), *transparency* (the unacceptability of secret trade restrictions and barriers), *consultation and dispute settlement* (resolution of disputes through direct negotiations), and *reciprocity* (the idea that all members should incur balanced obligations).

The free trade issues raised in the 1940s are instructive because they parallel and even anticipate the kinds of debates and problems that enliven the 2000s. The debate over the extent to which free trade should be an active part of American international economic policy stands at the vortex of the issue. Generally, there has been a domestic political debate with strong interbranch implications: The White House in the 1940s was the epicenter of free trade advocacy under Roosevelt and Truman and has been for the last decade under Clinton and Bush. On the other side of the coin, organized political opposition has largely come from elements in Congress with constituencies that would be harmed by free trade and thus are opposed to it. What is different is that in the 1940s, most of the organized congressional opposition was Republican, whereas much of the current opposition is Democratic.

This disagreement manifests itself in two distinct ways. One is the amount of discretion the Congress is willing to grant the executive to negotiate trade arrangements. The general outcome has been to give the president some tethered leeway. Congress granted the president limited authority to negotiate tariff reductions through the RTAA of 1934, but it restricted what he could negotiate and under what circumstances. Moreover, the RTAA was time-limited legislation that automatically expired in 1948. The Congress continued to renew the RTAA annually until 1962, but the threat of nonrenewal—presumably if the president exceeded his authority—provided the congressional tether. A parallel exists regarding the so-called fast track legislation, which authorized the president to negotiate trade agreements that Congress could only approve or disapprove but could not amend. That legislation was also renewable; it expired in 1993. The efforts to get it reinstated, first by President Clinton and later by President Bush, have been an ongoing interbranch struggle with strong free trade bases; the issue was resolved for now by extending the authority to Bush in 2002.

The other form of disagreement was over the international institutionalization of free trade. Congressional opposition effectively killed the ITO when Truman determined he did not have the votes in the Senate for ratification, and the issue remained dormant for over four decades. The call for an international organization, the World Trade Organization (WTO), emerged from the 1993 Uruguay Round of the GATT. In a changed economic atmosphere, where cutting-edge American industries in areas such as telecommunications and financial services would clearly benefit from institutionalization, the Senate passed the treaty forming the WTO (which took effect on January 1, 1995). The ITO was thus reborn as the WTO.

The other common thread of the two experiences is organized opposition to the idea of free trade. When opponents of the WTO took to the streets of Seattle in 1999 to disrupt its proceedings and carried their street tactics to meetings of such organizations as the G-8 in Ottawa and Genoa and the Asia-Pacific Economic Cooperation (APEC) and the Free Trade of the Americas (FTAA) in Washington, they reflected a long-standing opposition to the underlying free trade values of all those organizations. The focus of those objections has changed somewhat; for instance, there were no opponents of global warming theories in the 1940s. The tactics and forums have also changed. In the 1940s, opposition was expressed in the pinstriped suit–dominated halls of Congress, in contrast to the often rowdy street demonstrations of the 1990s and 2000s. The underlying sentiments, however, remain largely the same.

The Breakdown of Bretton Woods

For the first two decades following World War II, the U.S.-dominated Bretton Woods system prevailed in international economics. During this time, the United States dominated the international economic system basically because the U.S. economy was the dominant economic force in the world. Because countries needed American economic resources and goods, the dollar emerged as the only "hard" currency in the world (the only currency universally accepted in international trade). Regulating the supply of dollars in the international system provided a considerable source of leverage for the United States in international financial circles.

The attractiveness of the dollar was also enhanced because it was tied to the gold standard. As a matter of U.S. policy, every dollar in circulation was backed by gold, such that one ounce of gold was worth $35. The gold standard meant that, at least theoretically, anyone with $35 in cash could trade it in for one ounce of gold from Fort Knox, Kentucky, or some other federal gold depository.

The gold standard was always a fiction, in the sense that the United States never possessed enough gold to redeem all the dollars in circulation. In fact, there was never enough gold to redeem more than a few percent of those dollars, and as more and more dollars went into circulation, that percentage declined. Nevertheless, the promise of the gold standard created an aura of confidence around the value of the dollar that stabilized the entire financial system.

Because the strength of the Bretton Woods system was predicated on the preeminence of the American economic system and currency, the system was bound to founder as the relative position of the United States in the world economic order faltered, which began to happen in the 1960s. Some of these changes were the direct consequence of American actions in the world; others were the result of domestically based political decisions.

Part of the change was the postwar recovery in Europe and Japan. In the late 1940s, the American economy was producing about 40 percent of all the goods and services produced worldwide. Although this was a remarkable testimony to American productivity, it also reflected the absence of productivity in the other traditional industrial countries, all of which were struggling to recover and rebuild from the ravages of the war.

Faced with the geopolitical Soviet menace, it had been explicit U.S. policy, starting in the 1940s, to assist in the recovery of the European and Japanese economies through programs such as the Marshall Plan. The motivation for this was largely geopolitical—to increase the status of these countries as anti-Communist bastions and to ensure that Communism did not appeal to their citizens. (In 1948, for instance, the French Communist Party emerged briefly as the largest electoral party in France, raising fears of a peaceful Communist takeover.) Pumped up by American dollars, the European and Japanese economies did recover—as intended—and became economic competitors to the United States. In the process, the United States' relative share of global GNP began to shrink, moving downward to the low 20 percents in the 1970s, where it has essentially remained since. The United States did not cease to be the preeminent economic power in the world, but it no longer enjoyed the same overwhelming level of superiority it had once occupied.

Since purchases of goods and services in international trade are, by and large, made in the currency of the country from which those goods and services are purchased, there suddenly was a demand for currencies other than the dollar to pay for goods and services from other countries. In addition, political and economic events during the 1960s were making continuing adherence to the gold standard an increasingly impossible fiction.

Several domestic events and trends in the 1960s contributed to this problem. In the mid 1960s, President Lyndon Johnson made the fateful decision to finance the Vietnam War and the complex of entitlement programs known collectively as the Great Society simultaneously, without raising taxes. The result was the first sizable budget deficit and consequent accumulation of national debt in the United States since World War II. One result was a decline in confidence in the American economy which, coupled with rising inflation and competition from foreign goods and services, created a new atmosphere in which American economic predominance was actually called into question for the first time since the end of the war.

The ultimate event occurred in 1971, when adherence to the gold standard became such a burden on the American economy that it could no longer be sustained. The inflationary spiral of the 1960s had resulted in such a flood of dollars into circulation that the fiction of redemption of dollars for gold was increasingly and obviously hollow. Moreover, pegging the value of the dollar to gold resulted in overvaluation of the dollar against other currencies. That, in turn, made it difficult for American producers to compete with their overseas counterparts. (It took too many units of a foreign currency to buy enough U.S. dollars to purchase American goods.)

These factors combined to force the U.S. government to renounce the gold standard in 1971. Dollars would no longer be redeemable in gold. More important, the value of the dollar would no longer be determined against a set quantity of the precious metal. Instead, the dollar would be allowed to "float" against other currencies, with its value set at whatever price others were willing to pay for it in other currencies. The dollar thus essentially became a commodity like other commodities and would have to compete with other currencies in the marketplace. Almost instantly, other currencies (especially those from places such as Germany and Japan, which produced goods and services that were desired in world markets) became hard currencies. The global economic competition was on, and American preeminence was no longer to be taken for granted.

THE TRANSITIONAL PERIOD, 1971–90

The renunciation of the gold standard ushered in a period of change in the structure of the international economic system. The broad theme of the period was the apparent American decline in military and political power (largely the result of the Vietnam experience) and especially in the economic realm, followed by a resurgence by the end of the 1980s.

The 1970s was a difficult period of transition in the United States. Economic turbulence was assured by the oil shocks of 1973 and 1977. Led by its Middle East members, the Organization of Petroleum Exporting Countries (OPEC) took a series of joint actions that greatly raised the price of oil to all consuming countries. In 1973, these actions were accompanied by a boycott of countries that did not denounce Israel after the Yom Kippur War. The consequent shortages in the United States and the Netherlands (the only major states that refused to condemn Israel) resulted in long gas lines and higher prices at the pump in both countries.

The rise in the price of oil had structural effects on the global economy as well. When the rebuilding of Europe and Japan was undertaken, the decision was made to base energy consumption on petroleum. The reason was that Middle Eastern oil was plentiful and was largely controlled by the major Western oil companies (known as the Seven Sisters), thereby guaranteeing availability at a low cost ($3 to $5 a barrel). Most of Europe and Japan became heavily dependent on imported oil, since neither had domestic sources (the North Sea oil fields had not been exploited at this point). As the price of oil rose to $20 a barrel and more, the First Tier states became debtors to the oil-producing states, and successful competition in global markets to sell goods and services so as to buy petroleum became a much more serious business than it had previously been. Economic competitiveness in global markets became increasingly important for overall prosperity.

Other events in the United States were serving to undermine America's normally high level of self-confidence. In 1973, the United States removed its last combat troops from Vietnam, in effect admitting its failure to prevail in that conflict. Controversy over the U.S. participation in Vietnam reached a crescendo of recrimination. Shortly on the heels of that withdrawal, the Watergate scandal (the break-in of Democratic Party headquarters at the Watergate apartment complex in Washington during the 1972 presidential campaign by Nixon campaign authorities and the subsequent attempt to cover up and deny presidential involvement in the affair) broke into the open. In 1974, President Richard M. Nixon, facing an impeachment trial in the U.S. Senate, became the only president in American history to resign from office. American faith in and support for political institutions and leaders hit rock bottom.

American Decline

Economic bad news accompanied these political mishaps. One of the apparent legacies of the deficits created by financing the war in Vietnam was perpetual inflation. By the end of the 1970s, it had become "double-digit" (over 10 percent annually). Inflation eroded consumer buying power and created a sense of economic malaise. Worse yet, there was growing evidence that American industry was losing its competitive edge against other countries (especially Germany and Japan) and that the United States was in economic decline. The question in the minds of many Americans was not *whether* this was happening but how pervasive the losses were and how permanent the phenomenon was.

The evidence of economic decline seemed to cut across the board. American industries appeared to have become soft, no longer innovating, as competitors in Europe and Japan were. American industries were losing market share in a wide variety of products, from consumer electronics to heavy machinery, from hospital equipment to automobiles. Some dark predictions hinted that this condition might even worsen to the point that the United States would fade into second-class status. One prediction, put forward by Yale historian Paul Kennedy (see Amplification 5.2) went so far as to prophesy that the United States would fade as a world power due to imperial overreach.

In the context of the "go-go 1990s," when the United States reestablished itself as the central economic player, this pessimism seemed hard to imagine. At the beginning of the 1970s, the American electronics industry was supreme, and consumers greatly preferred American stereos or televisions to less expensive but "inferior" foreign models. The same was true of automobiles; American models predominated, and the major foreign competitors were European—either "cult" cars like the Volkswagen

Amplification 5.2

THE DECLINIST THESIS

The idea that the United States might be in a possibly irreversible process of national decline as a great power was most often associated in the 1980s with Yale historian Paul Kennedy, who published *The Rise and Fall of the Great Powers: Economic Change and Military Change from 1500 to 2000* in 1987. Given American economic woes during the 1970s and 1980s, Kennedy's "declinist thesis" found many receptive ears.

In the book, Kennedy puts forward as his central thesis the idea that "imperial overreach" is the trigger of national decline. Citing Great Britain and Imperial Russia as prime historical examples, Kennedy argued that great states had a tendency over time to overextend themselves militarily as they widened their imperial interests. This military burden, he contended, eventually placed such a strain on the economic underpinnings of the state that the power of the great state eventually went into decline. This, he argued, is what happened to the British and to the Russians, and he suspected that the same overreach had afflicted the United States and possibly also the Soviet Union. In circumstances where the American share of production appeared to be in relative decline and there was slippage in everything from scores on standardized mathematics and science tests to health standards, many found the Kennedy thesis compelling.

Others did not, and the declinist thesis never lacked critics. One of the loudest critics was Harvard political scientist (and Clinton administration official) Joseph S. Nye Jr., who, in his 1990 book *Bound to Lead*, maintained that the United States economy was much healthier than was argued by the declinists. He cited, for instance, the falsity of the amount of slippage of the American economy relative to others on the basis that the comparisons essentially "cooked the books" by comparing levels of productivity in the 1940s, when the American share was artificially inflated by postwar conditions, with the 1980s, when those levels were at more normal, and stable, levels. Time would prove Nye's projections to be more accurate than Kennedy's.

Beetle and van or luxury models from firms such as Mercedes-Benz and Jaguar. When the first Japanese models entered the market, they were dismissed as "junk," which might compete with the VW but certainly could not challenge the products of American automotive giants. The transformation in those markets to their present state was largely a product of the 1970s that continues to exist.

Driven by advances in high technology and changing policies and attitudes within the business and policy communities, things began to change in the 1980s. It was a quiet, virtually subterranean revolution. Much of the perception of malaise from the 1970s continued to dominate the public debate, and until the latter part of the decade, the Cold War continued to be the focal point of international concerns. One was much more likely to hear about the lack of competitiveness of American electronics or the seemingly endless military competition with the Soviets than about the crumbling of the Soviet empire or the resurgence of the American economy.

American Revival

Beginning in the 1970s and accelerating in the 1980s, policy and science coalesced to nurture positive change. In the policy arena, the 1980s were dominated by the efforts of the Republican administration of Ronald W. Reagan in the United States and the Conservative Prime Minister Margaret Thatcher in Great Britain, both of whom preached for and advocated a reduced role for government in the economic sector and a much more pure form of capitalism. Reagan's economic legacy is twofold and mixed. His domestic economic program is remembered most distinctively for the huge tax reduction he pushed through Congress in 1981, which resulted in runaway government deficits and a skyrocketing debt, the reduction of which became the centerpiece of domestic fiscal policy in the 1990s. The recurring theme of the Reagan policy was "getting government off the people's backs."

Reagan and those around him also believed that the less government interference in and control over the economy, the better. It was Reagan's general belief, supported by Thatcher, that in economic matters, the private sector almost always made better decisions than government officials did and thus should be as unfettered from government intrusion as possible.

This predilection resulted in two policy thrusts. *Privatization* involved getting government out of operating businesses and turning formerly government-operated functions over to private entrepreneurs and corporations. The idea was that privatization would result in increased efficiency and thus greater value for consumers. This thrust was particularly important to Thatcher, since the British economy had considerably more public intrusion into economic affairs than existed in the United States. In the United States, the breakup of government monopolies such as long distance telephone service illustrated this philosophy.

Deregulation was the other shibboleth. A major perceived cause of the supposed economic decline, the Reaganites believed, was too much regulation of the private sector by the government, thereby stultifying the ability of the private sector to be flexible and to compete both domestically and internationally. The claim was that by removing strictures on how business could be done, the result would be greater efficiency in operation and hence competitiveness. Airline deregulation is a primary example of this philosophy in action.

The Reagan administration's attitude toward so-called *industrial policy* demonstrates the ideas underlying these two principles. The idea of industrial policy is that the country benefits from the collaboration between industry and government (as well as academia for research purposes). In the process, the government influences the direction that the private sector takes on various initiatives, mostly by funneling government funds into specific research projects. The prime global example of this form of collaboration—and government influence and direction—is Japan, where the Ministry of Industry and Trade (MITI) was held up as the model for industrial policy–led economic success in the 1970s and 1980s.

The philosophy of Reagan and Thatcher (and their economist supporters) rejected the industrial policy model, claiming that it stifled individual initiative in the economic sector. Both privatization and deregulation are, in fact, direct refutations of the notion that collaboration between government and industry will maximize prosperity. Instead, these principles represent an embrace of market-driven economics. Thatcher stated the position most bluntly through the "TINA" principle: There Is No Alternative to the market.

Other forces were coming together to reinforce this set of policy predilections. A major source of change was emerging in the area of so-called *high technology*, where the fruits of advances in computing and telecommunications (and the merger of these two industries to create the information age) were changing the content and nature of what composed the cutting edge of economic and scientific activity. If the early post–World War II period had been dominated by the manufacture of goods, the impact of the information age was to change the structure of what was valuable. Services and the monopoly on the most desired information came to represent the "commodity" of greatest value in the evolving economy. Figuratively speaking, software replaced steel-belted tires as the symbol of productivity.

In the period of declinist malaise, the enormous advantage of the United States in this kind of transformation was not as obvious as it is now. The chief engine of change was the computer, and the countries with the most powerful computers would lead the way in generating the knowledge and technology by which the cutting edge would be defined. The supercomputer (the most advanced computer at any point in time) was an American preserve, which provided the basis for an American economic sector that was progressively attuned to exploiting this advantage. This American advantage was augmented by another traditional source of American preeminence—American graduate education in the sciences and engineering. American graduate schools are the most advanced in the world in the areas that contribute most directly to the artifacts of the telecommunications revolution and attract students and faculty worldwide.

The attractiveness of the American political and social system contributed to this growing American strength that became the basis for American resurgence in the 1990s. Fired by technological developments in computing, the birth of the Internet, and the like, the centers of American attraction emerged in the 1980s as magnets for the best young minds and the most ambitious entrepreneurs in the world. They tended to congregate in places where there were clusters of great universities and pleasant living conditions and lifestyles. The Silicon Valley in California, nestled between and nurtured by such great universities as Stanford and the University of California at Berkeley, became the model for the further development of emerging technology, followed by places such as the Route 128 corridor outside Boston (in the shadow of Harvard and the Massachusetts Institute of Technology, among other schools), the Research Triangle in North Carolina, and others. These enclaves became the seedbed of America's return to preeminence.

The private sector made its contribution as well. During the period of American decline, a major criticism was that the American manufacturing industry had gone soft and complacent and that industries in other hungrier and more ambitious countries had gained advantages, especially in the area of overseas trade. A primary invidious comparison was made between the American and the Japanese automobile industries.

This situation began to change in the 1980s, as the U.S. manufacturing community began to reform itself by imitating the practices of countries such as Japan and restructuring the "sunset industries" (those declining in importance) through actions such as the now-familiar practice of "downsizing." As traditional American industries began to narrow the gap with their ambitious foreign rivals and as new economic emphases in which the United States had a built-in advantage came to the fore, the United States became poised for the resumption of economic leadership in the world.

Both the American decline and the American resurgence in the economic realm were gradual and, for the most part, not very dramatic. If one's experience is limited to the bountiful expansion of the 1990s, it may be difficult to think of a time when there was a more fearful, less confident United States sitting astride the world of geopolitics and globalization, but this was indeed the case during the 1970s and most of the 1980s. For those Americans who lived through that time, it remains a benchmark against which to measure a return to the "bad old days," in much the same way that remembrance of the Great Depression conditions the perspectives of older Americans.

The events that ushered in the age of globalization were political, not economic, although many of the most noticeable effects in the long run have been economic. The most obvious manifestations of change came from the end of the Cold War and the demise of Soviet and world Communism as the 1980s made the transition to the twentieth century's last decade.

The end of the Cold War effectively ended the competition between economic ideologies. Socialist economics were so thoroughly discredited by the collapse of the politico-economic system that had enshrined Marx's and Engel's ideas that they effectively disappeared. For the moment, at least, we are at Francis Fukuyama's "end of history," in the sense that there is no current intellectual competitor to the supremacy of political democracy and capitalist economics. That is not to say that all countries have bought into the values; there are still political thuggeries in the world and countries that, for a variety of reasons, reject participation in the global economy. There are, however, with only a few exceptions, no open proponents of alternative systems. (Some fundamentalist Muslim systems, such as the former Taliban regime in Afghanistan, which recognize the cultural corrosiveness of joining the global system on their conditions, are the obvious exceptions.)

THE GLOBALIZING ECONOMY, 1990–PRESENT

The system of globalization resulted from a series of trends that came together in the 1990s, rather than from some traumatic economic event like the American renunciation of the gold standard in 1971. The collapse of Communism provides a political benchmark of that emergence, with some economic ramifications in the rise of globalism. The fall of Communism concluded the economic competition between socialism and capitalism, but the globalizing economy probably would have emerged even if the East had not collapsed when it did. Indeed, the economic disparities created by globalization might have been the economic force that toppled the Communist world in the 1990s, had it not fallen under its own geopolitical weight. Imagine the pressure on the socialist societies of Eastern Europe to join the general prosperity if they had remained on the wrong side of a still-existing Iron Curtain but still could see how the West lived. Even more dramatically, imagine the trauma for China, being a geopolitical enemy of the United States while simultaneously trying to participate actively in trade with this country.

The date the economic system moved from the transitional period to the globalizing economy may be blurred and arbitrary, but the international economic system that it produced is, by now, reasonably well established, with a structure that clearly distinguishes it from the transitional period. For one thing, its presence in all parts of the world make it a truly global system. It is also universal in that the only alternative to participation in it is economic isolation. There are no competing images or systems providing an economic alternative—no imperial preference system, as in the interwar years, or socialist world, as in the Cold War.

Globalization has a distinctive set of values; it was forged during the transition, and the value of trade was added as the most important contribution of the 1990s to its evolution. Acceptance of the rules and values of globalization is the *sine qua non* for membership in the global economy and thus, for most purposes, for participation in the prosperity that became part of the globalizing economy in the 1990s. Those countries that reject participation must suffer the economic consequences in terms of prosperity. Some countries have recognized these sacrifices and are struggling with them (Iran, for example); others continue to try to ignore the disparities (North Korea, for example). Moreover, the political freedom and prosperity associated with the globalization system creates popular pressures on governments outside the prosperity to try to join, sometimes with rocky and unpredictable results (Indonesia, for instance).

The emergence of the globalizing economy coincided with and helped contribute to the general global prosperity of most of the 1990s. At its height, the pressures toward globalization seemed ineluctable, and criticisms were weak and were overwhelmed by advocates—even cheerleaders—such as *The New York Times'* Thomas L. Friedman. The euphoria has proved at least somewhat overinflated, as was first demonstrated during the East Asian crisis of 1997 and 1998. That event slowed its movement as we approached the new millennium; and as chinks appeared in the armor, the critics came forward in increasingly public ways.

Although great shock has been expressed at the apparently radical nature of the objections raised by the so-called rejectionists and their political allies, the basic arguments go back to fundamental arguments in the U.S. political debate about the American place in the world (internationalism versus isolationism) and participation in the global economy (free trade versus protectionism), to say nothing of the parallel debate about national security (realism versus idealism). What goes around, it seems, comes around.

Characteristics and Values

The building blocks of the evolving "system of globalization" (to borrow Friedman's phrase) are central economic phenomena from the 1980s and the 1990s. The major contribution of the 1980s, as already mentioned, was the reassertion of the capitalist ethic of market-based economics stressed by Reagan and Thatcher. This philosophical underpinning proposed to free economies from the government meddling and interference that, it was argued, had been a barrier to entrepreneurial growth and innovation. Privatization and deregulation were the major tools of this policy change.

The major contributions of the 1990s represented both a continuation and also a reversal of some policies with their roots in the 1980s. The continuity came in the form of the election of free trader Bill Clinton to succeed free trader George H. W. Bush as president. The result was that free trade advocacy dominated in the executive branch of the U.S. government during most of the 1990s and beyond. The reversal in policy came through a commitment to wiping out budget deficits and reducing government debt as a way to improve the atmosphere in which economic entities do business in the 1990s, an emphasis at least partially derailed and abandoned after September 11. The combined effect was to create the so-called American model as the basis for the globalizing system.

A caveat to the legacy of the 1980s—market capitalism *within* national economies—must be added. The market capitalists rejected governmental management of economic activity, but they did *not* reject all governmental participation in providing a nurturing business environment. The specific areas of policy in which government participation is welcome are in governmental regulation, especially in overseeing the activities of financial institutions, and in adopting macroeconomic policies that facilitate how business operates.

The willingness to accept some regulation of fiscal activity—especially the actions of banks and other financial institutions—has its American roots in the so-called S&L (savings and loan) scandal of the 1980s. The scandal is significant because almost the same problems and solutions were encountered during the East Asian crisis of 1997 and its aftermath, when international institutions sought to enforce the same solutions on East Asian economies as the United States had adopted for itself. It will also be important as a precedent for future regulation of corporate accounting practices arising from the corporate scandals of 2002.

Prior to the S&L scandal, there had been very little regulation, especially public accounting, of this part of the banking industry. The "thrifts," as they were known, were limited-purpose financial institutions specializing in activities such as home mortgages and business lending. Their attractiveness to investors was that they generally paid higher interest rates than regular banks and were thus desirable depositories for small investors' savings. They were not, however, subject to the same standards of reporting of activities as regular banks were—a matter that was not of great concern because savings accounts were insured by the government, and no S&Ls had ever failed.

The scandal emerged when a number of S&Ls went bankrupt and threatened to dishonor investor accounts. The most famous bankruptcies were associated with the S&L empire of Arizona entrepreneur Charles Keating Jr. The investigation of a number of his institutions revealed a pattern of investor fund misuse through bad loans that could not be repaid (so-called nonperforming loans) and even bribes to public officials (five U.S. Senators, known as the Keating Five, received favors from the banker) that had been concealed because of lax accounting rules. As the modest savings of many Americans were threatened, the U.S. Congress passed legislation aimed at guaranteeing investor confidence by ensuring honesty and so-called transparency (making records of transactions, the financial conditions of financial institutions, and the like, available for public inspection) within these institutions. The reforms enacted in response to the S&L crisis restored public confidence and willingness to invest in institutions that lend funds to entrepreneurs. Over the objections of the Clinton administration, these rules were relaxed after 1994, leading to the corporate scandals of 2002, which stimulated yet another round of reform legislation—once again to create "transparency."

The same rationale—bolstering public trust—applies to other forms of macroeconomic policy. Proponents of the American model believe that the government has a limited useful role in the economy beyond making sure that bankers and others are honest. More specifically, the government can provide a useful service in creating a favorable fiscal climate for business and in providing services that it would be burdensome for the private sector to provide.

The major beneficial macroeconomic policy of the 1990s was deficit reduction and elimination, a direct reversal of the practices of the Reagan years. A major impact of the Reagan deficits was to force large-scale government borrowing to cover obligations for which there were inadequate tax receipts. This borrowing came from the private sector, to which the government had primary access before private enterprises. Much of the borrowed money came from foreign sources (a controversial matter in its own right), but a sizable amount came from American sources. With the government in effect skimming funds available for borrowing before private firms got a chance, the result was a smaller pool of financial resources available for private firm innovation and investment.

Reducing and ultimately eliminating deficits and beginning the process of reducing the overall debt reduction was largely the result of policies fashioned by Clinton Secretary of the Treasury Robert Rubin and enacted during the eight years of Bill Clinton's occupancy of the White House. Even some of Clinton's numerous critics have been forced to admit that it is no coincidence that these policies and the prosperity of the 1990s coincided. Whether the massive tax cuts enacted in 2001, large new defense-spending proposals, and returned deficits in 2002 by the new Bush administration will endanger this situation remains a matter of contention and concern but in the short run, massive deficits have returned.

The government also encourages entrepreneurial activity by providing a social net in the form of Social Security and related benefits for the general population. This not only frees private concerns from having to develop such systems themselves—thus becoming the social net for their employees—but it also provides considerable flexibility for firms in their operations. For instance, employees are no longer tied closely to individual companies upon which they must rely for such benefits as health care and Social Security upon retirement. Instead, devices such as portable health insurance and government-provided pensions frees companies to tailor and downsize their workforce without undue regard for the social consequences of laying off workers whose functions have been bypassed by change. Indeed, it is often argued that a major source of the rejuvenation of the American economy during the 1980s and 1990s was the ability to restructure and make leaner the operations of corporate entities because corporations were not locked into the social support of dysfunctional work forces that rely on them for the provisions of basic social support. Japan, which has an aging work force and increased demands for social services but insufficient government programs, is a victim of such a burden.

The other policy triumph of the 1990s was the victory of the free trade position. In concept, free trade represents the extension of David Ricardo's theory of comparative advantage to international economics. Politically, it represented the triumph, at least for the balance of the 1990s, of the free traders over the protectionists.

The triumph of free trade represented more of a practical than an ideological victory, as shown by the negative reaction to free trade at the end of the decade and beyond. When Clinton came into office, one of his first priorities was the passage of the North American Free Trade Agreement (NAFTA), negotiated through the Congress by George H. W. Bush. The traditional coalitions had lined up in support and opposition based on general preferences about American participation in international economics and the like. The authorizing legislation for NAFTA passed by a narrow margin in both houses of Congress. (As an economic agreement rather than a treaty, it required House as well as Senate approval.) NAFTA was followed by a flood of other activity supported by the free traders that, by the end of the decade, had locked the United States into a web of free trade associations from which extrication is now practically impossible. During much of Clinton's tenure, this process proceeded with virtually no organized or coordinated objections, with the major exception of the Congress's refusal to grant the administration so-called fast track authority (which, as noted, the Bush administration has renamed trade promotion authority and has achieved) on two occasions. Demonstrations at the World Trade Organization meeting in Seattle in 1999 heralded the return of protectionist sentiment, which has continued. Why?

The broad answer is that economic circumstances changed. When Clinton came to office, the recession of 1991 that had helped defeat the incumbent Bush in the 1992 election was lifting, replaced by an eight-year period of sustained growth in the local and global economy. One can debate the degree to which Clinton was responsible for or simply the beneficiary of this expansion, but it was a period of unprecedented growth from which the vast majority benefited economically. Trade was clearly a major element in the prosperity, as cheaper foreign goods poured into the country to benefit consumers. Although some American industries, such as textiles, suffered, in most cases there was enough prosperity to absorb most of those who were displaced. The argument that freeing trade was at least partially responsible for the prosperity was difficult to refute in that atmosphere—a situation that free trader Clinton exploited.

The slowing of the economy at the end of the 1990s and the revival of opposition to free trade coincided. The results have been to reduce support for the globalization process within the United States and to revive political opposition that was latent during the booming 1990s. As has always been the case, free trade and protectionism have varied bases and varying arguments. The political divide in the United States tends to be between the Congress and the Executive rather than along party lines.

The fate of fast track/trade promotion authority illustrates this tension particularly well. The proposal, by whichever name, is the successor to and an expansion of the RTAA of the 1930s. The authority, which was created as part of the Trade Act of

1974, authorizes the president to negotiate trade arrangements with foreign governments with minimal congressional ability to interfere. The "fast track" means that once the president presents an agreement to Congress, the Congress may vote only for or against the measure, *without amendment*, thereby shortening the amount of congressional perusal and virtually guaranteeing that the agreement will be approved.

The intellectual rationale for fast track is that economic agreements are so complex and complicated that they cannot be scrutinized in detail efficiently by a body the size of the Congress and that amendment of one provision might be highly destructive of the whole in ways the amenders might not anticipate. Politically, by placing constraints on how long the Congress has to consider agreements, the fast track authority precludes the Congress from effectively filibustering trade legislation by examining it in excruciating detail. Presidents desire the authority because it allows them to act decisively and authoritatively. Members of Congress who worry about presidents accumulating too much power oppose the authority for the same reason.

The issue became part of the debate in 1994, when it was up for quadrennial renewal. NAFTA had been negotiated under fast track, and its opponents united with traditional protectionists to oppose its renewal. Politically, the request to renew came from a relatively young and inexperienced Democratic president facing considerable opposition that resulted in the election of a conservative Republican majority in Congress in the off-year election that fall—and the Congress denied extension of the authority. The process was reprised in 1998, but the Clinton presidency, weakened by the Monica Lewinsky scandal and concern about the global impact of the East Asian financial crisis, allowed the Congress to deny the authority once again. In 2001, the new Bush administration tried again after renaming the authority, but it was 2002 before the authority was granted.

Although the political context has swung back and forth on globalization, the 1990s left a legacy of policies and practices that make a reversion away from the dynamics of the global economy virtually impossible for the United States, which has been the principal proponent—and beneficiary—of the process. Part of the reason for this has been the institutionalization of globalism through a web of regional and universal international agreements and organizations.

The Mechanisms of Globalization

The process of institutionalizing globalization accelerated during the 1990s and produced two distinct sets of institutions, agreements, and proposals. One set, to which the Bretton Woods process can be linked, involved the production of universal regimes, promoting global economics. The IMF and the World Bank are prototypes of this effort, as was the abortive International Trade Organization, the GATT, and now the WTO. At a less formal level, the G-8 also represents this tradition. The other emphasis, which has its concrete roots in the process that has evolved into the European Union (EU), has been regional. Its most prominent 1990s example has been NAFTA, although it has also been manifested in the APEC and, more recently, in the proposed Free Trade Area of the Americas (FTAA). With the partial exception of the EU, the United States has been a direct creator and supporter of all of

Challenge!

How Important Are Balanced Budgets and Free Trade?

Economic issues—especially the structure of economic policies of the Clinton administration during the 1990s—have been under indirect assault since George W. Bush became president and especially since the terrorist attacks of September 11, 2001. The new administration's emphasis on the "war on terrorism" has pushed the emphasis on free trade to the back burner, and a combination of the 2001 tax cut and additional defense spending after the Iraq War have turned budget surpluses into growing deficits.

How important is free trade to the United States? When President Bush first entered office, he called spiritedly for resuming fast track/trade promotion authority, which, as noted in the text, is a prime instrument for promoting American leadership in the globalization system. When Congress balked at his proposal, he vowed to fight their reluctance, but that promise was largely submerged in his transformation into a "wartime" president in the campaign against terrorism. In early spring 2002, he placed protective tariffs on imported steel to save American steelmakers from foreign competition while calling for the trade promotion authority he received. Was this a mixed message?

The same is true of balanced budgets. Before the terrorist attacks, the administration made a concerted effort to convince Congress and the American people that it was committed to a balanced budget and that the 2001 tax cut would not result in deficits. After the terrorist attacks, Bush proposed a $46 billion increase in defense spending that, combined with other initiatives, pushed the budget back into the red.

What do you think of these reversals? Are they justified by the need to combat terrorism? In the case of balanced budgets, do you think the increases can meaningfully be applied to the terrorism problem, or is terrorism simply being used as an excuse for more defense spending? Should an emphasis on free trade and balanced budgets occupy as important a place in national priorities as combating terrorism or the Iraq War?

these efforts, each with the goal of increasing global economic interdependence and, at least implicitly, of promoting the American model of economic organization.

Both sets of institutions share the common goal of promoting the prosperity of their memberships through the reduction of barriers to trade among them. They differ in the specific qualifications for membership—geographically, politically, and economically. In some cases, the goals may seem incompatible in the sense that the regional organizations are geographically defined, that they may be explicitly competitive with one another, and that they may even discriminate against goods and services from rival regional associations. The ultimate logic of both instruments, however, is to promote globalization. The institutional network propounded by the universal organizations is a one-step approach to that end, whereas the regional organizations can be thought of as the first of two steps toward the promotion and emergence of the global economy.

The Universal Emphasis.   System-wide international economic reform was clearly the intent of the countries that gathered at Bretton Woods in 1944, and freeing trade was one of their principal objectives. They were not instantly successful, of course, in institutionalizing this preference. At the time, protectionism was still strong enough to prevent American ratification of the ITO, forcing acceptance of the more limited and, from the vantage point of U.S. critics of free trade, controllable GATT process.

That situation gradually changed. Over the years, the original Bretton Woods institutions expanded their roles in ways compatible with the promotion of what we now call the American model. The IBRD, for instance, went beyond merely processing loan applications to performing what amounted to audits of national economies to establish creditworthiness. Many private lenders came to base their loan decisions on World Bank ratings, thereby adding additional clout to Bank assessments. The IBRD criteria were fundamentally compatible with American economic values.

The IMF has had a similar evolution. Using its ability to issue credits to stabilize currencies as its major lever, the IMF began to inspect economies to see if they were sound enough to absorb IMF credits productively. If they were not, the IMF issued dictates about the fiscal and economic policies that had to be put in place to receive IMF assistance. Because these criteria almost always include austerity provisions, they are often unpopular, particularly in poor Second Tier countries.

The universalist approach is most prominently associated with the WTO. Virtually identical in purpose to the ITO, its existence is testimony to the difference in timing and political balance of the late 1940s and the early 1990s. The objections to the two organizations were similar in both instances, but the environments were different. When the WTO proposal came out of the Ur   Round of the GATT in 1993, advocacy of and enthusiasm for the expanding   ssociated with globalization was on the rise, in contrast to the more re   al atmosphere that accompanied recovery from World War II and th.   iobalization through free trade was a much stronger force when the WTO   its doors in 1995. The critics, who were unable to block the organization when it was proposed, did not go away, and when the global economy began to appear to falter at the end of the decade, they were waiting to raise their banners at Seattle and beyond.

An intriguing part of this mix is the Group of Eight (G-8). It is not a formal organization at all, but rather a series of economic meetings between the world's most generally economically advanced countries—the United States, Germany, Great Britain, France, Italy, Japan, Canada, and, as a kind of honorary member whose economic status does not qualify it otherwise, Russia. The G-8 began meeting in the mid 1970s, originally with a secret meeting at the Plaza Hotel in New York, and has evolved into a highly publicized twice-a-year meeting of the heads of state of the participating countries. Some of these meetings have been little more than photo opportunities, but the fact that the most important economic powers in the world attend gives them potential clout in determining global policy across a range of subjects, including globalization.

The G-8's activities have become ensnared in the general controversy over globalization, as became painfully obvious at its summer 2001 meeting at Genoa, Italy, when noisy demonstrators attempted to shut the proceedings down. The G-8 had added an important element to its deliberations by inviting a series of Second Tier heads of state to join the group and discuss their economic woes and claims on the system. Although the G-8 members made no concrete promises to these leaders, they did listen, and they could respond in the future.

The Regional Emphasis.   The other institutional thrust has been through a series of regionally based international economic organizations. The oldest and most advanced of these, of course, is the EU, the basis for which was the Treaty of Rome of 1957, which created the original six-member European Common Market (West Germany, France, Italy, and the Benelux countries). The organization has evolved to the current fifteen-member EU and will undergo expansion into Eastern Europe in 2002 and 2004, and it has accomplished a long-sought goal of monetary union and the institution of a common currency, the euro. Additional regional organizations include the Asia-Pacific Economic Cooperation (APEC), encompassing most countries around the Pacific Rim; NAFTA; and the proposed hemisphere-wide FTAA (currently excluding only Cuba).

These organizations differ from the universal organizations in that the benefits of membership extend only to the member states, to the exclusion and even punishment of nonmembers. The proposed FTAA would create a free trading zone for all of the Western Hemisphere, but the benefits would not extend to countries—or regional organizations—outside the membership. With the exception of the EU, the regional organizations are also much less formalized and structured than universal organizations.

These regional solutions have several attractions. For one thing, the removal of trade barriers among the member countries is designed to stimulate trade among them. The APEC, for instance, has among its members countries that account for over half the world's trade; it includes such trade giants as Japan, the United States, and China, and such large potential markets as Indonesia and Russia. The FTAA, which has overlapping membership with the APEC, is advertised as potentially the world's largest free trade area.

These arrangements may influence the future greatly. One way this could occur is through the expansion of membership to embrace countries generally outside the heart of the globalizing economy. The EU, for instance, is already scheduled to embrace several countries of the former Soviet bloc, as already noted, and many see the gradual expansion of the EU as the final solution to European political division as well. The APEC has already expanded its membership to incorporate countries such as Vietnam, and the FTAA would be the most ambitious example of hemispheric cooperation ever.

These institutions may also be the stepping stone to universal globalization. They could well become negotiating units in and of themselves, particularly as vehicles for promoting agreements between themselves. Should the FTAA be fully implemented (a prospect not to be assumed lightly), it and APEC would almost certainly merge effectively into one unit because of joint membership of countries such as the United States, Canada, Mexico, and Peru. A combined APEC-FTAA free trade area would create a powerful economic bloc, which has prompted many in Europe to consider how to make arrangements with one or both organizations.

None of this progress is preordained. The formalization of associations is going to be an extraordinarily difficult process for the fledgling organizations. The APEC commitment to completely remove all barriers among the most advanced members by 2010 and among all members by 2020 and FTAA's promise of full implementation of free trade by 2005 are, at this point, intergovernmental resolutions requiring concrete implementing agreements that have yet to be negotiated and do not clearly represent the highest priority of member states. The process of negotiating NAFTA among three countries revealed how complex such a process can be; negotiating implementation among the thirty-four member states of FTAA or the twenty or so states of the APEC could be infinitely more difficult. NAFTA also proves, however, that such efforts are not impossible.

The role of the United States, a key member of both APEC and FTAA, is critical in this process. In one sense, this creates caution among members of FTAA, who fear that the "colossus of the North" will so dominate the organization as to minimize the benefits for the other members. That concern has helped spawn a rival organization among several South American countries, Mercosur, as a counterweight to FTAA.

The sheer size of the American economy (around one-quarter of the world's total) means that American leadership is crucial to the success of any enterprise. The problem, however, is political. For the United States to be a leading actor in negotiating these agreements, the executive branch of the U.S. government must have something like fast track authorization (an argument made by Bush in terms of FTAA). The reason is simple enough: What country would negotiate a detailed agreement, filled with compromises and potential problems, with the U.S. government, knowing that such an agreement would be subjected to a line-by-line review and veto in an unpredictable Congress?

The other side of the politics of globalization is opposition to the phenomenon and its effects within the United States and elsewhere. As the demonstrations against globalization-promoting meetings in recent years have clearly demonstrated, there is a reasonably broad array of opposition. Those who believe that the process of globalization will produce more harmful than beneficial effects want "progress" in that direction made more difficult, not less.

Barriers to Globalization

Before the general slowdown of the global economy that began in 1999 and extended into the early 2000s took hold, opposition to globalization seemed feckless—an enterprise that was attempting to arrest inevitable forces and thus was doomed to failure. The ability of a coalition of groups to intimidate political leaders and to slow the process has demonstrated that the logic and progress of globalization are not so inevitable; and it raises questions about both the desirability and the inevitability of the process. The question "Is globalization in America's best interests?" was largely unthinkable five or six years ago; it is now relevant.

The role and position of the United States as the remaining superpower is nowhere more evident than in the economic realm, and whatever position the

Amplification 5.3

THE REJECTIONISTS

The protests and protesters that were first seen in Seattle and have been a grim part of nearly every international economic event since represent a coalition of very different groups and individuals. If one does not place them in the context of the historic debate about free trade and protectionism, their grouping makes little sense. But the same coalition that has taken to the streets of Quebec City, Washington, DC, Genoa, and elsewhere represents a long-standing tradition of opposition that was clearly present in the 1940s (see Amplification 5.1). The tactics and actors may have changed, but the underlying positions remain very similar.

Who are the rejectionists? They are a single-issue coalition, bound together in their opposition to various aspects or implications of globalization but with very few, if any, other common interests. The interests they represent have, however, been present for a long time. First, there are the protectionists, who feel personally threatened by lowered trade barriers. In the 1940s, the protectionists were mostly conservative Republicans representing big business and commerce; today, they are predominantly Democrats representing the interests of trade unionists in industries that cannot compete successfully without trade protection. Then there are those who feel that efforts to institutionalize globalization are too timid. Environmentalists, for instance, believe that institutions like the WTO will not adequately regulate environmental degradation by international corporations and governments; they believe that globalization is dominated by private interests with little environmental sensitivity. Still others believe that the interests of Second Tier countries left out of the globalization policy are underrepresented. Finally, there are objections from groups that feel that globalization undercuts national sovereignty.

The coalition is conceptually quite similar to the group that successfully fought the ITO over a half-century ago. The major difference is the violent, confrontational tactics that are now employed in opposition to globalization. Although those tactics have not yet led to the successful blocking or slowing of the globalization process, they have succeeded in creating an atmosphere of intimidation that, among other things, caused the World Bank and the IMF to shorten their annual meeting for 2001 at their Washington, DC, headquarters to two days to minimize demonstrations.

United States takes will heavily influence the direction of the global economy. American leadership is expected and will be resented by some. Those who perceive that they will not benefit from or will be hurt by globalization, both internationally and domestically, seek to influence that position. At the same time, American citizens are among the most vocal opponents (as well as advocates) of globalization, which means that the outcome of the political battle over globalization in the United States will strongly affect the global process as well.

What are the major objections? Within the international community, three related problems tend to be raised, not so much about the desirability of extending the global prosperity but about how it is being done and the impact of imposing globalization in different places. These objections tend to focus, in turn, on the American model and the role of the United States in the globalization process.

One objection coming from the Second Tier is that the American model, which has dominated participation in the globalizing economy—especially since the East Asian crisis effectively discredited the Asian alternative—is too rigidly American and thus cannot be imposed uniformly on very different cultures and systems. For instance, one of the major requirements of the American model is transparency, an advocacy tarnished by the accounting scandals of 2002. Great secrecy is traditional, however, in the business practices of many Asian societies, as are activities that would be considered corrupt in Western societies. When the values clash, which should prevail? The United States and the international organizations that provide the funding and markets insist on the Western way, and other cultures are forced either to comply or to remain outside the system. It is a choice that breeds a certain amount of resentment, especially in light of revelations in 2002 that American corporations do not practice what the model preaches.

Much of the resentment, tinged with some envy, is directed at the United States. Beyond the cultural assault associated with the American-dominated economic system, there is further political resentment on other grounds. The constancy of American leadership is often raised; for instance, the United States insists upon conformance with American financial practices but refuses to conform to globally accepted agreements on matters such as banning land mines, accepting war crimes statutes, and even honoring the Kyoto treaty on global warming. This same United States that preaches global responsibility also has historically had the highest arrears to the United Nations of any country in the world. Which United States should the world follow—the responsible exemplar or the arrogant bully that obeys the international norms it favors and ignores those it does not? Furthermore, the 2002 corporate scandals exposed an American economy that operates far differently from the pious image the American model seeks to portray. Are the Americans hypocrites?

A final objection is the contribution of globalization to the growing gap between the richest and poorest countries on the globe. Although no one denies that those parts of the Second Tier that have become part of the globalizing system have benefited to some extent, it is increasingly obvious that not everyone has—or is likely to—become part of the prosperity. As has been widely trumpeted, over half the world's current population lives on $1 a day or less in income, and the gap between those who are becoming richer and those who remain desperately poor has widened. This trend is especially evident in Africa, where virtually the entire continent remains outside the benefits of globalization. The other side of this argument is that while benefit may be differential, virtually everyone is better off than they were before globalization—as the saying goes, a rising tide lifts all boats. Devising ways to extend globalization to those who are currently excluded is likely to become a major international priority.

The domestic debate is not foreclosed either. Although there is little support for the basic tenets of isolationism in any pure sense, there are enough piecemeal objections to the various aspects of globalization to produce a very noisy, and occasionally effective, coalition of opponents. These objections are not going to disappear, even if there is a return to the prosperity of the 1990s. There will always be, for instance, fierce advocates of the environment who will wonder how globalization subverts environmental concerns and promotes environmental degradation.

CONCLUSION: GLOBALIZATION AND AMERICAN SECURITY

Globalization in some evolving form is simply a fact of international life in the 2000s, and the only way it could be reversed altogether would likely be as the result of some catastrophic international event, such as a global war. That outcome may seem unlikely in the current context, but it is worth remembering that the same thing was widely believed at the turn of the last century.

Is globalization a good thing for the United States? That question is too simply put to be answered. It is too simple because it assumes that there is *a* globalism, when in fact globalization is an evolving condition whereby economic interconnectedness is gradually increasing. It is also too simple because the process is so multifaceted that it will almost certainly have some beneficial and some harmful effects on any country.

The real question is, on balance, does globalization add to or detract from the American place in the world and thus American security? And what can we do to improve those aspects with which we have concerns to make the process better serve those interests, including enhancing security? In the prosperous 1990s, when globalization was given credit—rightly or wrongly—for helping to create and sustain prosperity, the answer was likely to be automatically positive. In the more cautious economic condition of a postmillennial era that is more focused on the terrorist assault on physical security, the assessment is likely to be more guarded and critical.

One aspect of the question, which also provides an intellectual bridge to the next chapter, may illustrate the difficulty of reaching expansive conclusions. It is the connection between globalization and sovereignty. As noted in Chapter 2, the retention of state sovereignty is a core realist value that has always been particularly important to the United States. Guarding our sovereignty has sometimes forced the United States out of step with the rest of the world.

By definition, the retention of effective state sovereignty is a major element of the country's national security, making the relationship between sovereignty and globalization an important matter. At the same time, if globalization contributes to the greater economic well-being of Americans, is any dilution of sovereignty that results from globalization a good bargain? Moreover, a virtue of globalization has been to impose American economic values on others, bringing them into conformance with our ideals. Thus, is the question of *whose* sovereignty is compromised the way to phrase the concern?

An example may help us think about this. One part of the statute creating the World Trade Organization gives the WTO the power to investigate allegations of trade violations by member states and, where it finds violations, to prosecute and impose mandatory sanctions against violating governments.

In the ratification debate over WTO, this provision was widely condemned by defenders of American sovereignty, as was a similar provision in the proposed ITO in the 1940s. The counterargument was that most of the values the WTO would enforce were American values, making vulnerability minimal and assuring that others would be forced to conform as well. Conformance to the WTO charter thus cuts both ways: It dilutes the sovereign control of countries we seek to influence, but it also limits us.

The statute has indeed had both effects. A major argument for sponsoring Chinese membership in the WTO was that it would force China to reform its economic practices in ways that would lessen the ability of the Chinese government to maintain authoritarian control over the economy and ultimately, it was hoped, the political system. Although this would be a difficult step for the Chinese government, which is also a prime defender of state sovereignty, it is the price they would have to pay for full membership in the global economy. In this case, the U.S. government has used the international dilution of sovereignty to tie China more firmly into the global system and to increase American security.

But the statute does cut both ways. Shortly after the WTO came into force in 1995, the Clinton administration sought to improve its balance-of-payments situation with Japan by forcing the Japanese to buy more American automotive components to put into Japanese cars. To this end, Clinton announced his intention to place a high excise tax on Japanese luxury cars entering the United States, which would have made them uncompetitive with domestic models. The hope was that the Japanese would cave in and agree to import more American car batteries and tires to avoid these penalties. Instead, the Japanese cried unfair trade practices and threatened to drag the United States before the WTO, where the United States would certainly have lost any judgment rendered. Faced with that likelihood, the Clinton administration withdrew the threat to exercise its state sovereignty through the excise tax.

The purpose of this example is to suggest that the answers to apparently simple questions are rarely simple. For the most part, globalization has helped the United States reassert its position in a global economic system in which it had slipped in preeminence after 1971. Whether the United States will continue to benefit depends on how we define our international interests, the degree to which we are able to influence the system in ways that benefit the most Americans, and how we react to unforeseen and sometimes unforeseeable changes.

SELECTED BIBLIOGRAPHY

Antholes, William. "Pragmatic Engagement or Photo Opportunity: What Will the G-8 Become?" *Washington Quarterly* 24, 3 (Summer 2001), 213–26.

Barshefsky, Charlene. "Trade Policy in a Networked World." *Foreign Affairs* 80, 2 (March/April 2001), 134–46.

Dunn, Robert. "Has the United States *Really* Been Globalized?" *Washington Quarterly* 24, 1 (Winter 2001), 53–64.

Feldstein, Martin. "A Self-Help Guide to Emerging Markets." *Foreign Affairs* 78, 2 (March/April 1999), 93–109.

Friedman, Thomas L. *The Lexus and the Olive Tree: Understanding Globalization.* New York: Farrar, Straus & Giroux, 1999.

Fukuyama, Francis. *The End of History and the Last Man.* New York: Free Press, 1992.

Kennedy, Paul. *The Rise and Fall of the Great Powers: Economic Change and Military Change from 1500 to 2000.* New York: Random House, 1987.

Keohane, Robert O., and Joseph S. Nye Jr. *Power and Interdependence,* 2nd ed. Glenview, IL: Scott Foresman/Little Brown, 1989.

Luttwak, Edward. "From Geopolitics to Geo-economics: Logic of Conflict, Grammar of Commerce." *National Interest* 20 (Summer 1990), 17–24.

Noland, Marcus. "Learning to Love the WTO." *Foreign Affairs* 78, 5 (September/October 1999), 78–92.

Nye, Joseph S. Jr. *Bound to Lead: The Changing Nature of American Power.* New York: Basic Books, 1990.

Rothgeb, John M. J. *U.S. Trade Policy: Balancing Economic Dreams and Political Realities.* Washington, DC: CQ Press, 2001.

Sachs, Jeffrey. "International Economics: Unlocking the Mysteries of Globalization." *Foreign Policy* 10 (Spring 1998), 97–111.

Spero, Joan Edelman. *The Politics of International Economic Relations,* 4th ed. New York: St. Martin's Press, 1990.

PART II

THE CHANGING WORLD

The international environment is the setting in which U.S. national security policy is crafted to secure the country's interests in the world. In Part I, we looked at some of the historical factors that shaped how the United States looks at security matters, culminating in the rise and fall of the Cold War and the emergence of globalization after the first fault line was breached.

The second fault line—September 11, 2001—created another tectonic shift in the security environment; in Part II, we will explore various aspects of how the world is different and how those differences affect the American role in the world. Chapter 6 emphasizes the basic concepts around which security concerns revolve—security, interests, and power—and how these have changed. The basic message is that interests remain largely the same as they were before, but that there is a new configuration of threats to those interests and that those interests must be pursued in different ways. Chapter 7 attempts to assess the contemporary environment from two perspectives: (1) how we now depict the international environment in which we operate, and (2) how the U.S. government is organized to deal with changing circumstances. The last chapter in the Part, Chapter 8, looks at the traditional military means and roles that American force has taken and how they are relevant to today's world. It examines the changing role of both nuclear weapons and so-called conventional or traditional armed forces for dealing with the country's problems.

CHAPTER

6

Security, Interests, and Power

The shock of events such as those revealed by the opening of the fault lines tends to focus our concern on the trauma and extent of change rather than on how those events fit into the broader context of national concerns that transcend time and more strongly balance continuity with change. This first chapter on the contemporary world seeks to place recent traumas into the kind of analytical context with which national security policy grapples. Thus, we will analyze the impact of change on three basic categories of ongoing importance. First, what is the nature of security? Second, what impact has change had on basic interests? Third, what is the changing nature of effective power in the present and the future?

The contemporary national security environment contains elements of both continuity and change in the national security situation. From the perspective of any particular point in time, including now, the unique set of forces and events of the moment may seem to predominate and draw us to emphasize change and the uniqueness of the evolving system. Thus, we are drawn to the two major fault lines of the past decade and a half and their consequent effects on highlighting globalization or geopolitics as the principal system dynamic.

At the same time, some forces that seem unique in a narrow perspective appear less so within the general evolution of the international system and our place in it. The last century began with the belief that there was little likelihood of future violence. A general optimism prevailed, and much of the optimism was based on the perception of a growing economic interdependence driven by trade, which simultaneously was supposed to assure future prosperity and to make the recourse to war progressively less thinkable. The shock of the terrorist attacks makes it easy to forget that on January 1, 2000, most people felt basically the same about the future as their ancestors did on January 1, 1900.

National security analysis tries to determine what it is in the environment that may provide concern for the security and well-being of Americans and citizens of the world generally and to determine what, if anything, can be done to attenuate or eliminate the sources of disturbance. We ask the same questions today that we asked fifty or a hundred years ago; it is the answers that change to a greater or lesser extent, based on the flow of events.

The United States is clearly still in the process of reassessing the national security problem for a new century, particularly in light of our personal and intimate introduction to international terrorism, a force we had not previously had to confront. Before that introduction, the environment seemed less negative than it was during the Cold War. We questioned the amount of effort we should devote to the national security enterprise and, at a more personal level, the amount of effort or sacrifice that should be expected of us. Those commercial airliners slamming into their targets removed the complacency about our security that had developed in the tranquil 1990s. "Everything has changed" became the mantra after September 11, 2001—"nothing will ever be the same again." Dormant security concerns have been revived and now seem permanent parts of an environment that is unalterably changed. Or is it?

We live in a period that has been called the "long peace." If the first half of the twentieth century was arguably the bloodiest period in human history, the second half was relatively benign in terms of the toll of war. The consequences of general war may have been great during the Cold War, but the reality was that bloodshed was basically confined to the peripheries—the Second Tier—where the major powers became involved only when they chose to become involved, as the Americans did in Vietnam and the Soviets did in Afghanistan. After 1991, breaches of the peace were basically isolated to internal war in parts of the world outside the normal range of important American interests. The September 11, 2001, terrorist attacks that killed 3,000 Americans and many others darkened that sunny horizon and presented a new national security imperative. But is it a temporary interruption of the long peace or something more permanent and ominous?

In this chapter, we will begin to examine the face of national security in the twenty-first century. As a starting point, we will look at three related, enduring concepts by which judgments were made during the Cold War and which formed much of the base of the realist paradigm introduced in Chapter 2—security, interests, and power. We will examine the idea of security and how it may have changed in the contemporary context. That discussion creates some judgment about how the environment affects American interests in the world. The assessment of security and interests, in turn, leads to the question of how the United States can exercise power in the present and future.

THINKING ABOUT SECURITY

Security is a variable. What makes us safe or makes us *feel* safe (the physical and psychological dimensions of security) depends on two basic phenomena, each of which can vary or assume different values. The most obvious source of challenge to our security are factors that threaten the things that we value. As noted earlier, the most objective of these are physical threats, such as the ability of Russia to destroy the United States with nuclear weapons. Psychological threats—what makes us feel secure or insecure—are often less tangible and subject to individual interpretation; different people feel secure or insecure in the same situations. The degree to which we are personally threatened by the prospect of terrorist activity reflects that dimension.

This leads to the second security variable, which is our interpretation of the environment. Does the environment make us feel secure or insecure? What actions might we contemplate to change the environment and make it less threatening (increase our sense of security)? Clearly, the two variable aspects are related to one another: A more hostile physical environment will diminish our psychological feeling of security more than a more benign environment in which there are few adversaries posing fewer threats to our interests and our security.

The environmental aspect of security has apparently changed considerably since the end of the Cold War. With the demise of the Soviet adversary, the physical sense of insecurity diminished considerably for the United States. Russia still maintains a large stock of nuclear weapons but lacks any rationale to use them. As noted, the old Red Army has atomized into the armies of the various successor states, none of which individually pose any aggressive threat outside the borders of the former Soviet Union. The Cold War threat to American and allied security posed by the forces of Soviet Communism has disappeared and has not been replaced by any worthy successor—what the first (1997) Quadrennial Defense Review (QDR) called the lack of a "peer competitor" (true, worthy enemy), an assessment with which the second (2001) QDR was forced to agree.

Over the past decade, we have adjusted twice to this changed environment and what we still find threatening within it. We are thus in a period of security threat adjustment, in which both the hostility of the environment and how we respond to those sources of our insecurity will continue to be matters of debate and disagreement, even amid strong consensus about the focus of the threat of terrorism.

The discussion about these aspects of security can be divided into three sequential steps. We will first look at the changing balance between military and nonmilitary sources of security concern. This will lead to and be conditioned by the second step: the various levels of security that affect different actors in international politics. The final step will be an assessment of how concepts of security may be changing.

Military and Nonmilitary Elements of Security

Historically, national security and military security have been synonymous. Although other matters might threaten the well-being of the country, those threats about which policy makers and analysts were principally worried and which fell most obviously into the category of national security were military threats. Military elements were certainly the predominant form of threats during the Cold War.

The inclusion of nonmilitary elements into what was considered national security began to occur during the Cold War, particularly in the area of economic security. There had been previous occasions when economic and other concerns entered the national security arena: Trade matters with Great Britain, for instance, had been an important part of the conduct of the American Civil War, and a major threat to the United States of a German victory in World War I was the possible exclusion of American manufactures from the European continent. Likewise, suppression of the Barbary Pirates in the early 1800s may have been the first time that responding to terrorism became a national security concern.

The broadening of the areas we consider to affect our security has occurred gradually. Among the nonmilitary aspects (threats with no military component), for example, "economic security" has been broadened to encompass environmental security. To further muddy the distinction, we have added security concerns that are partly military and partly nonmilitary. A primary example of these *semimilitary* aspects of security and the responses to it is the problem of international terrorism. As the campaign against the Taliban and Al Qaeda in Afghanistan demonstrates, these problems can have a clearly military component, but significant aspects of terrorism and its suppression are also political and law-enforcement concerns.

Military, semimilitary, and nonmilitary elements have melded in the post–Cold War period. This has occurred partly because the purely traditional military elements of security are clearly less extensive and less intense than they were before. The virtually total absence of the danger of a major, system-threatening military conflict such as the world wars or the breakdown of the Cold War into a "hot war" is a major characteristic of the contemporary system, even after September 11. In some sense, the long peace continues to get longer.

Since no equivalent has replaced the Soviet military threat, the nonmilitary and semimilitary elements of security have risen in relative importance. For the most part, these are a series of smaller threats, some of which existed during the Cold War but received less attention then and some of which have emerged since. What they have in common is that none provides a direct, general threat to the United States physically in the way a potential Soviet nuclear attack did. As first discussed in the Introduction, the 2001 terrorist threat against the United States demonstrated that the American homeland has become vulnerable to harm that can kill many Americans but that these attacks do not currently place the integrity of the United States at direct risk.

Other than terrorism, the remaining security threats are at a lower level of urgency and importance, placing them squarely within the psychological dimension of security, in which people can and do disagree about the importance of the threat. Some of these threats existed during the Cold War but paled by comparison to the larger problem then. The danger and threat of the proliferation of weapons of mass destruction in countries in the Second Tier was a problem then and now, for instance.

Although purely military elements of security have been in decline, nonmilitary and semimilitary elements have been on the rise. Because of globalization, some of the most important nonmilitary elements are now in the area of international economics, where concerns such as conditions of trade have risen to a level of concern comparable to military matters. Whether it be the impact of the 1998 Asian financial crisis on the United States or the growing violence of anti–free trade demonstrators, economic matters have become increasingly important in the general flow of what makes us content or discontented. The semimilitary threat of terrorism has occupied a special place since 2001, but it is a concern that has been long held at a lower level of intensity.

The military and nonmilitary elements of security come together in concrete ways. The situation between the United States and China is an example. China was, of course, a Cold War military adversary of the United States, even if the threat it

Challenge!

Defining Terrorism as a Security Threat

What kind of threat does international terrorism pose to the United States? Much of the discussion of post–September 11, 2001, efforts by the United States to deal with this problem has been described as constituting a war, which suggests that the problem is a military one with a military solution. The "war on terrorism" was the way the Bush administration initially labeled the effort, and that designation was picked up and repeated by many of the electronic and print media.

Much of the initial effort seemed to justify this designation. The insertion of American forces into Afghanistan first to help topple the Taliban government and then to try to round up and destroy remaining pockets of Al Qaeda and Taliban resistance was clearly military in content. When American forces were sent to such places as the Philippines and Yemen to train local forces better to resist terrorists, this also represented a military response, albeit at the lower end of the spectrum of military responses.

This text disagrees with the assertion that countering terrorism falls within the category of military dimensions of security. Clearly, suppressing terrorism has a military element, as demonstrated by initial actions, and terrorism experts like Stephen Sloan specifically include military responses as part of dealing with terrorism. Thus, the response to terrorism clearly does not fall within the nonmilitary dimension either.

Thus, the text has placed terrorism in the category of semimilitary responses. The basic argument is that suppressing terrorism has some elements that involve various uses of military force, but that the effort also clearly includes elements that are either nonmilitary or quasi-military. Gathering intelligence information on terrorist plans and activities to frustrate the terrorists and arresting and prosecuting those who engage in or plot to commit terrorist acts are also important parts of dealing with the problem, and they are not military actions.

Is the distinction of dealing with terrorism within the semimilitary dimension of security important or just a matter of splitting hairs? In other words, if the problem is only partially military in origin and solution, does the analogy with "war" hold? If it does, that helps frame the public debate—for instance, the justification for greater defense expenditures. If the effort is only partly military, however, then the rhetoric of war—questioning the loyalty of those who question the effort as unpatriotic because we are "at war"—may be excessive and may run counter to democratic rule. What do you think?

posed was somewhat ambiguous after the split between China and the Soviet Union and the opening of Sino-American relations in 1972. Still, national security planners during the 1960s planned for two simultaneous major wars, one with the Soviets and one with the Chinese (the two-war strategy). The focus of Sino-American military rivalry was and is over the Nationalist Chinese government of Taiwan, which China periodically threatens.

After Deng Xiao-peng's announcement of the "Four Modernizations" in 1979 and their implementation during the 1980s and 1990s, an economic relationship began to emerge that faded the military rivalry. A major pillar of the modernizations was to allow the development of private enterprises in the so-called Special Economic Zones (SEZs) of the southeastern part of China. When the Cold War ended and the age of globalization came into full bloom, a burgeoning trade between the two countries developed and largely replaced the military rivalry.

Is China currently a national security threat to the United States? From a purely military viewpoint, one can make a small case for a "Chinese threat" in the form of a primitive nuclear capability and large conventional armed forces that cannot be projected far from China's shore. Taiwanese rumblings about declaring Taiwan's independence regularly bring Chinese saber rattling, and the spy plane episode of April 2001 (when an American reconnaissance plane collided with a Chinese jet fighter off the coast of China) caused some concern. Balanced against those problems, however, Beijing will host the 2008 Olympics (a major achievement that will likely have China on its best behavior in the interim), and the Chinese Communist Party announced in August 2001 that capitalists will be permitted to join the Communist Party (a seeming oxymoron). China continues to be a major provider of consumer goods for Americans and will become more fully integrated into the world economy when it becomes fully integrated into the WTO. Furthermore, the American spy plane was returned, amid some haggling over how much the U.S. government should reimburse China for having kept it. Thus, calculating Sino-American military threats is no longer an easy or clear-cut matter.

The Chinese example is not the only one in which the intersection of military and nonmilitary aspects of security have become blurred. When Iraqi forces invaded and conquered neighboring Kuwait in 1990 and the United States responded by forming the coalition that drove Saddam Hussein back to Iraq in 1991, it was American economic security that was most directly affected by the Iraqi action and that arguably justified an action we might not have taken if Kuwait was oil-poor. Iraq posed no more direct military threat to the United States in possession of Kuwait than it did before, but the Iraqi action did threaten the unfettered American access to Persian Gulf oil that was deemed necessary to fuel the American economy. In that situation, energy insecurity threatened economic security and activated the military dimension of security. Access to water could provide a similar dynamic in the relatively near future, as Amplification 6.1 suggests.

Amplification 6.1

ISRAEL, SYRIA, THE GOLAN HEIGHTS, AND WATER

One of the ways in which concerns over security have been changing in the contemporary environment is the expansion of situations and conditions about which states may feel insecure and thus may feel the need to take action to ensure their security. In other words, military security has been augmented by economic security, environmental security, energy security, and a variety of other concerns.

One scarce resource that will surely climb to the top of the agenda of security concerns in some places is secure access to adequate supplies of potable water. Nowhere in the world is this concern more evident than in the arid Middle East, where very few states have adequate water supplies, particularly to service populations expected to grow in the future and

place additional demands on dwindling supplies. (Turkey is the exception to this rule.) Although it receives little publicity outside the region itself, the problem of water remains a major barrier to the ability of Israel to reach an accord with the last of the countries that has opposed it in war—Syria.

The major remaining issue between the Israelis and the Syrians is the return of the Golan Heights to Syria. Before the 1967 Six Days' War, Syria had used the Heights, a series of low mountains that border on northern Israel, to launch mortar and artillery attacks on the Israeli settlements in the valley below. As a result, when Israel was occupying territories of its neighbors as a result of the war (the West Bank from Jordan, the Sinai Peninsula and Gaza Strip from Egypt), it also occupied the Golan Heights to assure that Syria could not physically resume its attacks.

The Golan Heights are also important because of water. Much of the water that Israel (and Jordan) uses comes from the Jordan River, the source of which is the Sea of Galilee. As the map shows, the eastern shore of the sea forms the border between Israel and Syria when Syria possesses the Golan Heights, thereby affording the Syrians the physical ability to interfere with that source of Israeli water. The problem is moot with Israel occupying the Heights, since the Syrians are physically kept away from the seashore. Return of the Golan Heights to Syria is the *sine qua non* for a peace settlement between the two countries. Before Israel agrees to transfer the territory back, however, it must have an iron-clad agreement covering military attacks from the Golan Heights and, perhaps more important, giving equally strong assurances that Syria will not interfere with Israel's water supply.

Levels of Security

The previous discussion was centered on the idea of state security, which is the primary focus of concern in a system in which the realist paradigm predominates. This focus is one of the more controversial consequences of a realist paradigm world, and it has caused many reformers to suggest that there should be a more balanced approach to legitimate security concerns both below and above the level of the state.

Competing levels of security arguments run closely parallel to the debate about sovereignty. The idea that there could be a source of authority superior to the state was, of course, a major issue in the Thirty Years War in the clash between papal authority and secular authority. A major reason for adopting state sovereignty as the core value of the Westphalian system was to preclude future discussions about where supreme authority resides.

There are parallels within the contemporary assertion that the security of subnational groups and individuals should be primary considerations. This assertion reflects the notion of popular sovereignty first put forward by such political thinkers as Locke and Rousseau, which also heavily influenced the writers of the American Declaration of Independence and Constitution. It is at least implicit in the rationale of other democratic systems (minimally, the idea that power and authority flow from the people).

The arguments are more than academic. Some of them, of course, reflect assaults on the sovereign base of the state system and tend to emphasize the negative consequences of a state-centered system that has state security as its underlying first principle. Others assert the need for and positive consequences of a reorientation of security around the individual or supranational concerns.

One line of reasoning questions the consequences of states' acting principally out of their own security concerns while ignoring other levels. A most basic formulation of this concern is something known as the *security dilemma*. In this construct, states may act in certain ways—such as building up levels of armaments—to increase their security against real or potential adversaries, regardless of the effect on the larger international system. The response of those targeted by the original action may be to respond in kind (building their levels of arms), which may result in an arms spiral wherein, in the end, all parties are left feeling less secure than in the beginning. Security dilemma situations represent the perspective of *international security*—the security of the overall system.

The security dilemma is not an abstract problem; it can be seen in ongoing, concrete situations. Currently, the debate over American construction of a missile defense system shows the dynamic in action. The proposed national missile defense (NMD) is clearly an American *national* defense proposition aimed at solving a perceived American security problem: the future vulnerability of U.S. territory to missile attacks by states that possess small numbers of missiles armed with weapons of mass destruction.

The states facing the United States with nuclear weapons, including those identified publicly as potential U.S nuclear targets in a 2002 Department of Defense nuclear weapons review, feel threatened by the proposal. China is a prime example. It has a very small nuclear arsenal, which it maintains to threaten retaliation should the United States launch a nuclear first strike against it (no matter how far-fetched such an attack might seem). China is concerned that the NMD is designed to intercept and destroy an attack of about the size and nature the Chinese might be able to mount after absorbing a first attack. Thus, the Chinese deterrent is compromised, and the Chinese are left to ponder how to respond if NMD deployment occurs. One obvious response would be to build enough additional rockets to guarantee overcoming the NMD regardless of the effectiveness of an American first strike. The result could be to make the United States more vulnerable to China than before NMD deployment—the security dilemma in action. India, the state that feels most threatened by Chinese weapons, might then feel the need to respond to a Chinese buildup—a ripple effect that could then extend to Pakistan, further destabilizing the system.

The American terrorism campaign also raises levels of security concerns. The American military response in Afghanistan was clearly framed in terms of American state security—removing the source of a threat to the American homeland. Very few in the world argued with this campaign. When the United States threatened to widen the campaign to other sources of potential threat—notably Iraq's suspected WMD program and the incumbency of Saddam Hussein—world leaders, from France's Jacques Chirac to Russia's Vladimir Putin, in effect raised the security dilemma in objection. Such U.S. actions to strengthen its own security, they (and others) argued, could so destabilize the Middle East as to leave everyone worse off.

The other level of concern is that of *individual security*, a primary orientation of security around individuals and groups. This emphasis is most often associated with the protection of the safety of people within states. The problem arises from traditional interpretations of the absolute power that state sovereignty provides for the state over its population. The consequences of this power become an international concern in the post–Cold War environment of internal wars that involve atrocities against victim populations and groups within populations.

Traditional definitions of sovereignty give the state total control over its territorial base, including the treatment of individual citizens and groups, and makes illegitimate any outside efforts to affect that treatment. In the cases of particularly tyrannical regimes, the result has often been state-sponsored or state-conducted campaigns against their own citizens, which the international community is technically incapable of preventing or alleviating; it is none of anybody else's business how a state treats its citizens.

An assertion of the validity of individual security challenges that assumption. It is related to the assertion of popular sovereignty, since presumably no one would delegate authority to the state to abuse them. The history of individual security, however, is relatively recent; it is based in two post–World War II phenomena—reaction to the Holocaust and the emergence of notions of individual, enforceable human rights.

The Holocaust was a terribly traumatic event for the international community and gave a black eye to advocates of the notion of total sovereign control. Among other things, it revealed the lengths to which unrestrained governments might go in mistreating their citizens—state sovereignty had run amok. Yet in the early war crimes trials at Nuremberg, a prominent participating American jurist opined that Nazis could be tried for killing non-German Jews and Gypsies (among others) but not German Jews, since they had sovereign authority over their own populations.

Reaction to the Holocaust boosted advocacies of universal human rights after the war and resulted in a number of international treaties asserting that individuals everywhere had certain rights that could not be denied by governments. Since the nondemocratic governments that existed routinely denied and repressed these rights, individual rights and a concept such as individual security reinforced one another.

Once again, the importance of this distinction is not abstract in the post–Cold War world. Although mass atrocities occurred during the Cold War (e.g., the Khmer Rouge slaughter in Cambodia during the 1970s), brutal civil wars have been a major part of post–Cold War violence. Ethnic cleansing—the displacement or extermination of ethnic, religious, and other groups—and the suppression of human rights have been a focus of violence within the international system, a problem that is discussed in Chapter 10.

Traditional conceptions of sovereignty and security (as well as international law) do not permit international involvement in such conflicts when they occur exclusively within the boundaries of individual states, as they most often do. In order to assert a "right" to alleviate the suffering of groups in the Balkans (Bosnia, Kosovo, Macedonia) and elsewhere, there has to be a broader concern for whose security the system has responsibility. The only way to argue a right or obligation to intervene on behalf of Bosnian Muslims, Albanian Kosovars, or East Timorese is to assert some form of the rightness of the notion of individual security. In most of the concrete cases, this assertion has been implicit, since its direct assertion also represents an attack on the primacy of claims of the superiority of national security *and* state sovereignty.

Changing Concepts of Security

The preceding sections have emphasized challenges to traditional conceptualizations of what constitutes security and, more specifically, national security as the focal point of national policy. Much of the criticism and hence advocacy for change has come from those who find fault with a state-centric system whose keystone is state sovereignty and which is, in a sense, made operational by a primary focus on defending the state, even at the expense of other values.

How profound have these advocacies of change been? In other words, has there been a fundamental challenge that has moved our thinking radically away from the traditional focus on national security conceptualized in military terms?

It is easy to overestimate the degree of change. Certainly, there is a greater acceptance of broadened conceptualizations of what constitute security, but these have come as additions to the list of things considered part of the security equations, not as alternatives. Adding environmental concern to what makes us secure does not diminish the importance of military security. Rather, it expands the realm of security. In some cases, new sources of security may actually increase the realm of military security. If free trade is key to globalization, as its advocates claim, and if economic security includes the prosperity that trade creates, then enforcing the freedom of the high seas militarily becomes an even greater concern than before.

The advocates of alternatives have become more vocal than they were during the Cold War. Some analysts argue that the emergence of global priorities is the product of greater global democratization and the emergence of the information revolution, which allows groups to communicate freely worldwide. This combination, it is argued, has the effect of pushing for greater sensitivity to nonmilitary aspects and other levels of security. The expanding role of the reformers in the 1990s contrasted with a relatively quiet military situation worldwide, wherein the defenders of traditional national security were reassessing their roles. The emergence of the suppression of international terrorism on the global agenda has thrust semimilitary security concerns into a prominent middle position between military and nonmilitary aspects.

There is no question that purely military security has become a less urgent matter than in was during the Cold War, and that this has given additional impetus to those who would change the focus of security concerns. The anxiety of the traditional community was no more clearly seen than in the angst of the new Bush administration as its Secretary of Defense, Donald Rumsfeld, conducted the defense review that the 2000 campaign of candidate Bush had promised would heal the neglect allegedly suffered under President Clinton. As the administration prepared to submit the congressionally required QDR, Rumsfeld concluded that reviving military health might allow for a modest reduction of conventional armed forces across the board, while he continued to undertake a more fundamental review aimed at potentially sweeping reform. This initiative was placed on the back burner, however, when the problem of terrorism was added to the military portfolio—to fight the "war" on terrorism—and has been brought further into question by the manpower requirements for occupying Iraq, which some argue requires a larger, not smaller, army.

The changing emphasis on aspects of security has important and confusing policy and philosophical implications. Military aspects of security normally dictate military concerns—deposing the Taliban in Afghanistan, for instance. Nonmilitary aspects such as environmental security equally imply nonmilitary solutions.

The debate gets murky in hybrid situations with both military and nonmilitary aspects. These semimilitary situations first became prominent when President George H. W. Bush declared the "war on drugs," emphasizing the military aspect of a far more complex problem with many nonmilitary facets. The "war" failed at least partly because it was not, in a real sense, a war at all.

In the contemporary situation, it has become fashionable to refer to the war on terrorism. As noted, terrorism suppression is a classic semimilitary security problem. As the campaign evolves, its military content is likely to decline, and its nonmilitary security aspects will likely expand. Will the implicit assignment of terrorism to the military aspect of security clarify or muddy the realization of our goals and make achievement more difficult?

THINKING ABOUT INTERESTS

Questions about the role and implications of interests mirror differences over what constitutes security in the contemporary order. The interplay of interests—whose are realized and whose are not—is central to the dynamics of international relations organized around the realist paradigm. The interests at the base of these calculations are invariably state interests. Constructed in this manner, the military aspects of security are prominent, because force is one of the options available to achieve the state's most important (or vital) interests.

For better or for worse, interest-driven calculations remain the criteria by which states operate in the anarchic international system. When the interests of states come into conflict, the question of which states' interests will prevail also arises, and this leads to an attempt to determine how important the interests are and thus what means will be employed to try to achieve them. Thus, the question of levels of interest must be addressed, although within a somewhat different context than the question of security. These levels, in turn, suggest different national security and military and nonmilitary implications, including economic implications connected to the theme of globalization. Finally, we will address the challenge to traditional concepts of national interest in the form of broader variants of what constitute vital interests.

Levels of Interests

The various levels and intensities of interest introduced in Chapter 2 need not be repeated here. The heart of that discussion, however, dealt with the critical traditional national security question of the boundary between so-called *vital* interests and those that are deemed less than vital. The salience of that boundary is that it is theoretically the demarcation point for the state to contemplate the use of military force to realize its goals. Interests that fail the test of vitality (major or peripheral interests) imply the use of means of lesser intensity than for those that are vital. Most of the economic methods of achieving goals that are compatible with globalization presumably are useful for less-than-vital interest realization. There are instances in which economic weapons may be applied to vital interests, such as the boycott and economic isolation of Saddam Hussein to gain his compliance with international norms of WMD inspection before 2003, but such actions have a very limited success rate and are relatively infrequent. In the case of semimilitary threats, the invocation of vital interests may suggest both military and nonmilitary responses.

This conjunction between interests and security can be depicted in matrix form, as in Figure 6.1.

Cells 1 and 6 are the most easily describable. They are the heart of the realist formulation that when vital interests are threatened, force may become an option if the situation is solvable by using force (military security, as depicted in Cell 1). At the same time, when less-than-vital interests come into conflict, they are normally solved nonmilitarily, because military force either is inappropriate or is more drastic than the situation dictates (Cell 6). An imminent attack on one's territory would be a clear Cell 1 situation; a dispute over tariff schedules would clearly fall in Cell 6. When vital interests are involved, the first inclination is to try to use nonmilitary means to resolve the differences—maintaining force as a "last resort" if all else fails (Cell 5). Applying economic sanctions would be an example.

The real debate is over the situation in which vital interests are not engaged but military aspects of security may be contemplated because they are the only means that may bring about a satisfactory resolution of situations (Cell 2). A strict interpretation of the realist paradigm is very restrictive in this regard: If American vital interests are not threatened, for instance, then American use of force should not be contemplated. This was the basic stance taken by the Bush campaign in 2000, when it argued that the United States should not be the "world's 911."

The continued application of realist criteria for using force rages in Cell 2 with strong national security and military implications. Because the United States possesses such an overwhelming amount of force, there is some temptation to apply it to

Figure 6.1   Interest Levels and Security Means Dimensions

		Interest Level	
		Vital	Less-Than-Vital
Security	Military	Cell 1	Cell 2
Means	Semimilitary	Cell 3	Cell 4
Dimension	Nonmilitary	Cell 5	Cell 6

a variety of situations. As Clinton Secretary of State Madeleine Albright once said, "What is the point of having armed forces if you never use them?" The retort from the realist paradigm is that you use them only when the situation is really important (vital interests) and when force is appropriate. Whether the removal of Saddam Hussein from power was important enough to justify invading Iraq is a Cell 1-Cell 2 dispute.

The role of force is more complicated in Cells 3 and 4 (semimilitary dimensions). When vital interests are at stake, force is justified to the extent that it can be effective. The military aspect of the war on terrorism is a clear Cell 3 application. The questions revolve around how much of a role force plays when it may be a necessary, but not sufficient, condition for success. The war on drugs arguably represents Cell 4, since drug use is an important but probably not system-threatening (vital interest) problem. In this case, questions can be raised about whether the problem is severe enough to invoke force as well as whether the use of force is appropriate for dealing with the problem.

Remember that the boundary between military and nonmilitary dimensions is not a fixed line and never has been. Rather, it is more like a movable confidence interval of changing widths and locations. Where the line should be, and just how wide the interval around it ought to be, is the heart of the national security debate about using force. It is a highly political debate about which reasonable people can disagree over specific situations, and it changes location as time passes and circumstances change. Although there will always be high levels of consensus on some items that are vital, there will equally always be disagreement about the exact location of the intellectual barrier separating those situations that do and do not justify the employment of U.S. armed forces. The existence of semimilitary situations only further blurs the distinction.

The debate within Cell 2 and in Cells 3 and 4 can thus be seen as a question about how much the change in the international environment of the post–Cold War world has moved the width of the band surrounding what is and is not vital and the extent and role of force in semimilitary situations. During the Cold War period, the location was relatively clear. The United States could and would use force when Soviet-inspired or Soviet-directed Communist movements threatened to come to power at the expense of American friends and allies. The clearest cases were where the United States had clearly important interests—Western Europe and northeast Asia (Japan and Korea)—or, of course, where the Soviets could threaten the United States directly with nuclear weapons. In cases where the physical survival or independence of the American homeland or the territories of our closest friends were at stake (the physical dimension of security), it was clear that military security was at stake and that force would be used (Cell 1).

Even during the Cold War, the demarcation was an interval, not a line, and this was most clearly seen in places that might be of interest to the United States in Communist–non-Communist terms, but where otherwise the United States had few interests. Those situations occurred most often in Second Tier areas such as Africa and much of Asia, and the American assessment became more debatable, falling within the psychological dimension of what makes one feel secure, about which reasonable people might disagree. These are the instances that fall into Cell 2.

Two potentially similar situations on which opposite conclusions were reached illustrates this relationship between interests and security. The first is the American involvement in Vietnam. When the United States replaced France as the principal barrier to Communist victory there after the Geneva Conference of 1954, there was relatively little debate about American direct interests in the outcome of that conflict. Rather, the prevailing criterion for some level of involvement was opposition to Communist expansion globally, of which Southeast Asia happened to be the then-most-current example. Opposition to Communism as a general proposition was viewed as important enough to ask the question "How will American interests be affected by the worst possible outcome (the unification of the country under Communist control)?"

In retrospect, it is probably unfortunate that the specific question was not raised in the public debate and fully considered at the time, because quite likely the assessment would have been negative. In the end, the worst possible outcome did occur, but except for the self-inflicted angst the country experienced because we "lost" the war, American interests otherwise were hardly affected at all; the answer to how interests were affected was "not very much." What looked at the time like a Cell 1 situation looks much more like a Cell 2 or even Cell 6 situation in retrospect.

The other example, initially raised in Chapter 2, is Nicaragua in the 1980s. How important Sandinista rule was to the interests of the United States was argued both as a matter of the competition between the Communist and non-Communist rule and on the basis of geography. At one level, a Marxist Nicaragua provided a foothold for Communism on the mainland of the Americas through which Soviet assistance could be funneled through Cuba into Nicaragua and on to destinations such as El Salvador, where the pro-American government was facing a Marxist insurgency. At another level, an activist Nicaragua might stir up trouble generally in the region, possibly eventually threatening control of the Panama Canal and even destabilizing the southern part of Mexico, where an incipient antigovernment insurgent movement was active.

Did the Nicaraguan situation rise to a threat to a vital interest, which justified a military response (Cell 1), or were the interests less than vital, in which case a military response might or might not be appropriate? There was disagreement between the White House and the Congress on this question, and the ultimate decision was to treat it as either a Cell 2 or Cell 6 situation, one not requiring the employment of American military forces. This determination was vindicated when the Nicaraguans voted the Sandinistas out of office in 1990.

Why engage in such a lengthy discussion of the relationship between security dimensions and interest levels? For one thing, it illustrates that, in the real world, such determinations are difficult and ambiguous. Were the world made up exclusively of clearly Cell 1 or Cell 6 situations, making and implementing national security policy would be simple. In fact, one of the sources of nostalgia about the Cold War is that the central confrontation between the United States and the Soviet Union was precisely such a Cell 1 instance. Because of that, building security policy from that central construct was intellectually straightforward and relatively noncontroversial. Having said that, the United States never used military force during the

Cold War in an unambiguously Cell 1 situation (the closest possible exception may have been Korea); Americans *deployed* forces to deal with Cell 1 contingencies (NATO forces in Europe), but they were *employed* in situations more closely associated with Cell 2.

The post–Cold War world is composed almost exclusively of situations in which there is debate about where the boundary between vital and less-than-vital interests should be placed and what kinds of responses—military, semimilitary, or nonmilitary—are most appropriate. Because of the interest–threat mismatch, there are hardly any clear Cell 1 situations for which to prepare and around which to base planning. If international terrorism truly threatened the physical integrity of the United States and was a force appropriate for military eradication, it might rise to Cell 1. American military preponderance makes it difficult even to think of potential Cell 1 situations in the near future, because no state or coalition of states poses a symmetrical threat.

The ongoing environment exists outside the realm of vital interests—in Cells 2, 3, 4, or 6. Part of the problem involves determining which of those cells is appropriate to describe any given situation and suggesting appropriate ways to deal with it. At the same time, arguably vital interests exist in areas outside national survival, where semimilitary solutions may be appropriate. Also, economic well-being, such as terms of trade with Japan, is the primary factor in situations where nonmilitary aspects of security are clearly more appropriate (Cell 5). In other words, there are more ambiguous decisions to be made than clear-cut determinations such as whether the country should be prepared to defend the Fulda Gap in Germany.

Security and Interests in the Contemporary Environment

It is an old saw that national interests rarely change but threats to those interests do change, and that is as true today as ever. A stable, free Western Europe, for instance, is just as important to the United States as it was a half-century ago; what is different today is that there are no realistic threats to the security of the countries of Western Europe (and increasingly Central and Eastern Europe). At the same time, new (or apparently new) threats to long-term interests may emerge, as the terrorist threat to American territory exhibits. In the terrorist case, interests and threats converge, and the only question is how to deal with them.

This situation creates an intellectual bind for those who think about and plan for national security, especially the military dimension of national security. Although there may be potential situations in which American vital interests could be engaged, the only one of these that has posed any substantial traditional military problem has been Iraq's refusal to obey international inspection norms for weapons of mass destruction programs and its occasional challenge to American and British jets patrolling the "no fly zones" in northern and southern Iraq. As long as Saddam Hussein did not invade someplace like Kuwait again or threaten American access to Persian Gulf oil, he posed only a potential threat. (Much of the post-war debate over the war has centered on whether Iraq indeed posed enough of a threat to justify the military actions that were taken.) Similarly, it is still possible that North Korea might try to cross the 38th Parallel into South Korea or that China might venture across the Straits of Taiwan to annex the island into the Chinese polity, but neither of these contingencies are especially likely.

Potential conventional military threats to vital American interests suffer from two debilitating characteristics. One of these is plausibility—a problem that is getting worse, not better. Even before being invaded Iraq lacked the military power seriously to menace the petroleum-rich countries on the littoral of the Persian Gulf and would have been crazy to do so if it could. The Iraqis had not been allowed to rebuild their military capabilities to any great extent since the end of the Persian Gulf War, and a feint southward toward the oil fields would have left them exposed on their long border with more powerful Iran and Turkey. Moreover, the precedent for frustrating such an action is already well established.

The Korean and Taiwanese scenarios are similar. Despite being one of the most secretive, reclusive regimes in the world, North Korea is showing steadily increasing interest in closer relations with the much more prosperous South Korea, and a reprise of the 1950 invasion could only destroy the economic base in the South that is the North's best (and possibly only) source of assistance in relieving the overwhelming poverty of that country. Based on any objective reading of the situation, it is much easier to project peaceful reunification of the Korean peninsula than it is to imagine an attempted reunion by the sword or by North Korean nuclear aggression.

A forceful Chinese annexation of Taiwan is similarly implausible. The Chinese lack the naval assets for an amphibious invasion (especially with the U.S. Seventh Fleet interfering with the operation—a virtual certainty in the event). Although China could reduce Taiwan to rubble in a rocket attack, it is hard to see the point, since virtually all the Taiwanese investment capital flowing onto the mainland would be destroyed in the process. Moreover, even limited military action against Taiwan would have serious repercussions—especially in trading—from the rest of the world, on which Chinese prosperity depends. It has already been argued that the Chinese will be on their best international behavior between now and the 2008 Olympics for fear that misbehavior would cost them the Olympic games, which they worked so hard to obtain. (The Chinese remember the Western boycott of the 1980 summer Olympics in Moscow after the Soviet Union invaded Afghanistan.) Furthermore, the decision to admit capitalists into the Chinese Communist Party may have been partially motivated by the desire to make unification more palatable to Taiwanese businessmen.

One may question any of these arguments, of course, and concoct an Iraqi, North Korean, or Chinese set of circumstances that is more negative and forbidding than described here, as many of the neo-conservatives have done. Under any circumstances, however, it is difficult to fashion a threat scenario for any of those situations that is important or plausible unless these situations change for the worse—as they could.

The terrorist attacks of 2001 and the continuing campaign to eradicate terrorism—the second fault line—adds a new element to the mix. Protecting the homeland is clearly a vital interest, but the threat is asymmetrical in size and the response is only semimilitary. At one level, interests and threats converge, but at another level they remain mismatched. Although destroying the bin Laden network's sanctuary in Afghanistan was a fairly traditional military mission, the post-Afghanistan campaign against terrorism will not be conducted on any battlefield with a climactic confrontation. Rather, it will be conducted by an opponent using unconventional methods, including acts of terror (asymmetrical warfare). At that point, responses will become markedly less military and the "war" designation even more problematic.

Beyond the direct attacks on American soil on September 11, 2001, the earlier pattern of actions carried out by bin Laden probably represents the nature and scale of response that the United States faces. Bin Laden's intent is to harm as many Americans as he can. His means of doing so has been to commission acts of terror against select American targets, such as the U.S. embassies in Dar es Salaam, Tanzania, and Nairobi, Kenya, or the suicide attack against the USS Cole in a Yemeni port. He probably was also involved in the attack against the World Trade Center towers in New York in 1993.

What defines these acts is their size and the responses to them. The African embassy attacks killed about two dozen Americans (as well as hundreds of Kenyans and Tanzanians), and seventeen sailors died on the Cole. Although these losses were tragic, they were not on a scale that threatens the basic integrity of the United States. It is also not clear how to respond to these kinds of acts. The United States retaliated for the embassy bombings by launching cruise missile attacks against suspected terrorist training camps run by bin Laden, but they failed either to kill the Saudi expatriate or to slow down his activities. (Reports suggest the attack hit its targets about an hour after bin Laden had left the complex.) Responses seem to fall outside the normal means for enforcing vital interests.

How to use armed forces when the kinds of situations for which they have traditionally been employed (securing vital interests) are basically absent or only partially appropriate is a major agenda item in the current debate about national security. Clearly, many of the real threats to American national interests fall on the less-than-vital side of the demarcation line. The clear implication is that there is not clear guidance about what military forces, especially conventional forces, should do in these situations. What, then, are the implications for the constellation of American instruments of power, including military force?

How does one deal with such circumstances? One way is to enforce the realist paradigm and accept the decreased saliency of regular military force in the current milieu. If American forces are to be used only when vital interests are at stake, then they will be used relatively infrequently in the near future, or they will only be a variable part of responses to worthy threats. Another solution is to broaden the criteria under which force employment is allowable. This amounts to moving the line between vital and less-than-vital interests more into the less-than-vital category of actions. The primary "beneficiary" of such a movement currently comes in the form of deployments of American forces into peacekeeping missions in places such as Bosnia and Kosovo under the justification of so-called *humanitarian vital interests*, to which we alluded in the Introduction. This has been a controversial use of force because it stretches forces thin and is even more problematic as forces are also called upon for far-flung deployments in the name of suppressing terrorists.

Amplification 6.2

SHOULD THE UNITED STATES BE IN KOSOVO?

Debate about whether the United States should have a military presence in Kosovo has been going on since Serbia launched its campaign of so-called ethnic cleansing against its Albanian Kosovar population in the late 1990s. That debate continued during the American-led NATO bombing campaign intended to force the Serbs to desist from their suppression in 1999 (Operation Allied Force) and then when the United States agreed to be part of the United Nations peacekeeping force in that province (the United Nations Mission in Kosovo, UNMIK). During the 2000 campaign, candidate George W. Bush suggested that the United States had no business in Kosovo and proposed a pullout as part of his general policy of reducing American overseas military deployments. Despite this pledge, a reduced American force remains on the ground in Kosovo, and there is little prospect that it and the rest of UNMIK will be removed from Kosovo in the near future. Not far away, American forces remain in Bosnia, where they have been stationed as part of a UN force since 1995.

How one answers the question of whether the United States should be in Kosovo depends on how one views American security and interests. From the perspective of a purely realist paradigm, it is difficult to reach a positive conclusion. In any direct sense, American national security is hardly affected negatively by any outcome to the conflict: How would Americans feel more or less secure regardless of who controls the territory? If the litmus test for whether an interest is vital is the intolerability of the worst possible outcome (presumably, resumed Serbian suppression of the Kosovars), it is hard to see how the situation rises to the level of constituting a vital interest.

Then why is the United States there? The rationale has come from two sources, each of which represents something of an expansion of the traditional definition of vital interests. On the one hand, it is argued that although what happens to the Kosovar population (or the former Yugoslavia or, for that matter, the Balkans more generally) hardly affects direct American interests, the situation is important to our European allies. The reason is that the area represents the one real trouble spot in an otherwise tranquil Europe, and it is also an area that has been a tinderbox for wider violence on the continent. Therefore, the Europeans have an interest in the situation, and the United States has an extended interest in what makes Europeans more secure, thus creating an indirect interest. On the other hand, it is argued that the campaign waged against the Kosovars represented a humanitarian disaster and that the defense of humanitarian vital interests (as discussed in the body of the text) creates the necessary justification.

Which of these arguments is compelling? The answer, of course, is that it depends on the philosophical position about the international system and the American place in it from which one starts. From the perspective of a narrow, realist-paradigm, limited view of the proper level of American activism, the United States clearly has no business intervening in the situation. The answer to the question posed in the title of this Amplification is a ringing "No!" From a more internationalist, expanded conception of when and for what reasons the United States can and should use force, the answer is more clearly "Yes!" It is all a matter of perspective.

These options cover the gamut of responses to the interest–threat mismatch but have been muddled in the current national security debate. The current Bush administration, for instance, entered office apparently committed to the dual, contradictory positions of a restrictive, realist position regarding when force should be used and a commitment to build up forces for which its own definition of force usage made the renewed forces unnecessary. Tying buildups to combating terrorism obscured some of this contradiction. Nevertheless, the result is a continuing commitment to conventional, symmetrical forces in an arguably increasingly asymmetrical threat environment.

APPLYING INSTRUMENTS OF POWER

The anarchic nature of international relations requires that states engage in self-help in order to realize their interests. A recourse to some superior source of authority before which they could adjudicate conflicts of their interests with those of others on the merits does not exist. There is no such authority, of course, because states have vital interests that might not prevail if some outside authority decided the outcomes of conflicts of interest. Since, by definition, a state will not willingly accept denial of its most important interests, the solution is to avoid having any body that can make adverse rulings that would probably be disobeyed.

This depiction is at the heart of the operation of the realist paradigm model of the international system. In such a system, states achieve their goals to the extent of their ability to coerce or convince others to comply with their goals or interests. Whether one applauds or decries that situation is interesting but, for present purposes, irrelevant, in the sense that this is the dynamic that energizes the system in the absence of some fundamental reform that has yet to occur.

The idea of instruments of power was introduced in Chapter 2 and need not be repeated in detail here. The term *instruments of power* generically refers to the array of methods a state possesses to gain conformance with its interests. Power situations (wherein one state seeks to get something it does not want to do that is in the power-applying state's interests) involve situation-specific relationships. This means that what will work to gain compliance in one situation will not necessarily have the same result in another, because power interplays involve discrete relationships between the players. Because of that, the more varied and robust the instruments a state has, the more likely it is to prevail more of the time. Operationally, one's rank among the powers refers to both the variety and the depth of its power across the spectrum of instruments.

Using the Instruments

The instruments of power do not exist in a vacuum; they gain their meaning in terms of whether their application accomplishes the purpose for which they are used. For an instrument to be potentially effective, it must possess two traditionally defined characteristics, to which we will add an implied third. First, a state must possess the physical wherewithal to take the actions it proposes—what is known as *capability*. The absence of capability renders a threat ineffectual if the threatened party recognizes the deficiency. A Chinese threat to close the strategic Straits of Malacca by interdicting shipping transiting the straits would be ignored, because China lacks the long-range aircraft (and refueling capability) or navy to sustain such action. Second, objects of threats must believe that the threatening state would actually employ those capabilities in the ways it says it would in order to accomplish its ends—what is known as *credibility*. Based on his perceptions of post-Vietnam unwillingness to use force, Saddam Hussein did not believe that the United States would use force to reverse his conquest of Kuwait. Beyond capability and credibility is the ability to apply the instrument in such a manner that the sought-after goal is achieved—what we can call *efficacy*.

These characteristics are clearly interrelated. Capability and credibility are linked. At the most obvious level, no state is going to believe a threat based in a capability the threatening state does not possess. Nicaragua, for instance, cannot threaten to invade Mexico, because it lacks the military capability to do so. Conversely, however, the ability to carry out a threat does not necessarily imply the willingness to use that power. The United States frequently becomes annoyed with France over its attempts to keep symbols of American culture, such as American popular music and films, out of the country (or to limit the amount of penetration into French culture). Although it would be physically possible for the United States to threaten a nuclear attack against France to force it to lift these restrictions, no one would believe such a threat—which means it lacks credibility. Moreover, a country may possess a variety of instruments that it might well employ that would not achieve the goal for which they are intended. The American economic boycott against Cuba for the past forty years, for example, has not accomplished its principal goal of removing Fidel Castro from power or removing Communist rule from the island state.

Orchestrating the uses of the instruments of power is a delicate activity and one that involves considerable uncertainties, because whether power is effectively applied is largely a complex psychological exercise. At one level, it is a duel between the state threatening to employ an instrument and the state receiving the threat. Assuming that the threatened party knows whether the threatener has the capability to do what is proposed (which the threatening party may seek to obscure), it then has to assess whether the threat is credible, which is an exercise in mind reading. There may be some evidence, based on how the threatening state has acted in similar circumstances in the past, to provide an indication of the threatener's will, but since no two situations are identical, that evidence may or may not be conclusive. Will he or will he not?

The threatening party must also make a psychological assessment of the party against whom it is seeking to apply power in a situation of less-than-perfect knowledge of the other party's mental state. Will the other party believe I would carry out the threat or call my bluff? Also, might the threat gain compliance without having to be carried out (the best possible outcome, since carrying out threats normally involves some harm for all parties)? If not, will carrying out the threat convince the other party to do what I wanted done in the first place, or will it fail?

The answers to these questions are generally not cut-and-dried in real-world situations. Such calculations sound like the reasoning in a poker game, where capabilities are defined by the hands the players hold but part of each hand is obscured (capability), where betting is a form of indicating credibility, and where the success of maneuvers such as bluffing measures the efficacy of the threats that raising bets represents. Employing power in the real world, however, has added complications such as the emotions of the interplay of national pride, different and largely nonmeasurable (at least in advance) factors such as national resolve, and the importance of outcomes to all the players.

During the Cold War, much of this calculation had been worked out, and the dynamics were reasonably clearly defined. Among the instruments of power, the military instrument was conceded to be of the greatest importance, at least in the relations among the contending superpowers. The economic instrument was clearly more important in the relations within the First Tier states headed by the United States, but economic sanctions and rewards had virtually no impact on East–West relations. The greatest ambiguities regarding which instruments had efficacy were in the Second Tier, both in the extension of the East–West confrontation and in First Tier–Second Tier relations over matters such as political and economic development.

How does the end of the Cold War alter the constellation of efficacious applications of power? One indication of change has been the reduction of military budgets for all the major powers (other than the United States). In addition, the economic instrument seemed to become more important as globalization spread—but how will that instrument be affected by the international economic turbulence that began in 1997 and threatened a global recession after September 11, 2001? How does the rise of terrorism as an instrument of power wielded by nonstate actors affect the environment?

The Contemporary Balance of Instruments of Power

Whether there is a real change in international relations today is largely a matter of the third criterion identified for applying instruments: efficacy. The question of change can be rephrased to ask whether the forces that induce change in the post–Cold War world are different from those in the Cold War era. Assertions of dramatic change will almost inevitably overshoot the truth, but there may be some discernible differences.

The efficacy of the traditional military instrument has clearly become more restricted. Military threats or actions among the major powers of the First Tier absolutely lack credibility. This is really not a change, however, because it was equally unlikely that the Western allies (including the market democracies of Asia) would have fought one another during the Cold War. If there is a difference, it is that what President Clinton liked to call the "ring of market democracies" has been gradually enlarging, including the addition of former authoritarian foes from the old Communist world. In these cases, positive military inducements may have supplanted threats as the instrument to advance American interests in spreading market democracy. Actions such as military arms sales, training programs, and membership and participation in military alliances like NATO are means to induce formerly non-democratic countries into the general peace.

The use of military force in the Second Tier has similarly undergone only modest, peripheral change. Most of the violence in the world occurs within (as opposed to between) Second Tier states, as was generally the case during the Cold War. What has changed are the incentives for outside involvement in these conflicts. During the Cold War, the motivation was to prevent the victory of Communist elements, and the calculus included the likelihood and intolerability of Communist success. In the contemporary environment prior to 2001, the incentives tended to cluster around humanitarian concerns. The calculus involved whether any lasting good could be achieved by physical involvement and what levels of sacrifice would be tolerable to accomplish various levels of good. These were less compelling interests than fighting Communism. Blunting and suppressing terrorism has provided a firmer basis for applying the military instrument; as a semimilitary concern, striking a balance between the use of military and nonmilitary instruments is the problem.

The major contraction in the efficacy of military force surrounds the avoidance of major war with potent and threatening adversaries. Only the utter failure of market democracy in a major state such as China or Russia could produce the underlying animosities necessary to produce a new "peer competitor" for the United States. Such a transformation would, of course, be carefully monitored from the beginning, and actions taken to reduce or contain such development would be certain. Moreover, the reversion could occur only by the failure of the economic modernization on which a potent military is built. Russia, for instance, cannot afford the military forces it has today. Were the Russian system to fail to the point of reaching a Faustian bargain to return to authoritarianism, what kind of military could such a totally failed system afford?

What this suggests about the military instrument is that its efficacy has shrunk in the most important and costliest area it formerly occupied. If that is the case and if the likelihood of a returned equivalent threat is unlikely, then those facts should have major implications for the capability component of the capability/credibility/efficacy equation that energizes the instruments of power.

It is easy to overstate how much the economic instrument has undergone change. Globalization has clearly expanded the arsenal of economic instruments of power. The emphasis on trade and the removal of trade barriers creates opportunities for countries with large markets such as the United States to obtain leverage among those who wish to compete in the American domestic market. Membership in the various universal and regional trading associations can provide the ability to influence economic decisions in various countries, and the ability of the IMF and other international monitors to guide the development of developing economies has clearly been enhanced as well. The desire to share in the general prosperity creates opportunities to shape the behavior of states that are outside but wanting to be in the global prosperity.

Three cautionary points should be made about too rhapsodic an assessment of the positive impacts of globalization. First, the enhancement of instruments of economic power is really the extension, possibly the intensification, of powers that were already there. Special economic preferences have always been part of foreign economic policy, for instance, and the IMF has been influencing governments for a long time. Second, the amount of leverage that globalization creates will be significantly related to how positively the phenomenon is perceived in the future. The decade of the 1990s was one of unrestrained enthusiasm and clamoring for inclusion—at almost any cost—until the crisis of 1997 occurred and the recession of 2001 took hold. How badly new members want in and what they are willing to do to get in will depend on how well the system operates and produces prosperity in the future. Finally, there have been and continue to be countries that resist the process and thus are impervious to its influence. This resistance is particularly strong wherever fundamentalist Islam is a major force.

New forms of power may blossom in the future. The telecommunications revolution has been a particularly potent force for economic expansion, information explosion, and a variety of other growth areas. The positive expansion of the information age to nonparticipants is an enormous positive inducement to change behavior. This positive aspect has a darker side, however, in the form of threats to disrupt the very fragile systems on which the telecommunications revolution rests. Cyberwar, a prospect raised in Chapter 2, may become an all-too-familiar instrument of power in the increasingly electronic nature of the international system.

CONCLUSIONS: THE CHANGING NATURE OF INFLUENCE

In this chapter, we have examined three related concerns about contemporary international politics and the transition from the Cold War environment to the present. The first concern was with security: We asked how a changed environment affects American national security in both a physical and psychological sense. Have the changes that have occurred enhanced or detracted from American security? The second concern was with national interests; it was phrased in terms of whether the most important interests were more imperiled or reinforced today. Can the United States better realize its interests today than previously? The third concern was with how those interests are realized in the form of changes in the effectiveness of the various instruments of power. In the changed environment, are different instruments more efficacious for realizing interests than before?

Overall, the major conclusion one must reach is that the post–Cold War world, despite the intrusion of international terrorism, is a more secure, less threatening place than before for the United States, and one in which the country is basically better able to realize its interests than it was during the Cold War. One can easily overstate both the pervasiveness of change and the improvement of the situation, but at least in a marginal sense, the generalizations seem to hold, even if one factors in the one major source of insecurity.

The chief cause of improvement is, of course, the end of the Cold War and thus the removal of the largest challenge to security—the possibility of a general systemic war in which the nuclear-armed superpowers confront one another on the battlefield with the fate of civilization in the balance. The vulnerability of American territory to terrorist attacks remains a significant threat, but not on the scale of the threat of World War III during the Cold War.

As large-scale military power has depreciated in value, economic leverage arising from globalization has expanded in the quiver of elements of national power. The reassertion of a robust American economy, which remains the world's premier market (chronicled in Chapter 5), provides the United States with considerable leverage to promote an international economy and national economies and polities based on the American value of market democracy. The world economic downturn in 2001 dampened some of the more effusive enthusiasm about how much globalization has transformed the international system, but globalization continues to be a positive force that benefits the United States.

What could cause a deterioration of the current situation and the American place in it? A cataclysmic turn of the global economy to a depression like the Great Depression of the 1930s would certainly represent the worst possible case. One of the fears surrounding the emergence of international terrorism, for instance, was the prospect that it might trigger a general economic downturn. Hardly anyone expects that to occur, but there are still potential dangers on a lesser scale.

Reaction to American supremacy probably holds the greatest potential for negative change. Many commentators have pointed out that the current epoch is remarkable because, unlike other historic periods when a single political entity dominated the world scene, no competitor or coalition of competitors has arisen to oppose and counterbalance American power. Initially, this seemed to be the case because, unlike other states, the United States is rarely viewed as a threatening power in the system. As time has passed, however, erosive influences have emerged in the form of reactions to what are perceived as inconstancy and even arrogance in American dealings with the rest of the world.

Where these concerns may become most evident is through the resurgence of American unilateralism, a trend most evident since the election of 2000 and in the American responses to terrorism. Such responses run counter to one of the contemporary trends in the international system, which has been to internationalize efforts—in the United Nations, through regional and universal economic associations, and through treaty obligations. This trend has all been part of a sort of democratization of international relations generally, wherein all states have the opportunity to participate in decisions about international norms and their implementation. The trend can be seen in areas as diverse as lowering tariffs, banning land mines, and raising air quality standards. For the United States (or anyone else) to exercise leadership and thus maximize its influence over matters within its interests that enhance its security, it must be a prominent part of that internationalization or be perceived as an arrogant, even overbearing, outsider.

SELECTED BIBLIOGRAPHY

Burton, Daniel F., Victor Gotbaum, and Felix Rohatyn, eds. *Vision for the 1990s: U.S. Strategy and the Global Economy.* Cambridge, MA: Ballinger, 1989.

Flanagan, Stephen J., Ellen L. Frost, and Richard L. Kugler. *Challenges of the Global Century: Report of the Project on Globalization and National Security*. Washington, DC: Institute of National Strategic Studies (National Defense University), 2001.

Luttwak, Edward N. *Strategy: The Logic of War and Peace*. Cambridge, MA: Belknap, 1987.

Nuechterlein, Donald E. *America Recommitted: United States National Interests in a Reconstructed World*. Lexington: University of Kentucky Press, 1991.

Pfaff, William. "Invitation to War." *Foreign Affairs* 72, 3 (Summer 1993), 97–109.

Rogov, Sergei. "International Security and the Collapse of the Soviet Union." *Washington Quarterly* 15, 2 (Spring 1992), 16–28.

Sloan, Stephen. *Beating International Terrorism: An Action Strategy for Preemption and Punishment*, rev. ed. Montgomery, AL: Air University Press, 2000.

Smith, W. Y. "U.S. National Security after the Cold War." *Washington Quarterly* 15, 4 (Winter 1992), 21–34.

Snow, Donald M. "'Let Them Drink Oil': Resource Conflict in the New Century?" in *Cases in International Relations: Snapshots of the Future*. New York: Longman, 2002.

———. *When America Fights: The Uses of U.S. Military Power*. Washington, DC: CQ Press, 2000.

The Foreign and Domestic Environments

How environmental changes affect policy and our approach and response to national security challenges is more than just an abstract matter. In this chapter, we will begin to apply the influences of the international and domestic political environments to substantive political problems. Because there is some difference in a generalized view of whether the environment is essentially benign or hostile (which has strong implications for viewing globalization or geopolitics as the dominant paradigm), we will begin by presenting and trying to reconcile two competing popular conceptualizations. We will then turn to the question of how internal political processes affect national security outcomes. We will then apply these insights to substantive problems: the creation of a Department of Homeland Security, military manpower, and military reform.

The way in which the United States (and other countries) deals with the world is a combination of several factors. One is an assessment of the international environment: Is it generally hostile or benign, and what, if anything, can and should the United States try to do to help create a world more to our liking. Generally, the United States prefers an international environment wherein peace and stability hold and, ideally, the American ideals of political democracy and market economics are taking hold more widely, a basic preference shared by traditional internationalists and neo-conservatives. This was, by and large, the environment of the 1990s, when globalization was the rising force in the world. But that generally benign set of conditions included circumstances in which radical international terrorism festered and grew and man-made disasters such as the genocide in Rwanda scarred Africa.

Deciding what to try to do about the world begins by assessing the environment. Our view has been jaundiced by the terrible events of 2001, which have rearranged our national priorities and arguably have distorted our overall view of the world. Beyond the focus on terrorism, there is less agreement about critical elements of the environment now than during the 1990s and before. In the wake of the terrorist attacks of 2001, the campaign against terrorism became the pivot around which many problems were perceived to revolve. How long will that focus remain?

The international environment provides contrasting images and impressions. The unifying influences of commerce and communications were the apparently ascending forces of the 1990s. How could one not look favorably on a world in which a Starbucks coffee house had been set up inside the walls of the Forbidden City of Beijing? At the same time, optimism was conditioned by negative phenomena such as the pestilence of AIDS that ravaged much of sub-Saharan Africa and the vicious civil conflicts that dotted the map of much of the Second Tier.

The confusion over the environment is also reflected in domestic politics. The debate is partly a philosophical discussion about the extent of American activism in the world, which reflects an assessment of what the world out there is really like and the degree to which the United States has some role, obligation, or ability to affect the environment. The 1990s was largely a period of American internationalism and activism under the Clintonian foreign policy sobriquet "engagement and enlargement." It featured an activist stance that included a great deal of international cooperation and commitments through forums as diverse as the United Nations, NATO, and various international conventions on international problems, ranging from the environment to human rights.

The domestic equation changed after the 2000 election, and even more dramatically after September 11, 2001. The new Bush administration initially professed a more limited approach to the American role in the world than its predecessor had, arguing that the United States neither could nor should attempt to involve itself everywhere and that it was willing to act unilaterally when it felt it needed to do so. The inclination to limit activism was doused by the actions of Al Qaeda. Unilateralism temporarily gave way to an international effort to combat the problem, but it returned when the international community disagreed with aspects of the American approach, as much of it did the forceful removal of Saddam Hussein, for instance, as the neo-conservatives gained greater influence over American policy.

Competing visions of the world and the American place in it spill directly onto the substantive national security question and its implications. The debate occurs when there is broad agreement in the national security community that the environment has changed enough to require rethinking and even restructuring American capabilities and approaches to confront that world. Responses to the terrorist attacks have added the concept of homeland defense and security to the lexicon of national security concerns and have resulted in major institutional adaptation. Two other areas that are especially affected by the outcome of that debate are military reform and modernization and military manpower recruitment and retention.

COMPETING IMAGES OF THE
INTERNATIONAL ENVIRONMENT

Predilections about the extent and content of the U.S. effect on the world reflect the convergence of four factors: philosophical views of the world, visions of general and particular assessments of the global condition, questions about American interests worldwide and in specific locales, and assessments of the efficacy of different American responses in individual situations. These assessments are more complicated on all four dimensions than previously. There is less general agreement on worldviews, assessment of the environment, American interests in a world of interest–threat mismatch, and the kinds of applications of power that work in different situations.

One's view on these matters is influenced by one's vantage point. Part of that vantage point is geographical. If one concentrates on the Pacific Rim as the direction of the future, the impression is of a basically benign international system of spreading commerce and cooperation, only slightly blemished by geopolitical concerns such as the China–Taiwan relationship or North Korean nuclear saber rattling. A Pacific Rim focus is likely to be optimistic about the future and to upgrade the role of globalization at the expense of geopolitics. If, however, one's focus is primarily on the poorest parts of the Second Tier outside the globalizing economy, then the shocking violence, poverty, and hopelessness of the situation is likely to result in a much more negative view, in which geopolitics rises to the fore. We have long ignored or downplayed this second image, but since it is the cauldron from which terrorism has emerged, we have had to begin to confront it.

Two sharply competing views of the general direction of the international system represent the geopolitical and globalization perspectives. For exemplary purposes, these can be represented by two international journalists, Robert D. Kaplan and Thomas L. Friedman, each of whom has traveled and written extensively about international trends; but they have reached diametrically opposed conclusions about the human condition.

Kaplan: The Coming Anarchy

Robert D. Kaplan is a long-time international correspondent, most of whose work has appeared in the *Atlantic Monthly*. His travel and coverage have been concentrated on the poorest parts of the world, those generally outside the First Tier and remote from the growing international economic activity associated with globalization. In particular, much of his reporting has been on Africa and the multiple calamities faced on that continent. Some of his more dramatic observations are contained in a slender volume of his essays, entitled *The Coming Anarchy*.

Kaplan's presentation is dramatic and provocative in its observations and conclusions, but many of them are shared by other analysts as well. Moreover, many of the dynamics he describes regarding Africa also apply clearly to conditions in parts of the Middle East that have produced international terrorists. His basic thesis is that the international system is becoming increasingly "bifurcated" between "societies like ours, producing goods and services that the rest of the world wants, and those mired in various forms of chaos." In the terms used in this text, he divides the world into the First Tier and aspirants to First Tier status (roughly the countries participating in the globalizing economy) and the countries at the lower developmental levels of the Second Tier. He argues that not only does a gulf exist between the two but it is progressively widening.

This thesis is not exceptional. In the past few years, there has been increasing publicity about the divide between the rich and the poor states, a recognition given greater urgency by the outbreaks of particularly vicious internal fighting and killing in such places as Sierra Leone and Liberia and, more recently, the recognition of the enormity of the AIDS pandemic throughout Africa.

Whereas many analysts point to the humanitarian tragedy of Africa and the moral and humanitarian obligations the rich countries have to alleviate the suffering, Kaplan sees the situation as a security problem for the international community. A major part of his emphasis is based on what he sees as an expansion of the security menu, not unlike what was suggested in the last chapter and elsewhere in the text. He believes that much of the instability and violence in the world will derive from unconventional problems already present in Africa, such as "environmental scarcity, cultural and racial clash, geographic destiny, and the transformation of war." In the latter category, he sees a continuation of the very chaotic, transnational forms of internal violence that have marked a number of African countries since the end of the Cold War and that could spread more widely in a geographic sense. This analysis applies equally well to places such as eastern Pakistan, which have been the breeding ground for organizations like Al Qaeda.

It is the implications that he draws from these trends that makes Kaplan's analysis provocative. Many analysts see environmental and other pressures, such as population expansion, as sources of future world problems and even of potential violence as scarcity increases along with demands for resources. Where Kaplan and his critics (who are numerous) part company is in the implications of change for the First Tier. Many Africanists, for instance, believe that the heart of African tragedy is the extreme marginalization and isolation of the continent from the rest of the world. As a result, African problems are left to be solved by Africans, who lack the wherewithal for the effort. In this view, the gulf will steadily widen, and Africa will simply be left out, with no recourse that will allow Africans to join the general prosperity.

Kaplan believes quite the opposite. He argues that the response to worsening conditions in the Second Tier will be their transfer to the First Tier. As the misery in the least developed countries becomes more intolerable, he believes that the result will be massive migration by the disaffected to the seats of power and prosperity—to the countries of the First Tier. He states this thesis in predictably dramatic form:

> It is time to understand the environment for what it is: *the* national-security issue of the early twenty-first century. The political and strategic impact of surging populations, spreading disease, deforestation and soil erosion, water depletion, air pollution, and possibly rising sea levels . . . will prompt mass migration

and, in turn, incite group conflicts [that] will be the core foreign-policy challenge from which most others will emanate.

Rather than silently suffering in isolation, in other words, those most deprived
will share their misery with the rest of the world in the hope of improving their
condition.

Kaplan's thesis is controversial in at least two ways. First, it is possible to argue
that he overstates the case factually—that things are not and will not become as dire
as he predicts. There is evidence on both sides of the issue. If he is correct or partially
so, however, the other question his prognosis raises is what to do about the problem.
The broad policy options follow the general contours of the U.S. debate over its role
in the world. The internationalist response suggests a concerted effort to alleviate
the conditions before they reach the proportions that could trigger the dire consequences that Kaplan prophesies. A more minimalist, isolationist approach suggests
that we have no business interfering in these natural conditions and that we lack the
resources or will to do much about them anyway. At any rate, Kaplan projects a very
grim, geopolitically centered view of the world.

Friedman: Globalization

New York Times foreign affairs correspondent Thomas L. Friedman has been among
the loudest and most consistent champions of the phenomenon of globalization and
what he likes to describe as the transition of international relations from the "cold
war system" to what he calls the "globalization system." The most elaborate description of this system and its operation is found in Friedman's 1999 book, *The Lexus and
the Olive Tree*.

Because we have already devoted a chapter to the dynamics of globalization, we
do not need to repeat that discussion. Rather, Friedman's basic argument can be summarized in his own words: "The driving force beyond globalization is free-market
capitalism—the more you let markets rule and the more you open your economy to
free trade and competition, the more efficient and flourishing your economy will be.
Globalization means the spread of free-market capitalism to virtually every country
in the world." Since that spread means the adoption of a uniform economic philosophy that implies movement to a common political idea—democracy—the virtues of
globalization include its integration of the countries into a commonality that should
spread and reinforce peace and stability.

If the claims of the advocates of globalization are accepted, the result should be a
more secure, peaceful world in which the recourse to violence will gradually subside
in the mutual acceptance of the mantra of market capitalism. Countries will have
progressively more in common than what may separate them, thereby moderating
international sources of conflict. States that accept the rules of globalization will
become prosperous and thus peaceful. Globalization will triumph over geopolitics in
this happiest of all possible outcomes.

The most optimistic descriptions and advocacies of the system-transforming
effects of globalization are products of the 1990s and a focus on Asia, especially

before the Asian financial crisis of 1997. Friedman presents a majority of his evidence from Asian examples, and when he shows how embracing globalization can transform countries not currently part of the global economy, most of his examples come from Asia and the non–Persian Gulf region of the Middle East, not from the parts of Africa that Kaplan decries.

In light of the Asian crisis and the slowing global economy as the century turned, enthusiasm about and belief in the inevitability of the triumph of globalization as the basis for a more peaceful world had become more restrained, even before our attention was refocused on terrorism. Although the criticisms are emerging and evolving—and any list is likely less than inclusive—we can present five of these arguments for exemplary purposes.

One argument is that we have heard all of these claims before, and they have always fallen short of fulfilling their promise in the past. The idea that states can be brought into a system from which they benefit to the point that old-fashioned geopolitics and the recourse to violence disappears is the basic argument made by the functionalists (such as David Mitrany) in forming the specialized agencies of the United Nations. (The idea was that having UN agencies providing basic services such as health care would cause people to abandon loyalty to the state as the functions of states were replaced by international providers.) It is also the basic argument of the advocates of complex interdependence (see Nye and Keohane), and globalization is—in a very real, linear sense—the current manifestation of that hope. At the same time, others (see Pettis) point out that we have had periods resembling what we now call globalization before, and they have not lasted.

A second argument is that globalization does not have the universal appeal its apologists claim. As pointed out in Chapter 5, those who feel they suffer from the process have arisen in noisy and destructive rejection, and they are not alone. Some countries and regions reject the cultural intrusion and destructiveness of globalization for local cultural, religious, or other practices. Strict Islamic countries are most often cited in this regard, and although advocates such as Friedman would argue that such resistance consigns those countries to the dustbin of the modern system, it is hard to see how many countries in the region could become part of globalization without a great deal of trauma, probably including major violence. Another group of rejectionists are those countries that, for a variety of reasons, are unlikely ever to be competitive enough economically to become members of the system. Friedman calls these countries the "turtles," implying that they can not gain the momentum to become full participants in the system. The most obvious examples are the very African countries that concern Kaplan, which may mean that globalization is not the answer to the problems Kaplan hypothesizes.

There is further question about the inevitability of globalization. Pettis, in a *Foreign Policy* article, argues that historical evidences of globalization have been cyclical and are tied to periods of monetary expansions and contractions. When money supplies have been expanding and investors have been optimistic, then globalization has been fed by supplies of capital that flow into the developing world. If history is any guide, however, cycles of monetary expansion are followed by cycles of contraction, when investor confidence wanes and resources are pulled from international markets. The result has been a decline in globalization. When Pettis asks himself if this cycle can be avoided in the present situation, he answers, "The outlook is not very positive." If, indeed, fluctuations in economic cycles have not been overcome, and if negative forces such as the American corporate scandals of 2002 can rock the American stock market, then one must wonder how firm a base globalization provides for anchoring the international system.

A fourth argument that derives from the others is that the impact of globalization is by no means universally benign. Globalization advocates claim that the spread of globalization homogenizes the international system by providing a common ideological underpinning in the economic and political realms. Such a benign acceptance of those ideas holds only if everyone benefits; it clearly does not make sense to adopt a set of ideas if one suffers from it. If, as seems to be the case, some benefit and others do not when globalization takes hold, then the values of globalization form their own oppositions among the losers as well as those who reject globalization for other reasons. In that case, globalization is not the unifying force that its advocates maintain it is.

Finally, there is the argument that globalization ultimately harms the state by undercutting state sovereignty. If one accepts the erosion of some degree of state sovereignty on the altar of globalization, one must raise the question of whether or not the benefits outweigh the costs. If, on the one hand, globalization leads to a more peaceful, prosperous world with decreased security concerns, then the bargain may be an acceptable—even good—one. If, on the other hand, globalization is subject to fluctuation, reversal, and thus instability, then the same bargain may not seem so good at all.

Reconciling Worldviews

The two foregoing assessments contain common and divergent points They largely agree that problems within the international arena occur primarily in the most unstable parts of the Second Tier, which of course is hardly a new concept. Internal conflicts within Africa and in parts of Asia are the core military problem facing the contemporary world. What is different in the two assessments is the severity of the problem and the ways to deal with it.

The globalization approach is inherently internationalist and activist. It sees the problem of world politics and instability primarily in economic terms, and the solution is the gradual spread of the process of globalization to those parts of the Second Tier that are not current participants. This is the essence of the Clinton policy of engagement and enlargement, but it comes with a caveat. The Clinton formulation said that the United States should promote market democracy in those places where it had the best chances of taking hold, and then hope that it spread beyond those bounds. It was not very specific about how that spread would occur in those areas—most of Africa, for example—that are most removed from the process of globalization or are the least able to compete (Friedman's turtles). It is also not clear how viable the strategy is if globalization falters.

The coming-anarchy assessment is more cautious and pessimistic in its approach. Kaplan projects a basic hopelessness about conditions in the poorest parts of the world and a virtual inevitability of the negative consequences he foresees.

This tone does not suggest that the levels of activism that are likely will make much difference and thus leads toward a more restrained approach to reforming the system. One can read a sort of neoisolationist message of trying to build up barriers against the onslaught that he sees in the future. The difference between the two visions is how fatalistic one is about conditions in the most wretched parts of the world and what can or should be done about them.

These arguments lost much of their abstract nature on September 11, 2001. The sources of the attacks came from the very kinds of circumstances that Kaplan describes: backwardness, poverty, and hopelessness in a hostile world. With the immediate problem of terrorism contained—if not eliminated—we now move toward the question of how places like Afghanistan and Pakistan can be made impervious to terrorist appeals in the future. Can they be drawn into the globalization system, or are they hopeless turtles that can never make the grade? How important is the effort to find out?

THE IMPACT OF DOMESTIC POLITICS

National security policy is among the most contentious political areas within the American federal system. It is politically charged for a number of reasons. For one thing, the content of national security policy is potentially very important, ultimately including choices that can affect the very physical survival of the country and, less dramatically, decisions about when Americans may be compelled to put themselves in harm's way to defend American interests.

National security policy is also highly political because it involves the expenditure of very large amounts of money. Until recently, defense spending was the third largest category in the federal budget, behind spending on entitlements (Social Security, Medicare, and the like) and service on the interest on the national debt. Full implementation of the 2002 Bush budget request moved it back into second place. During the Cold War, defense was consistently the second largest category of expenditures, involving roughly a quarter of the federal budget and 5 to 6 percent of gross national product (GNP). In the mid-1950s, before many of the entitlement programs were enacted, it accounted for nearly half of federal spending. Currently, it is about one-fifth of the federal budget.

Defense spending is highly political for other reasons as well. One of the important characteristics of the defense budget is that it is the largest *controllable* element within the federal budget. One way to distinguish items in the federal budget is to divide them into controllable and uncontrollable elements. A controllable element is one that must be appropriated annually; an uncontrollable element is one that is automatically appropriated unless there is specific legislation altering or rescinding the appropriation. Social Security is the best example. Nearly two-thirds of the controllable money in the federal budget goes to defense, meaning that attempts to increase, decrease, or alter the pattern of federal spending will often begin with the defense budget.

The political nature of defense spending also reflects the impact of national security spending on Americans. Not only is a lot of money spent on defense, those expenditures are made in a large number of locales, wherever concentrations of military installations and defense industries are found. The competition for defense contracts and the locations of bases or posts involves a highly competitive process wherein the financial health and prosperity of communities can be vitally affected by the effectiveness of congressional delegations that are able to win federal contracts for their states and districts.

National security spending is also contentious because much of the money is spent on highly durable procurements. The decision to build an aircraft carrier, for instance, not only involves appropriating several billion dollars for its construction (money that is fed into the local community wherever the ship is built, of course), but also involves investment in a weapons "platform" that is expected to be in the arsenal for thirty years or longer. Procurement decisions affect not only the arsenal characteristics of whatever administration commissions them but also the military capability available to a commander-in-chief a quarter-century or more in the future. The same is true of procuring new fighter or bomber aircraft, a new model of main battle tank, and the like.

There is an old saw that "policy is what gets funded." That truism not only holds for the national security area generally but is particularly true in the current milieu. Two things are coming together to create a sharp poignancy for the political, especially budgetary, elements of the national security decision process. One is the nature of the current military arsenal. The characteristics of the current military force include the fact that it was largely shaped to confront a Soviet military threat that no longer exists and that is not being replicated by any emerging potential adversary. Moreover, the force is getting old, and much of it needs replacement. A major question is how to modernize it. One group argues for the application of the *revolution in military affairs (RMA)*, applying very sophisticated technologies to warfare to produce such a qualitatively superior force as to be unassailable. Others argue against such a heavy investment, on the grounds that it would be excessive to any actual or likely threat facing the United States. Allies worry that the American force has already become so sophisticated comparatively as to render their own forces obsolete and expendable.

The other side of this debate is over more general spending priorities within the federal government. As the budget surpluses generated during the 1990s have evaporated in the early 2000s amid charges of raiding the Social Security fund to avoid future deficits, all areas of federal spending have come under close scrutiny. While the Bush administration has argued for enhanced spending on national security, the amount and direction of that spending has become intensely controversial. Because of the inherent vulnerability of the defense budget (its controllable nature), it will remain the subject of considerable political concern. The campaign against terrorism has muted this debate for now, but it will certainly return.

The politics of national security are played out at various levels that come together in the budget process. One level is within the executive branch of government, where the representatives of various government agencies and functions compete for priority within federal policy, including the budget. This competition extends to the legislative branch, where the same kind of competition occurs within the various layers of the committee system in hammering out whatever budget the executive will ultimately have to spend. Ultimately, decisions involve the interaction of the two principal legislating branches of the government (the judiciary is rarely involved).

The Executive Branch

National security policy within the executive branch of the government operates on two separate tracks that are, in some ways, conceptually paralleled within the Congress. The day-to-day conduct of national security (as part of overall foreign policy) occurs within the federal agencies with authority in the field—such as the State Department, the Department of Defense (DOD), and the Central Intelligence Agency (CIA)—at the direction of the president. Policy decisions are coordinated and implemented through the *interagency process,* the chief vehicle of which has been the National Security Council (NSC) and its subordinate bodies. This process of policy development and implementation is conceptually similar to the role of the authorizing committees of the Congress. The other track is the competition for funding, which is the heart of the budgetary process, and it pits parts of the national security community against one another and against competing functions of the government. The framework for this interaction, of course, is the constitutionally mandated roles for the various branches of government, as laid out by the Founding Fathers.

The Interagency Process.   The foundation of what has evolved, since the Eisenhower administration in the 1950s, as the interagency process was the National Security Act of 1947. In addition to creating the CIA as the country's first peacetime intelligence-gathering agency, a consolidated DOD, and an independent air force, the act created the NSC to coordinate foreign and national security policy.

The act was of great symbolic importance. It symbolized the growing importance of the United States in the world and the need for some formal mechanism to assist the president in dealing with this new, expanded role. It also implicitly boosted the centrality of defense matters within the hierarchy of foreign policy concerns by making the new secretary of defense (SECDEF) a coequal permanent member of the NSC with the secretary of state (the president and vice president are the other permanent members). In addition, the act established the director of the CIA and the chairman of the Joint Chiefs of Staff (CJCS) as statutory advisors to the NSC; others have been added subsequently. At a more informal level, the model and function of the NSC set the precedent for presidents to coordinate and focus on other policy areas. President Clinton created the National Economic Council in 1993 to emphasize his commitment to economic matters. President George W. Bush created the Homeland Security Council in the wake of the 2001 terrorist attacks; it became the institutional springboard for the cabinet-level Department of Homeland Security. The Homeland Security Council closely resembles the NSC in organization.

The NSC system in its present form as the interagency process came into being during the 1980s, and it is a fairly elaborate system. The NSC itself consists of the four permanent members and whoever else the president may designate to attend and participate for any particular purpose. The White House chief of staff is normally included, and on military matters, so is the CJCS. The purpose of the council is purely advisory. The members offer advice to the president that he is free to accept or reject. No votes are ever taken, so that the president will not be swayed by what the majority may favor.

Directly below the NSC is the *Principals Committee (PC)*. This group has the same membership as the NSC itself, except that the president does not attend. There are two basic occasions when the NSC meets as the Principals Committee. If there are matters that do not require direct presidential involvement and thus intrusion on his busy agenda, the others may meet without him. Also, the president will occasionally absent himself in order to facilitate a more frank exchange of views than might occur if he were present, and when he feels that the other members might be unwilling to champion views they think he might oppose. This latter reason was used by John F. Kennedy during portions of the Cuban missile crisis when the Principals Committee was known as the ExComm (Executive Committee).

The next layer in the system is the *Deputies Committee (DC)*. As the name suggests, this group is composed of the principal deputies of the members of the NSC. The meetings are traditionally chaired by the president's principal deputy for national security, the national security advisor (NSA), although in the early days of the George W. Bush administration there was an apparently unsuccessful attempt by Vice President Richard Cheney to usurp that role from NSA Condoleeza Rice. The Deputies Committee is more of a working-level body; its roles include formulating policy proposals for action by the NSC or the Principals Committee or figuring out how to implement decisions made in those bodies. Other members of the DC include the undersecretary of state for political affairs, the undersecretary of defense for policy, the deputy director of central intelligence, and the vice chairman of the JCS.

These levels of the process normally labor outside the public eye. When *Time* magazine revealed that plans for countering Al Qaeda had been developed in the Clinton administration but had become bogged down in the pre–September 11 Bush regime, the Deputies and Principals Committees were specifically singled out as institutional loci where the plans languished—a rare public exposure of the workings of the interagency process.

At the bottom of the process are the *Policy Coordinating Committees (PCCs)*, a series of committees formed along both functional and geographic lines. The functional committees are chaired by the assistant secretary (or equivalent) of the cabinet department with the most direct and obvious responsibility. There are, for instance, functional PCCs for defense, intelligence, arms control, and international economics. The geographic PCCs are all chaired by the assistant secretaries of state for the particular regions. It is the role of the PCCs to monitor their areas of responsibility (the PCC for the Near East and East Asia kept tab on the activities of Iraq's Saddam Hussein, for example), to provide options to the Deputies Committee and higher-level committees on assigned problems, and to carry out the detailed policies adopted elsewhere in the process.

Reflecting his own interests and perceptions about change in the international environment, President Clinton created a parallel body, the *National Economic Council (NEC)* by executive order in January 1993. It differed from the NSC in that it was not created by legislation and thus could be dismantled without congressional action. Clinton gave it four charges that parallel the duties of the older body: (1) to coordinate the economic policy-making process with respect to domestic and international economic issues; (2) to coordinate economic policy advice to the president; (3) to ensure that economic policy decisions and programs are consistent with the president's goals; and (4) to monitor implementation of the president's economic agenda.

The NEC was a prominent and important part of national security policy during the Clinton years between the fault lines and reflected the paramount importance of economic policy during the 1990s. The NEC was chaired personally by President Clinton, and it had its own Deputies Committee and staff capability through the Trade Policy Review Group and the Trade Policy Staff Committee. The first task assigned to the first director of the NEC, Robert Rubin (later secretary of the treasury), was Clinton's comprehensive budget reduction plan, which succeeded in balancing the budget in 1998. The NEC was also prominent in trade policy and multilateral negotiations on trade promotion. When he came to office in 2001, President George W. Bush threatened to do away with the NEC as an unnecessary relic from his predecessor, but has retained it at a much lower level of visibility.

Amplification 7.1

THE PRESIDENT, THE CONSTITUTION, AND NATIONAL SECURITY

Because the founding fathers did not anticipate a level of involvement in international affairs that even mildly resembles the extent to which the country interacts with the rest of the world today, the U.S. Constitution does not lay out an elaborate list of powers for the president in the areas of national security or foreign policy. Such specific powers as are provided are found in Article II of the Constitution and, as we shall see in Amplification 7.2, essentially are counterbalanced by contrary powers given to the Congress as part of the checks and balances system that characterizes the entire document. The result is an "invitation to struggle" (see Crabb and Holt) that is intended to make the two branches coequal in this area.

The Constitution lists six powers for the president that directly apply to national security and defense policy: the positions of chief executive, chief of state, commander in chief of the armed forces, treaty negotiator, nominator of key personnel, and recognizer of foreign governments.

Chief Executive.   In this capacity, the president is designated as the major presider over the executive agencies of the government, all of which report directly to the president. In the area of foreign and national security policy, these agencies include the Departments of State and Defense, the Central Intelligence Agency, and the various economic agencies, including the Departments of Treasury and Commerce, and the U.S. Trade Representative. These agencies collectively are the chief repositories of the expertise of the federal government on foreign matters, and the president's access to them provides an important advantage in dealing with foreign and national security matters.

Chief of State.   In this largely symbolic role, the president is designated as the chief representative of the United States government to all foreign governments. This means, for instance, that officials of foreign governments (ambassadors, for instance) are accredited to the president, and when the heads of other states interact with the U.S. government, it is with the president or a representative of the president.

Commander in Chief.   The president is designated as the commander in chief of the armed forces of the United States. This means, among other things, that he is the highest military official of the government, to whom all members of the armed forces are subsidiary, and that it is the president's authority to employ the armed forces in support of public policy, including the commitment of forces in combat (although this power is circumscribed by congressional limitation).

Treaty Negotiator.   Only the president of the United States or his or her specified representative (known as plenipotentiary) is authorized to enter into negotiations with foreign governments that lead to formal relationships and obligations on behalf of the U.S. government. Although only a small percentage of agreements between the United States and foreign governments come in the form of formal treaties, this nonetheless sets the precedent for presidential leadership in all arrangements with foreign governments.

Appointment of Key Personnel.   The president alone has the power to name key officials of his or her administration. Most of the important appointments are at the cabinet levels (the various secretaries of executive agencies), the National Security Council, and the various deputy and assistant secretaries, such as those who serve on the various committees of the National Security Council system.

Recognizer of Foreign Governments.   Only the president has the authority to extend or remove formal recognition of foreign governments by the U.S. government. This is one of the few powers of the president that does not require some form of formal supporting action by the Congress.

How the interagency process works is largely a matter of how the president wants it to operate. The NSC is assisted by the NSC staff, all of whom are members of the president's personal staff and thus not subject to congressional confirmation, review, or scrutiny. Because they serve at the president's pleasure, they are highly loyal to the chief executive and generally closely reflect the president's views. The degree to which the president utilizes this asset depends on presidential prerogative. Richard Nixon, for instance, had a long and deep-seated distrust of the State Department. State Department officials have civil service protection and cannot be fired (except in extreme circumstances), and most of them generally opposed Nixon's policies. As a result, he enlarged the NSC staff and used it, in effect, as an alternative State Department to ensure that his policy preferences would be implemented. Presidents who are highly active in foreign affairs, such as George H. W. Bush and Bill Clinton in his second term, rely heavily on the NSC to carry out their desires, whereas those with less interest (such as Gerald Ford) use the NSC less and rely more on the executive agencies to conduct policy on their own.

Funding Security.   The other dimension of policy making within the executive branch focuses on the competition for resources to fund various government functions and programs. The principal manifestation of this political battle is the formation of the presidential budget request to the Congress and its translation into the working budget of the federal government of the United States. The budget process is one of the most complicated, most arcane, yet fundamental political activities of the government. If one accepts the notion that policy is what gets funded, it is also the heart of the political process.

Unraveling the complexity of the process of allocating public monies for the various functions of government goes well beyond the purposes of this volume. Instead, we will look briefly at two aspects of the politics of national security budget making: the competition among the services for resources and the competition between defense and other government functions in the formation of the executive branch's request to the Congress. (Some of the politics of the congressional response to the president's budget request is discussed in the next section of this chapter.)

Budgeting is an ongoing process within the U.S. government. At any point in time, the Department of Defense, for instance, is working on at least three different budgets: the budget for the current fiscal year, which has been appropriated and is being expended; the budget proposal for the next fiscal year, which has been proposed to Congress and to which the Congress is responding; and the following year's budget proposal, which is being formulated for presentation to the Congress in the following fiscal year.

The competition between the services and between defense and nondefense spending is closely related to this process. Under the provisions of the planning, programming, budgeting, and spending (PPBS) system first introduced by the McNamara Pentagon in the early 1960s, initial planning for a budget begins approximately two and a half years before the first money is spent (assuming that the Congress and the executive branch agree on a budget before the beginning of the fiscal year in which spending is to occur). Thus, planning for spending in fiscal year 2004 (which begins on October 1, 2003) began in January 2002, when initial planning requests were sent to operational units within the DOD and elsewhere in the government. During the course of 2002, the requests from defense units, such as the military services, were compared with other equivalent requests and reconciled with one another, moving through the programming and budgeting phases during the late summer and fall of 2002. In turn, the DOD's proposal would be compared with requests from other executive agencies and reconciled into a budget request that would accompany the president's State of the Union address to the Congress in January 2003. Legislative enactment would occur between January and September of 2003, and if all went well, there would be a budget, agreed to by both branches of the government, that would go into effect on October 1, 2003. While legislative action was going on in 2003, the planning process for the fiscal year 2005 budget would be set in motion, while the Defense Department was spending resources from the fiscal 2003 budget.

Much of the politics within the executive branch occurs during the initial phases, when the president's budget request is being formulated. At the beginning, the military services are asked to formulate their individual requests. All units know that the aggregated requests (what is sometimes known as the "wish list") of the services will exceed by a large order of magnitude the resources that will actually be available to them. Nonetheless, each will request everything it wants, regardless of funding expectations, for two reasons. First, doing so creates a record of what the army, for example, feels it really should have to carry out its mission most effectively. Second, since all the services know that their requests will be cut—and, based on experience, approximately the percentage by which they are likely to be cut—submitting a request that combines what the services think they will actually receive plus what they assume will be cut reasonably ensures that after cuts are made, they will get roughly what they expected. Submitting a more modest and realistic request and having it cut probably would mean getting less than they expected and needed.

The politics of interservice competition is particularly important over military procurement of new equipment, especially for major weapons systems. During the process of proposal and negotiations, it is fair to say that the services provide a valuable public service to the budgeting process by offering detailed critiques of the requests of the *other* services in order to find weaknesses in the other services' requests that might be turned to their own advantage. The motivation combines self-interest and civic-mindedness, and it serves the useful purpose of providing a kind of informal check and balance within the process through expert monitoring of rival service requests.

Once the defense request has been formulated, the national security budget comes into direct competition with other spending priorities within the federal budget. As in the internal defense process, the requests from agencies representing the range of government activity invariably exceed the total amount of money the Congress is likely to be willing to appropriate in any given year, which means that budget compromises must be negotiated to get the total budget request within realistic parameters.

The defense budget is especially vulnerable during this phase of the process. The first and most obvious source of vulnerability has already been mentioned: The defense budget contains the largest controllable elements within the total federal budget and is thus a tempting target for budget cutters with other priorities. Whereas increases in Social Security benefits are mandated and appropriated automatically in the absence of specific legislation changing those benefits, the funding for new fighter aircraft for the air force must be expressly appropriated each year. Moreover, despite colorful political campaign rhetoric to the contrary, there is relatively little "fat" in other budgets that can easily be used to compensate for other priorities.

The politics of budgeting in the executive branch was dramatically demonstrated in the first year of the Bush administration in 2001. The new president inherited a budget request that was formulated in 2000, when Bill Clinton was president, and that reflected Clinton's priorities (as well as Al Gore's, who would have inherited the request had he won the election). This formulation contained modest but real increases in defense funding, much of which the military planned to invest in force modernization. As is always the case, the new administration had a short period to alter budget priorities before sending their request to Capitol Hill as part of the State of the Union. Usually these alterations are relatively minor, and it is normally assumed that the second year's budget (in this case, the budget request for January 2002) will be the first "true" budget of a new administration.

President Bush had different ideas. Inheriting a budget request that emphasized federal debt reduction (through maximizing government surpluses to retiring the debt) and bolstering Social Security, he introduced new priorities. The most dramatic of these, of course, was a massive tax cut that critics said would reduce the surplus dramatically and would mean curtailing other budgetary priorities. Bush, however, proposed budget increases in funding for education and for national missile defense and insisted that he would not compromise on either goal.

These changes had a direct impact on budgeting within the DOD. Secretary of Defense Rumsfeld, intent on implementing the president's NMD proposal, combed the defense budget as part of the QDR process in order to force the services to find ways to save money that could be diverted to the NMD. This change of emphasis meant potentially unraveling earlier budget agreements and modernization commitments that had been hammered out the preceding year for a missile defense program that had very little support within the uniformed services anyway. The result was a major, if temporary, confrontation between a new administration, which had campaigned partially on increased support for the military, and a military establishment that felt it had been rudely jilted by its former suitor.

The confrontation was defused by the terrorist attacks, which directed attention away from both the budget battle and the QDR. Defense budget increases became part of the homeland security effort in the fiscal year 2003 budget presented to Congress in 2002, which included a $46 billion increase above projected levels in previous budgeting cycles. The result was that the military services received most of the modernization requests from previous "wish lists."

The Congress

The parallel process within the U.S. Congress is theoretically simpler and more compact than that within the executive branch. The structure for congressional consideration of the budget request of the administration is more direct, consisting of three prescribed steps rather than the multiple steps in the formulation process within the executive branch. Compactness is facilitated because the Congress does not have to develop a budget on its own. It only has to respond to a presidential request, which it can accept, reject, or modify. The two houses of Congress are, however, two large and often unruly committees, consisting of 100 highly independent senators and 435 equally independent members of the House of Representatives. Unlike the politically appointed officials of the executive branch, they are divided by political party and by political philosophy. The disposition of the defense budget is particularly important to individual members, because defense dollars are spent in individual congressional districts and states. Members of Congress thus have an acute built-in self-interest in the outcomes. The result is quintessential politics.

The heart of congressional action in the area of national security is through the budget process. The process is important because it produces the resources that fund efforts to ensure the national security and thus provides much of the shape and nature of the national security effort. The budget process is also of particular importance to the Congress because it is the power embedded in the American constitution that gives it the most leverage over the executive branch in matters pertaining to national security.

The Committee System.   Because of its size and consequent unwieldiness, the Congress does relatively little of its most important business acting as overall houses of Congress. The real, detailed business of the Congress is performed by the committee system, wherein smaller groups of senators and congressmen, all of whom have volunteered for the committees on which they serve (although by no means do all members get membership on all the committees they desire) hammer out congressional positions, oversee the activities of the executive agencies they parallel, and respond to presidential budgetary and policy initiatives. When the Congress is working properly (which it does not always do), the agreements that are reached in committee are ratified by the overall bodies.

One might reasonably ask why committees are so important and powerful within the Congress. For one thing, the various committees (including their staffs) are the major repositories of congressional expertise on the area of their focus. Members of Congress typically volunteer for committee assignments in which they or their constituents are interested or in which they have particular expertise. Thus, a congressional district with a large concentration of military facilities or defense contractors will produce Congress members who will develop an interest and knowledge in defense matters, because the outcomes of defense issues may affect their constituents. The longer members of Congress stay in the Senate or House and remain on the armed services committee, for instance, the more expertise they acquire and the more influence they develop. The most prominent and knowledgeable members attain the status of congressional leaders in their areas of expertise. Former Georgia Senator Sam Nunn, for example, who served as chair of the Senate Armed Services Committee during the 1980s and early 1990s, developed a reputation as a defense intellectual both within and outside Congress.

These experts—especially the chairs and the ranking members of the minority party (who become chairs if their party attains majority)—become the chief congressional spokespeople in their areas of expertise. Members with less expertise than

Amplification 7.2

THE CONGRESS, THE CONSTITUTION, AND NATIONAL SECURITY

The U.S. Constitution is as compact in its enumeration of congressional responsibility over foreign and national security affairs as it is for the executive branch. The powers of the Congress are enumerated in Article 1 of the Constitution. Some of these are direct responses to and limitations on presidential powers; others derive from the application of more general congressional authority to the national security arena. These powers include lawmaking power, the power of the purse, war-making power, confirmation, ratification, and general oversight of the executive branch.

Lawmaking Power.   Nearly all actions taken by the government are the result of the passage of legislation by the Congress or the application of previous legislation. As noted in the text, all legislation must begin in one house of the Congress or the other and must have the concurrence of both houses. The president may, of course, veto any legislation he or she deems unacceptable.

Power of the Purse.   The Constitution specifies that all authorization of the expenditure of public funds must be initiated in the House of Representatives and must have the specific concurrence of both houses of the Congress. This is a particularly significant power in the area of national security because of the large amounts of money spent on national security and the fact that most of those funds are controllable and must thus be appropriated each year.

War Powers.   Although the president is the commander in chief of the armed forces, the Congress has important countervailing powers. The Congress sets the size and composition of the armed forces (promotions for officers, for instance, must be formally approved by Congress before they can take effect). The president can have no larger armed forces than the Congress authorizes. Moreover, the Congress is the only agency of government that can declare war. Although this provision has been used only five times in the country's history, it remains a strong limitation on the president's practical ability to place American armed forces into harm's way.

Confirmation of Officials.   Presidential appointees to high offices in the administration (with the exception of the National Security Council staff, who are considered part of the president's personal staff and thus exempt) are subject to confirmation by the U.S. Senate. The purpose of this provision is to ensure that the president does not appoint personnel who are personally obnoxious or politically objectionable in a policy sense.

Ratification of Treaties.   Although the president is the only official who can negotiate agreements with foreign governments, none of these can take force until they have the positive advice and consent of two-thirds of the U.S. Senate. This limitation is necessary because a ratified treaty is coequal to laws passed by the Congress. Because of the sheer volume of the relations between the United States and other governments, only a few of the dealings with other governments are in the form of treaties (most are executive agreements that do not require senatorial ratification), but most of the more important relationships are in the form of treaties.

Oversight.   Although it is not specifically enumerated in the Constitution, the power to review how laws are implemented by the executive branch and to examine how well executive agencies operate has long been an accepted form of congressional limitation on executive actions. The chief mechanism for this oversight is through the various congressional authorizing committees that mirror major executive branch functions (the Armed Services Committees and the Department of Defense, for instance).

the experts tend to defer to the judgments of these leaders (especially members of the same party) and vote the way the chairs recommend. The same is true of the major subcommittees of the major committees, in which the chairs develop great expertise in their narrower subject areas (military manpower, for instance). The rise in partisanship, especially ideological division within both houses of Congress during the 1990s, has made members more independent of their leaderships and thus has decreased some of the deference paid to the chairs, but their impact on legislation remains formidable.

Another reason the committee system is so powerful is because of the smaller and more manageable size of committees compared to the full houses of Congress. It has often been said of the houses of Congress that their size and organization make them great debating forums for the discussion of public policy, but that they are so large and unwieldy as to be terrible places to enact and especially to frame legislation. The major committees of Congress, normally composed of twenty or fewer members, are more compact and can give more thorough and knowledgeable consideration to matters of legislative review, including such techniques as calling on and considering the views of expert witnesses. The recommendations of the appropriate committees thus have a considerable impact on how the Congress as a whole acts on matters that come before it. If one wants to get a sense of what the Congress thinks about a particular matter, the person to listen to is the chair of the appropriate committee.

The Budget.   The budgetary process is the essence of the congressional committee system in operation. It consists of three steps. The first comes reasonably early in the legislative session that convenes in January and consists of actions leading to a *budget resolution*. When the president's proposed budget is submitted to the Congress, the budget committees of the two houses receive and analyze the request, both overall and by budget category (one of which is national defense). The review establishes likely budgetary ceilings for the overall budget and for each category. When the committees of the two houses reach agreement on these general goals and their acceptability is acknowledged by the executive, the result is the joint budget resolution.

This resolution is a nonbinding agreement about the general shape of the budget that is supposed to guide other congressional committees in legislating the details of the budget package. Sometimes the final budget conforms fairly closely to the guide-lines, but often it does not. In 2001, for instance, President Bush did not include unusual funding for missile defense in his original budget proposal, and it was not included in the budget resolution. When he added it later, many in the Congress cried foul and maintained this addition invalidated the original agreement (a posi-tion that was probably disingenuous, given the president's quite public advocacy of NMD in the 2000 campaign and subsequently). The 2001 budget resolution was passed in April.

After the budget resolution is in place, the serious work of budgeting begins in the Congress. This process is depicted in Figure 7.1. In a sense, this process is both simpler and more complicated than it may seem. The second and third steps of the congressional budgeting process occur through the actions of the so-called authoriz-ing committees of each house, the Senate and House Armed Services Committees (SASC and HASC) and the appropriations subcommittee on defense of each house. The role of the authorizing committees in budgetary action is programmatic: They review the programs requested in the budget and decide which of them to authorize and at what level of support. They do not, however, make specific recommendations about how much should be spent on individual programs or on the overall budget, although there are clearly budgetary implications in areas such as procurement; approving a program for a given quantity of a particular weapons system costs has predictable budgetary consequences.

Actual recommendations on the size of the budget and on what can be spent are made by the appropriations committee of each house—in the case of defense, the appropriations subcommittee for defense. The role of the overall appropriations committee is to develop the total congressional version of the federal budget, and the subcommittees', one of which parallels each functional authorizing committee

Figure 7.1   The Budget Process

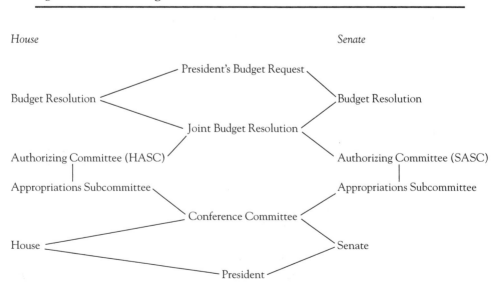

House   *Senate*

President's Budget Request

Budget Resolution   Budget Resolution

Joint Budget Resolution

Authorizing Committee (HASC)   Authorizing Committee (SASC)

Appropriations Subcommittee   Appropriations Subcommittee

Conference Committee

House   Senate

President

(including defense) is to make recommendations for that function, which are aggregated in the overall budget.

The process becomes political and controversial when there is disagreement among the various initiating and reviewing bodies, as there normally is. These disagreements can come about in three basic ways. First, the authorizing and appropriating committees in either or both of the houses can disagree on both programmatic priorities and budget size. The result is a mismatch between approved programs and the resources to fund them. Second, the committees in the two houses, when each reaches accord on *its* vision of the budget, can disagree. The results can be different programs or appropriations between the houses. Third, the president can disagree with the overall outcome. The more these possible points of disagreement come into conflict, the more contentious the overall process becomes and the more problematic is the outcome.

The authorizing and appropriations functions theoretically should be sequential. In a totally rational world, the authorizing committee would review the budget request programmatically and decide which programs are meritorious and worthy of funding. They would then pass their recommendations along to the appropriations subcommittees, which would allocate appropriate funding. In fact, the two forms of committee actions occur more or less simultaneously and independently within each house and with little formal coordination either within or between the houses. The result is often four more or less conflicting recommendations that require reconciliation before a budget bill can be passed along to either house for enactment.

If this seems a disorganized approach to enacting a budget, the reasons derive from the consequences of the outcomes. Members of appropriations subcommittees, like their counterparts on authorizing committees, commonly represent constituencies with interests in the outcomes and hence want to be certain that their interests are thoroughly represented. This is not only true regarding the defense budget; it has parallels in every area of budgetary and policy concern. The agricultural committees and subcommittees in both houses, for instance, overwhelmingly have members from farm states who want to protect the interests of their constituents.

When differences exist between the authorizing and appropriations subcommittees within the two houses, they are resolved by joint meetings whose purpose is to produce accommodations and compromises acceptable to all. Normally, there is informal contact with the parallel committee leaderships in the other house. In some cases, the president may well invite the leaderships of the committees to the White House to "jawbone" them into reaching agreements as close as possible to his position.

The ultimate outcome unfolds from this interaction. Each house passes a defense budget allocation based on the interaction of the authorization and appropriations committees. If these are identical (which they rarely are), they go directly to the president. If they are different, they are then sent to a conference committee composed of members of the appropriate committees of the two houses to reach agreement on identical bills, which are then sent back to the individual houses to be voted upon. When each house has approved the bill, it is then sent to the president for his signature. The president may accede and sign the budget, veto it, or ask for revisions.

This process has become especially turbulent, as the 2001 session of Congress demonstrated. The new Bush administration proposed major revisions in the budget it inherited from its predecessor, including changes at odds with the preferences of the military. The QDR produced some unconventional views of the threat and how to counter it that had strong budgetary implications (see later discussion). In 2002, the atmosphere of extreme partisanship was exacerbated by the fact that the two houses were controlled by different parties (conference committees featured a Democratic-led delegation from the Senate and a Republican-led House delegation). It is little wonder that the outcomes were so contentious.

APPLICATIONS: RESPONDING TO THE ENVIRONMENT

The interaction between the changing international environment and the vagaries of domestic politics can best be demonstrated by looking at actual policy arenas in which the two come into play. For this purpose, we will examine three matters of current concern: institutionalization of homeland security, military manpower, and responses to the implications of the 2001 QDR process for military reform. Although the current emphasis on terrorism has overridden virtually all other aspects of the defense debate, both manpower and reform raise concerns that are unlikely to disappear in the near future.

The Department of Homeland Security

One of the most important questions raised after September 11, 2001, was the institutional adequacy of the U.S. government in the face of terrorism. In the days and months following the attacks, information became available that intimations of the impending attacks had been circulating at lower levels of the government in the months before the actual attacks, and that there was even a planning document held over from the Clinton administration specifically aimed at Al Qaeda. And yet, the attacks appeared to come as an awful surprise. Why? Trying to sort out such questions led to the establishment of a congressionally mandated commission on inquiry in late 2002.

One answer familiar to those who had studied the problem of terrorism was institutional: Responsibility for some aspects of dealing with terrorism resided in more than forty executive branch agencies, atomizing the effort. Dealing with terrorism was not the primary responsibility of any of the major agencies, but was instead consigned to subagencies within the agencies. Moreover, there was a glaring lack of coordination of effort and information sharing among the three agencies with the greatest responsibility: the CIA, with major duties for collecting overseas information on terrorist efforts; the FBI, charged with monitoring terrorist activities within the United States; and the Immigration and Naturalization Service (INS), responsible for monitoring the entrance and exit of suspected terrorists into and out of the country.

The initial response to this problem was the creation of the Office of Homeland Security within the White House and the appointment of former Pennsylvania Governor Tom Ridge as its director. Ridge was given a position conceptually similar to that of the National Security Advisor (at least in terms of purported access to the president) and was charged with rationalizing and coordinating improved government capabilities for dealing with terrorism. Critics maintained that Ridge's position left him as little more than a figurehead, who could not compel agencies to do anything—especially to cooperate with one another.

In June 2002, the administration proposed a stronger way to institutionalize the effort—the creation of the Department of Homeland Security (DHS). The new department, with full cabinet status, was legislated into being in November 2002 and mandated to perform four functions: border and transportation security; emergency preparedness and response; chemical, biological, radiological, and nuclear countermeasures; and information analysis and infrastructure protection. To accomplish its tasks, the president proposed putting resources from a number of existing agencies under the control of the new department. Virtually no one opposed either the general proposition of this effort or its implementation in principle. Nevertheless, the proposal engendered enough criticism to assure that full implementation will take several years. These objections contain both international and domestic political elements—especially the latter.

The first problem was to determine which agencies would be drawn into the new department and which would not. Lead agencies such as the INS and Customs Service are now part of Homeland Security, but the CIA and FBI remained independent, with only directions to coordinate with the DHS. This raised questions about authority and the extent of improvement in communications. These questions were exacerbated by interagency turf battles as agencies tried to protect their anti-terrorist assets from usurpation, and by congressional committee chairs, who did not want to see agencies over which they had oversight removed from their purviews. The problem was made controversial by the preexisting pattern of organization: Virtually all of the agencies that might be included in the new department had terrorism as only part of their portfolios and could argue against inclusion because of their other duties.

The proposal also ran into unexpected opposition on another political issue—civil service protection of employees of the department. When he presented the proposal, Bush argued that the new secretary of homeland security should be given broad latitude to hire and fire personnel inherited from other agencies in order to shape the effort better. This meant that some inherited personnel might lose civil service protection they already held, which was universal throughout the federal service, and that some new employees would lack such protection. To many in Congress, this represented a dangerous precedent that delayed enactment of the legislation.

The Department of Homeland Security has come into being, however. The task of building a new agency to deal with a complex task that had been poorly handled in the past has proved to be a daunting task, and its eventual success will be determined in the future. As long as international terrorism remains a top priority in Washington, it will remain an important work in progress.

Military Manpower

The question of military manpower arises from two related concerns: the appropriate size of the armed forces and what must be done to ensure that adequate manpower resources are available to fulfill the country's needs. The necessary size of the armed forces is primarily a question of assessing the threat (the international environment) and the ways to counter the threat. The question of obtaining manpower involves how to recruit and retain an adequate force, which is normally a domestic matter. The two concerns are clearly related. The extent of the threat and the resulting commitments for the country help determine the needed manpower levels. At the same time, the number and quality of military actions undertaken can affect the attractiveness of military service for current and potential members and thus the ability to recruit and retain members. Although the patriotic response to terrorism provided a temporary spike in interest in military service, both aspects of the question have been controversial in the contemporary debate over national security.

During the 2000 campaign, the Bush team argued that the Clinton administration had overextended the armed forces through numerous deployments in places of dubious importance to the United States. One consequence of placing such heavy demands on military resources meant the neglect of investment in force modernization, a problem the Bush administration promised to remedy. In addition, placing so many U.S. forces in faraway deployments was said to affect morale negatively, thus lowering the likelihood of reenlistment.

Based on this assessment, the Bush administration proposed remedies during its first year in office that included both increases in defense expenditures and reductions in overseas deployments. These actions reflected an assessment of the international environment that downplayed the threats to American interests posed by vexatious internal wars of the type that had caused the Clinton administration to deploy troops in a number of countries. Simultaneously, Bush emphasized the future threat of exotic capabilities wielded by the so-called rogue states (or what are sometimes euphemistically referred to as "states of concern"). He also predicted that such a reorientation would make military service more attractive and thus help reverse a trend toward recruitment shortfalls that emerged in the latter 1990s.

Both positions were controversial and, in one case, reversible. Disagreement about the international threat assessment came from two basic concerns. Although there was little disagreement about the need to invest in force modernization, there was concern about the specifics of what needed procuring: Does the air force, for instance, really need a new manned fighter jet, the F-22, when the United States already possesses the most advanced fighters in the world and when many analysts believe the next generation of fighters will be unmanned drone aircraft (essentially cruise missiles)? Since most of the proposed items in the modernization package represented technologically sophisticated weapons systems associated with the revolution in military affairs (RMA), this raised the implicit assumption that such weapons would be needed against equally sophisticated opponents—a proposition at odds with most threat assessments (including the administration's own QDR), which projected most threats coming from reasonably primitive Second Tier states for the fore-seeable future. The administration raised these concerns even more with its obstinate insistence on missile defenses.

The other concern was with the pace of deployments during the Clinton years in places such as Kosovo and Haiti. The Bush administration argued that forces were overextended, harming morale due to long separations from families, and that the deployments did not advance important American interests. Although they backed away from campaign suggestions to withdraw American troops from Kosovo, they did promise to retard future deployments in similar situations. As the administration committed itself to widening its campaign against terrorism to new frontiers such as the Philippines, Georgia, and Yemen, however, calls for decreased overseas deployments were quietly shelved.

What the force will look like and where it will be used has an obvious linkage to manpower recruitment and retention. During the economic good times of the 1990s, the military had a difficult time competing with the civilian economy for recruits and keeping members in uniform through reenlistment. The military had to compete with a robust economy in which there were more jobs than there were entry-level workers to fill them and in which increasing percentages of eighteen-year-olds were going on to college rather than taking jobs or joining the armed forces. At the same time, skilled members of the armed forces (airplane mechanics, for instance) were succumbing to the temptations of higher pay for their skills in the civilian economy by failing to reenlist. Without menacing threats to create patriotic incentives to enlist and with deficient investments in equipment to promote reenlistment, the result was a manpower problem.

This problem burst on the public scene in 1998, when the U.S. Army, Navy, and Air Force all experienced manpower "shortfalls," largely due to insufficient enlistments. Although the problem had occurred periodically for the army (especially in the actual fighting force, the so-called combat arms), it was most unusual for the navy and air force. The problem continued through 2000, with the services attempting expedient solutions such as new advertising campaigns ("The Army of One") to try to appeal to the current generation of potential soldiers, sailors, airmen, and marines.

The situation improved in 2001, when each of the services reported that it had met its manpower goals for the year. The conditioning factor on enthusiasm for this turn of events was tempered by the explanation of why it occurred. The services credited the reversal to improved recruiting techniques and means to retain members of the force. As an example of the latter, the navy—which has some of the most severe retention problems because of extended tours at sea—began equipping all of its ships with readily available e-mail for all members of crews, to facilitate their ability to communicate with loved ones on shore.

Another explanation was the state of the American economy. It has long been an accepted fact that military service is more attractive in times of economic slowdown and recession, when there are fewer jobs at the entry level and more layoffs of workers with the least seniority—in other words, workers in the age brackets from which the military also draws. As the economy slowed in 2001, recruiting figures predictably improved. In addition, the patriotically motivated increase in enlistment after September 11, 2001, temporarily helped alleviate the problem. When the economy improves, however, the problem may well resurface.

The manpower problem thus has both international and domestic political roots. Internationally, the assessment of the threat leads to the use (or nonuse) of military forces more or less widely, with greater or lesser strain on military capability and consequent, if not altogether predictable, results. The Bush claims that deployments lowered morale and caused reenlistment drops were contradicted in 1999, when a study revealed that reenlistment rates were higher for forces serving in Kosovo than anywhere else in the army. The reason stated by soldiers was that their deployment gave them the opportunity to apply their training in an atmosphere where they were actually helping people, rather than just engaging in exercises. High levels of satisfaction have also been reported among personnel serving in Afghanistan. On the other hand, deployment of over one-half of the Army in Iraq in 2003 created problems of force rotation, with potential morale and retention effects. Domestically, the state of the economy affects the ability to recruit and retain military members, as does the ability of the government to provide attractive working conditions and a sense of urgency of mission to motivate people to make the sacrifices inherent in military service.

Military Reform and the QDR

In an atmosphere of constrained resources, the efficiency with which the military operates will always be part of their effectiveness. At times when the international environment is changing and the response to that environment is also undergoing change, the demand to improve military performance will naturally be an important factor in the amount and the nature of support the military gets to perform the tasks placed before it. These three factors—the environment (the threat), the nature and adequacy of capabilities, and responses to demands—were heated elements in the debate symbolized in the QDR that was produced in 2001.

An historical note is necessary. The effort to reform the military in the name of greater military efficiency—including budgetary efficiency—is by no means a product of the QDR process begun with the first document in 1997. In the modern era, the process dates back to the formative period of the Cold War defense effort. In 1948, James Forrestal, a retired admiral who was the first secretary of defense, sent the leadership of the services to Key West, Florida, to engage in a process of role and mission clarification that would remove the sources of redundancy, noncooperation, and inefficiency that had been noted during World War II. The resulting Key West agreement was the first modern attempt at military reform by the military itself, and it became the prototype of future efforts.

At Key West, the services divided up roles and missions, giving primary responsibility to one service or another, even forbidding services to engage in certain kinds of activities (the army, for instance, was not allowed to have fixed-wing warplanes). The process was dominated by the services' desire to protect their own prerogatives, even at the expense of the cooperation they were supposed to attain. As inherently

Challenge!

Military Service after September 11, 2001

No American who was not at least eighteen years old on January 1, 1972, has ever been subject to the possibility of involuntary conscription into the U.S. armed forces. One of the consequences of that condition—the result of negative reactions to the Vietnam War—is that few young Americans have had to give serious thought to the prospect of military service. Since exemption from involuntary service now spans two generations, this means that relatively few Americans in what used to be the "draft-eligible" age pool of eighteen to twenty-six years old even have fathers who served voluntarily or involuntarily.

The result has been that a military career—or service to the country—is chosen by progressively fewer Americans on patriotic or other grounds. Whether this is bad or good is a matter of individual conviction.

The attacks on the World Trade Center and Pentagon produced an increased interest in enlistment in the armed forces from young men and women across the board, including college students, who were heretofore among the least likely to enlist. By 2002, however, this appeared to have been a temporary reaction—enlistments by college students were not up appreciably.

How did you react to the terrorist attacks? Before the attacks, had military service seriously occurred to you? If it had, what did you conclude about joining one of the services? Was your attitude changed by the terrorist attacks? More specifically, did your view change enough that you gave more serious consideration to the service than before?

conservative institutions resistant to change, the services resisted reform and produced documents that contained as little change as possible. This set the precedent for the future.

The example of military aviation may help illustrate the dynamic of resistance to reform. In a totally rationalized, efficient system, it would seem reasonable to concentrate the functions of heavier-than-air flight to a minimum number of organizations. Instead, each branch of the American military services has its own air assets, which means that the United States effectively possesses four air forces. Although this is rationalized on the grounds of planned redundancy and discrete air missions, the well-publicized results are less than efficient.

Much of this arrangement, negotiated at Key West, reflected practices that had evolved during World War II and that the services were anxious to protect. The lead air force was the Army Air Corps, which became the U.S. Air Force and was given primary responsibility for air warfare (air-to-air combat and bombing). At the same time, World War II had seen the demise of the battleship as the main naval weapon and its replacement by the aircraft carrier. Thus, the navy had its own air force aboard the carriers for engaging in air combat with other ships. (This function was expanded to using carrier-based aircraft against land-based targets, in competition with the air force, and a land-based naval force to engage in reconnaissance and antisubmarine attacks along the coastline.) The marines had developed a small air wing for the purpose of close air support of ground operations, a function they were unwilling to give up and the air force was willing to give them. Thus, Key West produced three air forces.

The only major military service without an air force at the conclusion of Key West was the army. According to the agreement, the army could keep a small force of unarmed, fixed-wing aircraft for transportation purposes, but only with the stipulation that the fleet could not be armed or engage in combat. This prohibition was overcome in the 1950s and 1960s, when the Army semisurreptitiously began the transformation of helicopters from medical evacuation and reconnaissance aircraft (the functions they provided in Korea) to armed air cavalry (the function they carried out in Vietnam). Thus, by the middle 1960s, each military service had its own combat air force (the U.S. Coast Guard also has air assets but is not technically a military service, since it is not housed in the Defense Department).

Situations such as the four air forces and the resistance of the armed forces to other forms of change have always been vexatious to some, including many members of Congress who have the responsibility to oversee and fund defense efforts. In addition, there has also been the suspicion among some members that the armed forces and the DOD are less than innovative in how they approach the role of managing the military force. In the early 1980s, a group of about 100 senators and representatives (including such prominent "defense intellectuals" as Senator Sam Nunn, Senator William Cohen—later SECDEF—and Senator Gary Hart) founded the Defense Reform Movement, intent on promoting change. One outcome was the Goldwater-Nichols Defense Reorganization Act of 1986 (see Amplification 7.3), which shuffled power in the Pentagon. The Congress has also mandated that the president produce annually a document, *The National Security Strategy of the United States*. The reason for this requirement was the widely held belief that the country had no national defense strategy.

This same sentiment activated the QDR process, which requires the DOD to report every four years on the state of the military threat to the United States and on how the military establishment proposes to deal with the threat. Among other things, the report is supposed to provide major guidance in the procurement of military forces to blunt the threats it identifies.

The first QDR, produced in 1997, was a very conservative document that did not recommend enormous change. Its threat assessment was that the United States lacked a "peer competitor"—a truly threatening enemy—and that this condition would continue until at least 2010. Thus, there was no pressing need for reform of ongoing force structure or organization. At the time, many observers maintained that the document has a conservative tone because the staff that prepared it was dominated by retired officers who were mostly intent on protecting their services from unwanted reform.

The process for the second QDR in 2001 was different in two fundamental ways. First, it occurred at a time when all the services proposed major procurement upgrades—so-called big-ticket expenditures. The navy, air force, and marines, for instance, all favored major new aircraft programs, and the army was intent on upgrad-

Amplification 7.3

THE GOLDWATER-NICHOLS ACT

The Goldwater-Nichols Defense Reorganization Act of 1986 (named after its Republican cosponsors, Senator Barry Goldwater of Arizona and Representative Bill Nichols of Alabama) was a major attempt to reform policies and procedures within the Defense Department that the Senate had concluded the armed services would not remedy on their own. The bill was drafted and passed in a post-Vietnam atmosphere wherein the conclusion was that the military had not performed well, that many of its problems were structural, and that it was incapable of reforming itself.

The act had several noteworthy provisions. The first was to strengthen the Joint Chiefs of Staff and its chairman. The chairman (or CJCS) was designated as the chief military advisor to the president, the secretary of defense, and the National Security Council. The purpose was to unify advice to the executive and to restrain the individual services from appealing to the president on parochial service grounds. The entire Joint Staff was also placed under the direct supervision of the CJCS, rather than their individual services. Power within the defense area was further redistributed by adding to the responsibilities of the commanders of the unified and specified commands in areas such as budget requests, rather than funneling such requests through the various service departments. In addition, the act created a so-called procurement czar to oversee weapons acquisition and recommended an independent unified command for special forces (which had been the orphan child of the army). The effects were to move power and authority away from the individual services and toward cooperative interservice bases, a process now known in the armed forces as "jointness."

ing its main battle tank and field artillery piece (the Crusader cannon), among other things. Second, the process was dominated by the Office of the Secretary of Defense (OSD) and Secretary Rumsfeld to the point that the services complained—first privately, then publicly—that they had been effectively excluded from it. Since Rumsfeld and the Joint Chiefs of Staff were at poorly disguised odds over the missile defense proposal at that point, the process became more controversial and contentious.

This process was further complicated by the tragic bombings of the World Trade Center towers and the Pentagon on September 11, 2001. The initial confusion and response to this massive assault on the United States by foreign terrorists made the deadline date for the QDR of September 30, 2001, seem far less compelling than it had previously, and it simultaneously raised questions about both the appropriateness of the previous threat assessment and the relevance of the force modernization and programmatic suggestions that it contained. The country's focus quite naturally shifted to how to prevent a recurrence of such an act, which had demonstrated that American soil was significantly vulnerable to attack for the first time since the British attempted to burn down the country's capital in 1814.

The QDR was released on schedule and proposed some fairly thorough philosophical changes in how the country would view and respond to threats in the future. Systematic applications of these changes probably would lead to some fairly sweeping alterations in service-proposed modernization plans. Any such analysis and implication was drowned out by the response to the terrorist attacks and the "war"-driven increases in defense spending that embraced the military's basic vision of modernization. The actual content of the QDR recommendations is discussed in Chapter 8 in the context of conventional force modernization.

CONCLUSIONS: THE ENVIRONMENT SINCE SEPTEMBER 11, 2001

Our ways of thinking about and dealing with the environment were changed drastically by the events of September 11, 2001. Suddenly, a mostly benign and tranquil environment was revealed to have a very dark and hostile side, which had heretofore been only hinted at in the public debate. Before the attacks on major symbols of American military and financial power, the only instances of foreign-inspired and foreign-committed acts had been small and relatively primitive. The most notable example, ironically, was the 1993 attack on the World Trade Center towers by a single truck laden with explosives, which killed six people. The scale of the 2001 attacks and the enormous loss of life revealed a level and quality of vulnerability that few Americans had imagined in their worst nightmares. The body politic was thrown into convulsion about how it could have happened, how it could be avoided in the future, and how to punish those behind the atrocity.

The attacks indirectly reopened the old debate between the internationalists and the isolationists and neo-conservative unilateralists. The attacks on American soil meant that the United States joined a considerable list of countries that had proved to be victims of terrorism, and the internationalists quickly concluded that the only appropriate response was to abandon the unilateralist tendency and to plunge enthusiastically into an increasingly international effort to control terrorism. Others saw the attacks as evidence of what happens when the United States exposes itself too much to a hostile world and suggested a more neoisolationist approach and a more conscious retention of the options for unilateral action. The neo-conservatives saw it as an opportunity to press their regime-changing agenda. An arena for this debate was the openness of American borders and the permissiveness of the U.S. government in allowing foreigners into the country with allegedly inadequate scrutiny of their backgrounds.

The shock of the attacks and the ambiguity about appropriate responses confused the debate, raising many doubts but few obvious solutions. The conventional debate was particularly muddied. National security planning traditionally has concentrated on dealing with the concrete, conventional military threats posed by other sovereign states or groups within states. Although the importance of those threats and, hence, what we might do to counter them was tinged by a certain level of implausibility, at least the discussions could proceed within a common frame of reference that all parties understood.

   The massive attacks by nonstate actors engaging in the most unimaginable forms of "warfare" did not fit within standard categories. Shadowy private terrorist organizations that do not represent states and that have small, elusive organizations do not lend themselves to conventional military responses. The idea of using commercial aircraft heavily laden with jet fuel essentially as cruise missiles to attack urban, civilian targets had no precedent within military doctrine or practice and could only be found in escapist fiction. (Tom Clancy's *Badge of Honor* involves using an airliner to attack the Capitol.) How does one define such a threat? Moreover, how does one develop forces and capabilities that can counter and negate this kind of problem? The answers were and are not clear, but it became evident that one had to move beyond conventional thinking to formulate responses.

SELECTED BIBLIOGRAPHY

Crabb, Cecil V. Jr., and Pat Holt. *Invitation to Struggle: Congress, the President, and Foreign Policy*, 2nd ed. Washington, DC: CQ Press, 1984.

Elliott, Michael. "They Had a Plan." *Time*, August 4, 2002 (electronic edition).

Friedman, Thomas L. *The Lexus and the Olive Tree: Understanding Globalization*. New York: Farrar, Straus & Giroux, 1999.

Hilsman, Roger. *The Politics of Policy Making in Defense and Foreign Affairs: Conceptual Models and Bureaucratic Politics*, 3rd ed. Englewood Cliffs, NJ: Prentice-Hall, 1993.

Inderfurth, Karl F., and Loch Johnson. *Decisions of the Highest Order: Perspectives on the National Security Council*. Belmont, CA: Brooks-Cole, 1988.

Kaplan, Robert D. *The Coming Anarchy: Shattering the Dreams of the Post–Cold War World*. New York: Random House, 2000.

Keohane, Robert O., and Joseph S. Nye Jr. *Power and Interdependence*, 2nd ed. Glenview, IL: Scott Foresman/Little Brown, 1989.

Mitrany, David. *Toward a Working Peace System*. London: Royal Institute of International Affairs, 1943.

"Mr. Order Meets Mr. Chaos." *Foreign Policy*. May/June 2001, 50–61.

Pettis, Michael. "Will Globalization Go Bankrupt?" *Foreign Policy*, September/October 2001, 52–59.

Rosati, Jerel A. *The Politics of United States Foreign Policy*. New York: Harcourt Brace Jovanovich, 1993.

Snow, Donald M., and Eugene Brown. *United States Foreign Policy: Politics Beyond the Water's Edge*. New York: St. Martin's Press, 2000.

8

Traditional Military Problems

The thinking and planning for large-scale war between armed forces as they were developed for and fought in World War II—conventional forces for symmetrical warfare—predate and postdate September 11, 2001. The traditional purposes for which these forces were developed largely disappeared with the end of the Cold War, and only the United States retains a robust traditional capability that it proposes to augment through force modernization. At the same time, critics say these large, European-style forces are anachronisms in a world of shadowy asymmetrical threats. Before assessing these criticisms, it is necessary to describe traditional forces and missions—first nuclear forces and then conventional forces. The chapter concludes with some assessment of the continuing relevance of these forces.

Military planning did not begin on September 11, 2001, and most of that planning has not changed noticeably since. That second fault line, however, makes it easy to ignore or underplay the traditional purposes for which the United States has maintained armed forces in the past and will probably plan to use them again in the future.

What do we mean when we refer to traditional problems and conventional forces and solutions? Basically, we are describing the structure of the American armed forces in the European style—a structure that evolved through the formative period of the American military experience and congealed in World War II. Armies, navies, and air forces armed with nuclear and nonnuclear (conventional) weapons are designed to confront and defeat similarly armed and organized opponents in symmetrical warfare. These forces remain the backbone of American capabilities. A major issue on which they must be measured is their relevance in a world of asymmetrical threats. This chapter describes those forces; Chapter 9 assesses their relevance.

Why is this description important? There are four reasons. First, these forces and their uses have been important in the past. Second, they are still major components of the package of forces with which the United States confronts the world, and they are the components military planners best understand and are most comfortable with. Third, modernizing and enhancing the capabilities they represent is a major part of the additional defense expenditures proposed by the current administration. Finally, it may be necessary to use these forces again in the future against some currently unforeseen (or foreseen) foe. Any of these reasons would be sufficient to warrant a review and analysis of the traditional security components of national security; collectively, these reasons are compelling. These forces are the legacy of the highly geopolitical Cold War world.

In this chapter, we will examine the two major functions of armed forces during the Cold War competition with the Soviet Union and its Communist allies: thermonuclear forces and the strategies governing their potential use, and so-called conventional armed forces. Both capabilities were developed explicitly for a Cold War confrontation and environment that no longer exists, but the capabilities and plans for their use remain essentially intact today and greatly influence the current national security debate. Moreover, these forces frame what the United States can and cannot do militarily in the world, especially in the most militarily stressful situations we may face. They are quintessentially military capabilities in a world where there are few of the traditional threats for which they were originally devised; thus, they may have only marginal applications to contemporary problems.

The relevance of these traditional uses of armed force was a matter of debate before September 11, 2001. The series of events set in motion by the tragedies of that day quickly added the semimilitary nature of the terror to the menu and made us aware of an entirely different kind of war, which a few analysts had been predicting for a decade or more but which by and large had been downplayed within the national security community. The United States faced a new national security challenge that apparently could not easily be "fixed" using traditional military means, and new descriptors began to enter our vocabulary. Is this a new kind of war? Are traditional approaches adequate to defeat it?

In this chapter, we will address these questions by examining the traditional problems of national security sequentially. We will begin with nuclear forces and deterrence, the historically unique military problem of the Cold War. The possibilities of nuclear Armageddon, however remote, were of such enormous potential consequence as to receive the highest priority in defense planning and thinking.

The other side of the traditional balance is the continuing utility of conventional (or nonnuclear) forces. The Cold War's military competition featured very robust nonnuclear forces—large, heavily equipped armies; highly capable surface, subsurface, and aerial navies; and sophisticated bomber and fighter-based air forces—developed to deter and, if necessary, fight the "central battle" in Europe. The preparations undertaken came from a vision of an even larger and bloodier reprise of World War II. Of the two massive forces that conducted that competition, only American forces remain as large and are still configured with the kinds of capabilities the Cold War dictated.

NUCLEAR FORCES AND DETERRENCE

The nuclear age was formally born in the predawn hours of July 16, 1945, when the first atomic explosion lighted the skies around ground zero at the Trinity site at White Sands, New Mexico. The light from the explosion could be seen as far away as Albuquerque, New Mexico, a hundred miles or so away. Robert Oppenheimer, the physicist considered the "father" of the atomic bomb, was so overwhelmed by the event that he said later, "There floated through my mind a line from Bhagavad-Gita, 'I am become death, the shatterer of worlds.'" General Lesley Grove, the military commander of the Manhattan Project, which produced the bomb, intoned "This is the end of traditional warfare" as he viewed the explosion. His view was overstated, of course, and traditional warfare continued despite this monumental change in destructive capability. The clear difference, however, is that wars are now conducted under the shadow of the mushroom-shaped cloud, especially when nuclear-capable states are involved.

We are no longer consumed by the horror nuclear weapons represent, but some understanding of them remains important. We will thus begin by examining the evolution of the nuclear balance by looking at a series of seminal events that produced the capabilities that defined the Cold War nuclear balance. We will then turn to the nature of the competition that evolved between the superpowers, including how the relationship was conceptualized by the United States and how it evolved over time. We will then move to current issues that are residues of that competition.

This examination may have a broader importance in the contemporary context. In some important ways, nuclear weapons hung over the heads of the Cold War generation in ways similar to how the threat of terrorism hangs over us today. Nuclear weapons and the prospects of nuclear war frightened us and created the same sense of desperation and fatalism for the generations of the 1950s and 1960s that the fear of renewed terrorist attacks produces for contemporary Americans. In the 1950s and 1960s, we learned how to think about and control the problem and to get on with our lives without excessive morbidity about our futures. How we learned not to "love the bomb" (from the subtitle of the motion picture *Dr. Strangelove*) but to live with it may be a parable for our times.

Seminal Events of the Nuclear Age

The nuclear age did not burst upon us suddenly at White Sands. Scientific research into nuclear physics went back nearly a century through more-or-less independent investigations in Europe and North America. The impending clouds of World War II and intelligence reports that Nazi Germany was attempting to harness and weaponize nuclear physics alarmed Albert Einstein to the extent that he wrote a letter to President Franklin D. Roosevelt warning of the potential problem such weapons could pose in the hands of the Nazis. Roosevelt's response was to commission the Manhattan Project, which began the crash program that produced nuclear bombs shortly before the end of the war.

The first operational atomic bombs were used against Hiroshima and Nagasaki, Japan, on August 6 and 9, 1945, to shorten the war in the Pacific by forcing Japanese capitulation short of an anticipated bloody invasion of the Japanese home islands. (This vision was made especially vivid by the spirited Japanese defense of Okinawa which included Japanese soldiers wrapping themselves with explosives and committing suicide by blowing themselves up.) When the second bomb exploded, the American arsenal was temporarily exhausted; for the last time, the world had no nuclear weapons. In the next quarter-century, the nuclear world evolved from those primitive days through the impact of a series of nuclear events. Each of these events had the effect of making the nuclear balance more lethal and raising the potential stakes in a nuclear war.

The Atomic (Fission) Bomb.   The successful conclusion of the Manhattan Project was *the* seminal event of the nuclear age, since none of the other sophistications would have been possible without this first step. When the first atomic device was detonated, none of the participants had anticipated its enormity, and they were all taken aback at what they witnessed. In retrospect, however, it was only the tip of the iceberg of scientific discovery.

The original atomic bomb was what is known as a fission device: The basic physical reaction that makes the bomb explode and produce its deadly effects occurs through the breaking apart (or fission) of atoms of certain elements, in this case unstable isotopes of uranium. Fission weapons produce four deadly effects. The first is intense heat that comes from the release of energy from the split atoms and manifests itself in the ignition of fires and the production of a fireball and a firestorm. The second effect is blast overpressure, a massive change in atmospheric pressure radiating out from the explosion that creates enormous winds that topple buildings and anything else in the way. In addition, the explosion produces both prompt and residual forms of radiation. *Prompt radiation* is the release of deadly beta particles and gamma rays from the explosion itself, which kills or debilitates anyone directly exposed to the stem of the explosion but disappears when the explosion ends. *Residual radiation* (or fallout) is the residues of the atoms that have been split; many of these are highly radioactive, with very long half-lives, and can have deadly effects for long periods of time.

The atomic bomb represented a quantitative change in the deadliness of war. The delivery of an atomic bomb over a target could produce deadly effects that previously could have been produced only by literally hundreds or thousands of attacks by conventional bombardment. The campaigns against Dresden, Germany, and Tokyo with incendiary bombs had required many sorties, and the characteristics of those bombs were insufficient to create an undeniably qualitative change in warfare.

The Hydrogen (Fission-Fusion) Bomb.   The second major event was the successful development of a qualitatively larger form of nuclear explosive, the fission-fusion or hydrogen bomb. Known as the "Super" at the time because of its orders-of-magnitude increase in deadly effect, a prototype of the hydrogen bomb was successfully tested by the United States in 1952. The Soviet Union followed suit a year later. The nuclear arms race was escalated qualitatively in the process.

As the name implies, the physical reaction involved in this new form of nuclear explosion involves two steps—the explosion of a small fission "trigger" to induce the second step, which is fusion. This reaction involves the fusion of atoms of heavy hydrogen (deuterium or tritium), which produces the release of an enormous amount of energy, far in excess to that possible with a fission reaction.

The effects of a thermonuclear explosion are awesome. Fission bombs produced yields that were the equivalent of thousands of tons (kilotons) of TNT; fission-fusion devices produced explosions with destructive effects measured in *millions* of tons (megatons, or MT) of TNT. During the Cold War, the Soviet Union was reported to have tested a fission-fusion device that produced an 85 MT blast.

The entry of thermonuclear bombs into the arsenals of the two sides altered the calculus of nuclear weapons and their use in two ways. First, it altered the assessment of survivability in a nuclear war. A society might endure grievous damage as the result of an attack with atomic bombs, but it could reasonably anticipate surviving such an attack. The same attack with thermonuclear bombs—a quantum leap in destructive capability—meant that the new weapons represented a *qualitative*, rather than a quantitative, increase in the deadliness of war.

A parallel development amplified this distinction. During the early 1950s, scientists achieved considerable success in designing bombs that were more compact and much lighter than the Hiroshima and Nagasaki prototypes. As long as the delivery platform for nuclear weapons remained the airplane, this change did not represent a fundamental influence. When a means of delivering these weapons more efficiently was perfected that could be mated with lighter bombs, however, the change was profound.

The Intercontinental Ballistic Missile (ICBM).   The effort to weaponize rocketry began in the period between the world wars, when the first rockets were developed and tested in Germany and the United States, among other places. In World War II, the first prototypes, the V-2 "buzz bombs" were used against Great Britain in a desperate act by the Germans to break British will. These early designs were so grossly inaccurate as to have little impact on the war, and rockets were considered little more than terrorist weapons. By the 1950s, advances in rocketry allowed nuclear weapons to be transported over intercontinental ranges and to land close enough to their targets to destroy them.

The results of these advances fundamentally altered the impact of nuclear weapons on war more than any other of the other seminal events. The reasons were (and are) profound and cumulative. The thermonuclear bomb had removed the likelihood of surviving a nuclear war if a large number of these devices were used. The ICBM produced the perfect delivery device for such weapons, since there was (and arguably still is) *no known defense capable of defending against a nuclear rocket attack*. The result is total societal vulnerability to nuclear devastation; and when both sides have this offensive capability, the condition is known as *mutual societal vulnerability*. This description of human existence in a nuclear-armed world persists to this day.

Recognition of societal vulnerability profoundly changed our thinking about the existence of nuclear weapons without workable, reliable defenses against nuclear attack (discussed later); the only way to avoid being destroyed by a nuclear attack was to ensure that such an attack never occurred. The term *nuclear deterrence* suddenly became a matter of central concern to decision makers and strategists. The purpose of deterrence is to dissuade someone from doing something harmful to you—in this case, our convincing the Soviet Union and their convincing us not to attack one another with nuclear weapons.

The Multiple Independently Targetable Reentry Vehicle (MIRV).   The fourth development was a major increase in the deadliness and extensiveness of nuclear arsenals—the perfection of a means to dispense more than one nuclear bomb (or warhead) from the tip of a single rocket. This military capability was achieved by the United States in 1970, when it began to add MIRV capability to its arsenal; the same feat was achieved by the Soviet Union in 1975.

The MIRV had two major effects on the nuclear equation. The first was to multiply the size of nuclear arsenals without increasing the number of nuclear missiles within those arsenals, a phenomenon known as "fractionation." This meant that a single rocket's capacity could be increased by the number of additional warheads that the MIRV permitted to be added (or fractionated). The MIRVing of superpower arsenals had a second, anomalous effect. During the 1970s, arms control negotiations aimed at reducing the likelihood of nuclear war between the superpowers were particularly active, and one of their purposes was to place limits on the size and capabilities of the two offensive arsenals. The MIRVs, however, had been excluded from those discussions by the Soviets (who lagged in the technology and did not want to negotiate away their chance to catch up), and the process of converting arsenals to MIRV status meant that the number of warheads actually increased greatly during the decade. By the end of the 1970s, nuclear arsenal sizes approached the maximum size they would achieve, with both sides confronting one another with weapons inventories of more than 10,000 warheads aimed at one another. The MIRV was the reason.

Ballistic Missile Defense (BMD).   The fifth seminal event—defenses against missile attacks—is one that has not yet occurred. It is a high priority of the Bush administration, however, and could, in certain circumstances, alter the nuclear calculus as much as the others. The current round of debate about missile defenses is nothing new. In fact, investigation of how to try to destroy incoming ballistic missiles proceeded parallel to the development of offensive applications of rocketry, and all the theoretical problems of missile defense had been solved before the first ICBM was launched in 1957. The problem has not been the concept; the difficulty has been, and continues to be, execution of the proposed mission.

Missile defense has always had an instinctive appeal, but the idea has also been plagued by some level of disreputability. The appeal is clear: Since deterrence can fail at some time, we would all like to have some means to protect ourselves from the breakdown of deterrence and the ravages of nuclear attack. To some, missile defenses offer a supplement to deterrence; to others, BMD is an alternative. The disreputability of missile defense mostly attaches to the ability to achieve a workable, effective defense at an acceptable cost. When the subject first came up in the public debate in the 1960 presidential campaign, John F. Kennedy drew the analogy of the problem of missile defense as that of trying "to shoot a bullet with another bullet." Whether the analogy is apt or not is a matter of debate, but it is a description that has largely stuck in the popular mind.

Why would the development of effective defenses represent a seminal event in the nuclear age? The answer begins by defining "effective" in this context. In an absolute sense, an effective system should be capable of intercepting and destroying all of an incoming nuclear missile attack, with great certainty in advance of the attack that the system will perform as expected. This is a very exacting and difficult criterion to achieve. The need to destroy all of the attack is imposed because of the enormous destruction that could be caused if only a small portion of the attack evaded the defenses. During the Cold War, for instance, a 90 percent effective defense would have meant that about 1,000 warheads would have gotten through to their targets in an all-out Soviet or American launch against the other, with devastating effect.

A truly effective, reliable defense would remove dependence on deterrence as the only way to prevent the ravages of nuclear war. Rather than relying on the threat of robust retaliation after absorbing an attack (the basic threat under theories of deterrence as they have been practiced), a defensive system that worked could render such an attack ineffective and futile and make nuclear weapons "impotent and obsolete," in Ronald Reagan's depiction of the purpose of his Strategic Defense Initiative. A truly effective defense would rank with the ICBM in importance in nuclear evolution.

The Nature of the Competition

Conceptualizations of the nuclear problem changed during the course of the Cold War. The major variables were two interrelated factors: the size and deadliness of the superpower arsenals and the strategies of deterrence and potential use on which the thinking about these weapons was based.

The Evolution of Arsenals.   The deadliness and sophistication of nuclear arsenals increased greatly in the forty years or so of active competition, aided by the seminal events already discussed. The two sides built ever more sophisticated arsenals that were intended to counter one another's evolving deadly capability. In calculating what needed to be countered on the other side, the method was the estimation of adversary *capabilities* (the size and nature of the other side's arsenal) and *intentions* (the presumed reasons the adversary possessed those capabilities and what it intended to do with them). The problem was that each side knew a great deal more about the other's capabilities than about its intentions. Thanks to satellite imaging, for instance, it was impossible to hide the launching of a ballistic missile submarine; thus each side knew how many of these vessels the other side had. Knowing *why* the adversaries had the numbers of weapons they did was a different matter, since intentions are mental constructs that cannot be directly observed and thus had to be estimated.

The need to guess at intentions created *worst-case analysis* as the primary method of calculating why and for what purposes the enemy built the weapons capabilities it did. In this form of analysis, the array of possible intentions for a weapons decision was considered, and the most malevolent possibility (the worst case) was selected as that which was most likely and consequently needed to be countered. The result, of course, was a tendency toward the strongest possible reaction, which, in turn, accelerated the arms race as one side reacted to the actions of the other (something known as the *action–reaction phenomenon*).

Much of the competition was driven by technology. As already noted, it was technological invention that gradually made nuclear weapons more powerful (the atomic to hydrogen bomb progression) and overall arsenals larger and more indefensible (the ICBM and the MIRV). These same technological processes also gave those arsenals their ultimate force characteristics.

As time went by, nuclear weapons became deliverable in three different ways: by bomber aircraft, by land-based ICBMs, and by submarine-launched ballistic missiles (SLBMs). The Soviet Union never developed a real intercontinental bomber capability, however, which meant that the Soviets had basically two ways to attack the United States, while the United States had three means to attack Soviet territory.

The three-pronged mode by which the United States could launch an attack (or counterattack) became known as the TRIAD. Each "leg" of the TRIAD had advantages and disadvantages. The bomber (or air-breathing) leg carried large bomb loads that could be recallable during the course of a mission; their disadvantage was their vulnerability to being shot down by Soviet anti-aircraft defenses. ICBMs could carry heavy loads against which there were no effective defenses; their principal disadvantage was that they were located in known, fixed locations that could be targeted for preemptive attack by Soviet weapons. SLBMs evolved as the backbone of the arsenal because of the large number of warheads they could carry and their invulnerability to attack as they patrolled beneath the world's oceans. However, they were occasionally impossible to communicate with when submerged, and their warheads were relatively more inaccurate and smaller than weapons from the other legs.

The advertised virtue of the TRIAD was its planned redundancy. The practice of "cross-targeting" meant that every major target in the Soviet Union had a weapon from each leg aimed at it, on the assumption that at least one of the attacking methods would succeed, thereby guaranteeing the success of the mission. If more than one attacking method succeeded, the target would be pulverized more than once—making "the rubble bounce," as the British statesman Sir Winston Churchill said at the time. This redundancy also required a very large number of weapons to convince the adversary that if it started a nuclear war, it was effectively committing suicide by inviting an overwhelmingly deadly retaliation.

Theories of Deterrence

As the nuclear balance evolved, two broad conceptualizations of deterrence emerged to dominate defense theorizing and planning in the United States, including the development and deployment of nuclear arsenals. Both positions about nuclear weapons were first articulated in two works published in 1946, one very famous

(Bernard Brodie's *The Absolute Weapon*) and one not so well known (William Liscum Borden's *There Will Be No Time*).

These formulations sound strange, even macabre or bizarre, when taken out of the context of the times. Brodie's formulation evolved to the strategy of *assured destruction*, which a detractor modified by putting the word *mutual* in front of it to produce the acronym MAD. Borden's position evolved to a strategy known as limited nuclear options (LNOs) or countervailance; a detractor gave its adherents the title *nuclear utilization theorists*, or NUTS. The intellectual debate about what best deterred a nuclear attack thus became a dialogue between those who were MAD and those who were NUTS.

Assured Destruction.   The title of Brodie's book gave its thesis away. According to Brodie and his associates at Yale University who collaborated on *The Absolute Weapon*, nuclear weapons fundamentally changed the nature and calculation of war. The destructiveness of those weapons was so great that, in Brodie's opinion (which closely resembled that of General Grove, discussed earlier), conventional war—which could escalate to nuclear war—was now obsolete. Thus, the only reason states could have for maintaining military forces (including nuclear weapons) was to avoid their being used against them—in other words, deterrence. Borden disagreed, arguing that nuclear weapons were weapons, after all, and that weapons are eventually used. From this premise, Borden argued that the secret was to be sure these weapons were used only against military targets, thereby limiting their horror. Thus, the debate over the usability of nuclear weapons was joined, but not resolved, in 1946.

Much of the debate lay fallow for over a decade. The event that enlivened the question of deterrence was the successful testing and deployment of ICBMs in the latter 1950s. Since the only way to guarantee not being killed in a nuclear war when ICBMs were present was to make certain that a nuclear war did not occur, the question became: What kind of nuclear strategy best assures the avoidance of nuclear hostilities?

The Brodie position, the first answer to dominate the debate, was articulated in the early 1960s as assured destruction. The first premise of the strategy, which came directly from Brodie himself, was that all sides would lose in any nuclear war, which meant that only war avoidance was acceptable. The question was how best to assure that no one could ever miscalculate the possibility of succeeding in a nuclear war and thus decide to start one. The answer was the assured destruction threat.

The basic assured destruction threat was that any Soviet nuclear attack would be met by a fierce and destructive American retaliation that would destroy the Soviet Union and rob it of any possible calculation that it had "won" anything. ICBMs guaranteed the condition of mutual societal vulnerability under which such a retaliation would occur against an initial attacker; the upshot was that launching a nuclear strike became the equivalent of committing national suicide.

The implementation and implications of assured destruction are ghoulish, and they created a lively opposition. In order to convince the Soviets of the suicidal nature of an attack, the strategy featured *countervalue targeting* by American retaliatory forces against Soviet targets. This antiseptic term means aiming weapons at the things people value most—notably, their lives and the conditions that make life livable. The prototypical countervalue target is an urban complex, the larger the better, since the purpose is to convince the adversary's leadership and population that they will die for attacking the United States.

As the critics were quick to point out, this strategy amounts to no more than a promise to commit genocide in response to an initial attack—hardly a praiseworthy goal. Supporters of the concept replied in two ways. First, they argued that if a nuclear war ever began, both sides would likely become so vengeful that the assured destruction outcome would likely occur even if it was not the conscious basis for planning. Second, the threat was purposely hideous to ensure that no one could miscalculate: Assured destruction maximizes deterrence by guaranteeing the hideousness of its failure.

Limited Nuclear Options.   The murderous implications of assured destruction did not go unnoticed or uncriticized within the defense community. Arguing that such a threat was both gruesome beyond belief and incredible because of the ghoulish consequences, a second strand of thought emerged within nuclear strategy circles, based at least implicitly on Borden's formulation and suggesting a different role for nuclear forces. In the curious world of nuclear weapons and deterrence, the argument began with the belief that the assured destruction threat was unbelievable because of the moral abyss that implementation of the strategy promised, and it then posed a supposedly more humane alternative.

Richard Nixon was the first president to voice concern about nuclear strategy based in assured destruction, a strategy he inherited from the Johnson administration. His spokesmen wondered aloud—and largely rhetorically—if, in the event of a nuclear crisis, the president should be left with only the options of no response at all or an all-out, assured destruction response, inviting a similar, third-strike attack that would destroy both countries. In other words, should the president's options in the event of a nuclear attack of any kind or size be capitulation (no response) or Armageddon (assured destruction counterattack)? Based on that construction, the answer was straightforward: The president should have options other than the two extremes. Nevertheless, the outcome of the exercise was to expose the need for a different strategic formulation. The strategy of limited nuclear options was the response to that self-generated need.

The basic idea of limited options (known as the *countervailing strategy* under President Carter and *controlled response* under President Reagan) was proportionality as the basis of deterrence. The defenders began by arguing that the assured destruction threat was believable only in the event of an all-out Soviet first-strike attack against the United States. Since the Soviets knew the consequences of such an attack, it was the least likely form of attack for them to undertake. Thus, any nuclear attack they might actually contemplate would be less than all-out, leaving the president with only the options of doing nothing or launching the entire arsenal. As a result, the assured destruction threat emerged from this analysis as a credible threat against the least likely form of nuclear aggression and an ineffective threat against other and, by definition, more likely forms of provocation.

The limited nuclear options theory remedies this deficiency by creating within the Single Integrated Operational Plan (SIOP—the actual plan for implementing nuclear attacks) a series of options short of all-out response (hence the name *limited options*). The idea is to provide the president with an array of possible responses proportional to the original attack by the Soviet Union. Thus, if the Soviets were to launch twenty to thirty missiles against U.S. ICBM fields in North Dakota, for instance, the United States should have the capability and plan to respond by taking out a similar target in the Soviet Union. Presumably, the threat and the ability to follow through with it would have two salutary effects. First, a proportional response would be more believable than an all-out counterattack. Second, knowing that the United States could effectively play tit-for-tat in the event of any provocation, the Soviets would realize that any action they might initiate would be countered effectively; their attack would be trumped and would provide no advantage.

Limited options had different targeting and arsenal size implications from assured destruction. Following from Borden, limited options targeting concentrated on so-called *counterforce* targets, defined as military and military-related objectives. This emphasis was based on the dual assumptions that these would be the kinds of targets the Soviets would aim at in first strikes and that destroying military rather than civilian targets would be less inflammatory to escalating passions. (Since many military targets, such as bases, are located in or adjacent to cities, critics pointed out that the distinction was more philosophical than real.) The list of counterforce targets, particularly when it is extended to societal capabilities that allow a country to sustain a war effort (e.g., fertilizer factories to produce nutrients to grow crops to feed troops), is almost infinitely long, which means that a much larger arsenal is necessary to cover the entire target "set" than is the case with assured destruction.

As might be expected, adherents of assured destruction disagreed with this assessment. They argued that contemplating the use of nuclear weapons in less than the direst situations might actually lower the inhibition on using them in the first place (the major goal of deterrence), since it was possible to calculate surviving a limited exchange. Moreover, the calculation of limitation could prove wrong. It is possible that the exchange could be limited to a single attack and counterattack. It is also possible that the initial attack, of whatever proportions, would so inflame passions on both sides that an inexorable spiral to all-out assured destruction would occur. Assured destruction adherents argued that the cruelest irony would be to act on the assumption that an exchange could be limited when in fact it could not. They claimed that the only reliable way to avoid nuclear destruction was to avoid nuclear exchange altogether, which the absolute known horror of assured destruction would best guarantee.

The debate between advocates of assured destruction and limited options continued inconclusively for decades, because there was no hard evidence to prove which construction would best constitute deterrence. The central contention always boiled down to the question of whether nuclear war could be limited. The question and its answer were critical, since both sides agreed an all-out nuclear war would destroy both sides and thus had to be avoided at all costs. In the absence of any reliable evidence about the nature of a nuclear war, both deterrence camps could—and did—make their arguments with no danger of being refuted by facts that did not exist.

Happily, the debate between those who were MAD and those who were NUTS did end, indecisively, with the end of the Cold War and thus the end of the reason for the argument. In the end, deterrence prevailed, in the sense that nuclear war was in fact avoided. Whether this success was a result of enormous insight and persistence or the mere avoidance of what would have been the stupidest (and possibly last) decision in human history is a judgment to be left to the reader and to history. The entire enterprise did contribute to the end of the Cold War, however, and thus to the dismantling of the edifice of deterrence strategy in the end.

That such a bizarre drama would continue for decades given this knowledge of the consequences of its failure reflects the context and animosities of the times. To repeat a point made earlier, during the Cold War the only intellectually acceptable outcomes seriously considered by policy makers and analysts alike were to keep the Cold War cold or to let it "go hot" into World War III. With the possibility of a peaceful resolution of the competition effectively excluded from the menu of realistic future conditions, preparing for a war that both sides agreed had to be avoided at all costs made sense. The madness of the whole enterprise became possible to contemplate only when the unthinkable implosion of the Cold War occurred peacefully—with a whimper, not with the expected bang.

Nuclear Residues

Have nuclear weapons and our past experience with them lost all salience for dealing with the world? It is true that many of the calculations have changed significantly. The United States, for instance, still faces a large (although shrinking) *Russian* nuclear arsenal, but we no longer consider it a menace, since it is difficult to imagine circumstances in which the Russians would launch an attack against us. Since no other country possesses or is likely to build a nuclear arsenal large enough to oppose us the way the Soviets did, the problem of nuclear holocaust has receded, if not disappeared.

But that does not mean that nuclear considerations have simply disappeared from national security concerns. Indeed, there are at least two related concerns about nuclear weapons that remain on the agenda: problems of nuclear proliferation and the alleged need for ballistic missile defenses (BMD). In the most obvious sense, they are related in that problems associated with the spread of nuclear weapons to other states and nonstate entities provide one of the major justifications for missile defenses.

Nuclear Proliferation.   The spread of nuclear weapon capability to states or nonstate actors that have previously not had that capability—also known as horizontal proliferation—has been a concern of the United States for some time. This concern arises from the general assumption that the more states that have nuclear weapons capability, the greater are the chances they will use nuclear weapons, with unknown consequences for the rest of the system. When proliferation has occurred, it often comes in the spread of the weapons to historical rivals, such as India and Pakistan in 1999, raising the prospects that their ongoing military conflict could escalate to nuclear exchange.

In the current context, the more urgent problem deals with the possible spread of nuclear weapons to states considered unreliable, unstable, and hostile to U.S. interests. At the top of the list of such states stand Iraq and North Korea. Although the North Koreans very publicly renounced the intention to try to operationalize a nuclear capability in 1994, they became involved in a diplomatic imbroglio with the United States over resumption of nuclear activity that could lead to weapons capability in 2003, a problem not resolved at this writing in July, 2003. The fear about Iraq was not only that the country is a rogue, but that it might develop connections with nonstate groups such as Usama bin Laden's Al Qaeda, with whom it is feared that Iraq might share a nuclear device to aid in their terrorist campaign against the United States. These dual fears provided much of the official rationale for the American invasion and occupation of Iraq in 2003.

A question increasingly asked is whether concepts of deterrence developed in the Cold War competition can be translated into ways for dealing with nascent nuclear powers. Does the threat of nuclear retaliation dissuade a leader like Saddam Hussein or bin Laden in the same way that the Soviets and the Americans were deterred during the Cold War? Or is the new breed of enemies so different—including their being suicidal—that traditional deterrence concepts will be ineffective? As noted earlier in the chapter, one alternative to traditional deterrence is the ability to defend oneself from attack, which makes the missile defense option more attractive than it might otherwise be.

Missile Defenses.   The Bush administration proposal to build a missile defense system is not a new idea. In fact, the *national missile defense (NMD)* is the third generation of advocacy for developing and deploying a defense against ballistic missile attack. The first proposal was put forward in the late 1960s and early 1970s as the Sentinel and later as the Safeguard system. Its purported purpose was to guard against a Chinese nuclear capability that was projected for the future, and as such, it was similar to the current NMD plan in intent (see Amplification 8.1: The Chinese Threat).

In 1983, President Ronald Reagan proposed a much more ambitious system, the *Strategic Defense Initiative (SDI)*. The Reagan SDI had the grand purpose of providing a comprehensive, totally effective shield against a massive launch of nuclear weapons (essentially an assured destruction attack) by the Soviet Union. The impenetrability of the SDI screen would render nuclear weapons "impotent and obsolete," in Reagan's words. Reagan's longer view was that such a shield would make nuclear weapons themselves irrelevant and thus lead to nuclear disarmament, his real goal. The SDI program lost focus during the George H. W. Bush administration and was formally scuttled by President Clinton. What remained after the demise of SDI was research on a more limited form of defense. The current NMD proposal came from this ongoing program.

The Clinton White House never showed great enthusiasm for missile defense, and the program was kept alive largely because of congressional interest. President George W. Bush took up the cause of missile defense in his 2000 campaign and continued that advocacy once elected. The events of September 11, 2001, temporarily

Amplification 8.1

THE CHINESE THREAT

Current proposals to deploy a national missile defense (NMD) bear an eerie resemblance to similar arguments made over thirty years ago, when the People's Republic of China's fledgling nuclear capability was the major objective of the United States' proposed Sentinel and later Safeguard anti-missile systems. What critics of NMD argue was particularly instructive about the comparison was that the threat posed by China was potential rather than actual. At the time, China had nuclear warheads but no ballistic missiles capable of delivering them against the United States. The projected problem was the assertion that China would soon acquire such a capability, and that missile defenses were needed to deter a Chinese launch against the United States when they indeed acquired the capability.

In retrospect, the arguments appear nearly hysterical, although the state of U.S.–China animosity in the late 1960s made them appear more plausible than they do today. In 1967, after all, the United Sates had no formal relations with the Chinese (and had not since the Communists assumed power in 1949), and we had fought Chinese "volunteers" in the Korean War (Chinese forces sent to Korea were officially designated as volunteers to avoid a direct legal and political confrontation between the two countries). Moreover, Chinese leader Mao Zedung had publicly proclaimed after China joined the nuclear weapons club that China's huge population meant that it was the only country that could physically survive a nuclear war.

The irony of the rationale was that not only were the projections of Chinese acquisition of delivery capacity against U.S. targets premature, but the capability has never been meaningfully achieved. As of 2003, the Chinese arsenal remained minuscule, consisting of a handful of unreliable liquid-fuel land-based and sea-based missiles that cannot be kept at a high state of readiness because their means of propulsion cannot be stored in the rockets and would have to be "gassed up" before a launch. These missiles arguably pose a potential threat to neighboring Taiwan, but not to the United States. The question is whether potential acquisition of delivery capability by "axis of evil" countries such as Iraq and North Korea may be as fanciful as the Chinese "threat" against which the first missile shield was proposed.

sidetracked what had been active attempts both to gain support for the program and to overcome foreign (notably Russian, but also Chinese) objections to deploying such a system. The antiterrorist campaign has since been used both to argue the greater necessity of a missile screen and to argue its relevance as a tool to frustrate terrorist organizations from attempting to use a nuclear weapon against the United States.

There are several objections to developing and deploying the NMD, almost all of which have been raised against its predecessor proposals as well. The first and most fundamental objection is *workability*. Although the theoretical principles for missile defenses had been worked out before the first ICBM was fired successfully, developing a system that actually could shoot down missiles with any proven reliability has been and remains illusive. The Bush administration itself has demonstrated some public ambivalence on this issue. At times, it has said it would not deploy an NMD until a design had proved "workable," which presumably means that it has succeeded in knocking down offensive missiles in numerous realistic tests (something it has arguably not yet accomplished). At other times, Defense Secretary Rumsfeld has argued that demonstrated workability is not a defining criterion in a deployment decision.

A second critique deals with the *need* for a defense. As Amplification 8.1 points out, the original Sentinel/Safeguard system was designed to thwart a projected Chinese nuclear threat to the United States that has yet to emerge more than thirty years later. Whereas no one questioned that the Soviets posed a threat for which an effective SDI might provide a remedy, the NMD proposal is more similar to Sentinel/Safeguard than to the SDI. The NMD is designed not as a counter to an existing threat, but rather as a hedge against the emergence of a threat by "rogue" states or, in the wake of the September 11 terrorist attacks, by nonstate actors. Critics argue that, as the Chinese threat of the 1960s, this threat may never emerge, and if it does, it is far enough in the future to wait until a truly effective system can be designed.

The third objection is *cost.* A major characteristic of all three missile defense proposals has been widely diverging speculation about how much a system designed to fulfill its mission would cost. The numbers are always high. The most extreme case was the comprehensive SDI, the most ambitious of the proposals. The cost of deploying the SDI was estimated at anywhere between $500 billion and $2 trillion over a ten-year deployment period. Estimates for the NMD run upwards of $60 billion.

Controversies over cost vary with estimates of effectiveness and need and are conditioned by assessments of the state of the economy and thus the ability to bear the costs. Clearly, a costly defense whose effectiveness is unknown is harder to sell than a system of known high-quality performance, and the costs are easier to justify against a real and menacing threat than in a more uncertain environment. Moreover, the increased defense spending that deployment would entail (unless those costs are absorbed by cutbacks elsewhere in defense) are easier to justify in a vibrant economy such as that of the 1990s than in the softer economic conditions of the early 2000s.

The various missile defense proposals have had different fates in the face of these objections. Deployment of the Safeguard system actually began in the early 1970s but was rejected by the Congress on the dual bases of cost effectiveness and the absence of a demonstrable threat. The SDI advocates had no problem identifying a problem, but they were ridiculed on the question of workability and the enormous and uncertain costs of the program. The NMD has been under scrutiny on all three dimensions: workability, given the highly uneven results of testing; analogies with the Chinese threat that never materialized; and the current projected threats that also may not exist. It has also been derided as a waste of money, particularly given other priorities. As John Pike of the Federation of American Scientists, which has opposed missile defenses consistently over time, maintained the NMD is a "system that won't work against a threat that does not exist."

Two other problems have affected the NMD. The first comes from the international political environment. Virtually all countries (Israel being a notable exception) oppose deployment of the system as destabilizing and cite Bush administration insistence on building it as evidence of American unilateralism. The Bush administration mounted a massive diplomatic initiative in 2001 to overcome those objections, with some limited success, such as gaining a limited agreement with Russian President Vladimir Putin to allow the United States to test and develop the system while holding ABM Treaty prohibitions on testing in abeyance. Much of the international objection was based in the fact that deploying the system would force the United States to abrogate the ABM Treaty, which is viewed as the symbolic apex of Cold War arms control success. The United States' announcement of its intention to withdraw from the treaty in 2001, however, created little fanfare in the international community. Similarly, when the Bush administration announced its intention to begin construction of the first elements of the NMD system in Alaska in late 2002, there was muted adverse reaction.

The other problem is the impact of the terrorist campaign against the United States begun on September 11, 2001, and the need for missile defenses. Advocates of the NMD argue that the willingness of terrorists to attack American soil directly demonstrates the need for comprehensive defense of the homeland, including protection against possible future missile attacks. This kind of reasoning underlies much of the rationale for the "axis of evil" designation of Iran, Iraq, and North Korea, each of which has alleged nuclear ambitions. Critics counter that the NMD would have had no effect on preventing the attacks that occurred in New York and Washington, so that those attacks actually prove the irrelevance of the NMD in light of real threats. In other words, terrorists are unlikely to have missiles against which the NMD might be a response; they would likely smuggle a device into the country on a ship or truck, against which the NMD would have no effect. Moreover, the critics claim that coping with terrorism will require a broad range of national efforts, which will put large demands on government resources, and that the NMD should not occupy a high place on the list of priorities.

CONVENTIONAL FORCES AND THE FUTURE

Both of the fault lines have served to highlight the question of the future of conventional forces. As already noted in Chapter 4 and in the introduction to this chapter, the bulk of American conventional military forces and the expenses associated with them were devoted to maintaining and modernizing a force that was largely designed and configured to fight a potential World War III in Europe for more than forty years after World War II. The end of the Cold War made this kind of conflict extremely unlikely, and no realistic substitute has emerged to confront the United States in traditional symmetrical warfare, nor is one likely to emerge in the near future. Saddam Hussein was the last leader to challenge the United States on its own military terms in the Persian Gulf War, and he failed miserably. His experience was instructive for all who might challenge the West, especially the United States, on its own terms in the future. The end of the Cold War started the process by which the U.S. conventional power has become so great that it has made itself virtually obsolete, a kind of self-fulfilling prophecy wherein American prowess has eliminated the problem for which it was devised.

Challenge!

After Taking Out Saddam

The American-led invasion of Iraq succeeded in one of its major aims—to remove its president, Saddam Hussein, from power. In the wake of the war, however, a number of geopolitical questions remained. Beyond refusing to let UN inspectors monitor Iraq's supposed weapons of mass destruction (WMD) program, what had he done to merit such drastic action? Although his government was gone, with what would he be replaced? Could an American-sponsored replacement possibly have legitimacy in Iraq and the region? Would other Middle Eastern states oppose the American action on grounds of imperialism? Would inevitable comparisons to the Crusades undermine American objectives and promote those of hostile forces in the region? Would the result be to fracture Iraq into two or more successor states that would be easy prey for Iran? How would predictable Arab rage over the invasion spill over to the confrontation between Israel and the Palestinians? Would the aftermath stimulate more terrorism?

There were no easy answers to these political questions. No one doubted that American conventional forces could defeat the Iraqi army in symmetrical warfare, probably more easily than a decade earlier. The initial fear that the Iraqis would adopt asymmetrical, guerrilla tactics, as their Afghan neighbors did in the 1980s against a Soviet invasion, proved false when the invasion occurred. The Iraqis did not retreat to the mountains or the alleyways of Baghdad to engage in bloody urban guerrilla warfare. The active war itself was less bloody than feared and created a false euphoria in which President Bush announced major combat over, only to see the Iraqis respond with limited attacks on American forces that killed roughly one soldier per day. How long would the occupation of Iraq take, and at what price in treasure and blood? How long would the Americans have to stay? Would the result be a uniform front in the region in opposition to the American onslaught?

These kinds of questions make the aftermath of removing Saddam Hussein from office—an outcome most Americans support in principle—more difficult in execution. How important are these uncertainties? Can they be overcome? Is the United States in danger of being stuck in a Vietnam-style quagmire? What do you think?

The campaign against terrorism has simply accentuated this situation. Following the fairly conventional first phase (overthrowing the Taliban), the campaign in Afghanistan became a very different way of waging hostilities, which raises some further questions about the continued relevancy of traditional military forces in dealing with such problems. Where do conventional forces fit in this environment? In the remaining pages of this chapter, we will look at the traditional roles such forces have played and the fate of attempts to reform those forces; the question of force modernization in light of environmental changes and revised missions for the military, caused by dynamics associated with the fault lines; and the impact of recent events on the equation.

Traditional Roles

World War II was the major formative period for American conventional military forces as they are configured today. That conflict had as its purpose the defeat of Nazi aggression by large, heavily armed, mechanized forces fighting European style; the United States and its allies responded to that aggression with symmetrical forces. Although the structure of active-duty forces was largely dismantled in the years immediately after that war, that structure served as the model for the Korean conflict, with some peripheral modifications to reflect technological innovations (such as jet aircraft and helicopters). Since this conventional force remained in existence after Korea, rather than following the American tradition of mobilization for war and then rapid demobilization at war's conclusion, the force for the Cold War was one with which veterans of World War II were comfortable and familiar. Only the adversary changed, and since the Soviets were similarly organized and were likely to fight symmetrically, the model seemed vindicated. This force structure has largely survived reductions in size since the end of the Cold War but is under more intense scrutiny in a new century, the first and most dramatic national security events of which were the terrorist attacks of September 11, 2001 and their aftermath. There are, in broad terms, two models available for future structure.

The Heavy-Force Model.   The bulk of the nonnuclear armed forces can be fairly accurately described by two adjectives, heavy and conventional, that define what the military likes to refer to as *legacy forces*. The term *heavy* refers to the way the force is configured and how it is equipped to perform its mission. More specifically, it refers to a force designed to fight large-unit, concentrated-firepower combat by mobile, mechanized units against a similarly configured opponent in brutal, positional land, air, and naval warfare. The symbols of heavy warfare are tanks and mobile artillery on land, bombers with large payloads in the air, and large capital ships (battleships, aircraft carriers) on the sea. By contrast, *light* forces feature more lightly armed and mobile forces capable of engaging in various forms of warfare and generally not involving the kinds of direct confrontations between armies, navies, and air forces that are typical of heavy forces.

Heavy forces are designed to fight *conventional* warfare, the style we have called European, which was perfected during World War II. Sometimes referred to as the "Western way of war," its military purpose is to overcome the adversary's "hostile ability" (the capacity to resist the other side's armed forces physically) through the direct confrontation of armed forces. The military purpose is to destroy "in detail"— that is, to break the cohesion of enemy armies, sink enemy navies, and shoot down enemy air assets. Collectively, the objective is to gain military superiority over an adversary so as to impose whatever political objectives one has on that enemy by overcoming its physical ability to resist that imposition. Warfare that employs heavy forces is most closely attached to wars of total political purpose (where the objective is the overthrow of the enemy government) such as World War II, although in some circumstances these forces are effective in lesser contingencies. Heavy forces are designed and best suited for confronting similar forces of the opponent. They are the tools of symmetrical warfare.

A heavy force was appropriate for the Cold War confrontation with the Soviet Union and its allies. United States and Soviet armed forces were virtual mirror images of one another physically, and they shared similar plans in the event of war. The doctrines of both sides emphasized mass (having more force at the point of engagement). A war between them, it was assumed, would resemble World War II except that it would be much bloodier, and one side or another would be first to exhaust its weaponry and its ability to continue. Moreover, such a war would likely be total in purpose, with one side or the other having its government overthrown (unless, of course, the war escalated to system-destroying nuclear war, in which case both sides would lose). The heavy model proved durable for fighting and winning World War II and confronting the Soviet Union short of war during the Cold War.

The prospects for this kind of war have not survived the end of the Cold War. With the collapse of the Soviet Union, the United States and to a lesser extent its NATO allies stand alone in possessing heavy forces, and no country or conceivable coalition could mount a force that could challenge the American heavy force combination or is likely to try. In a very real sense, we have perfected conventional warfare to the point that no one can (or will) fight that way with us.

The Light-Force Model.   The alternative approach to building heavy military forces is the light-force model. Light force generally refers to military structures that do not include much large military equipment—in their most extreme, they are largely limited to equipment (e.g., rifles, small-caliber mortars) that can be carried by soldiers on foot or transported by helicopter or similar conveyance. The emphasis of light forces is on speed, maneuverability, and surprise. They are not designed to confront and "slug it out" with heavy forces, against which they stand little chance in symmetrical warfare. Rather, they are forces best adapted to rapid movement, to special assignments for which speed and deception are critical, and to accomplishing missions that heavy forces cannot because of their relative lack of speed and flexibility—such as capturing fugitives or rescuing hostages.

In the developing world, light forces are associated with guerrilla warfare, particularly in the heavy jungles of the mountainous "green belt" surrounding the Equator, where it is easy for such forces to maneuver and to engage in hit-and-run tactics in the face of more firepower-intensive heavy forces. The Viet Cong during the Vietnam conflict were classic practitioners of this style of warfare, and it consistently frustrated the efforts of the much more heavily armed American regular forces.

The light model has always been part of the Western tradition, although its relative importance has varied. Some would argue that the cavalry tradition is the prototype for light forces in the American system, whether it is the cavalry that rides horses or the helicopter-borne "air cavalry." Special Forces and Rangers are also examples of applications of the light-force model.

The chief criticism of light forces is their inability to match up with heavy forces in direct combat; a soldier with a rifle stands little chance against a tank. This criticism is valid and carries considerable weight when the opponent is heavy, in which case heavy forces are the necessary counterweight. A light force facing a heavy force can deal with it successfully only by avoiding the kind of direct confrontation in which the superior firepower of heavy force can be brought to bear to "frame" and destroy the lighter force. This was the lesson painfully learned by Taliban light forces that remained massed in the face of American air forces in 2001. Heavy forces have not always prevailed over light forces in unconventional asymmetrical warfare, however, as Vietnam provides ample evidence. If the future is likely to hold more asymmetrical than symmetrical foes, then the primacy of heavy forces is not to be taken for granted.

Light or Heavy Futures?   If the heavy model served the United States well in the twentieth century, is it equally durable and serviceable for confronting the environment of the twenty-first century? Clearly, the environment within which the use of armed forces is contemplated has changed. The prospect of fighting a symmetrical war against heavy forces using conventional means has all but disappeared. In the words of the original, 1997 version of the Quadrennial Defense Review (QDR), the United States lacks a "peer competitor" or foreseeable adversary that poses the kind of military threat for which those forces would be appropriate. The question becomes whether this type of force and this style of warfare is appropriate for the challenges ahead. The experience of the United States in Afghanistan, where both heavy and light forces were employed in both symmetrical and asymmetrical settings, does little to clarify this debate, as Amplification 8.2 explains. However, there is nothing really new in the debate, nor is it likely to be resolved definitively anytime soon.

Military Reform

Military reform—change in how and what the military does—comes in several forms, not all of which are relevant for present purposes. Reform may, for instance, refer to changing the rules about who can join the military (females, gays) and for what purposes (women in combat roles). It may also refer to proper military conduct or the relationship between civilian and military authorities and a broad variety of other areas of military concern.

For our purposes, we will limit our consideration to the questions of military missions and the appropriate and most efficiently configured forces to carry out those missions. The questions, generally, are logical and sequential. The first concern is with the kinds of situations the military will be forced to confront and the outcomes in mind. The second is with whether current forces are appropriate for achieving current and future assigned missions and, if they are not, what changes should be made to align missions and forces better. (One could, of course, reverse the sequence of these concerns and determine what to do based on what can be done, but that would be a self-limiting approach more appropriate for a smaller and weaker state with more limited goals in the world than for the United States.)

Military reform in this context is a dynamic and ongoing process, since situations are always changing, as is the ability to deal with the changes that occur. Military reform, however, is an especially wrenching task for military professionals to

Amplification 8.2

LIGHT *AND* HEAVY FORCES?

For a country with considerable resources available to it, the debate over heavy or light forces is not an either/or proposition. For very poor countries, there may be no affordable alternative to lightly armed forces. The United States, on the other hand, can afford both kinds of forces, and although there will always be a debate over which kind to emphasize at different times and in differing situations, neither form is likely to disappear.

There are several good reasons why the debate is about emphasis, not about the exclusive existence of one kind of force or the other. First, keeping both kinds of forces is politically the easiest solution, especially in the relations between civil authorities and the military. An emphasis on light forces has considerably more support within the civilian community than it does within the career military, most of whose leaders have emerged from backgrounds in heavy military specialties. Considerable political capital is preserved by arguing the need for both kinds of forces.

Second, it is difficult to argue for the elimination of either emphasis in an uncertain environment. As military apologists are quick to point out, for instance, no one foresaw as little as a few months before the fact that Iraq would invade and conquer Kuwait. In order to oust the Iraqis, heavy forces were clearly necessary to confront and defeat a heavy Iraqi opponent. Had the choice been made in advance to draw down American heavy assets, the effort would have been considerably more difficult and expensive. In other words, a wide variety of forces is a hedge against unforeseen contingencies.

Third, eliminating or drastically cutting back heavy armed forces would eliminate the principal military advantage the United States has in the world. Confronting the United States frontally in symmetrical combat may be unthinkable under current circumstances, but if the United States abnegated its advantage, then such warfare might once again emerge as a real and lively problem.

The arguments over which kinds of forces are preferable in any given environment are endless, and they are almost certainly going to be inconclusive. Heavy forces arguably may be anachronistic today, but that does not mean they always will be. Both light and heavy forces have long traditions in the American and other militaries. Neither is likely to disappear.

undertake. The nature of the problem for which military forces are developed is profoundly serious; ultimately, it is the protection of the population from harm, even its survival. That mission tends to make the military conservative in approach, more prone to tried and true methods than to untested innovations that might fail at critical points. Institutionally, most military professionals get into positions where they may be charged with assessing reform proposals only after they have served long careers in specific warfare specialties to which they have great allegiance and loyalty and which they believe are necessary to the successful prosecution of war. Moreover, the "American way of war" emphasizes the Western tradition in warfare, which has been relatively successful in warfare fought by forces with similar values and similar rules for fighting (what are sometimes called conventions of war). Military traditions and values are simply resistant, if not impervious, to reform efforts, unless truly traumatic experiences force change upon the military establishment of the day. This is not intended to be demeaning or insulting to those charged with reform, but only to reflect sources of and reasons for resistance.

The history of military reform efforts since the end of World War II reflects this resistance. As noted in the last chapter, the first reform effort was convened by new Secretary of Defense James Forrestal in 1948 at Key West, Florida, to rationalize military roles and missions. In the early 1990s, President Clinton's first defense secretary, Les Aspin (a former chair of the House Armed Services Committee) commissioned the "Bottom Up Review" (BUR) to conduct an exhaustive review of how the military should operate with the collapse of the Soviet threat. When that effort failed to produce meaningful reform, a frustrated Congress pushed through legislation requiring the QDR. The initial report was produced in 1997. When the George W. Bush administration entered office in January 2001, one of the first assignments facing Secretary of Defense Rumsfeld was to complete the 2001 QDR by September 30 of that year. Overwhelmed by the terrorist attacks of September 11, the new QDR was issued without fanfare on October 1, 2001.

Force Modernization and the 2001 QDR

Those formulating the 2001 QDR were faced with two major challenges. The first was to describe a national security environment that had changed markedly since the Soviet Union collapsed but remained murky, shapeless, and difficult to describe adequately. The events of September 11, which occurred after the document was in final draft, seemed to add a new dynamic to that environment. The operational implications of this "new kind of war" were not immediately obvious, but they were clearly unconventional, adding to rather than clarifying the essential amorphousness of a threat environment that was suddenly more compelling but no less confusing than before.

At the same time, the American military stood at a junction point in terms of force modernization. Critics of the Clinton administration had argued for several years that the numerous deployments of American forces in such places as Somalia, Haiti, Bosnia, and Kosovo had come at the expense of modernizing and reequipping a force in desperate need of replenishment and updating. Each of the services had impressive arrays of new and potent weapons systems they were anxious to field to increase their effectiveness. In the months before September 2001, however, the administration argued for economy and the devotion of new resources to missile defenses, leaving the military leadership with the disquieting impression that many of their force modernization needs would go unmet.

The political reactions to terrorism radically changed the fiscal situation for defense. Concerns about the part increased defense spending would play in returning the country to deficit spending (which had originally been raised over the Bush tax cuts earlier in the year) simply evaporated in the patriotic fervor the attacks created among Americans. Suddenly, resources for the "war on terrorism" were not in short supply—but on what should we spend the newly available resources? And for what purposes should the military receive these rewards? The QDR was intended to pro-vide major guidance in answering both of those questions.

The 2001 QDR does not so much provide answers to the issue of reform and the future shape and character of American forces as it raises questions. The document readily acknowledges that we are in the midst of a process of change, from which a different kind of force will likely emerge. In order to accommodate the notion of change, it develops a series of analytical categories by which to organize thinking about the changes it predicts will occur. However, apart from acknowledging that there is still no peer competitor and endorsing the national missile defense system, it provides little guidance about the direction the future is taking and how we should respond to it.

Part of the reason for this reluctance to predict future developments may reflect the political context from which the document emerged. When the Bush adminis-tration first entered office, Secretary Rumsfeld made a very public point of saying that he was undertaking a basic reevaluation of the defense sector and that the results of this investigation would provide basic reforms that would be reflected in the QDR. Since President Bush had campaigned on the promise to rejuvenate a mil-itary establishment whose needs he alleged had been neglected by his predecessor, the services took this to mean that the new administration would be highly sympa-thetic to their needs. In this spirit, the Joint Chiefs of Staff put together a "wish list" of new—and mostly heavy—equipment and systems they felt they needed, with a ten-year price tag of an additional $50 billion to $100 billion per year.

The new administration, more interested in tax cuts and missile defense than in force modernization, did not respond warmly to this initiative. Rather, it began to look to many in the service departments that the purpose of Secretary Rumsfeld's review was to find places in the service budgets to *cut* and *reduce* programs to free up funds to spend on missile defenses. The grumbling grew within the Pentagon to the point that many serving officers were predicting, with some anticipation, that Rums-feld would be the first Bush cabinet member to be relieved of his duties. His emer-gence as the highly articulate, tough-talking chief spokesman for military efforts in Afghanistan to fight terrorism stilled such speculation in 2002.

The confrontation between the services and the defense secretary over the con-tents of the QDR was, in a sense, abated by the terrible events of September 11. The QDR document was in final draft form and under final review, but reactions to the terrorist attacks pushed the review off the agenda. At the same time, the reaction to September 11 included a newfound willingness for large defense expenditures in the Congress, enough to assuage the president's interest in missile defenses *and* the ser-vices' interests in upgrading their conventional forces. A QDR with a vaguely worded vision of the future and responses to it served everyone's interests at the time it was released to the public.

The QDR document is best understood in this light. That it did not offer a detailed blueprint for force modernization should not come as a surprise. The propos-als being made by the various services were numerous and complex, and the new administration was forced to issue its report less than nine months into its term. Instead of trying to do what was probably the impossible, by picking and choosing among specific proposals, it offered an alternative framework within which future decisions could be made.

Using the terrorist incidents of September 2001 as its context, the document provides an assessment of the threat environment in which decisions will be made—a situation of considerable uncertainty. As the report puts it, "The attack on the United States and the war that has been visited upon us highlights a fundamental condition of our circumstances; we cannot and will not know precisely where and when America's interests will be threatened, when America will come under attack, or when Americans might die as a result of aggression." The Cold War comfort of a potent but known opponent has been replaced by lesser, but also less predictable, potential foes. As a result, the report argues the need "to establish a new strategy for America's defense that would embrace uncertainty and contend with surprise."

This assessment of the environment changes the context within which questions of force modernization must occur. During the Cold War, forces were developed on the basis of known, concrete threats that needed to be negated. Threat-based capabilities were matched to Soviet capabilities in a relatively straightforward manner—when the Soviets built more tanks, for instance, the United States responded by building more anti-tank weapons.

With no concrete opponent, there is no measurable threat against which to develop capabilities. Instead, according to the QDR, "the United States is likely to be challenged by adversaries who possess a wide range of capabilities, including asymmetric approaches to warfare, particularly weapons of mass destruction." With uncertainty as the backdrop, force planning will thus be based on capabilities rather than threats in the face of a potentially diverse set of requirements.

A capability-based approach to force development works in two ways. First, it attempts to identify the range of likely problems the country may confront and tries to develop forces to nullify that range of threats. An example is the projected problem of possession of weapons of mass destruction by rogue states or nonstate actors such as Usama bin Laden. The national missile defense system is advertised by its champions as an example of a capability-based response to such a capability. At the same time, the approach is also designed to exploit American technological superiority in weapons development through the revolution in military affairs. The environment, the QDR argues, "requires the transformation of U.S. forces, capabilities, and institutions to extend America's asymmetric advantages well into the future." As an example of exploiting advantage, the Bush administration's first announced modernization (other than its stated commitment to NMD) involves buying 3,000 units of the Joint Strike Fighter, a versatile fighter-bomber that will be used in various modified versions by the U.S. Air Force, Navy, and Marines to guarantee American air superiority well into the century.

One of the more interesting questions not fully discussed in the QDR regards military manpower. The numbers of Americans either on active duty or in the reserves and National Guard has shrunk from its Cold War numbers by about one-third. Partly in response to these reduced overall numbers, the armed forces have turned to the reserves for a variety of tasks formerly assigned to active forces. Reserves were prominent in the Persian Gulf War (the first major reserve activation since Korea), and they have played a major role since September 11 as well. As Amplification 8.3 explains, this increased role was also a conscious army response to Vietnam.

The QDR is essentially mute on the question of force size and the relative mix of active duty and reserve forces, other than to say that these questions will be part of the "ambitious transformation" of U.S. forces "to sustain U.S. military advantages, meet critical operational goals, and dominate future military competition." Presumably, the American experience in the campaign against the Taliban and Al Qaeda in Afghanistan will provide useful guidance for future substantive force modernization and reform considerations. Force modernization meanwhile remains very much a work in progress, with less then totally predictable outcomes.

CONCLUSION: THE CONTINUING RELEVANCE OF TRADITIONAL FORCES

There is clearly much more agreement that change is occurring in the role of military force than in its actual direction. In a speech in early November 2001, Secretary of State Colin L. Powell went so far as to declare that not only was the Cold War over, but the post–Cold War period had been surmounted as well. He did not, however, tell us what new era we are entering.

What seems clear is that the military requirements of the post–September 11 defense environment will be considerably different from those of the Cold War. We have clearly moved decisively away from the large end of the scale of threat, where huge arsenals of nuclear weapons and massive conventional forces faced one another in what could have been mankind's most destructive, and possibly last, war. Russia, the successor to the menacing Soviet Union, is now virtually an American ally; Vladimir Putin and George W. Bush have, in some ways, become closer friends than Bill Clinton and Boris Yeltsin were. The titanic clash that once seemed inevitable now seems a more and more fanciful possibility. The military artifacts of that confrontation seem oddly archaic as well.

We have moved toward the small end of the scale, where there is no "peer competitor" directly in front of us or on the horizon. Instead, the threats to American security come from more remote places, where American interests are less engaged and where the scale and the nature of American involvement are less well defined but generally more limited. The terrorism of bin Laden against the American homeland is the apparent exception to that rule, but it is not yet entirely clear whether his or some other form of terrorism will fill the center stage of our concern or prove to have been an historical aberration. We will begin to explore those possibilities in the next two chapters.

How relevant are the military concerns and forces of the Cold War for the present and the future? Certainly, the conventional forces and structures inherited from that era proved to be highly useful during the Persian Gulf War of 1990–91, which helps explain why a more thorough critique of future roles has not been undertaken. The defenders of tradition received a reprieve in the Kuwaiti desert. As the United States began to conduct military operations in Afghanistan in the fall of 2001, those

Amplification 8.3

CREIGHTON ABRAMS AND THE ROLE
OF THE RESERVES

In its postmortem of the military experience in Vietnam, one of the questions the U.S. military, especially the army, asked was why the military lost the support of the American public for the war effort. Putting the argument in Clausewitzian terms, the trinity of unity among the people, the government, and the army—which Clausewitz had argued was essential for successful prosecution of war—had been severed as public support for the war eroded to the point that American withdrawal from the war became inevitable. The question was both why this had happened in Vietnam and how the army could avoid a recurrence in the future.

The answers were sequential. After carefully reviewing the record, the army concluded that what allowed the tie between the army and the public to fray and eventually break was that the public had never been asked to commit to the struggle when the war was contemplated and that that lack of commitment eventually turned into outright opposition. The only overt display of political support for military action in Vietnam was the Gulf of Tonkin Resolution of 1964, when the Congress (acting as the people's representatives) overwhelmingly provided President Lyndon B. Johnson with the authority to take appropriate military action in retaliation for alleged attacks against American warships in the Gulf of Tonkin—a dubious mandate for an eight-year military excursion. The army, under the leadership of Army Chief of Staff General Creighton W. Abrams, further concluded that the reason public support was not solicited was the fear that the public would voice opposition that would effectively veto the military action before it could be mounted. There was no World War II–style call to war to which the population could reply "yea" or "nay," and Abrams and his colleagues concluded that parallel situations might arise in the future, potentially creating the same problem as occurred in Vietnam.

The army had a solution: the reserves. They reasoned that one effective way to ensure that the public had a chance to voice its opinion about potential military deployments was through the prospect of reserve activation in future conflicts. The prospect that reserves would be among the first forces called to action meant that the people, through their elected representatives, would in effect be asked to voice their approval or disapproval through their willingness to see their friends, neighbors, and loved ones activated and sent off to war. To ensure that reserve activation would have to occur, the Abrams-led Army took the lead in transferring critical tasks exclusively to the reserves, so that future deployments would be impossible without reserve participation. Thus, mostly noncombat functions—such as medical care, transportation, civic affairs, and aerial refueling—are now reserve responsibilities, and when deployments occur, the reserves are among the first to be called upon in the defense of their country.

Such deployments have become routine in the 1990s and 2000s, but they were not when they were proposed in the 1970s. The gap between the Persian Gulf War and the major deployment involving reserves in Korea was a span of forty years. That reserves have become a routine part of deployments in such places as Somalia, Bosnia, Kosovo, and Afghanistan since 1990 is a testament to the conviction by army leaders in the wake of the Vietnam experience that they would never be caught without public support again.

forces seemed adequate to the task as well. Whether either experience was reminiscent of the past or a harbinger of the future is less certain. Iraq fielded a symmetrical Russian-organized and -equipped force in 1990, and the Taliban initially refused to disperse and fight asymmetrically when faced with American airpower. Will future opponents be so cooperative and fight by American rules? Our analysis to this point suggests they may not.

The huge nuclear arsenals and the elaborate constructs for their deterrent roles seem particularly anachronistic, which is partly why Putin and Bush are moving forward on largely dismantling them. Nuclear weapons are not completely irrelevant, of course, because several states possess them and others, including terrorists, may attempt to get them. Both the United States and Russia will clearly maintain arsenals adequately large to promise that an aggressor contemplating attacking either country with weapons of mass destruction (WMD) will be given pause to face the suicidal consequences of such actions. In the meantime, the emphasis will be on arsenal reductions, the security of remaining forces from undesirable hands, and determining whether the threat from those undesirable others is sufficient to undertake highly expensive defenses against ballistic missile delivery of WMD.

The structure of conventional forces is also questionable. As noted, the heavy composition of American (and most other Western) forces was designed for a massive, Western-style World War III clash with like forces from the Soviet world. Now, the only countries that possess those kinds of forces are American allies or friends, and it is not clear how adaptable those forces are for other contingencies, especially the kinds of asymmetrical wars that may be the future. If we need any preview of how well conventional forces perform in the contemporary environment, we have only to look at Russian performance in Chechnya, where it has pummeled a rag-tag guerrilla force with everything in its conventional arsenal for nearly a decade but has been unable to bring the Chechens, reinforced with *mujahadeen* from other Islamic countries in the region, to their knees. American conventional forces are undoubtedly more capable than their Russian counterparts, but the question remains. Iraq is the current laboratory.

Conventional forces are buffeted from both ends of the spectrum. On one hand, their relevance in the face of unconventional forces bent on devising ways to negate their advantages has not been proven. If technological proficiency and mass always prevails, the United States must have won in Vietnam. At the same time, the RMA may well produce capabilities that make current capabilities obsolete or vulnerable. Although it is not reflected in the 2001 QDR, candidate Bush talked about simply leapfrogging a generation of weapons procurement for this reason—for instance, not building a new generation of manned fighter aircraft, but waiting for the technology to provide unmanned drone aircraft to do the same things fighters do without endangering human pilots. In the same vein, some naval critics see aircraft carriers becoming as obsolete as battleships did in World War II. Just as aircraft flying off carriers reduced battleships from dreadnoughts to targets, so too may advanced cruise missiles reduce current carriers to vulnerable targets.

If the continuing relevance of traditional forces is coming into question, there remains considerable uncertainty about what threats we face and how we must respond to them in the future. The assertion that the future will be different has to be addressed in terms of *how* it will be different.

SELECTED BIBLIOGRAPHY

Borden, William Liscum. *There Will Be No Time: The Revolution in Strategy*. New York: Macmillan, 1946.

Brodie, Bernard. *Strategy in the Missile Age*. Princeton, NJ: Princeton University Press, 1959.

————. *War and Politics*. New York: Macmillan, 1973.

Clark, Ronald W. *The Greatest Power on Earth: The International Race for Nuclear Supremacy from Earliest Theory to Three-Mile Island*. New York: Harper and Row, 1980.

Clausewitz, Carl von. *On War*. Princeton, NJ: Princeton University Press, 1976.

Jervis, Robert. *The Illogic of American Nuclear Strategy*. Ithaca, NY: Cornell University Press, 1984.

Quadrennial Defense Review. Washington, D.C.: U.S. Department of Defense, September 30, 2001.

Snow, Donald M. *The Necessary Peace: Nuclear Weapons and Superpower Relations*. Lexington, MA: Lexington Books, 1987.

————, and Gary L. Guertner. *The Last Frontier: An Analysis of the Strategic Defense Initiative*. Lexington, MA: Lexington Books, 1986.

PART III

NEW CHALLENGES

The contemporary environment described in Part II has created a new set of security problems with which the United States must wrestle in order to secure itself in the world. The purpose of Part III is to examine these problems, to determine why they are important to the United States and how they individually and collectively produce opportunities and challenges for the United States.

In the wake of the terrorist attack of September 11, 2001, Chapter 9 explores systematically what is sometimes called the "new kind of war." Although fighting against nontraditional opponents may appear to provide some unique problems, the basic argument is that nontraditional, asymmetrical warfare is not something new but is the repackaging of ideas and approaches that have given the United States and other countries problems in the past. Chapter 10 looks at some of the semimilitary problems facing the United States, which require a combination of military and nonmilitary solutions. The discussion begins by looking at the two most intractable regional conflicts in the world: Israeli–Palestinian and Indian–Pakistani (over Kashmir), then focuses on terrorism and drugs. One of the consequences of conflicts that are dominant in the world today is the need to rebuild and rehabilitate countries after the fighting stops, so Chapter 11 looks specifically at the problems of peacekeeping and state-building in war-ravaged countries. Chapter 12 concludes the part, examining how the dynamics of globalization fit into the geopolitical pattern of the contemporary environment and into the solutions of contemporary problems.

CHAPTER

9

The "New Kind of War"

The events of September 11, 2001, reintroduced the United States to a form of warfare it had experienced in the past, most recently in Vietnam nearly forty years ago. Because the United States prefers to engage in traditional, conventional (symmetrical) warfare and has had an undistinguished history against unconventional foes, the attacks were all the more difficult to comprehend. Had we, indeed, discovered a new kind of war that represents the future? This chapter examines such questions. First, we will define and describe asymmetrical and symmetrical warfare, with an emphasis on the more unfamiliar former. Following that examination, we will look at asymmetrical futures, in the forms of fourth-generation warfare and the new internal wars (NIWs). The chapter will conclude by discussing how "new" this kind of war really is.

The horrendous events of September 11, 2001, revived the public debate over the uses of American military force in the future. In the decade following the end of the Cold War, important American interests for which armed force might be employed were largely unchallenged; as a result, the debate over how and when to use force had been largely muted. The principal international dynamic in a national security sense was, indeed, the interest–threat mismatch, whereby American vital interests were hardly threatened anywhere and the threats that did exist were so peripheral as to be hardly interesting. No country on Earth appeared to pose a meaningful threat to basic American security. The only remaining superpower reigned supreme, and the only apparent needs for American armed forces were in "deployments of choice" (situations in which the United States chose but was not compelled to employ armed forces) in remote and obscure locales such as Haiti, Bosnia, and Kosovo to quell humanitarian disasters.

This seeming tranquility did not mean that questions were not being asked about the future of American military activity. Within the professional defense intellectual community, the future was a lively concern that centered on two related questions. The first question was the kind of circumstance in which Americans might have to bear arms, and the answers tended to suggest that the most likely scenarios were nontraditional conflicts occurring in the developing world. A few writers, as we will see, were even predicting the kinds of concerns that have been raised since September 11, 2001, although their exhortations were clearly not prevalent during the 1990s. The other question was how the United States should prepare for future contingencies, and it was focused on issues of force modernization and possible restructuring, introduced in the last chapter.

The future came home with a literal crash with the terrorist attacks against New York and Washington, D.C. The events themselves were galvanizing and shocking enough to raise basic concerns about national security. As the reaction to the airplane attacks settled in our collective consciousnesses, an immediate victim of the exposure of the second fault line was American complacency about a supposedly tranquil and nonthreatening environment. At bottom, the attacks revealed that the United States was indeed vulnerable to attack. Even if we lacked a major foe that could imperil our survival, our previously assumed invulnerability to harm was shown to be false and could not easily nor quickly be restored, and we lacked any clear consensus on the larger meaning of what had happened and what could be done about it.

In our immediate, shocked response, the analogy that dominated descriptions of our new situation was that of war. President Bush rapidly described the bombings as acts of war equivalent in their infamy to the Japanese attack on Pearl Harbor sixty years earlier. The media, especially the electronic news networks, promptly seized the analogy, with Cable News Network (CNN), for instance, proclaiming the "new kind of war" as the masthead of their news coverage for months after the fact.

The analogy of the attacks to war was never entirely comfortable. On the positive side, it galvanized the public behind a policy goal of attacking and subduing the perpetrators of these unspeakable acts. As reserves were activated and called to duty (see Amplification 8.3: Creighton Abrams and the Role of the Reserves), there was no question that public support for doing whatever was necessary to root out and bring to justice Usama bin Laden and his supporters was virtually unanimous. There would be no Vietnam-like breach between American citizens and their leadership on the righteousness of the actions that would inevitably follow. If war meant the mobilization of national resources—including military force—to confront and overcome the crisis, then we appeared to be in a war of sorts.

But the war analogy was uneasy as well. The situation was not completely analogous to past wars in which the United States had engaged. The "enemy" was not a state or even a movement within a state, but instead was a transnational terrorist organization with some ties to sovereign states—notably, Afghanistan—but no legal or political affiliation with any states. In an international legal sense, wars, after all, are between states or between groups within states seeking to gain control of government. Al Qaeda (the Base), bin Laden's terrorist organization, clearly did not conform to the stereotype of the kind of entity with which one went to war. If there was an analogy with the American past, it was with the effort to overcome the Barbary pirates of North Africa in the early nineteenth century, but even that comparison was imperfect (the pirates were sponsored by governments in the region, whereas Al Qaeda was sanctioned only by the government of Afghanistan).

It was also not clear *how* one went to this war. The objective was quickly identified as a "war on terrorism," the objective of which would be to eradicate the terrorist threat to the United States. But how? Al Qaeda lacked anything resembling a conventional armed force with which to become locked in traditional combat, and although military action would clearly be part of the effort, it was also clear that it would not be the sole or—as Secretary of Defense Rumsfeld warned—even the most prominent tool for making war on terrorism. Moreover, although bin Laden and his network were the initial objects of this war, it was also clear that suppressing them was not going to end the problem of terrorism (discussed more fully in Chapter 10). Since the campaign would clearly contain military and nonmilitary components, it was more properly what we have called a semimilitary problem, for which the formal term *war* does not clearly apply in any straightforward way.

Within a week of the attacks, French President Jacques Chirac suggested to President Bush that the term *campaign* might be a more appropriate way to describe the endeavor, since that term suggested a broader, more comprehensive approach to the problem, including diplomatic, political, and economic aspects (among others) as well. Although the president agreed to the amendment, the war analogy had grabbed the public attention and would not be relinquished easily.

The extension of the campaign to Afghanistan and the effort to remove the Taliban government shielding Al Qaeda from capture added to the conceptual confusion. In Afghanistan itself, forces loyal to the Taliban were waging a very traditional civil war against a series of opponents led by the Northern Alliance, as noted in the Introduction. It was traditional, or *symmetrical*, warfare in the sense that both sides were fighting in similar manners and for the traditional goal of maintaining or gaining control of the government. When the United States entered that situation, we were indeed involved in what quite properly could be described as a war, in which American airpower and special forces were employed in absolutely traditional ways to help overthrow the Taliban government. When the Taliban was overthrown and the objective returned to rooting out Al Qaeda from its hideouts in the caves of the Tora Bora mountains, the enterprise moved away somewhat from traditional warfare. In other words, the war analogy did not fit exactly when the United States joined the anti-Taliban effort, and although we were clearly engaged in a war during the months of American participation (the first phase of the struggle over Afghanistan), that was only a transitory phenomenon.

Whether the war on terrorism is war or not, the persistence of the analogy has helped to enliven a national security debate that goes beyond the defense intellectual community to encompass the public as well. The major question driving the debate is the symbolism of the September 11 attacks for the structure of the national security problem of the future. Is this really the *new* face of war, or is it a restructuring of some older, more traditional methods in new "clothing"? At the same time, the question of whether this is *the* form that war will take or *a* way in which hostilities will be conducted becomes an added element in national security concerns.

These are not merely academic concerns, and they must be taken in the context of the debate that was ongoing before the terrorists violated American soil. The future face of war has very strong implications for the future evolution of American forces and missions. As the war in Afghanistan began to take shape, for instance,

American special operations forces (SOFs) became very prominent early on, serving as advisors to the anti-Taliban forces and as spotters directing American air strikes to their targets. Later they helped organize and conduct operations against remnants of the Taliban and Al Qaeda hiding in caves in the Afghan mountains. Is the future one in which SOFs occupy a much more central place in the army than they have in the past? Because the Taliban forces chose not to abandon conventional war when the American bombers arrived—leaving them in concentrated, vulnerable positions—American airpower had its most successful showing since the Persian Gulf War, killing and helping to destroy the cohesion of those Taliban who maintained their positions along traditional military lines and ended up serving as fodder for the bombers. Does this mean that the future lies in the greater decisiveness of airpower, as its proponents have long argued?

The aftermath of September 11 raises more questions than it answers, but it has provided a new emphasis for the debate about war in the future. In the remainder of this chapter, we will try to answer some of the questions raised. For better or worse, the public debate has been infected by a whole new lexicon of terminology, some of which we have already used, that had hitherto mercifully been confined to professional circles, and that is where the discussion will begin. From there, we will try to assess how these ideas and forces fit into the broader pattern of national security concerns.

SYMMETRICAL AND ASYMMETRICAL WARFARE

A basic consideration in thinking about the nature of warfare is through the conceptualizations of war among the different participants. For most of the American experience, our wars have been fought by traditional, conventional military forces; both sides were organized in pretty much the same way, had largely the same (if opposing) purposes, served as representatives of sovereign states (or of groups seeking to gain or maintain control of states), and accepted the same general conventions (or laws) surrounding proper and improper ways to conduct war. The term we have used to describe warfare among similar opponents is *symmetrical warfare*, in the sense that the contending sides resemble or mirror one another along the axes of organization, purpose, affiliation, and intent. The world wars were the epitome of symmetrical wars.

The term *symmetrical warfare*, of course, suggests the existence of its opposite. One of the newer terms to enter the public debate is *asymmetrical warfare*, which in its broadest connotations represents the opposite of symmetrical warfare. In this form of combat, one side fights conventionally, but the other side organizes itself differently, may or may not share the same objectives as its opponent, may or may not represent a government or a movement aspiring to become a government, and rejects the conventions or laws of warfare propounded by the conventional side.

In the current context, symmetrical warfare is associated with the Western military tradition associated with modern Europe and, more recently, North America and other parts of the world that have adopted its norms. The salient characteristics of countries operating in this tradition include the fielding of mass armies, navies, and air forces that are similarly organized and configured (e.g., wearing regular uniforms, organized in traditional rank orderings), follow Clausewitzian principles regarding the subordination of war to its political purposes, fight as representatives of state governments seeking to realize the interests of states, and accept common rules about what is permissible and impermissible in war (e.g., treatment of prisoners, acceptability of purposely targeting civilians). Although not all wars fought in this tradition completely mirror all of these characterizations and not all conventions are honored all the time by all participants, it is the general and expected means of war. Those who hold these values view adherence to them as honorable and deviation from them as somehow less than honorable.

In the current debate, asymmetrical approaches are more closely related to what is described as the Asiatic (including Middle Eastern) approach to war. This tradition goes back to the beginning of recorded theories of war and is currently manifested in military conduct in which at least one of the opponents is organized in a manner different from a standard armed force (guerrilla fighters, for instance), may or may not have gaining or maintaining government control as its central purpose, may not represent governments or insurgents, and does not accept or practice warfare (especially limits on permissible actions) in accord with Western conventions.

There is nothing new about asymmetrical warfare other than the name. Its underlying motivations are clear and have deep roots. As already argued, asymmetrical approaches to warfare are attractive to those who cannot compete successfully using conventional methods and whose only chance for success requires changing the playing field so that they do have a chance. As Vincent Goulding Jr. put it in a recent article, it is the approach by which "weaker opponents have sought to neutralize their enemy's technological or numerical superiority by fighting in ways or on battlefields that nullify it." If you cannot win fighting one way, it makes sense to find another way with which you can succeed. The principle is as old as the first armed group that faced a superior enemy it could not possibly defeat if it fought according to the accepted rules of the day.

Put in a slightly different way, asymmetrical warfare is unconventional warfare. Symmetrical warfare is the preference of those entities that are advantaged under accepted forms of war, whereas asymmetrical approaches are appealing to those who cannot compete successfully within the constraints of those rules. In the current environment, the world's most vociferous champion of symmetrical warfare is quite understandably the United States, because the United States has overwhelmingly the world's most powerful conventional forces.

Evolution of Asymmetrical Warfare

As already stated, the term *asymmetrical warfare* is a good bit newer than the phenomenon it describes. Methods of warfare displaying some or all of this style of warfare have a long history, have been described with a variety of names, and have long been at least a small part of the American military tradition.

The idea of trying to negate the advantages of opponents fighting in whatever may be the conventional warfare of the day is as old as organized warfare. Although styles and tactics have changed, conventional warfare has almost always been conducted by massed, uniformed armies divided into ranks who used their weight and firepower to confront and overwhelm opponents. It is how the Roman Legions generally fought—although Belfigio (see Selected Bibliography) points out that they also occasionally engaged in what we would now call asymmetrical methods—and it is how the various combatants in World Wars I and II conducted war. Normally, this style of warfare is conducted in conformance with some broad set of rules of engagement that specify acceptable and unacceptable conduct in battle. Through history, there have been notable exceptions to this depiction—the Mongol hordes substituted maneuver for mass and ignored conventions on the treatment of prisoners, for instance. The tradition of this style of warfare, what we are now calling symmetrical warfare, is highly Western in content and values. More to the point, it is key to the "American way of war."

Normally, an opposing force that lacks the mass of a conventional armed force in either quantitative or qualitative terms cannot successfully confront a conventional force on its own terms and prevail. In that circumstance, the options available to the inferior force are either to quit the contest and surrender, to stand before and be destroyed by the superior force, or to adopt a style of warfare that negates the advantages of the superior force and provides an opportunity for success. In other words, the only possible avenue for victory is to fight asymmetrically.

The asymmetrical tradition is most associated with Asian styles of fighting. The original Chinese military manual, Sun Tzu's Art of War, is a virtual primer on how to shift the advantage from a superior to an inferior force. Many of the principles originally laid out by Sun Tzu were adapted and operationalized by Mao Zedung in his campaigns against the Guomintang led by Chiang Kai-shek in the twenty-plus years of the Chinese Civil War and were in turn adapted by the Vietnamese historian turned general Vo Nguyen Giap in his campaigns first against the French and later against the Americans between 1945 and 1975. Hundreds of years earlier, the Vietnamese successfully evicted Kublai Khan and the Mongols from Vietnam during the thirteenth century using similar techniques.

The style of warfare represented by the asymmetrical tradition has known different names across time. A parallel term is guerrilla warfare, used to describe a particular style of warfare involving highly unconventional tactics employed for the traditional end of gaining control of a government. Asymmetrical is to symmetrical warfare as unconventional is to conventional warfare. Terms such as partisan or people's war have also been used as synonyms. The purpose of this is not to confuse the reader, but to point out that asymmetrical warfare has known many names and that the names change more than the underlying principles on which they are based.

Asymmetrical warfare is part of the American military tradition as well, beginning in the earliest days of the white settlement of North America. Most of the Indians whom the settlers encountered fought unconventionally at the tactical level, engaging in ambushes—hiding behind trees and rocks—and otherwise behaving in ways that did not conform to the tactics of linear warfare practiced in Europe. Moreover, when the American Revolution began, it quite quickly became apparent that the fledgling Continental Army could not successfully contest the British Army in linear battles, and some of its tactics moved from the symmetrical to the asymmetri-

Amplification 9.1

SUN TZU ON ASYMMETRICAL WARFARE

Little is known about Sun Tzu, a Chinese military thinker who advised several warlords in China about 3,000 years ago. His classic military manual *The Art of War* (similar in intent to Machiavelli's political manual for Italian leaders in the sixteenth century) was little studied in the West until it became known that it was one of the sources of inspiration for Mao Zedung in his campaign to seize control of China over a twenty-year period ending in 1949.

The heart of Sun Tzu's military advice, which would be familiar to practitioners of what is now called asymmetrical warfare, was knowing when and how to fight. His statement of indirection and asymmetry is best stated in his advice to military leaders of his time: "When the enemy advances, we retreat; when the enemy halts, we harass; when the enemy seeks to avoid battle, we attack; when the enemy retreats, we pursue." In addition, he adds that the victor on the battlefield has a superior understanding of his opponent that allows him to deceive and thus alter favorably the battle: "All warfare is based on deception. . . . To subdue the enemy without fighting is the acme of skill. Thus, what is of supreme importance is to attack the enemy's strategy." Echoing that sentiment 3,000 years later, Goulding adds, "War might usually favor the side with the heaviest battalions, but it *always* favors the smartest." Does war really change?

cal. America's first great victory in the Revolutionary War, at Saratoga in 1777, was a classic linear clash, but its success was largely the result of attrition of the British expeditionary force coming down from Lake Champlain, caused by American militiamen fighting Indian-style. By the time General Burgoyne's army finally reached Saratoga, attrition had reduced it to about half the size of its American counterpart. The United States also faced asymmetrical opponents in the Seminole Wars in the 1820s in Florida, in the campaigns against the Western Indians after the Civil War, in the Filipino Insurgency at the turn of the twentieth century, and against Pancho Villa in New Mexico and Arizona in the 1910s.

The United States' most extensive and traumatic encounter with an opponent practicing a form of asymmetrical warfare was, of course, in Vietnam. The basic situation conformed neatly to the distinctions we have already made and, as we shall see, has some parallels in the ongoing campaign against the remnants of the Taliban in Afghanistan and the Iraqi resistance to the American occupation in 2003.

Consider the basic structure of the military situation in Vietnam. The Vietnamese insurgents (the North Vietnamese and Viet Cong) faced an American-organized and hence thoroughly conventional South Vietnamese opponent. Following the basic outlines of the Maoist mobile-guerrilla warfare strategy (see Snow, *Distant Thunder*, Ch. 3, for a description), the North Vietnamese Army (NVA) and the Viet Cong (VC) had worn down the Army of the Republic of Vietnam (ARVN) through a guerrilla war of attrition and, by 1964, had gained such a military advantage that it converted to conventional warfare, confronting the ARVN in a symmetrical fashion for the purpose of destroying it and seizing political power.

The United States entered the fray with combat forces in 1965. The South Vietnamese were in desperate straits when the intervention occurred, but American conventional military power quickly reversed the military situation. This change was first demonstrated in the two-day Battle of the Ia Drang Valley in November 1965, an encounter vividly captured in Moore and Galloway's *We Were Soldiers, Once. . . and Young* (which was the basis of the motion picture *We Were Soldiers*). On the first day of the battle, an NVA conventional force encountered and engaged a U.S. Marines force in a conventional battle. The overwhelming American advantage in firepower (mass) turned the confrontation into a deadly shooting gallery in which the NVA was severely bloodied. On the second day, however, the Americans began a march to the staging area from which they were to be evacuated that stretched the troops single file over three miles, and the NVA responded by reverting to guerrilla tactics of ambush and hit-and-run attacks by small units that could avoid the Americans' concentrated firepower. The result was a defeat for the Americans.

Although largely unrecognized at the time, the Ia Drang experience was a parable of sorts for understanding the dynamics of Vietnam and of symmetrical and asymmetrical warfare. Prior to the American intervention, the NVA and VC were fighting symmetrical (conventional) war against the ARVN, and they were succeeding. (The ARVN continued to fight that way, because although they were losing, it was the only way they knew how to fight.) When the United States entered the contest, however, the much more modestly equipped NVA and VC realized that they could not compete with American firepower in symmetrical combat, leaving them the choices of surrender, loss, or changing the rules to give them a chance of success.

The asymmetrical style they selected was the guerrilla phase of mobile-guerrilla warfare. Instead of standing toe-to-toe with the Americans, they reverted to guerrilla tactics such as ambush and avoidance of concentrations of American forces. Capturing and holding territory ceased to be a central concern; instead, they sought to wear down the American forces, to drag out the war until the Americans wearied of the contest and public opinion demanded they leave. It was the classic Vietnamese approach that they had used seven hundred years earlier to rid themselves of the Mongols, and it ultimately worked equally well against the Americans. And, of course, when the Americans left in 1973, the NVA abandoned asymmetrical methods and returned to conventional, symmetrical warfare to finish off the job the Americans had interrupted during their stay.

The Contemporary Setting

Proponents of the idea that there is a new kind of war argue that asymmetrical warfare is the overwhelming wave of the future, and even a brief examination of the contemporary environment suggests that there is some truth in the assertion. Aside from the demise of the Cold War, the contemporary setting differs from the environment surrounding Vietnam in one significant military way, the overwhelming and growing military disparity between the most advanced countries—especially the United States—and the rest, including the developing countries in which violence most often occurs. This trend was made evident to all serious observers originally in the Persian Gulf War, and it was reinforced in the campaign against the Taliban and Al Qaeda and in the Iraq war of 2003. The major implication of the trend is a likely increase in the adoption of asymmetrical methods when confronting Western— especially American—forces.

The Impact of the RMA.   The growing gap in qualitative military capabilities is largely the result of the revolution in military affairs (RMA). Without going into diverting detail, the idea of an RMA (there have been several of them historically) is the impact of a particular technology or series of technologies on the battlefield when those scientific discoveries are applied to warfare. The classic study of how new weaponry changes the nature and outcome of war was the Brodies' *From Crossbow to H-Bomb*. A good twentieth-century example of the effects of applying new technology to warfare was the impact of the internal combustion engine, which allowed the development of weapons such as the tank and the armored personnel carrier and made possible the *blitzkrieg* tactics introduced by the Germans in World War II and widely employed by all combatants in that war.

The current RMA features the application of advances in computing and telecommunications to modern warfare. The "computer revolution" was first applied by the United States in the Vietnam conflict in ways such as using electronic sensing of VC and NVA troop movements. At the time, the applications were fairly primitive (for example, the VC stymied the sensors by hanging sacks of human waste above them, which emitted heat and caused the sensors constantly to record troops going by when none were), and there was inadequate appreciation of the strategic implications of the application of technology to the war. The early attempts in Vietnam, however, were no more than the tip of the iceberg of contemporary applications.

The "weaponization" of so-called high technology began to mature in the years following Vietnam. Although technology has had a pervasive influence, it has been most dramatic in two related areas that have most widened capability disparities: reconnaissance and weapons accuracy. Reconnaissance has been enhanced dramatically by satellite imagery, which, when wedded with the most modern telecommunications equipment, allows the location of both friendly and adversarial forces over a wide area and in considerable detail. To aid in visualization of the battlefield, for instance, high-definition television (HDTV) was subsidized by the U.S. Department of Defense to produce the most vivid, detailed pictures of combat areas possible. Particularly when this kind of information is available to one side but not the other, the result is a considerable advantage for the possessor and an almost insurmountable disadvantage for the side that lacks the capacity. In its most extreme manifestation, the possessor knows where his opponent is and can target him all of the time, whereas the nonpossessor never knows where the enemy is or when and how that enemy is likely to strike.

The second advance has been in guidance capabilities that allow the precision delivery of munitions—usually airborne from cruise missiles or bomber aircraft— over long distances with astonishing accuracy. This capability makes it possible for the possessor, once he has found an enemy, to attack him promptly and with a very high degree of success. Because the munitions normally can be fired from distances outside visual range and at speeds such that they cannot be seen, the victim is help-less to protect himself. Because these weapons are often fired outside the range of the attacked party's weapons as well, the victims have no means of retaliation. In the most advanced instances, these weapons can approximate what is sometimes called a "one-to-one kill ratio" (a single weapon destroys the target).

Reconnaissance and precision delivery are just two of the more important aspects of the current RMA. All these applications have the effect of being *force mul-tipliers*, or enhancers of the effectiveness (lethality) of the force that possesses them. In addition, they all reduce dramatically the vulnerability of the warriors who possess them, thereby dramatically reducing casualty rates for the possessing state while increasing the rates for the victims. Reducing casualties is an important considera-tion, of course, for democratic countries, which are supposedly less willing to incur war dead than the nondemocratic states against which these weapons are often used.

The Persian Gulf War Example.   The first application of this growing disparity occurred in the Persian Gulf War of 1990–91. After the Iraqi invasion, conquest, and threatened annexation of tiny Kuwait in August 1990, a military coalition was organized to reverse that outcome. The United States took the lead in organizing the effort, under United Nations auspices, and eventually brought together a coalition of twenty-five states, including some Islamic countries from the region, to oppose Sad-dam Hussein.

At the time, there was great concern about how difficult the military task of dis-lodging the Iraqis from Kuwait would be. Iraq possessed the fourth largest army in the world, it was pointed out, and it was a battle-tested force, having fought for eight years in the Iran–Iraq war that ended in 1988. In those circumstances, many pre-dicted a stout defense by the Iraqis, and widely varied speculations abounded about, among other things, the level of casualties the United States would incur.

Those who predicted large numbers of casualties were proven wrong, as the war turned out to be a walkover in military terms, largely for two reasons. First, the appli-cations of the RMA to the forces of the major Western powers (the United States and, to a lesser degree, Britain and France) had created such a technological dispar-ity between the two opponents that the Iraqis stood no practical chance against the coalition troops. Second, Saddam Hussein misperceived both American will (he believed the United States was still so traumatized by Vietnam that it would not react decisively) and the relative strength of his forces against the Americans and their allies. As a result, he engaged his Soviet-trained and Soviet-styled armed forces in conventional, symmetrical warfare fought on the terms of the coalition, against which he could not prevail.

The major difference was the RMA. When the air war commenced, the Ameri-cans attacked and destroyed the Iraqi radar and communications infrastructure on the first day. For the rest of the campaign, the United States had uncontested control of the skies while the Iraqis were limited in their ability to monitor activities of the coalition literally to what they could see standing on the ground. Meanwhile, satel-lite images provided detailed images of Iraqi locations and movements. As an example, the global positioning system (GPS) meant that the Americans always knew where they were in the featureless Arabian Desert, whereas the Iraqis were never certain of their own, much less the enemy's, location. At the same time, the Americans were able to locate Iraqi targets and to direct precision munitions to them well out of range of Iraqi retaliatory capabilities. Although subsequent assessments have indicated that some of the more dramatic claims of superiority were inflated, nevertheless the results were an overwhelming coalition victory with very few coalition—specifically, American—war deaths (less than 150, not all of which were the result of hostile action). The implication for future developing countries taking on the United States symmetrically using American rules was clear to all concerned.

The Afghanistan Reprise.   The same dynamic occurred again in 2001 when the United States broadened its response to the terrorist attacks of September 11, 2001, to include deposing the Taliban government of Afghanistan. In order to achieve its underlying purpose—the destruction of the bin Laden organization, Al Qaeda, which was being shielded by the Taliban regime—it was determined that a prefatory step had to be the overthrow of the Afghan regime after it refused to turn over bin Laden and his followers to the United States for prosecution. The result was to involve the United States in what had been a reasonably conventional civil war between the Taliban and opposing factions, notably the Northern Coalition.

Prior to the U.S. entry into the conflict with special operations forces and air-power, the Taliban had been engaged in a conventional civil conflict with their opponents. Success and failure in that conflict was measured by territory controlled, and the clear purpose was for one side to maintain or the other to gain political power for territorially defined, clearly traditional purposes. The fighting itself was reasonably conventional, with thrusts and parries in one direction or the other, and fortified lines facing one another across the harsh Afghan vista. It was war the way it had been fought for centuries among Afghan factions, and it was a war in which the Taliban were holding their own or winning.

Enter the Americans. After the Taliban leadership refused to capture and relinquish bin Laden and his followers into international custody, the United States began to mount a military campaign the purpose of which was to force the Taliban to comply and turn over the terrorist or, failing in obtaining that goal, physically to assist in the overthrow of the regime, thereby removing that barrier to bringing the terrorist to justice.

The military campaign involved the use of both conventional and unconventional forces. The SOFs were among the first dispatched to Afghanistan, coordinating efforts with anti-Taliban rebel forces, securing crucial staging grounds such as airfields (a task for which marines were also used), and acting as spotters, directing the bombers to their targets. The real hammer of the operation, of course, was air-power, both from fixed-wing aircraft relentlessly bombing Taliban and, later, Al Qaeda positions and from helicopter gunships strafing suspected concentrations of enemy forces.

The Taliban apparently did not anticipate either the fury or the deadly effect of the American action. It is arguable that the Taliban failed to anticipate American actions because they believed bin Laden's assessment of prior American responses to terrorist attacks. In those cases, bin Laden had publicly claimed that the United States had either done nothing in retaliation, as occurred after the Khobar apartments attack in 1996 and the attack on the *USS Cole* in 2000, or had carried out a symbolic but ineffective response, as in the cruise missile attacks on supposed terrorist training camps in Afghanistan in 1998 after the bombings of the American embassies in Dar es Salaam and Nairobi. Bin Laden had also suggested in various pronouncements that he believed that the Americans were obsessed with avoiding casualties under any circumstances and that they clearly would not put American forces in harm's way.

Whatever the basis of their assessment, the Taliban were clearly wrong and did not respond appropriately to the American aerial assault. Past experience has suggested (at least to some) that airpower can be devastating to concentrations of exposed forces (in other words, forces fighting Western-style symmetrical warfare), but that it loses some of its effect if its targets take evasive action, such as dispersing and retreating into more impregnable positions, such as the Afghan mountains (in other words, adopting asymmetrical methods). To do this, of course, the Taliban forces would have had to abandon the lines they used to protect the physical areas under their control to the advancing Northern Alliance and other opponents.

The Taliban options were devil's choices. Beyond the option of surrender, they could either continue the war as they had been fighting it, which meant symmetrically, or they could stage a Maoist reversion to asymmetrical warfare. In either case, they were likely to lose, either by being pounded into submission by their airpower-aided opponents in a continuation of the conventional war or by retreating into the mountains, where they would become the hunted opposition that had abandoned the territory they controlled. They initially chose to stand and fight, leaving themselves ready targets for American bombs. The effect was predictable—if more rapid than anticipated. In addition to killing a large number of Taliban fighters, the sheer shock effect of the bombing apparently destroyed the cohesion of the Taliban forces, sapping their morale and will to continue fighting. With the Taliban bombed into disarray, they and the remaining Al Qaeda fighters retreated to the mountains, where they have managed to resist attempts to capture their remaining fighters by adopting long-held asymmetrical tactics such as evasion.

The Iraq War.   The impact of the RMA, combined with blitzkrieg-style maneuver techniques, was also felt dramatically in Iraq. The Americans and British were able to sweep through the country virtually unopposed except in a few cities like Basra. In addition to the "shock and awe" effects of massive precision bombing, the heart of the success was the extreme speed with which the forces moved, demoralizing and dispiriting those Iraqi foes who did not melt into the population.

The Strategic Effects.   The dual lessons of the Persian Gulf War and the Afghanistan and Iraqi campaigns should be clear, and so should their implications be clear for likely uses of American force in the future. The assessment is not without irony, as already noted. At bottom, the United States and its closest allies have become so proficient at conventional warfare that they are likely to be able to engage in such methods only against extremely foolish or masochistic opponents. At the same time, the maintenance of such force will continue to be necessary to remind potential future opponents of the folly of challenging the United States symmetrically and to punish anyone who does not understand and act according to that truth.

The three experiences clearly reinforce the gap in conventional capabilities that has been widened to a chasm between RMA-proficient forces and conventional forces that do not share those capabilities. In Kuwait, Afghanistan, and Iraq, the opponents of the United States stood and fought symmetrically in circumstances in which they realistically had no chance of prevailing, and in all cases they were thoroughly and efficiently routed. This gap in capability between the military "haves" and "have nots" will only widen further in the future, which means that the consequences will remain as well.

Much has been said since Vietnam about the failure of American will, especially the American aversion to accepting casualties. Saddam Hussein apparently reasoned in 1990 that the United States would not respond forcefully to his aggression in Kuwait out of a paralyzing fear of another Vietnam, and bin Laden and the Taliban apparently assumed that the militarily tepid nature of American responses to previous provocations were symptoms of that same reluctance. This perception has invaded even American military thinking, as in the dictate that American bombers fly above Yugoslav anti-aircraft range during the campaign to end the ethnic cleansing of Kosovo in 1999 (pilots were required to fly at 15,000 feet or above, thereby limiting the effectiveness of their efforts).

Two factors from the Kuwait, Afghanistan, and Iraq experiences should mitigate this perception and thus temper future assessments of how or if the United States will respond when provoked. One of the consequences of American conventional dominance that was first demonstrated in Kuwait and was reinforced in Afghanistan and Iraq has been the ability to reduce American casualties greatly through the application of technology. American losses in Kuwait and Iraq were, after all, less than 150 dead from hostile causes during organized fighting, and there have been only a handful of American casualties in Afghanistan. The mass of American firepower and the distance from which it can be employed not only devastates its opponents if they try to confront it directly, it also saves American lives. The old myth that an opponent can force an American withdrawal by killing a few American soldiers is very difficult to achieve when fighting symmetrically with the Americans. Whether the postwar Iraqi resistance will rekindle American aversion to casualties remains an open question at this writing.

The Afghanistan experience provides another angle on American willingness to accept battle losses. The reaction to the terrorist attacks reminded us of another factor—that Americans have always been willing to put lives at risk *if the cause was sufficient*. The question of the unacceptability of casualties has arisen when people thought the cause was insufficient to justify the sacrifice, as in places such as Somalia. In that sense, the analogy between the terrorist attacks on September 11, 2001, and Pearl Harbor are apt, as captured in Admiral Yamamoto's response when he learned that the Japanese ultimatum was not delivered until after the Japanese had attacked: "We have awakened a sleeping giant and filled him with a terrible resolve."

The lessons of these combined experiences for future potential American (or more broadly, Western) opponents should be fairly obvious. The most obvious lesson, of course, is that it is fool's work to challenge the Western powers at their own game; symmetrical warfare with the West is suicidal. It has been suggested that one way for weaker states to level the playing field would be to introduce weapons of mass destruction (WMD) such as chemical or biological weapons on the battlefield. Such a suggestion misses the essential point and actually reinforces the disparity. Should Saddam Hussein have introduced chemical or biological agents into the Gulf War (as it has been suggested he contemplated doing), the overwhelming Western advantage in WMD would have simply made his defeat all the more decisive—with the United States, for instance, responding to a chemical attack against its forces with a more or less controlled nuclear response. Fortunately for most potential opponents of the West, they lack the military resources for a symmetrical challenge anyway.

The other obvious lesson is how to fight the West if a clash becomes inevitable. The overwhelming weight of American and other Western might means that a challenger cannot confront that power directly and can succeed only by changing the rules in ways that allow some possibility of success. Vietnam again provides a model of sorts. The North Vietnamese government understood shortly after the American intervention that it could not defeat the United States symmetrically, so it reverted to an asymmetrical style (guerrilla warfare) that negated the American advantages in technology and firepower. It attacked the American will to continue the contest by inflicting a large enough number of casualties on the Americans (although the numbers were trifles compared to the casualties it incurred) to convince the American public and its leaders that persevering was not worthwhile. What ultimately undermined the American campaign was not, as Saddam Hussein and Usama bin Laden apparently concluded, an American unwillingness to incur losses, it was our unwillingness to do so in what we concluded was a *less than worthy cause*.

This assessment leaves some ironic implications for American preparation for the future. On the one hand, the only countries that could possibly confront the United States in conventional, symmetrical warfare are our closest allies (NATO) and other countries with which we have developed such close relations that war is unthinkable (Russia, China). All realistic potential foes either lack an armed force that could challenge us directly or realize that such a force would lose. Saddam Hussein taught the world that lesson. Thus, the very kind of application of force at which we most excel is the least likely kind of force we will have occasion to use in the near future.

That does not mean, however, that conventional force can be abandoned, dismantled, or substantially diminished. Although it may be debatable whether current American forces deter *all* kinds of attacks on the United States (future terrorist assaults, for instance), they certainly *do* deter conventional attacks that might be contemplated if they didn't exist. At the same time, Kuwait, Afghanistan, and Iraq demonstrate that situations can arise periodically in which such forces can be brought to bear with decisive effect.

What this analysis suggests is that, in the future, most of the situations in which the United States will have the opportunity to use force will be against an opponent that adopts asymmetrical methods to try to obviate the American dominance in conventional warfare. This would suggest an emphasis on light forces (see Chapter 8) and on special purpose forces, such as SOFs, as well as on precision airpower. On the other hand, the campaign against the Taliban would have been much more arduous and difficult in the absence of conventional applications of the RMA. Determining which kind of force will be necessary for what kind of contingency thus requires examining likely future conflicts based on our contemporary experiences.

ASYMMETRICAL FUTURES?

Although it is arguable that asymmetrical warfare is not as novel as some analysts and policy makers imply in the post–September 11, 2001, environment, it is nonetheless true that this form of warfare has not been as publicly prominent in policy discussions in the past as it is today. In order to get a better idea of what the dynamics of asymmetrical warfare are and how they may affect the future, we will look at two models. One of them is a more or less theoretical construct predicting what some analysts during the 1990s thought about the likely future of warfare and providing a generic description of that future—what has been called *fourth-generation warfare*. The other, about which I have written in *Uncivil Wars* and other works, is a description of the empirical nature of a series of chaotic civil wars of the 1990s and beyond that I have called the *new internal wars* (NIWs). They are basically similar depictions, with NIWs essentially serving as concrete examples of how the fourth generation of warfare may look in parts of the world. These constructs are important to examine in terms of whether they will become the dominant form of future conflict or just an additional element of the pattern of war.

Fourth-Generation Warfare

A body of thought among military historians and other analysts has for some time argued that conventional, Western-style warfare—especially warfare conducted along Clausewitzian lines—represents an aberration rather than a universal phenomenon. In particular, these analysts maintain that the kind of warfare we have described as symmetrical is a temporal oddity. Among the champions of this position has been the British historian John Keegan, who argues that there has been a kind of Clausewitzian interlude, beginning with the Napoleonic era and ending with World War II, when the trinitarian relationship among the people, the government, and the armed forces was dominant and when Western norms of warfare prevailed. Keegan argues that that era has passed and that the dominant pattern of warfare in the future, as it was in the past before the Napoleonic period, will be what we have identified as asymmetrical warfare. A persistent band of contemporary analysts agrees; for some of them, the dominant analogy is fourth-generation warfare.

The term *fourth-generation warfare* represents a conceptual and physical departure from the dominance of Western-style warfare. One of the earlier depictions of this change, described by a group headed by a former aide to Senator Gary Hart,

William Lind, in the October 1989 *Marine Corps Gazette*, examines the evolution of warfare from the Napoleonic period forward. The authors maintain that the first generation of warfare was dominated by linear formations of armies clashing in open fields, and the dominant weaponry was the smooth-bore musket. This form of fighting favored the offensive actions of the conventional armies in combat. The second generation was the result of the introduction of much more accurate rifles and muskets, which made the charges of tightly configured formations suicidal. The trench warfare of World War I is the epitome of this kind of defensively dominated war. With the weaponization of technologies such as the truck and tank and the storage battery (for propelling submarines), the pendulum swung back to the offensive advantage, as maneuver was reintroduced onto the battlefield. The epitome of this third-generation warfare was the *blitzkrieg* style of fighting mastered by Germany in World War II.

What is notable about these three generations is how geopolitically and militarily traditional they are. In all three cases, they describe warfare fought by Western national armies organized conventionally and with clear and identifiable political purposes for their actions. The changes from generation to generation are not radical but are largely the result of changes in weapons technologies and adaptation of strategies and tactics that reflect those changes. At the same time, this Western-style warfare features the clash of armies frontally when the major purpose of conflict is for one side or the other to defeat the enemy on the field of battle as a necessary preface to imposing its political will on the vanquished. It is fundamentally a Clausewitzian vision of war.

Those who suggest a new kind of war, either using the fourth-generation analogy or not, maintain that we are entering a period of radical change in warfare. One of the apostles of this change is the Israeli analyst Martin van Creveld, who described the magnitude of the change he foresees a decade ago in *The Transformation of War*. His basic argument is that the Western paradigm of war is being broken. The Clausewitzian base, for instance, is shattered because, "should present trends continue, the kind of war that is based on the division between government, army, and people seems to be on its way out." The result will be the crumbling of conventional nationally based military forces. As he puts it, "Much present-day military power is simply irrelevant as an instrument for extending or defending political interests over much of the globe."

What replaces conventional, trinitarian warfare in the van Creveld scheme? He argues that the change is fundamental in terms of the units that wage war, the methods of combat they use, and the purposes for which they fight. In his words, "In the future, wars will not be waged by armies but by groups whom we today call terrorists, guerrillas, bandits and robbers. Their organizations are likely to be constructed on charismatic lines rather than institutional ones, and to be motivated less by 'professionalism' than by fanatical, ideologically based loyalties." The new kind of war, in other words, turns the traditional warfare of the first three generations on its head both organizationally and in terms of its underlying purposes.

The arguments surrounding this alleged transformation are, of course, controversial. Although they have been debated for a decade or more, most of the discussions have been confined to places such as the war colleges, where they have been extensively argued and dissected. Because the arguments, if accepted, cut to the core of Western-style military values, there has been a tendency, if not a vested interest, in dismissing or denigrating their truth and their implications for how the professional military performs its functions in the future.

The events of September 11, 2001, have brought these arguments out of the shadows and onto center stage. The actions by bin Laden and his colleagues clearly meet parts of the description of future war described by van Creveld, and the popularization of the term *new kind of war* has sent many scrambling to find out what this newness is. There is no consensus at this point.

We cannot settle all the controversy here. What we can do is describe what the champions of the new form of war claim about it. Because the terrorist attacks and the subsequent campaign against the Taliban and Al Qaeda proved the stimulus for consideration of the fourth generation, we can also ask how an assessment of that experience reinforces or undercuts the claims of those arguing fundamental change.

Characteristics of Fourth-Generation Warfare.   Although there are other available depictions that differ in detail, the Lind et al. framework is useful for describing what people mean when they talk about fourth-generation warfare. What is interesting about their analysis is that it not only argues the change that marks the fourth generation, but it also points out how important elements of the new environment have their roots in the past and evolving kinds of war.

Lind and his colleagues argue that there are several characteristics of fourth generation warfare that can be traced to the past. In terms of the conduct of hostilities, for instance, they maintain in the future there will be no distinctions between civilians and military forces in terms of targeting: Society is the battlefield in the new environment. There will be an absence of definable battlefields or fronts, and the places where fighting occurs will be dispersed and undefined: Everywhere and nowhere is the front lines. The result is a much more fluid military situation, in which traditional concerns such as logistics and tallies such as land gained or lost will largely lose meaning as measures of military success.

The purposes of fighting will also change, at least for those who adopt the methodologies of the fourth generation. The goal will be not traditional military defeat, but the internal political collapse of the opponent and its will to continue. Manipulation of the media will be a skill that is highly sought by practitioners of the fourth generation, and the targets of much of this activity will be popular support for the government or whatever force against which the campaign is waged.

To this point, the description of fourth-generation warfare is still not terribly innovative. Although one can see elements of it in the terrorist attacks (not distinguishing between military and civilian targets, for instance), almost all of these characteristics could easily be ascribed to the NVA and VC asymmetrical campaign against the United States a third of a century ago. In fact, this part of the description is largely attributable to the postmortem of the American experience in Vietnam.

Lind and his colleagues extend these characteristics in trying to describe the basic nature of the fourth generation. First, they argue explicitly the non-Western, Asiatic (including Middle Eastern) basis of this form of warfare. In an article published in October 2001, Keegan embellished this connection:

The Oriental tradition, however, has not been eliminated. It reappeared . . . particularly in the tactics of evasion and retreat practiced by the Vietcong against the United States in the Vietnam war. On September 11, 2001, it returned in an absolutely traditional form. Arabs, appearing suddenly out of empty space like their desert raider ancestors, assaulted the heartlands of Western power, in a terrifying surprise raid and did appalling damage.

Second, they argue that terrorism is a standard tactic of practitioners of the fourth generation. Because they are militarily weaker in the traditional (symmetrical) sense, terrorist tactics provide an asymmetrical way to bypass the conventional strength of Western militaries and to strike at the homeland. They are aided in accomplishing these acts by the very openness of free societies, which makes them more easily penetrable. The third major objective of fourth-generation practitioners is the disruption of target societies—what Lind et al. call the "culture of order," which is the direct objective of the attacks. Finally, they argue that movements adopting fourth-generation warfare often will not be nationally based governments but will have a transnational and, on some occasions, even a religious base.

These descriptions, published twelve years before the September 11 attacks, have an eerily prescient ring in terms of what happened in New York and Washington. Van Creveld adds (once again, in 1991) other evidence of similarity: "There will be a tendency to treat leaders as criminals who richly deserve the worst fate that can be inflicted on them. Hence, many leaders will probably decide to remain unattached and lead a seminomadic life."

The Fourth Generation and September 11, 2001.   The descriptions of the nature and implications of fourth-generation warfare seemed virtually to predict the terrible events of September 11, 2001, a decade or more ago, which is, in large measure, why they are quoted here in some detail. Imbedded in these discussions, however, is the further assertion that non-state-based warfare, fought using asymmetrical methods and for nonconventional purposes, will become the dominant form of warfare in the future. Implied in that prediction is the further assertion that traditional, Western national military forces will become obsolete relics because of the new form of warfare.

Does the experience of the terrorist attacks and responses to them bear out these implications? In some ways, they clearly do. The attacks against the Pentagon and the World Trade Center towers clearly fit the descriptions and motivations of the purveyors of this new "model" of warfare. Not all the attributes were new, of course—terrorism is a decidedly old tactic, and terrorist acts committed by nonstate actors are hardly novel in the American or international experience. What sets the attacks apart in the contemporary context is their audacity and scale. Terrorist attacks, by individuals and groups with no formal state affiliation, that kill a relatively small number of people are, if not common, not entirely uncommon. When thousands of innocent people are killed in such attacks, the problem achieves another order of magnitude.

Did the attacks and the subsequent campaign to overthrow the Taliban, destroy Al Qaeda, and capture bin Laden vindicate the apostles of the fourth generation of warfare? In other words, were the ways in which America's asymmetrical foes fought sufficiently frustrating to the United States that we felt the need to reformulate how the military goes about its business in the face of future repetitions that may become the norm for future violence?

The short-term answer would seem to be overwhelmingly in the negative. Admittedly, the Taliban did not engage in a campaign of asymmetrical warfare after the Americans entered the civil war to bring about their ouster, which was a major mistake caused by the irony of their situation. At the same time, part of the reason for their defeat may also have been a seething, if repressed, hatred for their rule, which meant that most of their countrymen offered them neither aid nor comfort when they came under the relentless fury of the American bombers. Some of the ease with which the Taliban were dispatched stemmed from their lack of popular support at home.

Al Qaeda, on the other hand, did attempt to fight asymmetrically, and it did them slightly more good. While the Taliban remained in their conventional lines providing target practice for the bombers and the Northern Alliance, the Al Qaeda fighters headed for the cave-pocked mountains, where they went into deep hiding, emulating their Viet Cong predecessors.

Ultimately, Al Qaeda ended up in the Tora Bora Mountains and beyond, where they were pounded by the combined conventional might of the Americans and the various Afghan factions, but not entirely broken. All the adherence to apparently novel forms of warfare did not keep them from being forced to go deep underground, and bin Laden and his closest cohorts evaded the dragnet out to snare them. Conventional force was able to reduce Al Qaeda to a shadow of its prewar status but was not quite able to destroy it completely. The reason may be that the problem confronting the United States and its allies was a hybrid of conventional and unconventional elements. When the situation was conventional, traditional forces were effective. When the opposition adopted ways of war more compatible with the fourth generation, however, the results were more mixed. At any rate, the overall experience in this particular instance of the "new kind of war" does not decisively demonstrate the obsolescence of more traditional forms of warfare. In this case, the part of the war that was probably mislabeled (the terrorist attacks themselves and their aftermath) resembled the fourth generation, whereas the fairly traditional phase dealing with the Taliban and Al Qaeda in Afghanistan more resembled the older form of war. Assigning labels and proclaiming success are probably premature at this stage.

New Internal Wars

Although the events of September 11, 2001, have understandably held our attention more fully, another form of warfare has been raging over the last decade or more in parts of the developing world in the form of often grotesque and hideous conflicts that I have identified as the new internal wars (NIWs).

This kind of war broke onto the public scene during the 1990s, although there were a few internal conflicts during the Cold War that met all or most of the criteria for classification as NIWs. What sets these conflicts apart from previous internal conflicts is their disorderliness and the extreme violence and apparent senselessness of the suffering being exacted, mainly against civilian populations, by their country-men. Moreover, although they have occurred most often in places far from the geopolitical spotlight, the unrelenting eye of global electronic mediation has focused upon them as the "warts" in what, until September 11, 2001, had appeared a very benign international environment, at least in terms of threats and violence.

The end of the Cold War contributed to the emergence of the NIWs as a major phenomenon in the pattern of world violence. Internal conflicts were the dominant form of war during the Cold War, and in that sense, the NIWs represent a continua-tion of the pattern that occurred during the period of superpower competition. At the same time, civil conflict during the Cold War generally had the character of tradi-tional insurgency, in which the structure of the violence featured a government seek-ing to maintain itself in power, supported by one of the superpowers (usually the United States), and an insurgency employing some form of mobile-guerrilla war model that sought power and was supported by the other superpower (usually the Soviet Union). Superpower presence layered an often irrelevant Communist/anti-Communist aspect to contests more properly understood in other terms (ethnic or tribal dominance, for instance), but it also brought restraint to the fighting, since nei-ther superpower wanted its client (and by extension, itself) charged with atrocities.

The war in Cambodia in the 1970s between the Khmer Rouge and its opponents was the major exception to this rule (the contending sides were sponsored by the Soviet Union and China), and in many ways, it was the prototype for the NIWs. The brutal, genocidal campaign by the Khmer Rouge government to transform Cambodian society into a pastoral, docile condition produced a litany of horrors which war crimes investigators are still unraveling. They also provided a frightening portent of the future of internal war that was largely ignored at the time.

The list of the most prominent instances of these new internal wars is familiar. The post–Cold War prototype occurred (and in limited form is still going on) in Somalia, where a combination of a long drought and the use of international food supplies as weapons in the clan-based conflict for power threatened to result in mas-sive starvation until an international peacekeeping force intervened to interrupt the suffering. "Ethnic cleansing" was added to the language of international politics as Serbs, Croats, and Bosnian Muslims struggled to partition the Bosnian successor state to Yugoslavia—and that phenomenon was reprised half a decade later in Kosovo. Between those Balkan conflicts, the United States intervened in Haiti, and the Rwandan nightmare was added to the list in 1994. Simmering NIWs dot the map of Africa, notably in places such as Sierra Leone.

Arguably the dominant form of warfare in the 1990s, the NIWs sent contradic-tory signals to an international system that was enjoying peace and prosperity for the major powers and the apparently inexorable spread of globalization in the develop-ing world. On the one hand, almost all the NIWs occurred outside the band of coun-tries participating in the global economy. That created in those victimized countries a certain sense of marginalization in the developed countries that suggested they

Amplification 9.2

THE "BATTLE" FOR SIERRA LEONE

The civil conflict that has racked the small West African country of Sierra Leone for a decade and has only recently been terminated by the insertion of the United Nations–sponsored peacekeeping force UNAMSIL (United Nations Mission in Sierra Leone) is, in some ways, the epitome of the phenomenon of new internal war.

First, it is not a war in the common sense of the reasons for which war is fought. At various times, three different groups have been involved in shifting coalitions with one another: a weak and unsupported government, an equally weak Sierra Leone army, and the Revolutionary United Front (RUF). The objective of the war is only indirectly control of the Sierra Leone political system, especially for the RUF. The real objective is political destabilization of the country so that no legitimate authority can interfere in the criminal exploitation and smuggling of the country's primary resource, diamonds.

Second, the war is not military in any recognizable sense. The RUF do not even pretend to be soldiers, preferring the designation "fighters," and there have been no battles between the sides worthy of the name *battle*. The principal distinguishing mark of the RUF, before the peace was imposed, consisted of more or less random terror against members of the population. The preferred form of terror was amputation of hands and feet, leaving Sierra Leone with an enormous need for prosthetics, which nongovernmental organizations (NGOs) such as *Medicins sans Frontieres* (MSF, translated into English as Doctors without Borders) have only recently been able to begin to deal with. The result of the "battle" over Sierra Leone has been to leave a helpless, prostrate country that it will take years of concerted effort to rebuild.

could be ignored. Is it any of our business what goes on in East Timor, for instance? On the other hand, the publicity of global television gave full-blown coverage to the human suffering associated with these hideous conflicts and made them difficult to ignore altogether. Who could not be moved by the distended bellies of the starving children of Somalia? the gaunt faces of Bosnian detainees so reminiscent of the German concentration camps? the hacked bodies of Rwandan women and children? the hopeless, helpless visages of Kosovar refugees? the pitiful amputees of Sierra Leone? The security question of the 1990s was what the international community should do about these human tragedies, if anything. Although that question has been pushed from the center of the agenda for a time by the terrorist acts of 2001, the ongoing evolution of the situation in Afghanistan provides a bridge of sorts. Afghanistan was not an NIW (although it had some characteristics of one), but the solution selected for Afghanistan—state building—is also the prescribed solution for states in which NIWs have occurred, as discussed in Chapter 11.

Characteristics of New Internal Wars. The characteristics ascribed to NIWs have been derived differently than those for fourth-generation wars, making any precise form of comparison difficult. As noted earlier, the *Marine Corps Gazette* article from which the list of fourth-generation characteristics was derived combined historical observation of trends with extrapolations into the future. Although some of the characteristics of NIWs do come from past experiences, we have limited our characterizations here to experience to date with more contemporary instances of NIWs and have not tried to extrapolate those trends forward.

The characteristics can be divided into political and military categories. At the political level, the most striking feature of these wars is their nearly total reversal of the kinds of goals found in traditional insurgencies. Unlike traditional civil wars, the control of government is often not the clear objective of both sides. In a number of cases of NIWs, the "rebel" force articulates no political objectives or statements of ideological principles about how it would organize itself to rule. The Revolutionary United Front (RUF) of Sierra Leone, for instance, never issued a manifesto of any kind, and this is not unusual. The apparent reason for this is that the RUF movement has had neither the intention nor the desire to gain control of and govern the country, and this too is not unusual in NIWs. Rather, in a number of cases, the political purpose (to the extent one can call it that) is anarchical, in the sense of seeking to destabilize the country from governmental control by anyone. In these cases, most notably the narco-insurgencies of South America and some parts of Asia and the criminal insurgencies of parts of Africa, the real goal is to create a sense of total lawlessness that maximizes the group's ability to enrich itself either through thievery and worse or by controlling or protecting narcotics trafficking. Such groups often adopt splendid political ("revolutionary front") or otherwise high-sounding (the "Lord's Army" of Uganda) names to mask the basic criminality that forms their purpose.

There is another political characteristic that also helps differentiate NIWs from traditional internal wars and explain the savagery that often dominates these conflicts. Traditional civil wars, as noted, are fought for control of the government of a country, and a central factor in which side prevails is the loyalty of the country's population—the so-called hearts and minds of the people. This "center of gravity" is a point of competition for both sides, and neither side wants to drive the people into the other's arms by committing hideous and unacceptable acts of violence against the population. The need to appeal to the people thus moderates the violence, especially against noncombatant civilians.

Since the goal in NIWs is not to govern but to intimidate or kill those members of the population who might be in opposition, there is no such motivation toward moderation. In Bosnia during the first half of the 1990s, Bosnian Serbs did not seek to appeal to Bosnian Muslims (or vice versa); rather, their aim was to drive people from their homes, move in, and claim the land by virtue of possession. Similarly, the Rwandan Hutus were clearly not appealing politically for the support of the Tutsi as the rampage proceeded; they simply wanted to kill as many people as possible. This absence of a shared center of gravity that needs to be nurtured makes NIWs effectively like wars between states (interstate wars) rather than internal wars (intrastate wars) politically. Like interstate wars, the purpose is to subdue, not to win over, the opponent. Unlike traditional intrastate wars, there is no battle for the "hearts and minds of men" to moderate the slaughter.

The military characteristics of NIWs follow from these nontraditional political characteristics and provide a close parallel with the military characteristics of fourth-generation warfare. Since there are no clear political objectives for these affairs, they do not translate into strategic guidance to form conventional military objectives and operations. The military units that conduct these forms of hostilities are typically highly irregular, not uniformed or organized into coherent rank orderings of officers and enlisted soldiers, poorly trained if they have received any military training at all, and unaware or contemptuous of normal conventions of war. Furthermore, they normally lack a sense of military order or discipline. It is not unusual to have these troops referred to not as "soldiers" but as "fighters," since that is what they truly are. In a number of instances, these fighters have been little more than children, with members of the ranks reportedly no more than ten- to twelve-year olds, often kidnapped and forced into service by the fear of personal or family consequences if they refuse. (The Lord's Army of Uganda, for instance, kidnaps children from orphanages and threatens to kill them if they resist, as a recruiting "appeal.")

Given these characteristics of the forces, the savagery and atrocity associated with these wars should come as little surprise. Echoing the fourth-generation lack of distinction between civilians and military targets, they are marked by high incidences of attacks by fighters against unarmed civilians, notably women and children, the elderly, and other similarly helpless beings. In most NIWs, there are rarely any encounters between the organized armed forces of the two (or more) contending sides (as noted in Amplification 9.2, about Sierra Leone). The large reason for this pattern is that the sides are not organized into military forces that can contend with other organized forces; attacking, mutilating, or killing helpless, innocent civilians is their form of asymmetrical warfare.

The Prospects for NIWs.   One of the notable aspects of NIWs is where they occur. For the most part, internal violence, of which the NIWs are a prominent part, happens in the poorest parts of the world, where the lives of average citizens are among the most miserable and where there is little sense that things can get much worse. This is also the description of the places that have been the breeding grounds of terrorists—notably, the recruitment grounds for many of the fighters associated with Al Qaeda and other terrorist organizations. Although the practitioners of asymmetrical warfare may be motivated by different end states and aspirations, they do share a fairly common breeding ground (this is discussed in the terrorist context in the next chapter).

Before September 11, 2001, refocused our attention, there was a policy debate about whether it was wise for the United States to involve itself in these situations. A major observation about NIWs is that they generally cannot be ended internally, because neither the government nor its opposition possesses the physical capability for toppling the other side (which the "insurgents" may not want to do, preferring to have an ineffectual government than the prospect of an effective successor). It then becomes a question of whether there is sufficient outside interest in trying to do something to end whatever atrocity is occurring. This is an ongoing problem, which is examined in its operational and philosophical aspects in Chapter 11. The point is that the prospects for future NIWs, not unlike those for terrorism, are as good as the prospects for suffering in the world. The question is whether we care less, as much, or more about those prospects now than we did before asymmetrical warfare landed directly on our doorsteps.

CONCLUSION: NEW FORM OR NEW FACE OF WAR?

We conclude by going back to the question raised at he beginning of the chapter: Is the kind of warfare that appeared quite literally in America's face something new? Or is asymmetrical warfare a "back to the future" proposition (to borrow from the title of Goulding's recent article in the U.S. Army's journal, *Parameters*)? As the analysis here has sought to demonstrate, in a purely military sense, what is now called asymmetrical warfare does not represent a great change in war but rather is the approach that has been taken through history by weaker protagonists when facing superior forces. The American reintroduction to this kind of warfare in Vietnam, however, did not prepare us for an opponent who would change the rules of engagement so radically as to attack and destroy the kinds of civilian targets that were attacked on September 11, 2001. The innovation was not the dynamics of war but the physical object of attack.

If asymmetrical warfare as a generic concept is not really new, its manifestations in fourth-generation warfare and new internal war do show some differences from past experience. Clearly, the high level of irregularity of the forces we face—in terms of composition, style, methods, and objects of fighting—is a factor we have not encountered before. At the same time, fighting that is not directed at political goals of gaining or maintaining governance is a novelty in our experience; it creates wartime difficulties in sorting out the sides and postwar difficulties in reconstructing a peace. We understand people who fight like us for the reasons we fight; we are not quite so certain how to deal with people who accept neither our methods nor our ends. It is not clear that we have either military or political solutions to this phenomenon. The lessons of Afghanistan will likely provide little guidance in this regard.

We had better anticipate, however, that we will face more asymmetrical foes in the future. One of the other clear characteristics of the contemporary environment is the huge and growing chasm of conventional military capabilities between the countries of the West—especially the United States—and the rest of the world. The RMA means that no developing country or movement has any military chance against the United States or its friends and allies if it fights on our terms (symmetrically). The Iraqis did not understand that in 1991 and paid the price. The Taliban either did not understand it or could not adapt quickly enough when confronted by Western airpower in 2001. Not many others are going to make the same mistake.

That leads to the conclusion that, at a minimum, future opponents are likely to confront the United States with highly unorthodox, unconventional, and unanticipated problems. If what we learn from September 11, 2001 is how to combat terrorism (see Chapter 10) and no more, we will have missed the real novelty of the "new kind of war," which is the need to change and adapt and be ready for the unexpected. The alternatives are unattractive. As Goulding puts it, "Military forces like those of the United States and its allies who constitute the bulk of 'well organized and well

Challenge!

Is There a New Kind of War?

The initial, highly emotional reaction to the terrorist attacks of September 11, 2001, in the United States suggested that these attacks were somehow an unprecedented phenomenon, and the rage and smoldering desire for revenge could most easily be turned toward the analogy of militarily crushing those who had committed these atrocious acts. The idea that we were faced with a "new kind of war" was born of this conjunction of the apparent uniqueness of the act and the desire for a military reaction.

Is the analogy accurate? The theme of much of the analysis in this chapter has been that it is not. The central point has been that terrorism has long been a key manner in which weak groups attempt to assert their will over stronger groups. A major thrust of such efforts involves changing the rules of engagement between contending forces to remove some of the advantage the stronger party has and, in effect, to level the playing field or tilt it in the weaker party's favor. Since part of that leveling entails rejecting the rules and conventions under which the dominant player operates, the result is likely to be outrage when the weaker party attacks. This dynamic of fourth-generation or asymmetrical warfare dates back to antiquity. The uniqueness of the current application is its scale and the fact it has been visited directly against the American population. Would we have the same sense of rage and the same depth of reaction if airliners had attacked the 1,381-foot Jin Mao building in Shanghai, China, or the world's tallest buildings, the 1,483-foot-tall Petronas towers in Kuala Lumpur, Malaysia?

The question asked in the title of this *Challenge!* is really two related questions. Is the form of activity in which the United States is engaged properly described as a form of war? And is that activity something new? The answer to the second question is fairly clearly "no," but the answer to whether this is a form of war is not so clear. Is it more useful to think about this kind of campaign in warlike terms, or is some other framework more useful? What do you think? If you think war is not the best way to think about countering terrorism, what do you think is a better way?

paid regular forces' and generally play by the rules may, in their next battles, wish fervently that it was against soldiers of their own ilk they were fighting."

SELECTED BIBLIOGRAPHY

Belfigio, Valentine J. *A Study of Ancient Roman Amphibious and Offensive Sea-Ground Task Force Operations*. Lewiston, NY: Edwin Mellen Press, 2001.

Brodie, Bernard, and Fawn M. Brodie. *From Crossbow to H-Bomb: The Evolution of Weapons and Tactics of Warfare*. Bloomington: Indiana University Press, 1973.

Gallagher, James J. *Low-Intensity Conflict: A Guide for Tactics, Techniques, and Procedures*. Harrisburg, PA: Stackpole Books, 1992.

Goulding, Vincent J., Jr. "Back to the Future with Asymmetrical Warfare." *Parameters* XXX, 4 (Winter 2000–2001), 21–30.

Keegan, John. *A History of Warfare*. London: Hutchison, 1991.

———. "In This War of Civilisations, The West Will Prevail." *The Daily Telegraph (London)*, October 10, 2001.

Lind, William S., et al. "The Changing Face of War: Into the Fourth Generation." *Marine Corps Gazette*, October 1989, 21–26.

Mao Tse-tung. *Mao Tse-tung on Guerrilla Warfare*. Trans. Samuel B. Griffith. New York: Praeger, 1961.

Moore, Harold G., and James L. Galloway. *We Were Soldiers Once. . . and Young: Ia Drang—The Battle That Changed the War in Vietnam*. New York: Harper and Row, 1993.

Snow, Donald M. *Distant Thunder: Patterns of Conflict in the Developing World*, 2nd ed. Armonk, NY: M. E. Sharpe, 1997.

———. *Uncivil Wars: International Security and the New Internal Conflicts*. Boulder, CO: Lynne Rienner Publishers, 1996.

———. *When America Fights: The Uses of U.S. Military Force*. Washington, DC: CQ Press, 2000.

Sun Tzu. *The Art of War*. Trans. Samuel B. Griffith. Oxford: Oxford University Press, 1963.

van Creveld, Martin. *The Transformation of War*. New York: Free Press, 1991.

CHAPTER **10**

Nontraditional and Other Security Threats

As first suggested in the Introduction, not all situations with national security implications for the United States are military in content or solution, even if they are sometimes described in warlike terms. This chapter examines the inclusion of semimilitary and nonmilitary elements of the contemporary environment by looking at three important nontraditional security threats. The first is the problem of regional conflicts between neighboring states or groups that the participants are incapable of solving politically but in which military solutions could create great dangers beyond the regions—military problems that must be managed nonmilitarily. The second is terrorism, a recurring concern that represents a classic semimilitary problem. The third is the international problem of illicit drugs, a basically nonmilitary problem that was distorted to military proportions by the declaration of the "war on drugs."

National security no longer deals with problems that are exclusively conceptualized in military terms. Indeed, it is one of the evolving characteristics of the post–Cold War world that the national security menu has been broadened in recent years to include problems that are either semimilitary or nonmilitary in how they pose a threat and in their solutions, which may have no clear military content at all. Economic security, the object of the ongoing discussion of globalization, is the most obvious source of these new notions of security, and it is thus the heart of the discussion in Chapter 13. In this chapter, we will look at some other policy areas that are parts of the security environment that go beyond more traditional concerns with the direct military security of the United States.

We will begin with an area of concern that transcends the end of the Cold War but has taken on a new and different kind of meaning in the contemporary world. Regional conflicts are historic rivalries between neighboring countries within geographical regions that either have erupted or have the potential to explode into conflicts and that may have the potential to spread beyond their present boundaries and engulf greater parts of the international system. During the Cold War, these conflicts were numerous and inevitably had a Cold War overlay, with the United States supporting one party and the Soviet Union the other. Since the end of the Cold War, these regional conflicts have been reduced in number. Two of these conflicts, however—the Palestinian–Israeli and Indian–Pakistani conflicts—remain as serious threats to world peace, both because of their inherent explosiveness and because the interests of the United States are embedded in each of them. Because they transcend the transition from the Cold War to the contemporary period, they are clearly traditional in the sense of having a central military content that, should it get out of hand, could threaten American interests. What is notable about these particular regional conflicts, however, is their intractability. Both involve such deeply held animosities and differences as to be irresolvable to the point that the best that can be done is to contain them below the level of traditional warfare that could conceivably escalate into something larger and potentially threatening to the international community.

The chapter will then examine two other security problems that have traditionally been thought of as nonmilitary or semimilitary but that in some ways have been militarized. We will begin with the newly poignant problem of terrorism, including, at least briefly, the danger of the proliferation of weapons of mass destruction (WMD) to terrorists and others in the process. We will then move to a brief consideration of the impact of narcotics trafficking, a particular problem for the United States, which consumes an estimated 60 percent of the world's illicit drugs. A major and growing international dimension of this problem is its effect on the criminalization of societies in which narcotics become a major factor in the economy.

REGIONAL CONFLICTS

Animosity between neighboring political units that occasionally turns violent is certainly not a novel phenomenon in human history. Instances of animosities between neighbors, which we now call regional conflicts, are as old as recorded history, and they were a prominent feature of the pattern of violence during the Cold War. What has happened is that in the last decade or so, regional conflicts have decreased in number or become dormant in many places that used to trouble us. At the same time, those that remain have become more volatile elements in the international political equation, with potential linkages to other problems.

Regional conflicts must be seen in perspective. Since the end of World War II (which was, in significant ways, the penultimate European regional conflict, with a significant Asian theater), most regional conflicts have occurred primarily in the areas that had won or been granted independence from European colonialism. In most cases, these outbreaks represented the revival of rivalries that had been suppressed for decades or centuries by colonial rule. The Southeast Asian rivalry between Vietnam and its peninsular neighbors Cambodia and Laos predated the arrival of the French in the 1860s and 1870s, for instance, and was rekindled when the French departed in 1954. Similarly, once independence was granted to separate states, Hindu India and Muslim Pakistan renewed a confessional conflict that dated back to the arrival of Muslims from Arabia a millennium earlier and was interrupted by the reign of the British Raj. Some of these conflicts have remained within the boundaries of states and are thus internal wars. The long African conflicts in Angola and Mozambique, for instance, have a largely tribal basis, and the ongoing tribulations among parts of Indonesia are another example.

Although Cold War rivalries exacerbated most of these internal conflicts, the Cold War competition had its strongest effects on the regional conflicts—a mixed influence in both cases. As the consequences of direct confrontation between the Cold War rivals became progressively less acceptable, proxy involvement in situations among regional rivals became a safer, less expensive forum for conducting the competition for global influence. On the positive side, neither superpower wanted regional conflicts to become so heated that they might explode beyond their control, engulfing the sponsoring parties and impelling them into a direct showdown they both sought feverishly to avoid. Thus, both superpowers put pressure on their clients to moderate their behavior in much the same way and for many of the same reasons that they sought to moderate the conduct of civil wars where they supported opposing sides.

Superpower involvement also impeded the solution of regional conflicts in several ways. Although maintenance of the status quo minimized the likelihood of direct superpower confrontation, keeping regional conflicts alive but below the boiling point served the interests of both the affected states and their sponsors. The parties themselves, by definition, disfavored the status quo. They were under no real compulsion to accept a settlement that did not favor them, because they could always retreat to their sponsor for comfort and support. At the same time, the superpowers would likely lose influence without continuing conflict, as their clients would no longer need them to provide weapons and political or economic assistance. Continuing, if controlled, conflict served all sides.

The end of the Cold War has changed the equation. As the Soviet Union crumbled, the regional "game" with the United States became an unaffordable luxury from which the Soviets and their successors, the Russians, progressively withdrew. As they did, the United States realized that its interest in most of these areas had been limited largely to countering the Soviet influence, and it withdrew as well. In the process, the Americans were able to divest themselves of some unsavory leaders with whom they had been associated, such as Zaire's Mobutu Sese Seko, but they left behind a void that has left the regional parties on their own. When President Clinton began his activist campaign of peacemaking in places such as Northern Ireland and in the Israeli–Palestinian confrontation, the combatants found they had no alternative power to hide behind when the Americans laid down the terms of settlement.

The result has been that regional conflicts have decreased in number. The one area that is an exception to this contraction is the old Soviet Union. As former Soviet republics have gained their independence, some have undergone processes of conflict revival similar to those in the Afro-Asian world in the 1960s and 1970s. In addition to internal conflicts in Chechnya, Georgia, and Tajikistan, this process has included the outbreak of a new, post–Cold War regional conflict between neighboring Christian Armenia and Muslim Azerbaijan.

Two regional conflicts that dominate the current landscape deserve at least a brief review because of their potentially disruptive international implications. They are the conflict between the Israelis and the Palestinians as the remaining aspect of the Arab–Israeli conflict, and the ongoing conflict between India and Pakistan, which centers on Kashmir. Both may be problems too difficult to solve and, as a result, can only be managed.

The Israeli–Palestinian Conflict

The conflict between Israel and its neighboring states and peoples was born with the declaration of an independent Israeli state in 1947. In panicked response, most of the Muslim inhabitants of what they called Palestine fled into neighboring political jurisdictions, and most Muslim states declared war upon and attacked the new Israeli state. Their efforts were repulsed by the Israelis, resulting in the addition of more territory as part of Israel. The structure of regional conflict was also established.

Background and Evolution. Over the quarter-century after its birth, Israel fought three major wars against a shifting coalition of Muslim states (erroneously called Arab, because not all of the opponents trace their lines back to Arabia—the pure sense of being Arab), including Egypt, Jordan, Syria, and Iraq. In 1956, the Israelis joined the joint British-French expedition to seize the Suez Canal from Egypt, their reward being possession of the Sinai Peninsula. Due to international reaction led by the United States and the Soviet Union, all three were forced to withdraw without accomplishing their goals. The Suez War was followed in 1967 by the Six Days' War, when Israel was attacked both from the west by Egypt and from the east by Syria and Jordan. In a brilliant campaign, the Israelis repulsed their attackers in six days. In the process they occupied strategic territory from each opponent that has been the object of subsequent negotiations—the West Bank of the Jordan River from Jordan, the Sinai Peninsula and Gaza Strip from Egypt, and the Golan Heights from Syria. Continued occupation of Gaza and the West Bank remains a central contention between Israel and the Palestinians that has to be resolved before any form of enduring peace is possible in the region.

The climactic Arab–Israeli war came in 1973. Another Muslim coalition attacked Israel during the Jewish religious holiday of Yom Kippur (which coincided with the Muslim Ramadan holy month). Unlike previous wars, the Muslims were initially successful, to the point that Israel allegedly authorized the arming of its clandestine nuclear arsenal. The Israelis finally reversed the military situation, leading to the major confrontation with Egypt and the Soviets mentioned in Chapter 4. As a consequence, the Egyptians broke their client relationship with the Soviets, leaving Syria as the only place in the region where the Soviets maintained significant influence. The United States quickly jumped into the breach, replacing the Soviets as Egypt's chief armorer and source of economic assistance. This action gave the United States the dominant outsider position with both sides and the conviction

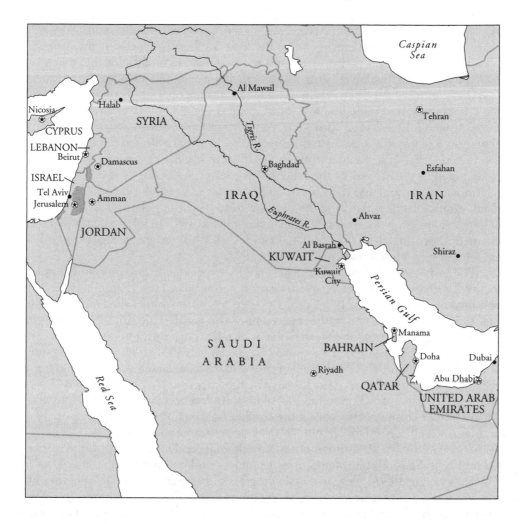

that the ongoing situation—which had come close to superpower war in 1973—was intolerable. The peace process was thus born, first when Egypt's president Anwar Sadat visited Jerusalem in 1977 and then when American President Jimmy Carter convened the Camp David talks in 1978.

Camp David I and Beyond. The Camp David process was begun to attempt a peaceful settlement to the effective state of war that had been going on between Israel and its neighbors for thirty years. Initially, it involved the Israelis and the largest of its opposing states, Egypt. If peace could be made between these two rivals, Israeli security could be increased dramatically: Future conflicts would come from only one direction rather than two, and Israel's opposition would be limited to the relatively less powerful Syria and Jordan, a much more manageable military task.

The original Camp David Accord was, in retrospect, simple and straightforward. Israel wanted a peace settlement ending the long conflict that included the recognition by Egypt of Israel's right to exist and the establishment of diplomatic relations between the two states. Egypt's price for meeting these demands included the return to Egyptian control of the Sinai Peninsula and Gaza *and* negotiations between Israel and the Palestinians that would lead to a sovereign, independent Palestinian state. Before they left Camp David (and with some very considerable arm-twisting by President Carter), a deal was struck between the historic enemies that reflected these terms.

Camp David I caused a firestorm in the Muslim Middle East. Egypt was roundly condemned by virtually all of the other Islamic states, including severed diplomatic relations with several and the suspension of economic assistance by others, notably Saudi Arabia. Despite exacting the promise to resolve the Palestinian question (a major and ongoing source of Muslim unhappiness with Israel), Sadat was condemned as an infidel to the anti-Israeli cause, and his actions contributed to his assassination by Muslim fundamentalists in 1981.

The provisions of the Camp David accord were gradually and peacefully implemented, with one exception: Egyptian territory was returned to Egyptian jurisdiction on schedule, and Egypt and Israel signed a peace accord and established relations, but the sticking point was, and is, the settlement of the Israeli–Palestinian relationship.

Although Israel was subsequently able to reach accord with Jordan, it remains at odds with both Syria and the Palestinians. The conflict with Syria is about the return of the Golan Heights and the control of the headwaters of Israeli water supplies from the Sea of Galilee and the Jordan River (which border on a Syrian-controlled Golan Heights). Because of Syrian military weakness and preoccupation with its physical occupation of Lebanon, that part of the conflict has remained largely dormant. The problem of the Palestinians has not.

The question of Palestinian autonomy or independence has continued since Camp David I as both an internal Israeli problem and an international hot potato. Throughout the 1980s, there was little progress in negotiations, amid loud cries by the Muslim states that Israel was reneging on its Camp David obligations. In 1993, the Israelis and Palestinians met clandestinely in Oslo under the auspices of the host Norwegian government and produced a basic agreement on principles to create a Palestinian state. These Oslo Accords were followed by a concentrated American effort to move the situation to final settlement. That effort culminated in President Clinton reconvening the Camp David talks in July 2000. Camp David II came close to producing a settlement but ultimately fell short. After its failure, relations between the sides gradually deteriorated to the state of warlike hostilities between Israel and the Palestinian authority in 2001, which featured a brutal invasion of Palestinian-controlled areas of the West Bank by the Israeli army and suicide bombings against civilians in Israel by Palestinian terrorists. The ongoing confrontation has threatened to break out into general conflict in the region. This combustible situation maintains the status of this situation as an important regional conflict.

Irresolvable Differences.   In the end, Camp David II failed because the parties could not agree on three issues that are so basic and in such complete and fundamental disagreement that accord could not be reached then and may prove impossible in the future. Although the weaknesses of the leaders (especially Palestinian leader Yassir Arafat) have been cited frequently as the cause for failure, it is really the structure of the disagreements that has prevented progress. The three outstanding differences are the nature and size of a Palestinian state, the status of the Old City of Jerusalem, and repatriation of the Palestinians to their former homes in Israel. There is little room for compromise on any of these issues; all must be resolved before anything resembling a durable peace is possible.

The first issue is the Palestinian state, including its relationship with Israel. Interim agreements between Israel and Arafat's Palestinian Authority after the Oslo agreement had produced a gradual turnover of jurisdiction and control of parts of the West Bank to the Palestinians, and on the eve of Camp David II, about two-fifths of the West Bank was part of Palestine. The question left to be decided was how much more of the West Bank and Gaza would be included in the new Palestinian state. After a good deal of wrangling on the subject, the Israelis agreed to cede 95 percent of the territory to Arafat, leaving Israel in control of a handful of Jewish settlements that had already been established on the West Bank and Gaza.

Both sides were criticized for this division. Militant Israelis argued that Prime Minister Ehud Barak had given away too much, compromising plans for additional settlements on the West Bank in the future to accommodate Jewish immigrants to Israel. Arafat also rejected the territorial settlement as inadequate, as part of his overall rejection of the Camp David II package, for which he was severely criticized internationally for turning down the best offer that he could reasonably expect the Israelis to make.

The issue of Jewish settlements on the West Bank was at the heart of the dispute over the future Palestinian state. To many Israelis, the option of building additional settlements (housing areas) is necessary for the future health of the Jewish state, and they saw the deal Barak proposed as an unnecessarily generous abandonment of that future. Many Palestinians, on the other hand, see *any* Jewish settlements as an affront, reminding them of their inferior status and guaranteeing an Israeli police or military presence to safeguard the security of the settlers. When Ariel Sharon replaced Barak as prime minister of Israel, he renounced the territorial offer made by his predecessor and announced that the only division of land that would be acceptable was the status quo, which leaves Palestine with a little over 40 percent of the occupied lands. Although it is difficult to imagine how Arafat and Sharon can come to any mutually acceptable division of the lands given the diametrically opposing positions, the extent of the size of the Palestinian state is probably the *least* intractable of the three issues dividing the two sides.

The second issue is Jerusalem—more specifically, control of some of the holiest shrines of Judaism, Islam, and Christianity within the Old City of Jerusalem. Even more specifically, the issue hinges on control of the site known as Haram al Sharif by Muslims and the Temple Mount by Jews, because colocated on that site are the mosque from which legend has it that Muhammad rose to heaven and the ruins of the second temple of Judaism (the Wailing Wall).

There is no reservoir of goodwill about who shall control these sites. In the twenty years between Israeli independence and the Six Days' War, the area was controlled by

Jordan, and no Israeli was allowed to visit the Wailing Wall. When the Israelis occupied the West Bank in 1967, they also gained control of the Old City, and Muslim access to the Haram al Sharif was only possible with Israeli permission and after being inspected by Israeli soldiers or police. When Sadat visited Jerusalem in 1977 and made a pilgrimage to the Haram, it was the first time a Muslim leader had done so since the Israeli occupation had begun.

Some progress was made on this issue at Camp David. Proposals were made and accepted in principle that would create divided jurisdictions over the several neighborhoods (the Jewish, Muslim, Christian, and Armenian sectors), but agreement could not be reached over the Haram/Temple Mount. The Israelis, citing their historical experience with Muslim control, adamantly refused Palestinian control, and the Palestinians equally adamantly rejected Israeli control. In the end, discussions were being conducted around a principle of "joint sovereignty," but this concept disappeared with the breakdown of negotiations. Sharon has foreclosed further progress on this issue, declaring in 2001 that the Old City is "the united and indivisible capital of Israel—with the Temple Mount as its center—for all eternity." The Palestinians also claim Jerusalem as their capital.

The third and least publicized issue is Palestinian repatriation, or "the right of return," and in many ways it is the most difficult, emotional, and intractable of the divisions between the two sides. As noted earlier, when Israel declared its independence in 1947, most of the Palestinians who had lived in what was now the Jewish state fled in a panic, leaving their homes and belongings behind. The state of Israel appropriated the property of those who fled, but the former Palestinian land owners have never given up the dream of returning to their homes—of being repatriated.

This issue has enormous geopolitical importance. Currently, the population of Israel is about five million, of whom approximately one million are Palestinian Muslims. The number of Palestinians living outside Israel who have claims to repatriation number about 4.5 million. If all the Palestinians with such claims were allowed to return, Jews would instantly become a minority within Israel—an absolutely unacceptable outcome from the Jewish perspective, because Israel would then cease to be a Jewish state. In addition, the displacement of Israelis as Palestinians reclaimed their ancestral lands would create a level of political chaos that no Israeli government could possibly survive. Moreover, allowing a Palestinian return would also create living-space problems and make it much more difficult, if not impossible, to nurture further Jewish immigration to Israel—the Zionist dream.

Although most Palestinians harbor no illusions about the likelihood that repatriation will happen anytime soon, it remains a long-term aspiration that no Palestinian political leader could possibly renounce. Israel, given the geopolitical and internal political consequences of Palestinian repatriation, is equally insistent on a renunciation of repatriation as a precondition for an overall settlement between the two parties. This is an issue on which there can be no compromise (letting *some* but not all Palestinians return is not an option) and ultimately was the rough shoal on which Camp David II crashed. Those who have criticized Arafat for not taking what he could get fail to acknowledge that renouncing the dream of his people to return to their homes was not something he could possibly do.

The peace process has broken down completely. Within days of his coming to office in February 2001, a spokesman for Sharon announced that "everything in Camp David is null and void unless it was signed, and nothing was signed." Instead, conditions have deteriorated into open fighting between Israeli forces and the Palestinians, and the situation resembles a war zone in all manners except for a formal declaration of a state of war. In November 2001 the Sharon government cut all ties with Arafat, signaling that a negotiated settlement could not even be discussed as long as Arafat was leader of the Palestinian Authority. Palestinian suicide bombers continue their martyrdom, and the Israeli army continues its deadly incursions, in a vicious cycle that only gets worse.

The Bush administration reopened the process in 2003 with its "road map" for peace, but will it succeed? The fundamental divisions between the two sides are so deep and intractable that they have proved impossible to overcome even in the best of circumstances. The fighting and killing are only adding to the bitterness between the Palestinians and the Israelis, making the emergence of effective peacemakers even more unlikely. Moreover, the three-step process must overcome the same problems that could not be surmounted before. Step one (to be accomplished in 2003) requires an Israeli cessation of new settlements and an end to Palestinian terrorism. Step two (2004) calls for a provisional Palestinian state. Both these steps have been proposed or accomplished before. Step three (2005) requires resolving "remaining differences" (in the Bush administration's words), notably the final boundaries of Palestine, Jerusalem, and repatriation, the Camp David II deal breakers.

The Indian–Pakistani Conflict

The other great regional conflict shares three major characteristics with the battle between the Israelis and the Palestinians: It is about disputed territory, it has religious divisions at its core, and it has proved to be absolutely intractable. Given these characteristics, the conflict between India and Pakistan that centers in the mountainous Indian state of Jammu and Kashmir has raged in the northernmost tip of the subcontinent in the high Himalayan Mountains for over half a century. There is no resolution in sight.

Background and Evolution.   Like the Israeli conflict with its neighbors, the regional conflict on the Asian subcontinent has its roots in 1947, when both India and Pakistan gained their independence from Great Britain. The underlying concept of the division of the Indian subcontinent that resulted in the creation of the two countries was that the predominantly Hindu areas of the former British Raj would become India and the primarily Muslim areas would become Pakistan. In a highly complex region of the world like the subcontinent, operationalizing that concept proved to be especially difficult in a number of places. The basic plan created two parts of Pakistan, for instance, divided by 1,000 miles of Indian territory (East and West Pakistan, now Bangladesh and Pakistan), and the border separating Muslims and Hindus in the west was so imperfect that between eight and ten million people fled from one country to the other to be with their coreligionists.

Nowhere was the problem more difficult than in the princely state of Jammu and Kashmir (hereafter Kashmir). By virtue of the rules for partitioning the subcontinent laid down by Lord Mountbatten, the chief British negotiator, the princely states (of which there were over a hundred) had the options of joining either Pakistan or India, but not of independence. In most cases, these states were either clearly Hindu or Muslim, simplifying the decision process. In some states, however, including Kashmir, the composition was not so simple. Kashmir's population was about three-fourths Muslim, but its traditional ruler was a Hindu maharajah. The majority Muslims, supported by Pakistan, argued that the decision should be reached through a popular referendum, which, of course, would mean accession to Pakistan. The Indians preferred association through intergovernmental agreement. As tensions mounted, the maharajah agreed to make Kashmir a state of India.

Kashmir has been a prime source of tension and at least a proximate cause of fighting ever since. In addition to the continued sporadic fighting, the two countries have fought three wars. In 1948, shortly after they were established, they fought directly but inconclusively over Kashmir. In 1965, war broke out over a bleak disputed piece of territory along the West Pakistan–Indian border called the Rann of Kutch, after there were unconfirmed (and as it turned out, false) reports of large petroleum deposits under the soil. After Pakistan had some success in early fighting, it opened a second front in Kashmir, where fighting bogged down inconclusively. In 1971, war broke out again, with the major effect of splintering East and West Pakistan when the east declared its independence as the state of Bangladesh.

During the Cold War, it was possible to exercise some outside control over the evolution of the conflict, although that ability was always less than complete. In some ways, the major outside parties were not the Soviets and the Americans but the Soviets and the Chinese. China and India are historic enemies, having fought a border war in 1962 and with ongoing tensions between the world's two most populous countries. Chinese–Indian and Indian–Pakistani animosities make an alignment between Pakistan and China a marriage of convenience and mutual interests (from the old saying "the enemy of my enemy is my friend"). India, the world's largest democracy, tried to retain neutrality in the Cold War competition but was forced at various times to turn to both the Americans and the Russians for assistance in its struggle against its adversaries. As one Indian analyst pointed out in discussing India's need for nuclear weapons, India is the only country in the world that lacks a major ally to assist in deflecting its enemies. Because the Soviets were successful in mediating the end of the 1965 Rann of Kutch war, they gained some preeminence with the Indians. In 1971, the United States "tilted" in favor of Pakistan during that war as part of the strategy to use Pakistan as a go-between in the Nixon administration's initiative toward China. The result was minimal U.S. leverage in the region during the Cold War, especially with India. The tenuousness of American influence was demonstrated as well after the end of the Cold War. In 2000, President Clinton became the first American chief executive to visit the subcontinent, in an attempt to energize the peace process over Kashmir; his efforts were largely ignored by the two countries.

Two recent occurrences have made the Kashmir issue more intense. The first was the 1998 detonation of nuclear weapons, first by India and then by Pakistan.

The effect was overtly to "nuclearize" the conflict, which meant that a subsequent war over Kashmir could become the first nuclear war in world history fought when both sides possessed these weapons. The tests caught the world off guard (especially the United States, whose intelligence sources did not know of the plans in advance—a measure of the state of U.S. influence and presence in the region) and caused heightened concern that the highly volatile contest over Kashmir could escalate dangerously in the future. In a manner not entirely dissimilar to the reaction to near-escalation in 1973 during the Yom Kippur war in Israel, the international system's interest in seeing resolution has been piqued by these developments.

The other occurrence was the post–September 11 campaign by the United States in Afghanistan. Because of the relationship between Pakistan and the Taliban (whom the Pakistanis had helped put in power and had supported), enlisting the Pervez Musharraf government's support in Pakistan was critical to the American dragnet against both the Taliban and Al Qaeda. The Americans thus proposed and had accepted close cooperation with the new Pakistani leader. This apparent "tilt" once again toward Pakistan elicited a flurry of activity in India to counterbalance Pakistani friendship with the United States. When Islamic extremists attacked the Indian parliament building and killed a dozen people, tensions rose rapidly, as the Americans were now a more direct part of the situation, poised hundreds of miles from Kashmir in Afghanistan as 2002 dawned.

The Ongoing Issues.   The realization that another war over Kashmir could escalate to the nuclear level would seem to add urgency to finding a solution to this conflict that has hung over the region for over half a century. For the first time since partition, there were direct talks between the leaderships of the two sides in 2001 that held out some hope, but any optimism was literally blown apart by the terrorist attacks against India in December 2001. The guns continue to fire at one another at the top of the world, and in January 2002, India began to erect an Iron Curtain–like fence along the so-called line of control (see map) that symbolizes the intractability of the situation. The flirtation with negotiations was followed by a breaking away and hardening of positions, demonstrating the immense difficulty of finding grounds for resolving the fate of Kashmir and thus the simmering conflict on the subcontinent.

Two issues are of paramount importance between India and Pakistan, and both mix geopolitical and emotional elements that make resolution difficult. One has to do with the geopolitics of the disposition of control in Kashmir and requires crafting some geographic division of Kashmir. The other is the physical fate of the Kashmiris, especially those who desire independence. In addition to the question of Kashmiri desires, this issue has geopolitical importance for both India and Pakistan and beyond to China.

The first issue is geopolitical. As the map shows, the location and control of Kashmir is crucial to both sides, if for different reasons. For Pakistan, Kashmir is critical because the headwaters of the Indus River system all rise in Kashmir before flowing across the border into Pakistan. Because Pakistan is a semiarid country, the flow from the rivers is absolutely critical to Pakistani agriculture. Despite the fact that India has no physical way to interrupt the flow of the three rivers from Kashmir into

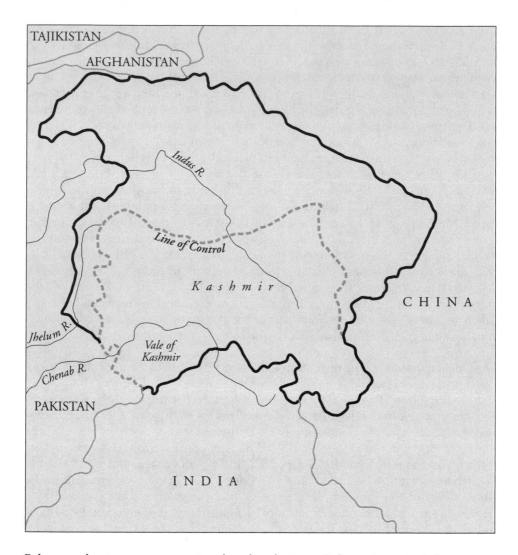

Pakistan, the issue is so emotional and so basic to Pakistani survival that no Pakistani government would dare relinquish control of those rivers within Kashmir.

The Indian side of the geopolitical issue has to do with geography. Kashmir forms a significant part of the boundary between India and China. More specifically, the traditional invasion routes between the two countries go through Kashmir. Given the relationship between China and Pakistan, no Indian government would dare negotiate a settlement that would leave these crucial invasion routes under the jurisdiction of the Pakistani government.

The second issue centers on the fate of the Kashmiris, and it has several aspects. At the most obvious level, there is the matter of religion, which has been a problem since 1947. On the Pakistani side, the fate of their fellow Muslims is an emotional matter, although the Indians question the sincerity of some of that concern. The

Indians, on the other hand, fear for the fate of the Hindu minority population in the region and feel that they cannot abandon their coreligionists either.

What happens to the Kashmiris has significance beyond this emotional level, however. There are separatist movements within both India and Pakistan that are watching the outcome of the struggle over Kashmir with a good deal of interest. Were the Kashmiris able to gain their independence by seceding from India, this could spark enthusiasm for a similar status among several ethno-religious groups within India, notably the Sikhs and the Tamils. The general instability of Pakistan has been heightened by the fall of the Taliban in Afghanistan with the assistance of the Pakistani government, since the Taliban have many supporters in the Pakistani population and many Taliban have fled into Pakistan. An unfavorable turn of events in Kashmir could only increase pressure to bring down the Musharraf government in Islamabad. After a terrorist attack against the Indian Parliament building in December 2001, the Indian government declared the event an example of the American war on terrorism and precipitated a military confrontation with Pakistan for allegedly aiding and abetting the terrorists. The regional conflict over Kashmir and the campaign against terrorism were thus dangerously joined.

The fate of Kashmir has implications beyond its borders. The Chinese are particularly concerned about the possibility of an independent Kashmir because of the close parallel between advocacies of Kashmiri self-determination and similar demands for Tibet—and possibly, by extension, other western, Muslim provinces of China. Although China generally sides with Pakistan on this problem, it does not want to see Kashmir break off from India and become an independent state.

Irresolvable Differences.   Breaking the cycle of violence over Kashmir must be considered in light of the current physical situation. Following the 1971 war, there was a de facto partition of Kashmir along what is called the line of control. Under this arrangement, all of Kashmir remains technically an Indian state, but Pakistan (or Pakistani-affiliated "rebels") maintains control of the territory on the Pakistani side of the line and India maintains physical control of the rest. Under this arrangement, what is sometimes informally called Pakistani Kashmir includes the headwaters of the Indus Rivers, and the Indians control the Himalayan invasion routes from China. It is along this line of control that India is currently erecting its barrier. Although this arrangement solves one aspect of the problem informally, none of the parties finds the status quo altogether satisfactory.

A durable solution requires placating three separate parties: India, Pakistan, and Kashmir. For a long time, the Pakistanis and the Kashmiris were considered to be one actor, since Kashmiri opposition to continued Indian rule was considered part of a Pakistani-operated subversion to add Kashmir to Pakistan. A pro-independence movement has emerged, however, which seeks Kashmiri union with neither side and instead favors a sovereign Kashmiri state.

Analytically, there are thus four possible outcomes to the current situation, none of which is currently acceptable to all parties. The first is a pro-Indian outcome that reasserts Indian sovereignty over all of Kashmir. This solution is unacceptable, of course, to the others involved: Pakistan will not concede control of the headwaters to its foe, and abandoning fellow Muslims would be political suicide for any Pakistani government that acceded to it (parallel to the fate of any Palestinian leader who renounced repatriation). The Kashmiris, whether they favor independence or union with Pakistan, find this outcome equally odious; removing Indian sovereignty has, after all, been the purpose of the struggle all along. India has abandoned this option, in effect, by fortifying the status quo along the line of control.

The second solution is to allow Kashmir, through a plebiscite or some similar method, to become part of Pakistan. This is the solution preferred in Islamabad, of course, but not elsewhere. The Indians oppose it on at least three grounds. It would mean ceding the invasion routes to an unreliable Pakistan. It would mean abandoning the Hindu citizens of Kashmir, a political disaster for any Indian government. And it would set a dangerous precedent for other separatist areas of India. Moreover, Kashmiris who favor independence (an option specifically ruled out in 1947) find union with Pakistan not a great improvement over their current plight.

The third option is an independent Kashmir. It is not clear what part of the Muslim majority in Kashmir favors this option, but some do not, and certainly the Hindu minority does not. Pakistan is less than enthused over this possibility, because it leaves the headwaters outside Pakistan's sovereign control and because it believes there is economic potential in Kashmir. The Indians, of course, oppose this outcome because it involves abandoning their coreligionists and because of the precedent it would set (one of the few things about which they agree with the Chinese).

That leaves the status quo as the final option. As already noted, this is a solution that none of the parties embraces and that has provided the framework for over fifty years of violence. But it may also be the only solution that is possible short of the cataclysm of an all-out, possibly nuclear, conflict that allows the imposition of one of the three other outcomes by whatever country comes out standing up (if either of them does) at the end. Given the uncertainty about the chances of escalation beyond the region should the nuclear bombs begin to fly, such a method is clearly opposed by all those outside the region. As long as the positions of the various parties remain diametrically opposed and mutually exclusive, managing an unsatisfying status quo may be the only acceptable (or least unacceptable) outcome to this irresolvable conflict.

TERRORISM

Terrorism, and how to make Americans secure against it, initially became a matter of public policy concern for most people in the United States in the 1990s, when the first public terrorist incidents had an impact on American citizens. The first attack on the World Trade Center in 1993, the bombing of the Murrah Federal Building in Oklahoma City in 1995, the attack against American service members at the Khobar Towers apartment complex in Dharan, Saudi Arabia, in 1996, the attacks against the American embassies in Kenya and Tanzania in 1998, and the suicide bombing of the American warship USS Cole in a Yemeni port in 2000 all helped to raise the public level of awareness from the abstract to the concrete. Events of this sort had been predicted by experts in the terrorism community for years. By and large, these warnings

Challenge!

Dealing with Irresolvable Differences

The two regional conflicts we have examined may be unresolvable. The Israeli–Palestinian conflict, with which we are more familiar because of the amount of coverage it has received in the media, hinges on the ultimately irreconcilable poles that the Palestinians can or cannot be allowed to emigrate back to their former homes in what is now Israel. A decisive outcome in Kashmir is blocked by Pakistan's insistence on controlling the headwaters of the Indus Rivers, and India will not give up control of the strategic invasion routes. No outcome, including restoring the integrity of Kashmir, is possible under these circumstances.

Assuming that a decisive defeat of one side or the other in these conflicts is impossible or would not be allowed by the international community (Israel defeats the Palestinians and reoccupies the West Bank and Gaza, or India crushes Pakistan and reunites Kashmir, for instance), what can be done? We Americans are used to the idea that problems are to be surmounted, solutions are simply to be found—but in these cases, what are the solutions? As former West German Chancellor Helmut Schmidt once observed, "You do not solve real problems. You work them." By this he meant that real problems simply cannot be solved and thus must be managed at as low a level of tension as possible.

The Indians have affected a workable solution of sorts by erecting their "iron curtain" across Kashmir, thereby solidifying the status quo that nobody likes but no one can overcome. The repatriation problem in Israel is even tougher, and the only way it seems possible to handle it in any peace settlement is to ignore it, so that Palestinians can continue to dream of going home and Israelis can deny that will ever happen. The result will undoubtedly be continued tensions, but not as severe as the consequences of trying to reach a definitive resolution. What more can be done?

had gone unheeded outside the policy community, however, because these incidents, horrible as they were, appeared isolated and unconnected (although it has since been revealed that the 1993 attack was part of a larger international terrorist conspiracy probably associated with bin Laden and Al Qaeda).

Complacency and inattention were brought to a halt by the awful events of September 11, 2001. Beyond the horror and shock at the acts of the suicide bombers (not all of whom apparently realized that suicide was part of their mission)—seizing and crashing airliners into the towers of the World Trade Center in New York and the Pentagon in Washington, D.C., incinerating thousands of passengers in the airplanes and workers in the buildings in the process—the attacks demonstrated American physical vulnerability to terrorist activity and propelled the "war on terrorism" to the very top of the national security agenda, a position it is likely to retain for some time to come.

The September 11 events remain inexorably embedded in our consciousnesses, but it is now possible to begin to assess them more objectively as part of the national security process than we could do immediately after they took place. To that end, we will examine terrorism in three ways: We will look at the characteristics of terrorism (including the virtually textbook application of those characteristics by Usama bin Laden and his associates on September 11, 2001, and before), the actions that can be taken to deal with terrorist threats and acts, and the location of terrorism within the constellation of national security concerns. Along the way, we will assess more directly than previously the appropriateness of the war analogy for dealing with terrorism.

Characteristics of Terrorism

What exactly is terrorism? Unfortunately, definitions of the term abound, leaving one in a quandary when assessing whether certain acts do or do not constitute instances of terrorism. For our purposes here, we will expand on the distinction raised in the Introduction and define the term as *the commission of atrocious acts of violence against a target population in order to gain compliance with some set of demands or conditions that the terrorists insist upon* (this definition is lifted from my book *September 11, 2001: The New Face of War?*).

The heart of the dynamic of terrorism derives from the Latin root of the word *terrere*, which literally means "to frighten." Terrorists engage in random acts of violence against randomly chosen targets for the purpose of frightening the overall target population with the prospect that, if it fails to comply with their threats, more acts of violence will follow. The randomness of the acts is pivotal, because it guarantees that no member of the target population can predict how the terrorists will strike and whether that individual will be the next victim. Fright is produced to the extent that people fear they may be among the next victims of the terrorists' attacks. The purpose of the terrorists is to raise the level of apprehension and anxiety among members of the target population to the point that they capitulate and accede to the terrorists' demands rather than endure the anxiety and continual fear of being the next victims.

The history of terrorism is not one of great success. Terrorists often succeed in carrying out initial acts because people are unaware of their existence and thus do not prepare adequately for the terrorists' initial gambit. Once terrorism is committed, however, that awareness is raised, and the instruments of society designed to deal with these kinds of criminal acts are engaged, making future commissions more difficult. More to the point, acts of terror indeed frighten people, but reactions are often quite the opposite of what the terrorists intend. Instead of being cowed into submission, a more frequent response is outrage, resolve not to bend to the terrorists' will, and determination to deal harshly with those who commit terrorist acts.

Understanding terrorism is difficult for someone who comes from an open, Westernized society. The will to engage in terrorism generally develops in social settings of great frustration and despair, and although some level of frustration is certainly present in open societies, it is unlikely to be of sufficient depth to spawn the terrorist instinct. (The Unabomber, Theodore Kaczynski, and Oklahoma City bomber Timothy McVeigh demonstrate that it is not missing altogether.) Terrorist acts, which often involve the hideous murders of people whose only guilt is membership in the target population, are clearly antisocial and aberrant to the point that most people cannot conceptualize actually committing such acts, nor can they empathize with anyone who could. Moreover, the major virtues of an open, free society make its members uniquely vulnerable to such attacks, and some of their reactive instincts challenge the values on which our society is based: Just how many liberties (if any) should we sacrifice to frustrate these strange, fanatical people who penetrate our society? It is all very confusing.

We cannot answer all of the questions that arise about terrorism here. What we can do is to describe terrorism through a series of characteristics of the phenomenon (borrowed from *September 11, 2001*). More specifically, we will look at terrorist objectives, justifications for terrorism, sponsorship of terrorism, and forms of terrorism. Where appropriate, examples will be drawn from the September 11 experience.

Terrorist Objectives.   Terrorism is normally a political act carried on for political purposes that its champions believe cannot be achieved in other, less extreme ways. Sometimes these purposes are overt and articulate, and sometimes they are not. Moreover, the overt purpose of terrorism may obscure hidden motivations that impel terrorists to commit the actions that they do.

The Prussian strategist Carl von Clausewitz said, "War is the continuation of politics by other means" (the quotation is paraphrased in various ways by different translators). Clausewitz meant by this that when policy issues cannot be resolved through conventional political processes, war provides an alternative way to decide which side is successful and which side is not in gaining the ascendancy of its policy preferences. In some ways, terrorism is similar. Generally, groups choose terrorism to achieve their ends because they are unable to achieve them in any other way. Most of the time, the reason is that the terrorist objective has little, if any, appeal in the target population. Thus, the population will not embrace the terrorist political demands voluntarily, and the unpopularity of the demand means that it will not be achieved through normal political channels. When the group seeking change also lacks the conventional military power to impose its will symmetrically, asymmetrical acts such as terrorism may seem to pose the only possible means of success. Palestinian suicide bombing exemplifies this line of reasoning.

The political objective of terrorism often gets overlooked because of the nature of the actions taken in its name and the obscurity or bizarre nature of the demands from the perspective of the target population. Before the airplane attacks on New York and Washington, for instance, very few people outside the terrorism community had even heard of bin Laden's demands that the United States leave the "holy lands" (Saudi Arabia) and abandon Israel in its struggle against the Palestinians. The focus of attention was instead on the horror of the events, especially the wanton murder of the airline passengers and office workers and military personnel. When various videotapes made by bin Laden surfaced in which the United States was demonized as leader of the "Jewish-Crusader" conspiracy that deserved the fate of the victims, people could not equate this demand as a political activity as we understand that term.

Sometimes the terrorists' political objectives are purposely obscured. The various narco-terrorists of South America justify the brutal acts in which they engage against the government of Colombia as acts intended to promote social justice and liberation. In fact, they are basically hired agents of the narcotics traffickers whose purpose is to protect their employers from prosecution by the government. In the case of bin Laden, there has been intriguing speculation that the real reason for his attacks on the United States was to channel Islamic rage against the West (which is very real in many places) into support for himself, and that his real political agenda is to ride a wave of regional support that would propel him into political control of his native Saudi Arabia (which has revoked his citizenship) and possibly leadership of the entire region. Dutch professor Rob de Wijk speculates, "His objective seems to be to unite the Islamic world under a political-religious figure, or caliph, by removing pro-Western regimes, the state of Israel, and the United States presence from the Islamic world." Presumably, bin Laden envisages himself in that role.

Justifications for Terrorism.   Is terrorism a legitimate means to achieve political ends? If the analogy between terrorism and war is correct and is taken literally, then there is a case to be made that terrorism is a legitimate act of war and that its perpetrators must be accorded the same status as practitioners of war who employ more conventional methods. Indeed, most of the arguments underlying asymmetrical approaches to war include terrorist acts as part of the repertoire of the unconventional warrior and as part of the way in which the asymmetrical warrior seeks to change the rules of war to his or her advantage. At the same time, terrorist acts are criminal acts (they violate criminal laws) everywhere they are committed. The victims of the September 11, 2001, attacks were, after all, murder victims, and those who took a hand in killing them are murderers, regardless of the rationales for their acts.

There is a significant disagreement on the question of whether terrorism is an act of war or simple criminality, and the position one takes affects both how one judges the legitimacy of terrorism and the legal treatment of terrorists. To apologists of terrorism (or at least specific terrorist acts), the familiar "one man's terrorist is another man's freedom fighter" summarizes the argument that terrorism is a political act akin to war. On the other hand, there is the equally passionately held belief that terrorists are no more than common criminals and should be treated as such. A subpart of the argument that terrorism is no more than common crime is that the elevation of terrorism to the status of the equivalency of war is a terrible mistake. As British military historian Michael Howard puts it, "To declare war on terrorists or, even more illiterately, on terrorism is at once to accord terrorists a status and dignity that they seek and that they do not deserve."

Whether terrorists are thugs or warriors affects both their legitimacy and their legal status. If terrorism is simply crime, then terrorist acts, regardless of their motivation, are no more legitimate than any other crime. If terrorist acts are considered acts of war, the status terrorists generally desire, then they are legitimate means to conduct war in asymmetrical situations where acting according to traditional conventions on war would ensure failure. The distinction is also important in legal terms.

If terrorism is crime, then terrorists have recourse to all the protections afforded by the legal system, and these protections, in such areas as rules of evidence, are considerably more stringent than in military courts. The Bush administration found itself caught up in this distinction when it sought to demonize Al Qaeda as criminals but to bring them swiftly to justice. The administration position, articulated by Attorney General John Ashcroft, was to shunt these criminals off to closed military tribunals, thus calling them criminals but treating them as military personnel. Terrorists, showing equal inconsistency, wanted to be thought of as soldiers but tried as criminals to maximize their chances of a successful defense. The loose use of the war analogy to describe the American campaign against the terrorists behind the September 11 attacks only adds to the legal confusion.

Evolving international law finesses this distinction. Under the general heading of war crimes is a category called crimes against humanity. Encompassing such acts as the systematic killing of members or groups within society, genocide, and mass murder, the law makes no particular distinction between military and civilian perpetrators. Thus, both former Yugoslav President Slobodan Milosevic and his leading military officers were charged under the same statute before the War Crimes Tribunal in The Hague, Netherlands. Now that the Statute of the International Criminal Court (ICC) has been ratified by enough countries (sixty) to enter into force, it may well become a useful forum for trying those who commit mass murder (and the September 11 attacks clearly fall into that category) without taking a position on the justification of terrorism in criminal versus warlike terms.

Is terrorism crime or war? The answer is that it is both. Clearly, terrorist acts that result in the killing of people violate criminal laws and are thus, by definition, criminal offenses. But can they be justified by the reasons for which they are committed? The answer is largely a matter of perspective, both philosophical and political. Can the killing of innocents, for instance, ever be justified? But is there any meaningful difference between combatants and civilians in modern warfare? It is a matter of perspective, as the discussion of asymmetrical warfare in the last chapter suggested. For the "rebel with a cause" practicing asymmetrical warfare, there is one answer to that question. For the object of terrorist acts, operating from a Western, conventional view of the justification of violence, the answer is quite different.

Sponsorship of Terrorism.   The issue of who organizes, encourages, nurtures, and provides monetary incentives, direction, and physical space for terrorists—in other words, who sponsors terrorism—encompasses a wide range of entities that fall along a continuum. At one end is direct state sponsorship, whereby the governments organize and fully control the acts of terror committed by their agents. In some cases, governments may use their own agencies, such as the secret police, to commit acts of terror either against their own citizens (normally for the purpose of political suppression of opponents in closed societies) or against foreign enemies. Examples of terrorism used in this way include the systematic elimination of regime opponents by the Khmer Rouge in Cambodia during the 1970s and the murder of Iraqi Kurds by the regime of Saddam Hussein during the 1980s. Also during the 1980s, the government of Libya was widely accused of sending its agents out on terrorist missions, such as bombing a bar in Berlin and blowing up Pan Am Flight 103 over Lockerbie, Scotland.

The other end of the continuum contains terrorist groups with no formal affiliations with any government, which can be thought of as the private entrepreneurs of terrorism. Since such independence generally (but not always) means a lack of access to funds from a sponsoring government, these groups are normally smaller and their activities more limited in scope than groups with formal affiliation and support by governments. But that is not always the case. A prime example of a terrorist organization unsponsored (even renounced) by governments but with considerable financial support is the Irish Republican Army (IRA). The IRA cannot be typified as small and poor, as it has received generous amounts of private support from individuals in the United States and elsewhere to support its activities. Similarly, Usama bin Laden's private fortune reportedly was used largely to underwrite his campaign of terrorism.

There is a third form of sponsorship between total state sponsorship and no affiliation at all. It is into this category that Usama bin Laden and Al Qaeda fall, at least until their essential eviction from Afghanistan. This category is composed of relationships wherein states provide some of the services associated with state sponsorship but the terrorist organization maintains a total or substantial level of autonomy in conducting its activity. This form of relationship is referred to as state-*sanctioned* terrorism. In this form, terrorist organizations are not arms of any government, taking orders on who to attack, how, and why, but they are provided physical sanctuary and other assistance by governments sympathetic to their cause.

This form of relationship is most often found in the Islamic Middle East. Governments that have historically sanctioned terrorist organizations, as identified on the U.S. State Department's annual terrorism list, have included Syria, Iran, Iraq, Libya, and Afghanistan as prominent examples.

The relationship between the former Taliban government of Afghanistan and bin Laden's Al Qaeda richly illustrates the dynamics of state sanctioning. In 1996, when bin Laden and his followers were evicted from Sudan at the request of the Saudi government, they migrated to Afghanistan, where the Taliban had recently come to power. Bin Laden had an historic relationship with the Taliban leadership, since they both had served as *mujahadeen* opposing the Soviet occupation during the 1980s. Moreover, both bin Laden and the Taliban preached a violently anti-Western, fundamentalist view of the world, and both recruited heavily from the *madrassa* system of Islamic schools described in Amplification 10.1. In other words, they had much in common.

The Taliban government neither directed nor financed bin Laden, but it did provide a sanctuary, or safe haven, from which bin Laden could operate without fear of interference or suppression. He did not need Afghan financing (which they probably could not have afforded anyway), since his private fortune, contributions from wealthy Saudi citizens who shared his hatred for Americans, and profits from legal and nefarious business dealings (such as facilitating the heroin trade that is a staple of the Afghan economy) provided him with financial resources the extent of which is still being revealed.

The existence and viability of this relationship was burst by American military reaction to the September 11 attacks. As a centerpiece of the declaration of the war on terrorism, President Bush issued a firm warning that those countries that did not stand with the United States in opposing and eradicating terrorism effectively stood with the terrorists and would be treated accordingly—what has since become known as part of the Bush Doctrine. When the Taliban refused to turn over bin Laden and his associates for prosecution, they became the object of American military action.

The American action, carried out under the broad sponsorship of the United Nations, raises interesting questions of precedent about future dealings with state sanction (to say nothing of state sponsorship) of terrorism. Does the U.S.-led coalition's effort signal a precedent for similar action against others in cahoots with ter-

Amplification 10.1

SCHOOLS FOR TERRORISTS: THE *MADRASSA* SYSTEM

One of the phenomena that has come to light in the wake of the September 11 terrorist attacks has been the existence of Islamic schools in Pakistan (and more recently in Indonesia) that have been the breeding and recruitment grounds for "freedom fighters" *(mujahadeen)* in various places (Chechnya, for instance) and for terrorists in support of Usama bin Laden and his Al Qaeda network.

The *madrassas*, as they are known, serve a useful social service. The students who are recruited into them are, by and large, the discarded boys of the Islamic Middle East: orphans, street children, and the like. The *madrassas* take them in, feed and clothe them, and provide them with shelter and an education. The *madrassas* are financed privately by wealthy individuals in the region, especially people from Saudi Arabia. Because of the desperate financial straits in which the government of Pakistan perpetually finds itself, it lacks the ability to provide equivalent services to these youth on its own.

The problem lies in what is taught in the *madrassas*, which number upward of 1,000 and have a student population of between three-quarters of a million and a million. The curriculum consists primarily of memorizing the Koran in Arabic (which is not the native language of most of the students) and listening to fundamentalist Islamic lecturers, who spew out a steady stream of fundamentalist, especially anti-American, diatribes. At the end of their "education" (which generally does not include even rudimentary schooling in subjects such as mathematics or reading and writing), these young people are so conditioned to hate the West, especially the United States, that they are willing recruits for terrorist missions. Any rebuilding effort in the region that does not include the transformation of these schools and the takeover of their legitimate functions by other institutions is unlikely to relieve the problem of terrorism.

rorists? Buoyed by their success in Afghanistan, the Bush administration has considered expansion of efforts against other states with connections either to Al Qaeda (Somalia, for instance) or with terrorism generally (notably Syria and Iran). There was notably little enthusiasm internationally for either proposed enterprise, suggesting that there is not—at least yet—any broadly based, general global mandate on the subject.

Forms of Terrorism.   One of the great frustrations of dealing with terrorism is the wide variety of forms it may take. Most of the visible acts of terror that have been publicly recorded have involved bombing something—office buildings, airplanes, and subways, for instance—but such activities by no means exhaust the wide range of actions that future terrorists may take against target populations. In a 1992 book, *Low-Intensity Conflict*, James J. Gallagher provides a representative list of other potential terrorist acts. The list includes hijacking; arson; kidnapping of public officials, corporate executives, or common citizens; hostage taking; assassination; raids against installations; property seizure; and sabotage.

Two points should be made about this array of targets. First, the range of physical locales—particularly in a large country like the United States—is staggering. Many of the targets may be in or adjacent to urban areas, where security and pursuit of perpetrators is very difficult because of the sheer number of potential targets. How many cities and towns, for instance, use reservoirs, which are susceptible to contamination, as the basis for their drinking water supply? In addition, a wide variety of targets, such as electric power-generation plants and hydroelectric dams, may be in rural areas. The potential list of targets vulnerable to attack is probably too great to be comprehensively protected simultaneously, no matter the level of diligence.

Second, the range of means available could be expanded greatly in the future, with ominous implications. The acquisition and use of weapons of mass destruction (WMD)—including nuclear, chemical, and biological (NBC) munitions—has been widely publicized and its potential dangers defined and decried. In a *Foreign Policy* article, Thomas Homer-Dixon adds an interesting twist to these possibilities in his discussion of what he calls "complex terrorism." His basic argument is that the nature of modern, postindustrial society makes it a tempting target for terrorists who are interested in disrupting society. As he puts it, "We're easy prey because of two key trends: First, the growing technological capacity of small groups and individuals to destroy things and people; and, second, the increasing vulnerability of our economic and technological systems to carefully aimed attacks." The upper end of the technological spectrum he describes is what we referred to earlier as *cyberwar.* The lower end could encompass actions as simple as introducing pathogens into grain reserves that could be passed through the food chain. The array of possible means and ends is stunning and daunting for those charged with preventing or suppressing terrorism.

Dealing with Terrorism

Because the terrorism problem itself is so complex and difficult, the problem of dealing with it—finding means to reduce vulnerability to terrorist attacks and to reduce or eradicate the terrorist threat—is concomitantly difficult. What can we do? What should we do in the face of a problem that is unlikely to disappear and that may become a more commonplace occurrence in our daily lives?

The answers are less clear than the questions. To understand the dimensions of the problem, we will proceed sequentially. We will begin by examining, once again, the war analogy. Does the equation of means to deal with war clarify or muddy the waters of our understanding and the effectiveness of our efforts? We will then move to the two standard categories of response to terrorism: antiterrorism and counterterrorism. What are they? Which is most effective and under what circumstances? Can an effective strategy be devised that does not incorporate elements of each?

The War Analogy.   The problem of conceptualizing the effort against terrorism as a war is that it is a partly accurate and partly inaccurate analogy; that is, it is semimilitary in nature. In the emotional heat of reaction to the September 11 attacks, it was probably natural to want to dramatize our resolve and commitment through such a rallying cry, even embellished with the subanalogy of equating the attacks with the Japanese attacks on Pearl Harbor in 1941. And indeed, the equation of the terrorism campaign with the war on drugs or similar entities was not much of a stretch if war meant, in Howard's terms, "the mobilization of all available resources against a dangerous, antisocial activity."

Unfortunately, the analogy represents yet another extension of the idea of war to another object beyond its traditional meaning. If the meaning is simply allegorical—such as the war on poverty—and everybody knows that, the designation is harmless. No one thought of sending the marines into Appalachia, for instance, to eradicate the grinding poverty of that region.

When the designation is given a military content, the trouble begins. We have precedent in this direction in the war on drugs (discussed in the next section). The term *war* in that case meant turning over primary jurisdiction to the military to solve a problem that was more social and psychological and criminal than military. This task was given to—and reluctantly accepted by—a military establishment that was unprepared physically and psychologically for such operations. That it did not do particularly well in the drug war should have come as little surprise.

There is an analogy between the wars on drugs and terrorism, although the nature of the post–September 11 campaign has obscured it. The confusion was created by two things. First, after September 11, there was a large-scale mobilization of American reserve forces to carry out a variety of tasks that normally would be assigned to civilians, such as airport security, and to perform the kinds of military duties that resulted from the Abrams reforms (see Chapter 8), such as aerial refueling. Second, the campaign to dislodge the Taliban from power and to destroy and pursue bin Laden and Al Qaeda was conducted through the application of thoroughly conventional military power.

Beyond those applications of military power, the use of continued military power—and thus the relevance of the war analogy—is marginal. Military forces will play some supporting role in the overall campaign against terrorism in ways such as improving the security of American embassies and other governmental facilities overseas. Occasionally, elite, nonconventional force elements such as the army's Delta Force or Navy SEALS may be asked to conduct specialized activities such as raids or the capture of known terrorists—a possibility that was under active consideration initially in 2002. As long as Al Qaeda forces are on the loose, military forces will pursue them. For the most part, however, dealing with terrorism will be a civilian enterprise, dominated by law enforcement, intelligence gathering, and political and diplomatic activities.

The adoption of the war analogy by virtually all American media has colored perceptions and thus has tainted the debate about how to respond. Taken in its literal, international, legal sense, there has never been anything resembling a state of war between the United States and anyone in the wake of the terrorist attacks, although it can be argued that the new forms of asymmetrical war (fourth-generation warfare) render such definitions archaic. Although the Bush administration warned that there could be no military "victory" at which point triumph could be declared, the image of war has not faded and has continued to flourish in the public mind.

Antiterrorism and Counterterrorism.   There are basically two ways to try to thwart terrorism. One is antiterrorism—defensive measures used to reduce the vulnerability of potential targets to attack and to lessen the effects of terrorist attacks that do occur. Antiterrorism, in other words, is based on the presumption that efforts to prevent terrorist assaults from being mounted will not always succeed and that, as a result, efforts must be made to lessen their impacts on the targets. In a world where there is such a wide variety of potential targets for terrorists and means by which terrorism can be carried out, antiterrorism clearly must be part of any overall strategy.

As the definition suggests, antiterrorism entails two kinds of activities: those actions that make terrorism more difficult and those that make it less effective. Examples of antiterrorism aimed at making terrorist acts more difficult are enhancing airline security procedures to make it harder for terrorists to board airliners or gain access to cockpits, or armor-plating the vehicles of corporate executives (installing solid rubber tires or bullet-proof glass) to make kidnappings more difficult. An example of making such attacks less effective is the practice of not allowing vehicles to park near public buildings or putting up barriers and closing streets, as has been done to Pennsylvania Avenue in front of the White House in Washington, to prevent car bombings.

A terrorist act that is prevented is one for which antiterrorist efforts need not be mounted, and that is the purpose of counterterrorism. Counterterrorism is defined as offensive and military measures taken by the military and other agencies against terrorists or their sponsoring agencies to prevent, deter, or respond to terrorist acts. The major emphasis of counterterrorism is to disable or dissuade the potential perpetrator by eliminating his or her physical ability to carry out these acts. Although counterterrorists may use offensive actions to carry out their missions, counterterrorism is usually reactive, responding to some terrorist act or to a revelation about a terrorist plan. The emphasis of counterterrorism is thus highly attuned to intelligence gathering and analysis (penetrating terrorist organizations or monitoring the movement of known or suspected terrorists, for instance) and to military or paramilitary actions (such as destroying terrorist facilities or capturing or killing terrorists).

Counterterrorism is intuitively appealing, because it is active—"terrorizing terrorists" to dissuade or punish them—and clearly much of the American response to the September 11 attacks falls in the category of counterterrorism: the military targeting and destruction of Al Qaeda's physical and human assets, for instance. The campaign's difficulty in tracking down and capturing bin Laden, however, also points to the difficulty of engaging in counterterrorism. Had there been adequate intelligence analysis on the Al Qaeda operation, we might well have known about the September 11 attacks in advance and might been able to thwart them. After the fact, a better quality of information might have assisted in locating and capturing or killing bin Laden. Similarly, a better knowledge of bin Laden's movements might have meant that American cruise missiles launched against his training camps in retaliation for the 1998 embassy bombings in Africa might have arrived while he was still there.

The problem is that competent terrorists are adept at countering counterterrorism. By their nature, such organizations are small, secretive, highly compartmentalized (i.e., one component knows little or nothing about the others), and are located somewhere where they have the sanction of the host state. In Afghanistan, there was a thirteen-year period, between January 1989 and the reinstitution of relations in early 2002, when the United States had no functioning embassy in Kabul and thus no platform from which to organize and launch intelligence operations. Since most terrorist acts will by definition be planned and initiated from locations hostile to the United States, the problem of intelligence penetration and surveillance will always be difficult.

This discussion suggests two imperatives in dealing with terrorism. The first is that any strategy must contain elements of both antiterrorism and counterterrorism. Although counterterrorism may reduce the number of assaults aimed at the United States (or at American facilities or citizens overseas), it is unlikely to eliminate all of them, which means that antiterrorist capabilities will always be needed to absorb those attacks that cannot be prevented. Counterterrorist actions can reduce the number of such attacks that must be absorbed, however, simplifying the antiterrorism problem. Neither strategy alone can manage the problem in its entirety.

The other imperative would seem to be that international terrorism can be contained only by an international response. This is particularly true in the area of counterterrorism—especially the intelligence function, which is crucial to successful counterterrorism efforts. The pooled information gathered by several national intelligence agencies will always provide a superior informational base than that obtainable unilaterally, the movement of people can best be monitored through surveillance wherever they go, and the successful penetration and destruction of terrorist organizations is most likely to occur when several entities are involved. International cooperation—especially among naturally secretive intelligence agencies—is easier said than done (because intelligence agencies fear that sharing information may compromise their sources, for instance), but it cannot help but aid the effort.

Terrorism and National Security

The events of September 11 clearly increased the importance of the issue of terrorism. Because so many American lives were lost and because the prospect of more carnage remains a potential, the safety and security of Americans are involved as well. Terrorism has arrived as a central matter on the agenda of national security.

Will it remain an important component of national security concern and strategy? If it does, how will it be treated? Will it occupy a position within the traditional hierarchy of national security threats, as one more essentially military problem with which the United States must contend, or will it occupy its own unique place? In other words, is terrorism a new form of security problem or an extension of more traditional forms?

How central terrorism is to future American security is, in a sense, up to the terrorists and to the success of those in the U.S. government and the international security community in suppressing them. The problem of terrorism is not, after all, entirely new in our historical experience. We have had assassins who have murdered

American presidents, and the 1990s demonstrated through the actions of people like Timothy McVeigh that we are capable of producing our own, homegrown terrorists. Likewise, Americans overseas have been victims of terrorism before. What has created the enormous emphasis on terrorism today is a single, horrendous event and a strident response to it, which have galvanized our attention. It may be beside the point that we had been warned that such an event was likely coming by a terrorism community to whom we gave little heed.

But it is not entirely beside the point. The academics and others who have warned for years of impending terrorist atrocities were largely ignored and their recommendations unimplemented because the warnings had been largely unfulfilled until 2001. A common thread through the warnings and the responses is the need for sacrifice, whether it be something as trivial as losing curbside check-in of luggage at airports or as profound as the suspension of civil liberties for some categories of residents, as suggested by Bush and Ashcroft in the initial, emotional response to September 11. The American people have demonstrated the willingness to suffer inconvenience in the face of clear public danger, but what about the future?

What happens if the threat appears to abate? After all, September 11 represented not the climax of a campaign of terror but a single, awful event. What if it is not repeated, on a similar or even smaller scale? This could happen if the terrorists are incapacitated by the onslaught against them in Afghanistan or if they conclude that they cannot succeed because our efforts make their nefarious plans impossible to carry out. In the latter case, the public will probably not even know of our successes in thwarting terrorist efforts, because revelations of such successes could compromise intelligence sources. In the meantime, the Department of Homeland Security issued terrorist alerts that did not materialize. At some point, the population may decide officials are "crying wolf" and may begin to chafe at the restrictions this "war" imposes.

What this suggests is that dealing with terrorism is unlikely to disappear from the range of national security concerns but that it may not occupy indefinitely the centrality it has enjoyed since September 11. Moreover, as the immediate threats fade, the shape of the response is likely to be much less public and notably less military. If Afghanistan is effectively pacified and governance is restored there, the emphasis on keeping Afghanistan on the list of antiterrorist states turns toward alleviating the wretched conditions that were the breeding ground of Al Qaeda. That effort is a matter of state-building, including the reconstruction of a country torn by twenty years of violence. A similar effort will undoubtedly be proposed for neighboring Pakistan. Neither effort will be especially warlike.

Nevertheless, the campaign will undoubtedly move more centrally to the political and diplomatic level, where the United States and other Western states will seek to establish ties in developing-world states much more closely to monitor the emergence of terrorist threats. This involves expansion of intelligence linkages, among other things, and once again the content will not be particularly military. Only if the planned response is overtly military, as in proposals to attack the sources of terrorism in such places as Iraq and Somalia (see Amplification 10.2), will there be a traditional national security content.

Amplification 10.2

SHOULD FORCE BE USED
TO ROOT OUT TERRORISM?

The obvious success of applying American air and ground force against the Taliban and Al Qaeda in Afghanistan has triggered proposals to extend the treatment to other countries suspected of harboring terrorists or engaging in terrorist activities. The first "candidate" identified for this treatment has been Iraq and its renegade leader Saddam Hussein. Other countries often mentioned because of their suspected ties to the remnants of the Al Qaeda network include Somalia and the Sudan. Moreover, American forces have been dispatched to the Philippines to assist in training their army to suppress supposed terrorists.

Is the Afghan experience a good precedent for other applications of American force? Going after terrorists wherever they exist is certainly congruent with the Bush Doctrine's assertion that any country not actively opposing terrorism is the enemy and President Bush's professed intent to root out terrorists wherever they may be.

Whether the precedent applies to other cases relies on a positive answer to two questions. The first is whether the tactic will work. In Afghanistan, the approach had two advantages that might not be present elsewhere. First, the opposition refused to resort to unconventional methods that might have made the attacks less effective. They did not disperse when the bombers came. Second, there was an operating opposition on the ground in the form of the Northern Alliance and other anti-Taliban factions that engaged the opposition and made it unnecessary for American forces to do that bloody work. The two conditions were reinforcing, of course, since the presence of the Afghan opposition made it more difficult for the Taliban and Al Qaeda to take evasive action. Neither of these conditions would likely hold elsewhere.

The second question has to do with international support. Because American military actions in Afghanistan were clearly responses to the terrorist acts against American soil, they were accepted and supported by most of the world. Since none of the countries often included on the candidate list (the "axis of evil" states of Iraq, Iran, and North Korea, for instance) can be clearly linked (if linked at all) to the September 11 attacks, that critical item in gaining international support is missing. Almost all countries have counseled the United States against expanding the campaign elsewhere, advice not always accepted. Because the extension would appear to be an act of American unilateralism, the effect might actually be to weaken the response to terrorism, since it might weaken the international solidarity and cooperation that most analysts argue is crucial to dealing with the problem.

THE PROBLEM OF DRUGS

The national security agenda has been further complicated by the addition of areas that threaten some sense of American safety and thus appear to enter the list of concerns that fall under the rubric of national security. Terrorism represents a kind of transition from problems such as the regional conflicts, which have a large and prominent military content and thus qualify in a traditional sense, to those concerns that are marginally military in any sense. The response to terrorism may be semimilitary in content, but it does have some military content, and it represents a clear challenge to the physical and psychological security of Americans.

Dealing with drugs does not so clearly meet those criteria. The "war on drugs" that was declared by the George H. W. Bush administration became a military exercise because it was so designated, and a reluctant U.S. military undertook a feckless attempt to impose a military solution to a social problem. There was even some question of how the problem of drugs rose to the level of security threat. A related concern arising from the drug problem is the political destabilization of countries where illegal drugs are prominent—a potential national security problem.

Drugs as a Security Problem

When President George H. W. Bush came to office in 1989, there was a general consensus that illicit drugs posed a serious threat to American society. The concern centered on the use of cocaine, and it was estimated that there were upwards of eight million cocaine addicts in the country and an additional twenty-five million so-called recreational users of cocaine. The drug enterprise was estimated at around $100 billion a year in untaxed revenue, and the cost of apprehending and incarcerating those guilty of drug-related crime was putting serious strains on the criminal justice system. Bush inherited this concern from his predecessor, Ronald Reagan, whose wife Nancy had spearheaded the "Just Say No to Drugs" campaign that had been spectacularly ineffective in confronting the problem. Bush upped the ante and declared "war" on drugs.

As a visible public priority, the drug war has largely vanished from the public eye, but the problem of drug usage has not. The underlying premise of the war on drugs was that the problem of drug usage was eroding the foundations of American society to such a significant degree as to pose a threat to American national security. As a result, Bush elevated the concern to a high priority of his administration, appointing a special assistant for the drug war (the so-called drug czar) and turning significant parts of the initiative over to the military—specifically, the Southern Command (SOUTHCOM), which has military responsibility for the southern part of the western hemisphere, which was the focus of the effort. Bush's successor, Bill Clinton, downplayed this war but appointed a high profile former SOUTHCOM commander, retired General Barry McCafferty, to serve as drug czar. During his tenure, military aspects of the war were downplayed. The continuing effort has not been a major priority in the current Bush administration, with its emphasis on terrorism. Since the war on drugs bears some structural resemblance to the war on terrorism, however, perhaps the Bush team should analyze the similarities.

The War on Drugs

The problem that the war on drugs addressed was the flow of cocaine from the Andes Mountains region of South America to the United States. As such, it was not a comprehensive campaign against drugs, since most heroin, for instance, comes from

Asia (notably Afghanistan), and other addictive substances, such as methampheta-mine and marijuana, are produced indigenously as well as overseas. South America was the target because it was where most of the cocaine, deemed the most serious and visible problem at the time, had its source.

The war on drugs developed two distinct focuses, one of them heavily military and one decidedly nonmilitary. One emphasis was on the *supply* of drugs entering the United States and sought to reduce the amount of cocaine entering the American market. The other emphasis was on *demand*, concentrating on trying to convince the population not to consume cocaine. Supply became essentially a military prob-lem, demand a nonmilitary issue.

Attacking the supply was assigned to the military, formally operating in cooper-ation with such nonmilitary elements as the Drug Enforcement Agency (DEA) but often, in fact, working independently or at cross purposes. There were three aspects to the supply-side campaign, one of which was shared with the demand-side cam-paign. One focus was on *source eradication*. This effort centered on the destruction of crops of coca, from which cocaine is distilled, and on attempting to interrupt the transshipment of unprocessed coca to Colombia for manufacture into cocaine and destroying the cocaine "labs" where the drugs were manufactured. These efforts were made difficult by the rugged, mountainous topography of the regions of Peru and Bolivia where coca is grown, the negative effects of killing coca plants (groundwater contamination from the defoliants employed), cooperation between farmers and Shining Path guerrillas in Peru, the ineffectiveness of local forces, and the difficulty of successfully interdicting the small aircraft used to transport the crop to the labs.

The other response assigned to the military was *interdiction* of processed drugs being smuggled into the United States. This effort involved all the major American military services: the navy and Coast Guard to try to intercept drug-laden boats skim-ming across the Caribbean Sea and the Gulf of Mexico, the air force to try to intercept airborne shipments, and the army to attempt to patrol (along with the INS) shipments overland, principally from Mexico. Given the amount of potential entry points into the United States through which drugs can be smuggled (the Florida coastline alone is over 1,000 miles long, and the border between the United States and Mexico is over 2,000 miles long), efforts at interdiction had spotty success, at best.

The other effort, partly shared with demand-side initiatives, involved vigorous *enforcement of drug laws*. From the supply side, the assumption was that if enough drug dealers and users were arrested and taken off the streets, the amount of drugs available would decline. From the demand-side perspective, it was hoped that if enough average citizens were arrested, and their arrests publicized, the largely recre-ational users would conclude that the risk of public embarrassment overrode what-ever pleasure they got from drug purchase and use. This part of the effort, of course, was assigned to law enforcement, and its consequences, in terms of a bloated prison population and demands for additional correctional facilities at the expense of other priorities such as schools, remain part of the contemporary policy scene.

The other side of the effort concentrated on reducing demand for cocaine. The basic premise was that if people could be educated to the dangers and health conse-quences of drugs, they would conclude that drug usage was wrong and there would be a drop in demand. Advocates of demand-side approaches also argued for more aggressive treatment programs to try to reduce recidivism among addicts. Neither effort was very successful: Educational efforts reached the middle- and upper-middle-class recreational users, but not the inner-city, hard-core addicts (who were also not deterred by the prospect of arrest). The success of treatment programs in preventing recurrence of drug usage was also very low, generally in the 15 to 20 percent success rate range.

The war on drugs was hardly a ringing success. Like the war on terror, it became a priority because the cause was adopted by an administration, although it lacked the dramatic impetus of September 11. But the response was in some ways similar. Calling for a war on drugs had the effect of militarizing the problem and its solution, even though it was not clear at the time that the military was the proper instrument for the task. At the same time, the appointment of a highly visible leader for the effort, the drug czar, created the appearance of a real focus, even though the drug czar never had the institutional position within a complex bureaucratic environment to coordinate effectively an effort that might not have succeeded under the best of circumstances.

Ongoing Problems

Although drug usage has never been officially removed from the list of threats to American national security, its treatment in the current list of security concerns has clearly declined. People still take drugs, and we no longer seem to feel so threatened by that fact.

Drugs remain a more indirect concern, however, because of the impact they have on the countries where they are produced and through which they travel. What has emerged in a number of countries is the destabilization of states because of the corrupting influence produced by the drug money used to bribe or otherwise control political figures. The prototype of this *criminalization* of the political process is Colombia, where the drug cartels effectively control large parts of the country and engage in a civil war of sorts, pitting narco-insurgents against government forces in a competition where the insurgents are advantaged in terms of capital and firepower.

When the countries affected by this erosion of governance are far distant—in Colombia or Afghanistan or Laos—there is arguably not much at stake for the United States in a security sense, but the problem has spread as close to the United States as its southern border. Although the statistics are notoriously unreliable, large parts of the Mexican political system have been compromised by drug money, and despite the attempts of Mexican President Vicente Fox to root out corruption, some argue that the situation is so far out of hand that no one is quite certain how to exorcise the problem.

The case of Colombia is illustrative. The Colombian government is engaged in a campaign to reduce the influence of the *narcotraficantes*, but it has been an uphill struggle. The government has specifically rejected direct military intervention by the Americans on the dual grounds that such an effort would be ineffectual due to Colombian geography and that such an act of "Yankee imperialism" would drive many Colombians into the arms of the "rebels." Moreover, a successful campaign would only drive the traffickers into adjacent countries such as Venezuela and Brazil, thereby providing a contagion effect, the prospect of which has aligned the countries of the region in opposition to an increased American role.

The problem of drugs becomes united with the threat of terrorism in Afghanistan. Historically, Afghanistan has been a major producer of the poppies from which heroin is made, as well as an important link in the transportation of illicit drugs between Asia and Europe (indeed, a portion of Al Qaeda and Taliban funds apparently came from drug trafficking). One of the important priorities in Afghanistan for the United States and the international community is to reestablish some productivity into an economy ravaged by war and Taliban rule. A temptation among the Afghans will undoubtedly be to return to the traditional role of heroin as a source of funds in a cash-poor country, and the question is whether the West is willing to expend enough resources on other forms of development for the Afghans to resist that temptation. The failure to arrest the drug trade in Afghanistan could have the same corrosive effects as those in South America, which is clearly undesirable and potentially could undercut American efforts. On the other hand, promising the volume of developmental assistance needed for Afghan recovery and prosperity and delivering it without drugs are very different propositions.

CONCLUSION: EXPANDED ROLES AND MEANS

The fact that the United States involves itself in a significant way in the three areas covered in this chapter suggests the expanded role of the United States in the world and the practical impossibility of American aloofness from the world in which it finds itself. Partly, of course, that involvement is the result of more or less purposeful actions taken by the U.S. government or individual Americans. There would be no need to combat drugs, for instance, if some Americans did not consume them, and the likelihood of terrorist actions against Americans originating from the Middle East would certainly be less if our addiction to Persian Gulf oil did not dictate a prominent ongoing presence there. Our concern with the containment of regional conflicts reflects the interconnectivity of the world and the possibility of being drawn into others' fights.

These nontraditional areas of concern go well beyond historical notions of national security grounded in the military defense of the United States against outside intrusion. Terrorism is an exception to that statement, of course, but even there, the means to combat terrorism go well beyond traditional military instruments of national policy, encompassing a variety of other means and roles. The U.S. involvement in the Palestinian–Israeli conflict or the struggle over Kashmir has virtually no American military aspect, unless the explosion of either conflict somehow draws the United States into the maelstrom or American forces are necessary to enforce some form of settlement. The inappropriateness of the war analogy for dealing with the problem of narcotics has already been demonstrated.

Treating these difficulties within a national security framework is made more difficult by our equation of national security and military force. Our loose usage of the term *war* to describe efforts that are only peripherally military adds to our confusion and to the confusion of matching roles and missions to appropriate instruments of national power. National security is the province of more than the armed forces; it now encompasses most of our national assets in some way.

The three areas discussed here have two things clearly in common. First, they are relatively recent but increasingly prominent parts of the menu of real concerns with which national security must deal. This is at least partly the case because more traditional forms of national security concern have receded in importance—the idea of major war in the twentieth-century sense is no longer a major consideration. Instead, we worry more about asymmetrical concepts, of which terrorism and combating drugs certainly are examples. Second, these are all concerns between the United States and areas of the developing world. They are all problems that have their seedbed in the unfortunate, even wretched conditions in some developing world areas. The crops from which drugs are produced, for instance, are grown not by gentleman farmers but by poor peasants, whether in Peru or in Afghanistan. Terrorism has as its breeding ground the wretched conditions of those who are drawn to it. The Palestinians and the Kashmiris yearn for relief from their meager conditions.

These problems are likely to continue into the future and to remain matters with which the United States will have to come to grips. A common theme in all these concerns is the need to improve the material and living conditions of people around the world. One of the major manifestations of dealing with this dynamic is peacekeeping and state-building, formerly obscure concepts that are becoming increasingly commonplace parts of the security debate.

SELECTED BIBLIOGRAPHY

Betts, Richard. "The New Threat of Mass Destruction." *Foreign Affairs* 77, 1 (January/February 1998), 17–30.

Deutch, John. "Terrorism." *Foreign Policy,* Fall 1997, 10–23.

de Wijk, Rob. "The Limits of Military Power." *Washington Quarterly* 25, 1 (Winter 2002), 75–90.

Douglass, Douglas D., Jr. "The War on Drugs: Prospects for Success." *Journal of Social, Political, and Economic Studies* 15, 1 (Spring 1990), 45–57.

Gallagher, James J. *Low-Intensity Conflict: A Guide for Tactics, Techniques, and Procedures.* Harrisburg, PA: Stackpole Books, 1992.

Ganguly, Sumit. *The Crisis in Kashmir: Portents of War, Hopes of Peace.* New York: Cambridge University Press, 1997.

Gorritti, Gustavo. "The War of the Philosopher King." *New Republic* 3, no. 935 (June 18, 1991), 15–23.

Hazleton, William A., and Sandra Woy-Hazleton. "Sendero Luminoso and the Future of Peruvian Democracy." *Third World Quarterly* 12, 2 (April 1990), 21–35.

Hedges, Chris. "The New Palestinian Revolt." *Foreign Affairs* 80, 1 (January/February 2001), 124–38.

Hendrickson, Ryan C. "American War Powers and Terrorists: The Case of Usama bin Laden." *Studies in Conflict and Terrorism* 23 (September/October 2000), 161–76.

Hertzberg, Arthur. "A Small Peace for the Middle East." *Foreign Affairs* 80, 1 (January/February 2001), 139–47.

Hoffman, Bruce. *Terrorism.* New York: Columbia University Press, 1998.

Homer-Dixon, Thomas. "The Rise of Complex Terrorism." *Foreign Policy*, January/February 2002, 38–50.

Howard, Michael. "What's in a Name? How to Fight Terrorism." *Foreign Affairs* 81, 1 (January/February 2002), 8–13.

Lewis, Bernard. "License to Kill: Usama bin Laden's Declaration of Jihad." *Foreign Affairs* 77, 6 (November/December 1998), 14–19.

McDonald, Scott B. *Mountain High, White Avalanche: Cocaine and Power in the Andean States and Panama*. CSIS Papers No. 137. New York: Praeger, 1989.

Reeve, Simon. *The New Jackals: Ramzi Yousef, Osama bin Laden, and the Future*. Boston: Northeastern University Press, 1999.

Schofield, Victoria. *Kashmir in the Crossfire*. London: I. B. Tauris, 1996.

Sloan, Stephen. *Beating International Terrorism: An Action Strategy for Preemption and Punishment*, rev. ed. Montgomery, AL: Air University Press, 2000.

Snow, Donald M. *Cases in International Relations: Portraits of the Future*. New York: Longman, 2002.

———. *September 11, 2001: The New Face of War?* New York: Longman, 2002.

Viorst, Milton. "Middle East Peace: Mirage on the Horizon?" *Washington Quarterly* 23, 1 (Winter 2000), 41–54.

11

Peacekeeping and State-Building: The New Dilemma

Violence and instability leading to terrorism and new internal wars are concentrated in select parts of the Second Tier where the wretchedness of the human condition breeds the despair that leads to such instability. In the 1990s, American involvement in these situations was justified on largely humanitarian grounds; today the rationale is suppressing terrorism. The question is what, if anything, can be done to alleviate those conditions and thus reduce the inclination to humanitarian atrocity or terrorist attractiveness. To address this problem, this chapter begins by identifying vulnerable societies—the so-called failed states. We will then look at why and how the United States may intervene in the future. The possibilities for improving the situations, peacekeeping and state-building, are then examined, and the chapter concludes with the likely effects of these actions for the future.

Almost all of the national security challenges in the contemporary international environment come in the interaction between the West (with the United States as its normal leader) and specific parts of the developing world. In previous chapters, we have attempted to identify some of the kinds of problems that exist. In the area of globalization, for instance, which states are more or less poised to participate in the global economy (a subject to which we will return in Chapter 12)? At the level of more traditional, military national security threats, we have identified problems as diverse as new internal wars and asymmetrical threats, including terrorism. In this chapter, we will shift our emphasis from what the problems are to what we can do about them in those instances when we decide to do anything at all.

The debate about American involvement with force in the developing world has been skewed by the events of September 11, 2001. Prior to the terrorist attacks, there was a lively, partisan political debate about the degree of American activism in the developing world. During the 2000 election campaign, then-candidate George W.

Bush and his close advisors, such as current National Security Advisor Condoleeza Rice, actively derided American intervention and continuing involvement in such Second Tier locales as Kosovo and Bosnia, maintained that the United States should cut back its involvement by scaling back or withdrawing American troops where they were present, and publicly promised that the United States would no longer be "the world's 911." More to the point, the commitment of American forces to missions such as peacekeeping and American resources to state-building was derided as a misapplication and overextension of scarce and valuable American assets.

During the 1990s, the United States became involved in a number of these developing-world conflicts and avoided others, with decidedly mixed results. In 1992, the United States joined the international response to suffering and atrocity in Somalia, which ended with American withdrawal after eighteen of our soldiers were slaughtered in an ambush in the country's capital, Mogadishu. In 1994, the United States launched an "intervasion" (part intervention, part invasion) to restore the elected government of Haiti, but we sat out the slaughter in Rwanda that same year. Operation Restore Democracy (the Haitian operation) restored democracy only in the most generous sense of that term. Nearly a decade later, conditions remain nearly as wretched as they were before American involvement, and only the faintest hints of representative government exist. President Clinton deemed U.S. failure to act in Rwanda one of the worst mistakes of his foreign policy. In 1995, the United States was a central player in negotiating and enforcing a ceasefire among the warring parties in Bosnia, an action it reprised in 1999 in Kosovo. The latter two involvements are notable because they required American military participation in ongoing, open-ended peacekeeping missions.

All of these were low-priority operations, but they also entailed relatively modest investments and risks for the United States. The United States, at least after Somalia, could indulge in the inclination to "do something" when faced with atrocity on national cable news, because the costs in blood and treasure were modest. In the Haitian, Bosnian, and Kosovar involvements, for instance, there have been *no* American casualties from hostile action. That we cannot measure great benefit from these operations (how much difference does it make that Haitian democracy remains an elusive chimera?) has been less important than the absence of losses.

This whole question appeared to change fundamentally when the United States set its sights on Afghanistan in the fall of 2001. The United States had tolerated the repressive, virulently anti-American stance of the Taliban regime there since they came to power in 1996, on the grounds that no American interests were affected by their objectionable attitudes and actions. Their sanctioning of terrorism was regrettable, of course, but until their refusal to hand over the terrorists dictated their removal from power, they were not very high on the American agenda.

The apparent need to change terrorist-prone societies changed the calculus of involvement in poor, unstable developing-world countries for the Bush administration. In the period between the fault lines, the motivation to become involved was primarily humanitarian, trying to alleviate great human suffering because it was, in President Clinton's justification for intervention in Bosnia, "the right thing to do." Terrorist-proofing similar societies became Bush's reason for involvement. Mohamed Zarea, an

Egyptian human rights advocate quoted in the November 14, 2001, *New York Times*, captured the rationale: "This war on terrorism may eliminate a few terrorists. But without reform, it will be like killing a few mosquitoes and leaving the swamp."

It can be argued that the American mission to Afghanistan is totally unlike our involvement in Bosnia, for instance, because of the emergence of truly vital American concerns associated with rooting out terrorism there. In other words, the United States has had no choice but to do what it has done, making Afghanistan a deployment of necessity and thus unlike the Kosovo deployment of choice. Although that is true during the active military phase of involvement, the package of responses that the United States and its allies have suggested for the longer haul (phase three) includes the same imperatives as those in Bosnia, Kosovo, and other places: peacekeeping to restore order and a healthy amount of state-building to stabilize the situation so that Afghanistan joins the ranks of stable, antiterrorist states. We are committed to doing the same thing in Afghanistan and Iraq that we promised the Kosovars. Only the motivations are different.

Is the Afghanistan case typical or atypical of what the future will hold? The answer largely depends on the lessons that other states take from the American response in Afghanistan and its effects. Countries assessing likely future American responses may conclude that the United States will respond when obviously vital matters are involved (suppressing terrorists, but not humanitarian motives). They may also conclude that American resolution to root out evil in the world is now sufficiently aroused that provocation of the United States is unwise in any circumstance. Whether the United States has become selectively or generally activist will be partially revealed by its actions against other states accused of harboring terrorists, in the name of the Bush Doctrine. Whether responses to terrorism set a precedent that also applies to involvements in new internal wars is something the U.S. government itself probably cannot answer with any real certainty.

Assessing the likely future of American activism requires making two judgments, both of which are controversial and both of which apply equally to terrorist-suppressing and humanitarian motivations. The first is what the United States and its developed-world allies seek to accomplish in the developing world. If we want to hold the troublesome parts of the world essentially at bay, that may suggest a fairly limited approach. If we want to incorporate the developing world—especially its more troublesome members—into the globalizing economy and general prosperity in the hope that it will end their troublemaking, that suggests a much more activist course.

The other judgment is about how much we *can* accomplish. Our experience in transforming developing states into modern or postmodern states is limited and spotty. We succeeded in South Korea but failed in Iran. Moreover, most of our experience has been in countries that were not among the most destitute, whereas most of the candidates in the future will be in such difficult places. Afghanistan is almost a textbook case of the difficulties we will likely face more generally.

The simple answer to what we can accomplish is that we do not know. The activist path has been attempted only in Kosovo, and that effort is too embryonic to yield a judgment about whether it works (or what, if anything, does work). Afghanistan will be a follow-on experiment that we have not really started. If we succeed in helping to transform Afghanistan into an exemplar in the region—more like Turkey than Iran—we will likely herald the experience and try it elsewhere. If we fail, we may not know exactly why. Was it the method that failed? Did we pick the wrong place to try that model? Is another model more applicable? Will *any* approach succeed? Should we try again or abandon the effort?

All these questions apply equally well to potential terrorist-suppressing and humanitarian situations, because the West believes that the same underlying set of circumstances breeds terrorists and practitioners of new internal war. Those conditions are poverty, despair, and oppression, which we believe constitutes the swamp that, once drained, will cease to be the breeding ground for future instability and violence.

To begin to come to grips with (if not conclusively to answer) some of these questions, we will proceed in steps. First, we will look at the kinds of places where intervention is likely to occur. In examining the "failed states," we will look at why they fail, what characteristics cause failure (and thus must be remedied), and how we might attempt to intervene. Second, we will raise questions about intervention in terms of the purposes for which it may be undertaken and the forms that it may take in different situations. We will then turn to the proposed solutions—notably, peace-keeping and state-building, two different but interrelated approaches and goals. We will conclude by speculating on how this complex of problems fits into the "new world order."

FAILED AND FAILING STATES: THE CONTEXT

Almost all of the violence that currently plagues the developing world and boils over occasionally into the developed world, as the events of September 11 did, comes from parts of the developing world. For our purposes, the developing world can be divided into two useful categories: those countries that are part of the globalizing economy and those that are not (for a more detailed discussion, see Snow and Brown, *International Relations*). Membership in the globalizing economy includes those countries that are part of the regional and global economic associations that became prominent during the 1990s: APEC, NAFTA, the EU, and the proposed Free Trade Area of the Americas. Geographically, this encompasses the Western Hemisphere (other than Cuba), most of Europe (including Russia, a member of APEC), and most of East Asia and the Pacific. The areas outside this network are principally found in Africa and parts of Central and South (including Southwest) Asia.

Using these categories to understand where violence is occurring, we find that it is overwhelmingly located in those parts of the developing world outside the globalizing economy. With the exception of Indonesia and the Philippines (both members of APEC), there are hardly any exceptions to this rule. Although not all states outside the globalizing economy are violent and unstable, almost all the violent and unstable states are outside the global economy.

To understand why this pattern exists and persists, we must look at the kinds of states where violence is the norm. We will thus begin by defining the so-called failed states and the characteristics they tend to have, using my own distinctions to define failure and Ralph Peters's characteristics of that failure. We will apply these distinctions to the kinds of conditions that must change for the emergence of stability and entrance into the globalizing economy, criteria for which we will borrow from Thomas L. Friedman.

What Is a Failed State?

The term *failed state* was coined in the early 1990s to describe a phenomenon occurring in parts of the developing world. The prototype was Somalia, a state that had simply collapsed as a viable entity in 1991 following an overthrow of the government and the inability of any other group to assume political control. Thus, as Helman and Ratner define Somalia and states like it, a failed state is "a state utterly incapable of sustaining itself as a member of the international community."

In most cases, failed states have legacies of authoritarian rule but possess unstable regimes in which authoritarian rule has eroded but no viable alternative has emerged. These states thus slide from a condition of authoritarianism to one of anarchy, from which they are incapable of extracting themselves on their own. In the most notable and troublesome cases, this anarchy is manifested in inconclusive, but often spectacular and bloody internal wars.

State failure has both a political and an economic dimension. The political dimension may include anarchy, or it may be manifested by a weak, venal, and corrupt political system that has little control over its population, cannot allocate societal resources nor maintain a civil order, and thus is not accorded legitimacy by sizable parts of its population. In most cases, this ineffectiveness is structural as well as political, in that important governmental institutions (law enforcement, courts, public services, etc.) are nonexistent, hopelessly corrupt, or unable to operate effectively. Probably the most important shortfall is the absence of a criminal or civil judicial and law enforcement community that the public believes treats all citizens equitably and that those citizens are therefore willing to support.

These countries, generally but not exclusively located as they are outside the globalizing economy, are typically economically poor as well. In a number of cases, the reason is structural and endemic: There are few human or physical resources on which to build a viable economic condition. Haiti, for instance, is poor because there is essentially nothing in the country around which to build wealth; and it is hard to imagine how Bangladesh, which essentially is a flood plain of the Ganges River system, can ever develop a viable economic base. In other cases, either whatever economic base exists is systematically misused (the looting of the diamond fields of Sierra Leone) or maldistribution of wealth leaves a tiny elite in possession of fabulous wealth while the masses toil in abject, crushing poverty. In some cases, the ravages of war add to the misery; twenty-four years of war in Afghanistan have left that country's modest prewar infrastructure in absolute ruin.

These two dimensions are interactive and reinforcing. Among the assets that weak or nonexistent governments fail to manage effectively is the economy, and their ineptitude or the resulting chaos their rule produces makes them especially unattractive to potential outside investors. Since living conditions are so poor and the government appears incapable (or uninterested) in changing that situation, there is little reason for people to support a system from which they clearly do not benefit. If the government has enough coercive power to stifle dissent, there may be no practical alternative to sullen acquiescence. If the government is weak, the alternative may be active opposition either to overthrow and replace the regime or to benefit personally from the resulting chaos. Essentially, these countries are unable to provide basic security for their citizens, the sine qua non for all other forms of progress.

Not all states that show signs of failure fall into the same category. The worst cases, such as Somalia, Haiti, and arguably Afghanistan, have failed on all dimensions and have little prospect of changing their situation by themselves. Other states have not quite achieved the status of full-scale failure but are demonstrably showing signs of failure. The most prominent example of the potentially *failing* state is post-Suharto Indonesia, as depicted in Amplification 11.1. In addition, other states have shown signs of potential failure and thus can be designated as *failure-prone*. North Korea is an example.

Ralph Peters provides an interesting and valuable methodology for identifying what he calls "noncompetitive states." These noncompetitive states are not exactly the same as the failed states we have defined already. What he has developed is a set of criteria that can be applied to states in looking at their potential for useful participation in the international system and in determining stability within states and the potential for state failure.

Peters's attributes of noncompetitive states highlight generally failed conditions. Three underlying factors in such societies underpin the list: They typically do not have a reliable and fair rule of law that applies to all citizens; they are generally rife with corruption (which is both a consequence of and reinforcement for a preference for the absence of law); and their economies are usually overly managed, particularly to favor those in power. They do not, in other words, produce a uniform sense of justice and security around which the population can gravitate.

Peters's list is also a warning guide of places to avoid. It includes seven indicators that individually and collectively demonstrate noncompetitiveness and in effect raise red flags about involvement with such societies. The first is a restriction on the flow of information within the society. As many others have also argued, control of the information available to a citizenry has historically been a major source of power, particularly when restricting information that might indicate that people in other places have a better existence. Although such products of the information age as computers and televisions make restriction more difficult, some states continue to try, and their effort is an indication of their backwardness. It has been argued that some of the distorted views held by some Middle Easterners about the United States—which result in the virulent anti-Americanism that justifies terrorism—are the product of the manipulation of information by the government-controlled media of the region.

Amplification 11.1

INDONESIA AS A
POTENTIALLY FAILING STATE

Indonesia, the world's largest archipelago and the fourth most populous state in the world, has experienced a downward political and economic spiral since it was one of the countries hit by the East Asian financial crisis in 1997. In Indonesia, the financial crisis triggered a political crisis that brought down the government in 1998 and left observers speculating about whether Indonesia might move through the categories of state failure.

The financial crisis revealed major weaknesses in the Indonesian economy, as banks failed, savings were destroyed, economic expansion halted, and inflation ran rampant. The Suharto regime, which had been in power since 1966 and was widely regarded as one of the most corrupt regimes in the world, bore the brunt of the criticism, and charges of cronyism and nepotism arose as the economy's weakness was revealed. Suharto was forced to resign, and between 1998 and 2001, two successors struggled in an atmosphere of recriminations regarding corruption. Some calm was restored when the daughter of Achmed Sukarno, who led the Indonesian movement for independence from the Netherlands in the 1940s, was elected. Whether Megawati Sukarnoputri (known popularly as Mega) can restore confidence remains to be seen.

Beyond political crisis, two factors cloud the future. One is the continuing economic crisis, which includes an active element that wants Indonesia to withdraw from the globalizing economy, a prospect most observers believe would further harm the country's economy. The other is a series of separatist movements in the far-flung archipelago that began publicly in East Timor and includes the Free Aceh movement in the Aceh province of Indonesia, where there are large deposits of natural gas crucial to the economy.

Source: Donald M. Snow, "Debating Globalization: The Case of Indonesia," Chapter 9 in *Cases in International Relations: Portraits of the Future*. New York: Longman, 2002.

Second, noncompetitive states tend to subjugate women, restricting their rights in areas such as education and the workplace. This restriction may be an historic cultural artifact or it may be a means to ensure male control, but its practical impact is to remove half a country's talent from the productive process. Any society that creates such restrictions will, he argues, be uncompetitive with counterpart societies that do incorporate women. Resistance to such inclusion is in itself an indication of noncompetitiveness.

Third, noncompetitive states are unable to accept responsibility for their own failure to compete in the world. Rather than recognizing that they are the problem, the leaders are more likely to project their ills onto hostile others outside, using these outside forces as scapegoats. A society that is unwilling to bear this responsibility is particularly unlikely to reform itself and make progress in the world. The United States has been a particularly useful "whipping boy."

Fourth, noncompetitive states typically either have the extended family, a clan, a tribe, or some similar entity as the basis of social organization. In many cases, this traditional social structure creates a crippling duality in terms of interpersonal dealings, with societal consequences. In such settings, Peters argues, relations within the social unit may be very open and honest, but the structure creates an us-versus-them mindset that makes relations between groups much less forthcoming and honest. The upshot is that this traditional form of social organization encourages corruption within the society as a whole and impedes formation and development of the kinds of societal mechanisms necessary for progress into the contemporary globalizing world.

Fifth, the dominance of a restrictive religion is often a characteristic of a noncompetitive state. Such a creed helps to reinforce the us-versus-them mentality and the denial of responsibility for the shortcomings of state performance. Restriction of religious belief not only binds the group together against others but makes more plausible the claim that hostile outsiders (infidels) are responsible for one's own fate. Sixth, this tradition-laden restriction tends to create and reinforce a low valuation of education, especially education that goes beyond the transmission of orthodox, and often fundamentalist, theology. States that devalue education dilute the potential value of their intellectual talent pool, thereby rendering themselves less competitive. Restriction of educational access and inequality only adds to this crippling effect.

Finally, noncompetitive states also tend to place a low value on work. In these generally male-dominated societies, menial tasks are usually assigned to women and children, and men gain prestige not because of what they produce, but somehow on the basis of who they are. As long as this condition persists, the incentives to excel through productivity are largely missing.

Is this checklist remarkable? In many ways, it is no more than a kind of quick visualization of the conventional wisdom about traditional, predeveloped societies. Most of these societies were, and are, authoritarian or at least patriarchal, with women subservient, in an extended family–based society where few were educated and work was avoided. The justification for conditions was often based in a religious credo extolling the status quo, and information about the outside world was restricted to avoid contamination. Breaking the cycle that this represents is the essence of beginning the developmental process.

What do these largely socioeconomic conditions have to do with American national security? The short answer is that these conditions are what produces terrorists and human rights–abusing insurgents, and alleviating them is prerequisite to possible stabilization. Application of American force to crush terrorists or human rights abusers that does not take these problems into account will likely fail in the long run.

In contemporary terms, these factors also reflect state failure. Societies exhibiting these characteristics are likely to be either authoritarian or, where the coercive veil has been lifted, anarchical, lacking reliable political institutions. The human wastage that restricting the role of women or downgrading education creates clearly contributes to the economic misery that typically marks the failed states.

The Peters list also creates a checklist of things to change in moving away from failure, or at least a set of indicators that more basic deficiencies are being addressed.

It is probably not productive to try to scale the deficiencies, arguing, for instance, that a truly *failed* state is one where all these characteristics are present, whereas a *failing* state exhibits only three or four. What the list does, however, is chronicle, in a way that is fairly easily observable and suggestive. (Peters argues, for instance, that a good way to tell about the status of women is to observe how, or whether, men and women interact in the terminal of the country's major airport.)

Although Peters published *Fighting for the Future* in 1999, well before Afghanistan was catapulted onto the world's center stage, it is remarkable how well his categories illustrate the deficiencies of Taliban-ruled Afghanistan and how rapidly the provisional government of Hamid Karzai moved to reverse these factors. Although the early indications are positive, it is the longer-term implementation that is most important.

Information Flow Restriction.   One of the major efforts of the Taliban was to shut the country off from the outside. A very visible symbol of Taliban rule was outlawing radios and televisions, often manifested in dramatic smashing of TVs or computers. One of the first images of Kabul and other cities after liberation was the marketing of replacements for those destroyed instruments of communication with the outside world.

Subjugation of Women.   There was probably no country in the world that suppressed women as much as the Taliban. Women not only had to be fully covered (including wearing the most impenetrable head coverings, or *burkas*, possible), they were also systematically denied access to schools or the workplace. Within weeks of liberation, the *burkas* were virtually gone, and females were prominent in education and the workplace. When the first post-Taliban motion pictures were shown in Kabul after the liberation, however, only men were allowed to attend.

Inability to Accept Responsibility for Failure.   This fairly common symptom of modern Middle Eastern Islamic states was especially pronounced in Afghanistan, where the fundamentalist rantings of Usama bin Laden and others were particularly filled with blaming the West, especially the United States, for the region's ills. Bin Ladenism quickly faded as bin Laden and the Taliban were driven from power.

Social Organization on an Extended Family or Clan Basis.   Afghan society has always been based on clan membership. The Taliban came principally from the Pashtun tribe, which is the country's largest ethnic group and comprises about 38 percent of the population, according to the CIA *Factbook*. Not all Pashtuns, of course, were Taliban, but the majority of the Taliban were Pashtun. Sorting out tribal concerns in the attempt to form a broadly based, multitribal form of governance is possibly the greatest challenge to establishing a legitimate government for Afghanistan—one that the history of tribal animosity and fighting suggests may not succeed for some time.

Dominance of a Restrictive Religion.   A particularly fundamentalist form of Islam underlay the attractiveness and purpose of both the Taliban and bin Laden. According to Michael Doran in a *Foreign Affairs* article, this view sees outsiders and even some Muslim state leaders as defilers of Islam. As Doran puts it, "In bin Laden's imagery, the leaders of the Arab and Islamic worlds today are Hypocrites (people who extol but do not adhere to the faith), idol worshippers cowering behind America, the Hubal (the symbol of pre-Muslim polytheistic idol worship) of the age." These views are highly restrictive and intolerant. Since many Muslims share this view of the West's negative influence but not bin Laden's actions, transforming these beliefs will be a difficult issue to handle, even though the outward forms of repression claimed necessary by the Taliban are removed.

Low Valuation of Education.   Clearly, the education system suffered under the restrictive attitudes of the Taliban against women (including female teachers), and the emphasis on the *madrassa* system in Pakistan is further evidence of devaluing the kind and quality of education that might be put toward making Afghan society more competitive. One of the first institutions to be revived in post-Taliban Afghanistan was the schools, but war-gutted school buildings and the absence of even rudimentary educational materials handicapped the effort.

Low Prestige for Work.   During the days of Taliban rule, the economy essentially did not function, some indication that work and progress were less important than piety within the hierarchy of Taliban priorities. Reviving the economy, which necessarily includes making hard work a valued trait, is also a major challenge for the post-Taliban rulers.

What this discussion suggests is that removal of many of the outward symbols of noncompetitiveness has been a major emphasis in Afghanistan after the Taliban. Much of this change arises from a very grassroots appeal—from women shedding their coverings and men shaving their beards, to street vendors selling boom boxes, to schools resuming as teachers (including women) and students simply return to their old buildings—that at once symbolizes the absolute lack of appeal of the Taliban's creed and the desire to embrace modernity. Whether washing away these vestiges of noncompetitiveness will result in removing the causes of state failure partly depends on the will of the Afghans to embrace fundamental change and the willingness and perseverance of the United States in providing the necessary resources on which to build that change.

Failed States and American National Security

Failed and failing, or noncompetitive, states are places that are obviously in trouble, and their troubles may make some of them unstable and violent. As a result, they present problems for themselves and potentially for others who may be drawn into their difficulties for one reason or another. These are states that rank high on anyone's index of misery. The questions for national security are whether these problems make any difference to *us*; if so, how much difference; and what efforts, if any, we are willing to undertake to try to alleviate the misery.

These questions must be put in historical perspective. There has always been a wide gap between the richest and poorest countries of the world and, thus, the places that have known plenty and those that have experienced unrelenting poverty and deprivation. Peters's conditions are broadly illustrative of the precolonial status of much of Africa and Asia, as well as parts of the Western Hemisphere. The kinds of indicators he attributes to the noncompetitive states are, in large measure, indications either of resistance or failure to move past traditional organizations of society to modern and postmodern forms that allow competition in the globalizing international system. This gap has existed for centuries, even millennia, but it was generally hidden by the isolation of the poorest from the richest. The poor knew they suffered but not that they could alleviate the problem.

The post–Cold War world has caused the perception of inequity to continue to expand. The surge of globalization has improved the status of many peoples, but it has bypassed others, and the gap between the richest countries and the rest has actually widened. In an age of global television and the Internet, these disparities are increasingly impossible to hide from those who do not enjoy the material benefits. Where governments have tried to conceal the truth by restricting access to outside information, they have generally failed spectacularly. Post-Taliban Afghanistan is only our freshest and most vivid reminder of the futility of trying to hide the outside world from one's own populations.

There have been two broad responses to the impact of globalization. Many developing countries have embraced modernization and have entered the globalizing system, with generally favorable results. As Wright points out, "There is . . . a clear connection between a nation's per capita gross domestic product (GDP) and the average happiness of its citizens." The process of benefit from globalization is not linear and tranquil, as the East Asian shocks of 1997 and the global recession of 2001 have demonstrated. On the other hand, countries that have embraced globalization have generally seen both economic progress and at least some political liberalization, which has translated into increased societal stabilization.

The other group of developing states has not embraced globalization, as a matter of either circumstance or choice. Haiti represents the former; many Haitians would like to partake of the general prosperity, but the country has so little to offer that not many outsiders are interested in helping them make the transition. This adds to the misery of Haitian existence, of course, and further destabilizes a Haitian polity whose instability is already one of the reasons no one wants to invest there—clearly a vicious cycle. Liberia is similar. Afghanistan under the Taliban represents the second reaction, rejectionism. The Taliban clearly believed that the intrusion of the West would be culturally intolerable, according to their preferred model of Koranic purity. For a time, they succeeded in isolating their country from the rest of the world, but they ultimately failed. After the fact, it was clear that most of their countrymen did not share their vision.

Those developing countries outside the globalizing economy define the national security problem for the United States. The situation in Afghanistan after September 11, 2001, created a national security concern with the rejectionist states. The desire for revenge against and repression of bin Laden and his associates produced a deployment of necessity that made Afghan isolation from the world unacceptable. Afghanistan as a failed, noncompetitive state minding its own, if bizarre, business, did not previously register significantly on the American national security list. When that isolation and failure also amounted to sanction of terrorists who attacked us, then the status of Afghanistan changed. The country had to become a bulwark against terrorism.

The effect is to add another criterion to our interest in developing-world internal instability. Previously, the major criterion was the intolerability of atrocity, including international outrage, and the result of those humanitarian concerns was ambivalent. We stumbled into Somalia when we had no interests beyond the humanitarian but before we knew to ask what other interests we had there. Afghanistan was the first place where vital American interests were added to the mix. We applied the same logic in Iraq.

Will the Afghanistan case add a permanent second criterion to future American decisions? Put another way, is our experience in Afghanistan *sui generis* or symptomatic of broader, ongoing concern? If it is a special case, the debate over future American activism will revert to pre-Afghanistan terms after the process is completed there (although the debate will clearly be influenced by our success or failure to convert Afghanistan into a viable state). If there are more Afghanistan-style problems out there to be confronted, then the impact on terrorism becomes a stock part of the debate. At the same time, the "humanitarian disaster" in Liberia in July 2003 demonstrates that the more "traditional" cases persist as well.

CONCEPTS AND FORMS OF INTERVENTION

The effort in Afghanistan by the United States and the UN peacekeepers (the International Security Assistance Force, or ISAF) has attracted more attention than previous peacekeeping missions because of the much higher profile of the situation. The missions in which the United States was involved in the 1990s—Somalia, Haiti, Bosnia, and Kosovo—generated some initial publicity when we embarked on them and, in the case of Somalia, when the United States withdrew under less than ideal circumstances and with a less than favorable outcome. Interest faded, however, when our focused interest in the outcomes decreased.

These missions had peacekeeping and, at least implicitly, state-building as objectives. In Haiti, the mission involved restoring Jean-Bertrand Aristide to the elected presidency from which he had been removed by a military coup and creating the conditions for future stability. The first objective was achieved during the four years the United States remained in the country as the lead party of the Operation Uphold Democracy coalition. The second objective is hard to label a success, because Haiti still lacks the basis of a stable, prosperous state.

In Bosnia and Kosovo, the United States was part of a UN-sanctioned peacekeeping mission with the purpose of restoring order and preparing the countries for postmission stability. In the case of Kosovo, the mission explicitly included state-building. The Stabilization Force (originally Implementation Force) entered Bosnia in 1995, and the Kosovo Force was formed in 1999. Both are still in place, and no one thinks they can be withdrawn without an almost certain return to violence.

Although the same terms, peacekeeping and state-building, are used to describe our role in Afghanistan, the situation is so different as virtually to defy comparison. The effort arises out of very different situations. In Kosovo and Haiti, repressive governments were suppressing the population, and the first goal was to end the suppression. In Bosnia, the problem was to separate warring parties as the first step in implementing the Dayton peace accords, calling for a separation of factions. In Afghanistan, there was a conventional civil war going on between the Taliban government and its opponents, which the United States pushed in favor of the insurgents (although prior to the stimulus of the terrorist attacks, we had essentially ignored that war). In Liberia, the country teetered on virtual chaos.

The structure and purposes of intervention are also different. The United Nations initially authorized the ISAF to restore and enforce order in Kabul, but its mission beyond that was not clear. The Afghans themselves expressed interest in a long deployment, providing security for more of the country while the situation stabilized. The United States, meanwhile, set up its own longer-term presence both by establishing and maintaining control of airfields and the like in Afghanistan itself and by establishing bases in adjacent former republics of the Soviet Union (e.g., Uzbekistan) while opposing the extension of the ISAF mission and declining to participate in it. The bases established outside Afghanistan were rather clearly hedges against outliving America's welcome in Afghanistan itself. Meanwhile, international leaders were pledging support for rebuilding an Afghanistan ravaged by over two decades of war (in other words, state-building), without being very specific about what that entailed. By the late summer of 2003, hardly any developmental—or even relief—assistance had arrived, to the growing frustration of the Afghans.

Basic Distinctions

Outside interference in the affairs of other states is always problematic. Although the motives underlying interference may be noble and pristine (or they may not be), they are never going to be viewed by those in whose countries the interference occurs in the same way they are seen by the intervening parties. The initial motivation among interveners since the end of the Cold War (usually under the flag of the United Nations) has always been publicly humanitarian, and helping the suppressed and suffering is always part of the honest motives that impel the actions. Such efforts are always likely to meet some initial opposition, however, which will increase the longer the operation lasts and the intervening parties stay. This is true because intervention always has the effect—if not the intention—of providing advantage to some internal factions at a cost to others, and the losers eventually will not appreciate the effort or view it as benign. How many Taliban welcomed the American intervention in the Afghan civil war, for instance? Moreover, lengthy interventions, especially in the formerly colonized world, will almost certainly begin to look like recolonization and will create rumblings of imperialism.

This uncertainty of reception helps create the frame within which outside interference is contemplated. What outsiders propose to do really consists of two determinations. The first is what it will try to accomplish—its concept. To this end, the basic alternatives are between conflict suppression and state-building. The other question is how to accomplish the task—its form. Here we will look at a continuum of actions, with peace imposition and peacekeeping as its poles. We will briefly define each of these and then examine them in some detail.

The first distinction is between conflict suppression (CS) and state-building (SB). One of the frequently recurring criticisms of American involvement in developing-world conflicts in the past has been the open-endedness of these missions. Part of this criticism is focused on the lack of a clear initial objective to be accomplished. This criticism, in turn, leads to the more frequently alleged shortcoming, which is the absence of a clear point at which we can declare that the mission is accomplished—sometimes called an end or exit strategy, which tells us when we can go home. The absence of such criteria causes us to remain apparently endlessly and even aimlessly in places such as Bosnia and Kosovo. In the worst cases (Somalia is generally regarded as the prime example), the result is an evolving and gradual unplanned expansion of the mission, what is derisively called *mission creep* (unintentional expansion of the purposes of the mission), sometimes with unanticipated and negative effects, such as the attack on U.S. Rangers in Mogadishu, depicted in the book and motion picture *Black Hawk Down*.

When entering the chaos of a war-torn developing-world country that has been unable to terminate the violence itself (which is why a mission is called for in the first place), one can have one of two missions. The first is conflict suppression (CS), which involves either stopping the ongoing fighting (peace imposition) or making sure that a recently established but volatile ceasefire remains in place (peace enforcement). These actions do no more than cause the fighting and killing to stop; they do not in and of themselves assure postwar domestic tranquility. The simplest measure of success is whether the fighting is discontinued.

Conflict suppression does not, of course, address or solve the problems that led to the fighting in the first place. A more ambitious definition of successful CS is that it results in a situation in which peace continues after the force has been withdrawn. Unless the underlying causes of fighting are addressed, the reasons remain and the fighting is likely to be rekindled after the intervening parties leave. In other words, CS deals with the symptoms of violence, not the underlying disease. It is a bandage to stanch the wound, not a cure.

Since intervention occurs in failed or noncompetitive states, success means leaving behind a stable, nonviolent environment in which the return to violence will seem unappealing to the formerly warring parties. As already noted, the societies that tend to collapse into violence generally require both political reform (institution-building, political reconciliation, etc.) and economic development to create a sense of present or future tranquility and prosperity that is clearly preferable to war and that thus commands the loyalty of the population (in other words, results in the conferral of legitimacy to the regime). The collective actions taken to accomplish this goal is what we call state-building.

Where both of these concepts are instituted, they are clearly sequential. A conflict must clearly be terminated before any state-building can begin. One can engage in conflict suppression without engaging in state-building, although the outcome is likely to be a reversion to war after the conflict-suppressing force withdraws. State-building cannot be undertaken unless successful conflict suppression has occurred; it would not be safe to try.

This leads us to distinctions in the forms of intervention. Commonly, these forms are known collectively as *peacekeeping,* although the term is misleading in its generally accepted form and only describes part of what is undertaken in an intervention.

The forms of intervention can be thought of as encompassing three distinct activities that form a continuum. At one end of the spectrum is peace imposition (PI)—actions taken to stop the violence in a war zone. In most but not all cases, PI will be undertaken for neutral purposes to stop the fighting and killing—what may be called neutrality of intent. The effect of stopping the fighting will never be neutral in effect, however, if for no other reason than that stopping the fighting halts the military success of whoever was winning and the likely failure of whoever was losing.

At the other end of the continuum is peacekeeping (PK). In its classic sense, peacekeeping consists of monitoring and observing an established ceasefire between warring parties when the peacekeepers' intent and effect is to oversee a situation of peace conducive to discussions intended to produce a lasting, stable peace. In the terms introduced above, a peacekeeping setting is one in which state-building activities can be undertaken with the relative assurance that the peacekeepers will not be the victims of violence while they build or rebuild the economic and political infrastructure of the target country.

Lying between these two extreme forms of activity is peace enforcement (PE). It is an activity undertaken when war has been concluded but it is uncertain that peace would be sustained in the absence of the outside force. Whereas PI and PK represent responses to concrete, finite situations (states of war, peace desired by all parties), PE encompasses a wide range of situations, from a near state of war, in which most of the participants prefer war to its alternative, to a situation in which most, but not all parties prefer peace. Most real situations in which outside forces are committed rightfully fall in the category of peace enforcement.

Why are these basic distinctions necessary as a preface to a more detailed discussion of what we can and should do? The answer is that language is often used imprecisely when describing the options available, leading to confusion and misplaced actions and expectations. Afghanistan is a prime example.

Even before the last bombing run and the last organized shots were fired in Afghanistan, there was agreement about what the international community would help with in that war-ravaged land: We would send in peacekeepers to make sure peace held (at least in urban areas such as Kabul), and we would rebuild the country and assist its transition to stable rule (which roughly meant creating a government that opposes and will not harbor terrorists)—state-building.

Is this language applicable to Afghanistan (or, for that matter, was it applicable to Bosnia or Kosovo)? Is the situation into which international peacekeepers were placed one of general tranquility, in which peace was the overwhelming desire of virtually everyone? Of course not. The fact that the United States has felt the need for a continuing military presence in the country and surrounding countries clearly indicated the assessment that war could break out again, which meant that the situation was a peace enforcement problem. The only question was where to place it on the war–peace continuum. Similarly, building the Afghan state in the state of chaos existing in Afghanistan when the goal was articulated in late 2001 seemed fanciful in the short run. Afghanistan is likely to be a model, however, for how we engage in what we will call peacekeeping and state-building in the future, including in Iraq.

Peacekeeping

The term *peacekeeping* has its contemporary origins in a specific set of United Nations operations conducted during the Cold War that constituted one of the few notable successes of the world organization during that period. Those activities basically conform to the definition of peacekeeping given earlier, emphasizing the observation and monitoring of ceasefires between formerly warring parties. In most cases, these PK forces were put in place between sovereign countries and had the passive purpose of making sure the terms of ceasefires were honored. They succeeded when the parties truly preferred peace to war and thus preferred maintenance of the status quo to a return to violence. In those circumstances, peacekeepers could be neutral both in intent and in effect, thereby adding positively to the situation for all concerned. Peacekeeping works, in other words, when the parties want peace roughly in conformance with the conditions the peacekeepers are assigned to enforce.

That set of circumstances rarely holds in internal wars, as the United Nations learned in its two major Cold War intrusions into domestic fracases in the former Belgian Congo (later Zaire, now the Democratic Republic of Congo) and Cyprus. In the Congo in 1960, UN peacekeepers opposed the attempted secession of Katanga (now Shaba) province and found themselves in the position of partisans rather than neutrals, to the organization's discomfort and the mission's ineffectiveness. In Cyprus in 1967, the United Nations was so successful in imposing peace and a ceasefire line that the Greeks and Turks concluded there was no real need to settle their differences as long as the UN Forces in Cyprus (UNFICYP) remained in place. The UN mission is still there, with no real prospect of being withdrawn.

When the Cold War ended, these distinctions and limitations were largely lost. In the euphoria of the UN-sponsored Desert Storm coalition, the security role of the world body seemed to have been enhanced, and it appeared likely that the UN role would become central to international security. In 1991, the Security Council instructed Secretary-General Boutros Boutros-Ghali of Egypt, to draw up a blueprint for UN participation in the promotion of international peace in the post–Cold War world. In 1992, he produced *An Agenda for Peace*. Among other things, it labeled almost any international intervention, regardless of whether it was in wars between states (which have been virtually nonexistent since the Persian Gulf War) or internal (which virtually all wars have been), as peacekeeping. The confusion over roles and missions has been ongoing ever since.

The problem, of course, is that the wake of internal wars rarely resembles the tranquil situation for which traditional peacekeeping is designed. In most cases, missions are not contemplated until violence has been going on for some time, and the trigger for international action is usually the public revelation of hideous, often grotesque atrocities (such as in Rwanda). In those circumstances, the impulse for reconciliation will likely be overwhelmed by the desire for retribution, which peace-keepers can only interrupt (Albanian Kosovar reprisals against their Serbian former persecutors is an example). The situation is normally a tentative one of peace enforcement at best, wherein intervening forces must work actively to sustain the absence of violence rather than simply observe and monitor an established peace. The ability to remain neutral in effect, so crucial to successful peacekeeping, is nearly impossible to attain.

This situation has operational consequences as well. Classic, traditional peace-keepers are lightly armed forces (normally with only hand-held weapons, to be used only in self-defense) that require a minimum of physical or military support, since it is not anticipated that they will be placed in harm's way. This also makes them rela-tively inexpensive, an attribute that makes them appealing to the United Nations, which must rely on the often fickle collection of member-state contributions to support their activities. Peacekeeping is cheaper than fighting a war, making the characterization of situations as peacekeeping appealing to a perpetually financially strapped organization like the United Nations.

A problem arises when a force designed for peacekeeping (and so conceptual-ized) has been thrown into a war zone. This is exactly what happened in 1992 in Bosnia, when the United Nations Protection Force (UNPROFOR) was charged with monitoring a ceasefire between the Serbs and Croats that almost immediately (and predictably) broke down, leaving the peacekeeping force at the mercy of more heavily armed oppositions. In the most embarrassing situations, UNPROFOR sol-diers were kidnapped and chained to military vehicles by Bosnian Serb forces to keep American and British bombers from attacking them.

The tasks and complexities surrounding generic peacekeeping take on added meaning if we add two other dimensions to the PI-PE-PK continuum, as shown in Figure 11.1. In the figure, the situations and missions are as already described, and the term *unstable peace* is added to describe the range of situations in which peace enforcement is needed. Clearly, the peace is decreasingly unstable as one moves away from war and toward the consensus that peace is most desirable. The figure also shows the kinds of military skills that are required in various stages of the operation. When war is ongoing and peace must be imposed, the need is clearly for combat sol-diers, with all the wherewithal necessary for self-protection and for imposing their will on a hostile enemy by brute force. These are the kinds of forces that were neces-sary to defeat the Taliban, and most of the foot soldiers were Afghans. When peace is achieved, the monitoring function is largely a police function, and the peacekeepers

Figure 11.1   Situations, Missions, and Force Requirements

Situation:	War--------------Unstable Peace------------------Peace		
Mission:	PI----------------------------PE-----------------------------PK		
Force Required:	War Fighters-----------War Fighters/Police-----------Police		

essentially make sure the "laws" represented by the terms of the ceasefire are obeyed. The tools of their trade are light sidearms and observation aids such as binoculars. Combat soldiers may or may not be proficient at policing; police officers are rarely prepared for combat.

The problem lies in the hybrid situation of unstable peace, which is the condition into which most outsider forces are actually interposed (occasionally after imposing the peace in the first place) and are likely to be called upon in the future. Clearly, when peace is fragile and fighting could resume, both combat and policing skills are needed, and in varying mixes as the situation changes. When the experience of war is still fresh, combat soldiers will still be needed to intimidate the parties so that they do not begin fighting among themselves or attack the peacekeepers, presumably the initial role of ISAF in Afghanistan until the situation stabilizes (if it does). That role may provide a kind of shield behind which other, more positive reconciling activities can take place, but in that role, soldiers do not contribute to the positive attainment of peace. The soldier, unlike the beat cop, does not befriend the neighbors where he patrols; doing so may get him killed.

Ideally, the same people can fulfill both the combat and the policing roles, adapting their behaviors, chameleon-like, to changing conditions. Unfortunately, the character and skills that make a good combat soldier generally are not the same as those for a good police officer, and developing the second set of skills may degrade the primary skill: The soldier-cop becomes a less lethal soldier, and the cop-soldier becomes a less compassionate, more ruthless cop. This dynamic is explored in Amplification 11.2. The bottom line is that real peacekeeping in the contemporary world includes a variety of roles that shift over time, suggesting the need to alter and fine tune the composition of the force across time and as progress is attained.

Even when the complexities of actual peacekeeping are recognized and addressed, they speak to only part of the problem. Almost all of the conditions to which peacekeepers contribute fall within the category of conflict suppression. As the situation moves toward the peace end of the continuum, the peacekeepers as police may make some positive contributions to restoring public confidence in the criminal justice system, but this will occur mostly when they are handing off their duties to the natives recruited to replace them.

Moving the situation to one of stable peace requires restoring (or creating) confidence and loyalty to the existing order in the country itself. The changing roles assigned to peacekeepers may contribute to that goal and may even be a necessary condition for success. Peacekeepers cannot create the conditions necessary for a stable political system and economic prospects of prosperity. That is the province of individuals and organizations engaged in state-building.

State-Building

The rationale for state-building is a logical extension of the justification for conflict suppression. A state intervenes in the internal affairs of another for one of two reasons: Either the target state is engaged in a civil disagreement that it seems incapable of solving itself and that manifests itself in great suffering (the humanitarian argument), or the intervening state has some interest in a particular outcome (the realist

Amplification 11.2

THE TALK-SHOOT RELATIONSHIP
IN PEACEKEEPING

The kinds of troops that should be employed in peacekeeping has been a matter of disagreement since the United States began participating in these enterprises, and it is an especially difficult matter in situations in which the duties go beyond simple observation and monitoring to actual or potential combat operations. Should peacekeepers be lightly and defensively armed observers on the model of military police? Should they be fully armed combat troops ready to respond to any situation? Or should the same peacekeepers be used to fulfill both functions?

The official position of the American military is that regular combat forces can be trained to be peacekeepers as well as combatants, and official military sources frequently assert that "any good soldier can do peacekeeping." But is that assertion true?

One way to look at the roles of passive peacekeeper/police officer and combat soldier/peace imposer or enforcer is what we can call the "talk-shoot relationship." For the policeman confronted with a potentially dangerous situation, the procedure is to try to resolve the situation peacefully and to fire only as a last resort in self-defense (talk first, then shoot). For a combat soldier, the failure to attack in a dangerous situation may be to put his or her life in peril, and the appropriate response is to defend one's self (shoot first, then ask questions). The peacekeeper who fires first may be a murderer; the soldier who fails to shoot first may be dead.

Can the same personnel perform both functions, making the right decisions in stressful situations? What does the combat soldier on patrol do when he sees someone about to throw something at him, not knowing if the object is a rotten tomato or a grenade? The decision is particularly difficult if the assailant is a child, as is increasingly the case and for which the military has few developed procedures (see the Singer article listed in the Selected Bibliography for an assessment of this aspect of the problem). Also, can soldiers effectively make the transition back and forth from one role to another? If involvement in other people's internal conflicts is to become a common part of the future, answers to such questions must be found.

argument). The first justification underlay American involvement in such places as Bosnia, Kosovo, and—earlier—Somalia. The second justification formed the basis for American involvement in Afghanistan and Iraq and may be extended to other places as part of the expanded "war" on global terrorism (e.g., in the Philippines).

State-building is a logical part of these motives, because simple conflict suppression will not by itself solve the root problems from which the violence has arisen in the first place—the conditions of the swamp. Somalia illustrates this problem. The roots of Somali anarchy lay in clan divisions that were deep-seated and historical and that had been magnified by several years of drought and starvation. The international effort there was limited and short-sighted, however, at least partly because it was the first time the international community, with the United States in the lead, had tried to save a failed state. The initial effort was limited to conflict suppression designed to reinstate the flow of food supplies donated by the international community until the end of the drought began to result in crops being harvested.

The effort succeeded as far as it went, but it did not go far enough. Conflict suppression had eased the food crisis within weeks and, by the estimates of American officials such as Chester Crocker, had saved well over 100,000 lives that would otherwise have been lost to starvation. Unfortunately, stanching the wound did not address the real underlying problem, political chaos and structural economic misery, which the participants in UNISOM had no plans to address. Instead, they engaged in incremental acts of what we now call state-building, including trying to disarm competing warlords, a prominent example of mission creep. The attempted disarmament of one clan leader's forces (those of Muhammed Farah Aideed) created such animosity that it produced the ambush in which eighteen Americans perished, which sent us scurrying away. The result has been that Somalia has largely remained in a state of desperately poor anarchy.

The idea of state-building came into disrepute after Somalia, enshrouded as a form of the hated mission creep that had led to American failure in that campaign. That charge was uninformed. The United States failed to produce a stable situation in Somalia not because of what we did but because of what we did not do, which was to attempt to engage in state-building. (Of course, the effort might have failed had we done so, in which case we would *truly* have failed.) It was not until the end of the decade of the 1990s that we decided to try again, declaring the building of a stable state as the goal in Kosovo, a promise that was reiterated for Afghanistan in 2001.

Can state-building turn a failed, noncompetitive state into a stable, contributing member of the international community? The answer is that we do not know, because we have never systematically tried to do so in the kinds of countries where attempts at state-building are likely to occur in the present and future. It is sometimes suggested that we engaged in state-building in Germany and Japan after World War II, but the problems were not the same. In the former Axis countries, the problem was to clear the rubble and rebuild the physical infrastructure. The price we exacted was acceptance of democratic constitutions, the success of which we made highly likely with the generous influx of cash. If there is any parallel to the present situation, it may be the Republic of Korea, which became a priority after the Korean War, but we need resources there proportionately far in excess of the amounts that will be available in contemporary failed states.

The inability to predict success confidently, combined with the frank admission that it will be a long, expensive, and difficult process, make it difficult to sell state-building. Moreover, the places for which it is mostly but exclusively proposed—the failed and failing states—are simultaneously the most in need and, by definition, the most unprepared for the process. Just as the "great game" (Russo-British competition for influence) in nineteenth-century Afghanistan ultimately resulted in failure for both, American-led state-building may also fail. The same dynamics and uncertainties are present in efforts to rebuild Iraq.

Nevertheless, the last two American presidents (Clinton in Kosovo, Bush in Afghanistan and Iraq) have committed the United States to engage in state-building.

To help assess what lies ahead for these efforts, I will borrow three questions that I originally asked in *When America Fights* for organizing the discussion: Where to go? What to do? and How to do it?

Where to Go?   For the immediate future, that question has largely been answered. The United States is already part of the United Nations–led effort in Kosovo, and will be part of similar, if as yet unnamed and unstructured efforts in Afghanistan and Iraq. The "sample" has the virtue of representing the two motivations underlying intervention: humanitarianism in Kosovo, realism and geopolitics in Afghanistan and Iraq. These two countries also represent the various levels of desperation state-builders will encounter: Kosovo, as a province within European Yugoslavia, is much more developed than Afghanistan. However, the outcome in Kosovo does not have the same urgency and priority that Afghanistan has by virtue of being subsumed in the category of the war against terrorism. American-led development of Iraq democracy is supposed to demonstrate the neo-conservative principle of benign hegemony—that U.S. force can be used to promote democracy.

The determination of places in which to intervene and engage in state-building is only partially our own choice. There may be other places like Afghanistan where an apparent deployment of necessity leads to a state-building mission of equal necessity. More opportunities are likely to present themselves in states where failure and noncompetitiveness have their primary, even wholly negative impact on the citizens of the country itself and where involvement and subsequent state-building must be justified on humanitarian grounds, deployments, and missions of choice. What they will all share is the enormous, daunting problems that state-builders will encounter.

Recognizing how difficult circumstances are likely to be is crucial to determining whether to engage in state-building. In most instances, there will be no functioning government that has the loyalty of any sizable portion of the population (by design, in some cases, as in the criminal insurgencies). Instead, there are likely to be competing groups eager to ingratiate themselves with the state-builders to benefit themselves but unable to cooperate or uninterested in cooperating among themselves. Institutions are likely to be in ruins where they exist at all, and basic service providers are likely to be in short supply. (During the Serb ethnic cleansing in Kosovo, for example, public servants such as clerks and mail carriers were systematically targeted and killed to break down the Kosovars' ability to self-govern.) Moreover, no regime or group is likely to have legitimacy in the eyes of the general population, a problem likely exacerbated by atrocities committed during the violent stage of the civil unrest. Sometimes these problems will be structural and historical, as in the tribal, clan-based warlord systems in Afghanistan and Somalia; sometimes it will be the result of the excesses of the civil conflict, as in Bosnia and Sierra Leone. Others, like Iraq, may be the result of regime change.

Economic travail is likely to be present as well. It is generally true that political peace and stability accompany prosperity and economic improvement, not poverty and misery, but the lack of peace and prosperity are major causes of failed and noncompetitive status. Infrastructures either are nonexistent or have been destroyed by years of war (a central problem in Afghanistan) and must be built or rebuilt before other services can be addressed. In cold climates (Kosovo and Afghanistan) where winter is a problem and many homes have been destroyed, simply providing a warm space in which to live may be a top priority.

What to Do?   Although the generalized goals of state-building are easy to articulate, actually doing it is more difficult. It is made more difficult by two problems (one discussed in this section, the other in the next). The first problem is determining what exactly needs to be accomplished, which is made more difficult by the absence of a comprehensive list of characteristics or a plan for achieving them. The second is our general lack of detailed knowledge about local conditions and people, making it difficult to know with whom to deal and how.

Building or rebuilding an internal war–ravaged country requires action on at least four dimensions, all of which must be accompanied by and must reinforce efforts by peacekeepers. The first dimension is *political*—somehow bringing a sense of order and eventually legitimacy into a setting that probably lacks both. Within this category, the first and most vital task is the simple establishment of order, creating a condition wherein citizens can expect peace and the absence of crime in their daily lives. Initially, this role will likely be assigned to peacekeepers (such as the ISAF in Kabul), but if the situation is one of peace enforcement and the peacekeepers are in fact combat soldiers, they need to be replaced rapidly by police when conditions allow. This problem was faced by U.S. forces facing the looting of Baghdad.

A major first task is the recruitment of a police force, initially internationally and later from within the population. This task seems obvious, but it is not necessarily easy. Finding foreign police willing to serve in war zones is difficult; a force of 13,000 was authorized for Kosovo in 1999 but the number has never been achieved, even at premium salaries of over $90,000 for a one-year tour. Finding locals may also be hard; when the United States recruited a gendarmie for Haiti in the mid-1990s, it turned out that many of the officers hired were former members of the terrorist *tonton macoutes* who wanted to be police so they could extract bribes from drug traffickers operating in the country. At the same time, the criminal justice system must be revamped so that people view it as fair, and other governmental institutions must be created or restructured and personnel recruited to operate them. Preparations for turning governance over to citizens must be undertaken simultaneously. In many cases, this entails helping to draft constitutional documents and finding the appropriate people to hold a constitutional convention in a place where we know relatively little about the candidates and there is a long and well-established tradition of mistrust and noncooperation between groups in the political arena. Somalia and Afghanistan are both examples of this problem.

The second dimension of the problem is economic. When international interveners arrive on the scene, they are likely to encounter wretched economic conditions, reflecting the destruction of the economy or the absence of developed economic structures. In some cases, what little economic activity that does exist may be criminal, as in Afghan poppy and heroin production. In virtually all cases, conditions are likely to be sufficiently chaotic and unappealing that foreign investors are almost certainly going to be unwilling to come in, establish themselves, and create the kinds of jobs necessary for prosperity.

The first task is basic infrastructure development and rehabilitation. Where they exist at all, roads are in disrepair, bridges have been damaged or destroyed, railroad tracks are in disrepair, and airfields are pockmarked or mined or both. All of these need attention for normal activities, including commerce, to resume. In addition, electric power and water supplies have probably been disrupted; schools, hospitals, and other public buildings have been burned or bombed; stores have been looted; and private homes and apartments have been damaged. All of these problems are urgent, especially in cold-weather climates where winter adds to human misery. Until basic conditions of survival can be secured and the most basic services necessary for commerce and economic activity are reinstated, little progress can be made on other fronts.

Military personnel attached to peacekeeping units can be useful in alleviating some of these miseries. Just as soldiers (especially military police) can help establish order and civic affairs units can aid in institution-building, so too can soldiers and military engineers repair and secure runways, roads, and bridges. These personnel are unlikely to be available in sufficient numbers or for long enough periods of time to make more than a dent in the problems (many of the American service personnel with the requisite skills are reservists who are likely to be deployed for short tours), but they can contribute to getting the process started. At some point (presumably after order is restored), private contractors will have to take up the task of longer-term development.

Longer-term economic success almost certainly will require outside capital in the forms of foreign direct investment, location of manufacturing facilities, and the like, in the target country. In order for this to occur, however, the target country must make itself attractive to investors. Besides overcoming a likely unsavory reputation from the past, this means the development of policies and laws friendly to investors, financial and educational institutions to support business, and a condition of tranquility and peace to reassure potential investors that their investments will not literally blow up in their faces.

The third dimension is social. In most of the failed states, there is social cleavage within the population that may be racial (Haiti), ethnic (Sri Lanka), clan or tribal (Afghanistan or Somalia), religious (Indonesia), or some combination of those (Bosnia, Kosovo), wherein identification with one group and targeting of one or more of the other groups has been the basis for violence. The violence, often aimed at innocent noncombatants, inflames hatreds that are already present, leaving a postwar condition of animosity, distrust, and a desire for revenge that must be overcome. Doing so is usually easier said than done.

These emotions often run very deep, especially in countries where there was pre-conflict physical mixing of communities. When the violence pits neighbor against neighbor, reconciliation after the fact can be especially difficult to accomplish. In Rwanda, for instance, Hutu tribal members identified their Tutsi neighbors for slaughter. In Bosnia, after marauding "militias" had driven particular ethnic groups out of villages, members of the offending group would occupy or destroy their homes.

The Bosnian government and international peacekeepers are still trying to return the dispossessed to their former homes.

The residue of hatred and distrust in these communities will linger, in some cases for a generation or more. In some instances, it may be possible to partition the states in ways that leave ethnic or other groups together and secure. Cyprus is an example of such a solution. In most cases, however, the partition solution is not possible or is more traumatic than not separating groups. In a country like Bosnia, for instance, commingling of population groups and the absence of natural physical boundaries (e.g., wide rivers) to create secure separation means that there are no easy ways to partition the country. At any rate, such solutions that create ethnically pure communities almost certainly involve uprooting and moving people. The history of such forced migrations does not commend partition as a method for broader application. The aftermath of partition of the Asian subcontinent in 1947—where eight to ten million Muslims and Hindus were uprooted and forced to flee to countries where they were in the majority—is stark testimony to this problem.

The fourth dimension is psychological. Although many assessments of statebuilding ignore or play down this dimension, it is clear that the atrocious conduct of many of these wars scars many of the survivors, often for life. People, especially children, see acts of gruesome violence committed before their eyes. When it is personalized—a child watching the gory execution of a parent—the result can be deeply traumatizing and may require considerable counseling to assimilate. Even hardened soldiers experience debilitating mental problems under such circumstances.

It is almost universally true that in the countries that experience these traumas there is an inadequate supply of doctors and psychologists to deal with the problem. It is also usually the case that the health care system in these countries was one of the first victims of war. Since these health systems typically were fairly primitive before the violence, the result is to make a bad situation even worse. An ABC television report on January 17, 2002, revealed, for instance, that there were only eight psychiatrists and three mental health wards in all of Afghanistan to treat the psychologically disabled there. The ward in Kandahar was little more than an open courtyard in which patients were chained so that they could not harm others.

How to Do It?   The preceding discussion has only touched on the tip of the iceberg of substantive problems with which state-builders must contend. This formidable list of tasks must be carried out in a situation in which multiple actors with very different perspectives and affiliations must cooperate with local officials in a place with which the state-builders are only generally familiar. The environment is likely to be competitive and chaotic, and not all of the groups providing services will trust one another or the target groups whom they are trying to assist. To add to the problem, there is no guidebook for organizing such operations, and the international system lacks enough experience to suggest comprehensive useful precedents.

The first concerted state-building exercise identified as such was mounted for Kosovo. As Amplification 11.3 indicates, it is not a model that one would necessarily impose on other situations, such as the effort in Afghanistan. Creating a monolithic effort in which all helping groups are operating together in a spirit of cooperation,

Amplification 11.3

KFOR AND UNMIK

At the end of the campaign to drive the Serbs out of Kosovo in 1999, the United Nations announced that the goal of the mission would be to build a stable, prosperous order in that province that could decide either to unite within a newly constituted Yugoslavia or to become independent. The mission there is thus state-building. The structure intended to implement the goal clearly shows the complexity and difficulty this kind of operation entails.

Although the entire effort is officially under UN control, this is not entirely the case. Indeed, there are two separate entities operating in Kosovo, each part of a different command structure. The military peacekeeping element is the Kosovo Force (KFOR), a North Atlantic Treaty Organization (NATO) force, commanded by a NATO general and reporting to NATO headquarters. The state-building element of the operation is the United Nations Interim Mission in Kosovo (UNMIK), which is headed by the Special Representative of the Secretary General (SRSG) of the United Nations, and he or she reports to the United Nations. The SRSG, in turn, oversees the operations of four activities, designated the four pillars, that constitute the major emphases of the state-building enterprise. Each function is administered by a different international organization. Civil administration is the responsibility of the United Nations itself; the development of political institutions is handled by the Organization of Security and Cooperation in Europe (OSCE); economic development is the job of the European Union (EU); and refugees are dealt with by the United Nations High Commission on Refugees (UNHCR). Each of these organizations has somewhat different memberships and reporting requirements. The relationship between KFOR and UNMIK is informal, based on the personal ability of the KFOR commander and the SRSG to cooperate.

working toward commonly accepted goals, is the obvious purpose. Accomplishing these goals is far from easy.

At a minimum, state-building will have two different groups performing different tasks. On the one hand, there will be a military element that is engaged in peace enforcement or peacekeeping. The primary task of the military is, of course, to keep order and to prevent the recurrence of violence, effectively acting as a shield behind which state-building can move forward. Their secondary mission, which is sometimes ignored by those planning or executing these missions, is self-protection—making sure that their own members are not subject to lethal attacks from groups that suffer because of their presence.

The military component cannot be considered a single, monolithic entity, and it may have differing priorities. In most cases, the peacekeeping force will be a coalition of forces drawn from several countries, under the auspices of either the United Nations or another organization, such as NATO. These countries will be present for a variety of reasons. Some have a philosophical commitment to this kind of mission (Canada and Norway, for example), while others will be there to collect the $100 per diem allowance provided by the United Nations (Ghana and Bangladesh, for example). Although a commander will be identified for the mission, the individual country contingents generally report to their own governments, which will instruct them on which orders from the command structure to carry out and which to ignore. When national and international orders contradict one another, national priorities prevail.

The United States has a unique position in these efforts. As the world's remaining superpower, the United States will almost certainly be involved at some level, usually including the provision of some troops. An American presence is often insisted upon by the target government, and it may be the sine qua non for acceptance of a mission by the host country, as was the case in Bosnia. American participation will generally be somewhat reluctant and will come with at least two conditions. One is maximum participation by other states to demonstrate that the United States is not shouldering a disproportionate share of the burden. The United States will also insist that its forces remain under American command, to avoid being placed in unnecessarily risky situations where casualties might occur. Often the Americans are called upon to provide logistical support, such as getting supplies and personnel to the locale (which means, at a minimum, that some American soldiers will be on the ground to protect airfields and ports) and providing satellite and other signal intelligence that only the United States has the physical capability to provide.

National control of peacekeeping forces and the mandate to limit exposure to danger mean that the military side of the operation will be difficult and also virtually guarantee some level of friction between the peacekeepers and the civilian statebuilders. The civilian element will also be a hodgepodge of different groups with different priorities. Representatives of governments providing developmental assistance will be on the scene identifying projects and making sure that the private contractors with whom they do business are fulfilling their obligations. Representatives from whatever international body is in charge of the state-building enterprise will have to try to coordinate national efforts to be certain that the process is orderly and that vital priorities are being addressed. In addition, nongovernmental organizations (NGOs) will be on the scene, either caregivers such as *Medicins sans Frontieres* (Doctors without Borders), ministering to medical needs, or monitors such as Amnesty International, on the lookout for human rights violations. The media will also be present, at least in the early stages, while the mission is still "news."

The ingredients for organizational chaos are clearly present and are made worse by two other factors. The first is dealing with the citizens of the country who are the supposed beneficiaries of the effort. Who are their legitimate representatives? What do they want, and why? Will international efforts benefit one formerly warring group at the expense of others, thereby making things potentially worse rather than better? Do the state-builders know enough about the country and its people to make valid independent judgments on any of these problems? The answers to these questions are often less than absolutely clear to the state-builders.

There is also rivalry between the various groups that make up the state-builders. There is a general tendency for all groups to think that their own part of the enterprise is most important and should receive the highest priority. Moreover, priorities may contradict one another. Doctors without Borders, for instance, believes that its mission to minister to health needs is paramount, especially in remote areas that may not be entirely pacified. They will demand military protection, which military commanders, motivated by the desire to expose their troops to minimal danger, will be reluctant to provide. The military will feel the same way about assisting the press or human rights monitors.

CONCLUSION: THE NEW ORDER?

The purpose of this chapter has been to present a particularly prevalent problem facing the international system—how to deal with the internal violence that marks the principal challenge to a peaceful world—and what may be done about such problems. As the analysis has indicated, neither the problem nor the possible solutions are easy, and we are still learning how to approach and surmount these difficulties.

Prior to September 11, 2001, much of this analysis would have seemed remote, even academic. The new internal wars happen in remote parts of the world, where there are few American interests and thus where the United States can engage itself or not without great repercussions for the American people—deployments of choice, in which humanitarian concerns are central to the decision of whether to intervene and for what purposes.

The decision to take action against the Taliban government of Afghanistan *and* to engage in state-building afterward changes that calculation. That change is further amplified in Iraq. The underlying assumptions in Afghanistan were apparently twofold. First, the division of the world into those who oppose terrorism and those who apparently do not means that terrorism sponsors or sanctioners are fair game for military actions—intervention, in other words. The effect is to widen the range of places where we will contemplate military action. The second assumption, on which the determination to engage in state-building is based, is that converting these former terrorist states into the antiterrorist coalition requires "terrorist-proofing" their countries through improvements in their conditions—that is, draining the swamp.

Both of these assumptions can be challenged, as can their implications for how the United States will use force in the world in the future. In the wake of the September 11 events, there was a consensus in much of the world that terrorism should be rooted out wherever it exists, but as the list of states condoning or protecting terrorism expands, that consensus may erode. How much of the world is likely to support attacking Iraq, Iran, Sudan, Somalia, and Libya, all states tainted by past or present association with terrorists? Many states may conclude that the assumption that the world is divided into those who support and those who oppose terrorism is little more than an American excuse to beat up on those with whom it has issue. Certainly that charge has been leveled at the neo-conservatives. It is not abundantly clear, however, that the terrorism-proofing premise is valid either. The chief problem is whether successful state-building is possible and, if it is, whether it will accomplish the goal set out for it: Can we create countries that will resist terrorism? No one knows at this point.

The implications of these assumptions regarding how to fight terrorism are also controversial. As noted, the imperative of going after terrorists shifted the reasons

Challenge!

What Should We Do in Afghanistan?

The removal of the Taliban government from power and its replacement by the interim Karzai government—supported by American and other foreign forces—represented the conflict suppression phase of the international effort in Afghanistan (phase one). With the election of a transitional government in mid-2002 and the beginnings of international efforts to build and rebuild that war-torn country, an international state-building campaign has begun. The extent of that effort and its effects are still not clear from the vantage point of mid-2003.

There has been clear rhetorical support for draining the Afghan "swamp" and building a stable country that will resist terrorist appeals and join the antiterrorism coalition in the future. As of the middle of 2003, that rhetoric had not translated into the massive assistance program that most agreed was necessary to produce a stable and hopefully democratic Afghanistan.

All four dimensions of state-building need attention. Progress in the military dimension is most advanced, as an Afghan armed force and constabulary have been initiated; whether they will run afoul of traditional Afghan tribal rivalries remains to be seen. In 2003, there were persistent reports of renewed Taliban activity. The economic dimension has hardly been addressed at all. There is wide agreement that massive amounts of money are necessary to build the Afghan economic infrastructure and to rebuild the country after so many years of war. Beyond more or less vague promises of assistance, however, the flow of resources has been slow to come, and Afghan patience is being tested. The social and psychological dimension likewise suffers from years of privation and violence. Exacerbating the situation is official government repression of the one major cash crop that could pump money into the economy: heroin-producing poppies. Prior to the Taliban regime, nearly 70 percent of the world's heroin was grown in Afghanistan poppies; after the Taliban were overthrown, peasant farmers planted new crops that had been forbidden by the Taliban. At the prodding of Western governments, those crops were destroyed (with compensation) in 2002, but a record crop reportedly was being harvested in 2003.

What should we do for Afghanistan? How many American tax dollars should be spent on rebuilding the Afghan infrastructure and in building a prosperous society—especially since the results cannot be guaranteed? It is one thing to call for making an antiterrorist bulwark out of Afghanistan, but what budgetary sacrifices should Americans be forced to endure to produce such a state? Also, the degree to which we respond to Afghanistan's plight will create a precedent for what other states may expect from the United States in the future. How seriously committed are we *in fact* to the continuing campaign against terrorism if it threatens to attack our own wallets? If we are not serious about Afghanistan, will anyone believe we are any more serious about neo-conservative dreams to build Iraq into a stable, prosperous democracy that will act as a regional role model?

for which the United States would contemplate intervention in civil disturbances from a humanitarian to a geopolitical, realist base. As if to reinforce this change, the Bush administration committed more than 600 special operations forces (SOFs) to assist the Philippine government in early 2002 to suppress a terrorist organization with alleged connections to Al Qaeda but was not directly linked to the attacks against the United States at all. It is one thing to justify military action after a direct military attack against the United States or against Americans; a broader onslaught on terrorism would increase the instances where American force may be contemplated in the internal affairs of other states.

These developments are particularly puzzling coming from an administration that campaigned on the pledge of reducing the number of American deployments around the world. In its first year in office, it authorized deployments in Afghanistan and the Philippines, sent agents into Somalia to assess the possibility of deploying there (on the assumption that the Somalis might provide bin Laden safe haven there), forged a military arrangement with several former Soviet republics, and invaded Iraq the next year. In all of these places, at least part of the justification was its war on terrorism.

Finally, there is a domestic element in this area that has two aspects. There was not great enthusiasm in the United States for our involvements on humanitarian grounds in Bosnia, Haiti, and Kosovo, but there was not a great deal of objection to President Clinton's justification of Bosnia that "it's the right thing to do." The reasons probably had to do with the relative inexpensiveness of the operations and the absence of casualties incurred in carrying them out. The Bush charge that these deployments overextended American forces did not have great impact on the election campaign and rings a bit hollow, given his administration's willingness to deploy forces widely in the name of antiterrorism. The new deployments, however, are both more expensive and more dangerous than those in the 1990s. In light of the expense of Iraq, how much treasure and how many lives are we willing to expend to put alleged Filipino terrorists out of business?

The other domestic aspect is the competition for resources. A sustained American presence in Afghanistan, especially participating in state-building, is going to be a great deal more expensive than American expenses in Bosnia or Kosovo, and those expenses will grow geometrically if we attempt an earnest state-building program in Iraq. The American people clearly supported the expense and sacrifice in response to the direct assault against the country in the Afghan campaign. Will they be willing to bear as much when the direct connections are more tenuous? If we renege on our commitment to Afghanistan (which we largely had as of summer 2003), will we truly honor our commitment to Iraq?

SELECTED BIBLIOGRAPHY

Boutros-Ghali, Boutros. *An Agenda for Peace: Preventive Diplomacy, Peacemaking, and Peace-Keeping.* New York: United Nations, 1992.

Crocker, Chester. "The Lessons of Somalia: Not Everything Went Wrong." *Foreign Affairs* 74, 3 (May/June 1995), 2–8.

Doran, Michael Peter. "Somebody Else's Civil War." *Foreign Affairs* 81, 1 (January/February 2002), 23–40.

Durch, William, ed. *The Evolution of UN Peacekeeping: Case Studies and Comparative Analysis*. New York: St. Martin's Press, 1993.

Friedman, Thomas L. *The Lexus and the Olive Tree: Understanding Globalization*. New York: Farrar, Straus & Giroux, 1999.

Gurr, Ted Robert. *Why Men Rebel*. Princeton, NJ: Princeton University Press, 1973.

Helman, Gerald B., and Steven R. Ratner. "Saving Failed States." *Foreign Policy* 89 (1992–93), 3–20.

Peters, Ralph. *Fighting for the Future: Will America Triumph?* Harrisburg, PA: Stackpole Books, 1999.

Sachs, Susan. "The Despair Beneath the Arab World's Growing Rage." *New York Times* (electronic edition), October 14, 2001.

Singer, P. W. "Caution: Children at War." *Parameters* XXXI, 4 (Winter 2001–02), 40–56.

Snow, Donald M. *Distant Thunder: Patterns of Conflict in the Developing World*, 2nd ed. Armonk, NY: M. E. Sharpe, 1997.

———. "Saving Failed States: The Problem of Haiti." In Donald M. Snow, *Cases in International Relations: Portraits of the Future*. New York: Longman, 2002.

———. *When America Fights: The Uses of U.S. Military Force*. Washington, DC: CQ Press, 2000.

———, and Eugene Brown. *International Relations: The Changing Contours of Power*. New York: Longman, 2000.

Wright, Robert. "Will Globalization Make You Happy?" *Foreign Policy*, September/October 2000, 54–64.

12

The Geopolitics of Globalization

Globalization as the predominant dynamic of the 1990s was given a severe geopolitical jolt by the terrorist attacks of 2001. In this chapter, we will assess the strength and durability of those globalization dynamics according to their impact on American predominance in the international system and how the outbreak of terrorism changes the realities of the international condition. We will argue that despite initial apparent incompatibilities between globalization and terrorism-induced geopolitics, there is a growing possibility of their compatibility in the longer run. Finally, it is possible to assert a long-term national security strategy for the United States that combines both concepts to confront an international environment that is based on neither the geopolitics of the Cold War nor the globalization of the 1990s.

The decline of significant international military confrontation and globalization dominated the international political landscape of the 1990s. The relative decline of international military and political confrontation was symbolized by the implosion of operational Communism and the end of the Cold War, as well as by a general decline in the frequency of international conflicts. The economic and political homogenization of much of the world, symbolized by the spread of political democracy and free trade–based economic capitalism, appeared ascendant.

Those trends are nowhere nearly as sharply evident at the beginning of a new century. The events of September 11, 2001, have jolted the system out of the bliss of apparent peacefulness and have reminded us of the continuing relevance of the military instruments of traditional geopolitics. The East Asian financial crisis of 1997, the clear rejection of the ideals of globalization in parts of the Middle East, and the global recession that began in 2000 make the linear ascendancy of globalization as the central feature of the global system much less certain than it was before the terrorist attacks.

Although it is hyperbolic to argue that "everything changed" on September 11, 2001, the events of that day clearly have cast a shadow over the international system and have helped raise questions about the direction in which the decade of the 2000s will lead us. One question that quickly emerges is whether the attacks and the subsequent figurative declaration of a war on terrorism means a return to the national security–oriented international politics of the Cold War (or something parallel to that), a retrenchment of the movement toward a reduced role and importance for globalization, or some new *modus vivendi* between globalization and traditional national security concerns. Almost no one suggests the possibility that the globalizing trend of the 1990s will survive (or return) in the way it existed during the heyday period of the 1990s. The question is how much of globalization will survive.

GLOBALIZATION AS A GEOPOLITICAL PHENOMENON

Exactly how to consider globalization as a force shaping future international relations was an unresolved issue at the turn of the twenty-first century. There was considerable disagreement, for instance, on the extent to which the globalizing economy had in fact permeated the economic life of the countries that had embraced it and thus how deep and abiding its effects were. Advocates of globalization argued that the influence was profound and growing and that positive trends such as democratization and economic interdependence would progressively render war less likely in the future. Critics pointed to statistics that showed far less change in international life than supporters argued. Thus, critics maintained that globalization in fact was much less pervasive than globalization in theory. A growing minority even pointed to the pernicious effects in such matters as environmental degradation, job loss and displacement, and underlying American imperialism that they said accompanied globalization.

This debate had both domestic and international elements. Domestically, the rise of globalism was tied inextricably, if differentially, to America's changing economic situation. Clearly, the dynamics of globalization had provided the fuel and direction for American reassertion as the preeminent global economic power and had contributed greatly to the enormous American prosperity of the 1990s. Not all Americans had shared equally in this prosperity, as already noted: The same wind that blew fair over large segments of the American economy also moved to destroy those elements of the economy that could not meet the Ricardian dictate of comparative advantage. Thus, domestically, the globalization of the 1990s bred both staunch advocacy and just as strong opposition to globalization and its consequences at the domestic level.

Internationally, the process of globalization and U.S. dominance in global affairs became virtually synonymous. As globalization spread, it was clear that the American model of economic organization was the clear victor in the competition with other alternatives (notably, the so-called Asian model). Globalization was making those places in the world where it intruded look increasingly American, a prospect with mixed implications for the foreign cultures on which it was imposed.

On the positive side, the fact that so many international students attended school in the United States meant that, in most countries, there were young elites anxious to emulate the American way as a means to achieve the prosperity and wealth of the American system and the political freedoms that attach to the American model. On the other hand, there were more traditional elements in most of those same states who opposed the spread of the American gospel. For some, it was evidence of what many viewed as a heavy-handed, arrogant imperialism seeking to reinforce the American position as a unilateralist hegemony. To others, the intrusion of the American system and American values was a direct threat either to their worldview or to their places in their respective societies. To many traditional elements in those societies, American cultural imperialism was as bad as its economic imperialism. Just as in the domestic debate, the rise of globalism sparked both a negative and a positive reaction within the system.

Globalization thus emerged from the turn of the century as a mixed bag in terms of its impact and desirability. It provided economic opportunity, but its power had been tainted by the economic slowdown. It was also widely associated with a perceived American geopolitical thrust that was offensive to some who sought to resist American power. If globalization was the Trojan Horse for the intrusion of the United States into the affairs of other states, then the assessment of the desirability of continued global economic integration was at least partly a reflection of what one thought about the United States more generally. The corporate shenanigans in the United States revealed in 2002 tarnished the glow of the American economic model, which had been considered as somehow more virtuous that its supposedly more corrupt alternatives.

This debate had not nearly reached closure when the first airliner plowed into the north tower of the World Trade Center. The worldwide economic downturn triggered by the Asian crisis had dampened economic growth and prosperity worldwide and thus had stifled part of the enthusiasm for globalization. The anti-globalism movement of the latter 1990s, which caught most officials initially unprepared, was having a major disruptive effect on world economic meetings that were extolling and solemnizing globalization. In the United States, the election of George W. Bush, a free-trader who was less demonstrative in his advocacy of globalization than his predecessor had been, did little to rekindle the fires of globalization rejuvenation. It was not unfair to say that globalization had already lost some of the luster it had gained during the previous decade. There was even growing suspicion that the apparent prosperity of the 1990s was an economic bubble of overinflation and overvaluation ready to burst.

Globalization and traditional geopolitics are not, of course, an either/or proposition. In the narrow sense, the term *geopolitics* has always referred to the relationship between geography and politics. Even when it was expanded by the Nazis in the 1930s to include the notion that politics is dependent on geography, the "theory" included the assumption that economic success required geographic control of territory and that economic strength was key to political success. The concept of globalization represented the same dynamic from the other end of the spectrum, arguing that maximizing economic commerce required overcoming barriers to trade based in both political restrictions and geographic impediments to the movement of goods and services. The term *geopolitics* had, over time, been expanded to be nearly synonymous with national security, which was clearly germane to the Cold War period but not so obviously relevant to the postwar period. By 2000, the two concepts were thoroughly intertwined with one another.

The disagreement was not so much whether globalization had superseded geopolitics as the heart of international politics as it was over which paradigm was dominant in an environment in which they coexisted. The traditional geopoliticians had suffered a bad decade during the 1990s, as the realist paradigm seemed decreasingly relevant to dealing with a generally tranquil international environment wherein cooperation between states in the economic realm seemed more important than rivalry among them in the area of national security. Traditional geopolitical symbols such as military force seemed increasingly applicable mainly for such marginal concerns as peacekeeping.

The interaction between globalization and traditional national security concerns was muted during this period. Occasionally, the realms of global economic expansion and traditional security concerns would overlap and rub against one another. The case of China and Taiwan, discussed in Amplification 12.1, seemed an exception to the general rule, as the Chinese rattled their sabers over the prospect that Taiwan might opt for formal independence at the same time that Taiwanese investment on the Chinese mainland was increasingly vital to the economic well-being of both countries. In fact, there were and are points of both compatibility and incompatibility between the two forces that were not explored fully when globalization seemed supreme and national security less obviously vital.

Because of the terrorist attacks on the United States, traditional national security concerns have once again risen to the top of the American foreign policy and world political agendas. In the process, the sources of potential inconsistency between the twin thrusts of national security (symbolized by the war on terror) and globalization have begun to emerge. At the core of that incompatibility is the question of the openness of American (and global) society, leaving Kurt M. Campbell to warn, "A U.S. crusade against global terrorism is likely to place the U.S. national agenda, featuring homeland defense, major military strikes, and heightened security, more squarely at odds with the powerful forces of globalization."

It is premature, of course, to judge how the clash between globalization and geopolitics will work out in the long or even the short run. Before even trying to establish the parameters of that struggle, it is first necessary to review how globalization became the geopolitical force of the 1990s and the implications of that emergence for the international system, especially attitudes toward the United States. In that context, we can look at some of the major points of disagreement between the two approaches that have emerged in the aftermath of the terrorist attacks.

Globalization and the American Decade of the 1990s

It is tempting to equate the globalization decade of the 1990s and the emerging geopolitical decade of the 2000s with the presidents and parties that oversaw the development of American policy emphases in one direction or another. There is some merit in such type-casting. President Clinton had economic matters clearly at

Amplification 12.1

CHINA, TAIWAN, GUNS, AND BUTTER

The dispute between the People's Republic of China and Taiwan has been going on ever since the Nationalist Government of China was defeated by Mao Zedung's Communists in 1949 and forced to flee to the island off the Chinese coast. Although the threat of armed conflict is always present, the dispute has evolved into a classic instance of the relationship between traditional geopolitics and globalization.

The political basis of the dispute is the status of Taiwan. Both the mainland Chinese and the government on Taiwan agree in principle that Taiwan and China are a single country (in effect, Taiwan is a province of China). The only dissenters from this assessment are the native Taiwanese who inhabited Taiwan before the Nationalists arrived and who favor Taiwanese independence. The disagreement is over who constitutes the legal government of China-Taiwan: The Chinese on the mainland claim they do, and the Nationalists say they do. Resolving the issue only becomes a high priority when the Taiwanese threaten to dissolve their ties to the mainland and declare their independence. When this suggestion was made formally in July 1999, China mobilized forces, and there were hints of war.

The major problem with a forceful resolution was that it would have been extremely bad for business—the result of the globalization that has extended itself to both Taiwan and mainland China. In particular, the decade of the 1990s witnessed considerable investment in enterprises on the mainland by Taiwanese businessmen, in the amount of a reported $39 billion by 2001. Moreover, war to put down Taiwanese independence would badly damage the advanced economy on the island, which China considers a future cornerstone of Chinese economic might. In the end, economic interests prevailed: Advocacies of Taiwanese independence subsided, the People's Republic stopped rattling their swords, and business returned to normal.

the forefront of his political agenda from the moment he entered office and even before. President George W. Bush campaigned on a pledge of strengthening the U.S. defense posture as well as promoting free trade, the latter a position he had advocated consistently as the governor of Texas. Moreover each was the beneficiary or victim of events. Bill Clinton's emphasis on economics was rarely diverted toward matters of national security—certainly not in any fundamental way that would force a reorientation back toward geopolitics. George W. Bush had his priorities thrust forcefully upon him by the events in New York and Washington. Preferences and events colored both leaders' priorities.

Clinton's preference for emphasizing international economics as the core of foreign policy was apparent before he was elected president and entered office. The 1992 campaign was waged in the context of a global recession, the American part of which was rightly or wrongly blamed on the administration of George H. W. Bush and which the Clinton campaign promised to remedy. After Clinton's nomination, the rallying cry invented by Clinton aide James Carville—"It's the economy, stupid!"—became a major focus of the campaign. After the election but before his inauguration, Clinton convened an economic summit in Little Rock, Arkansas, in December 1992, at which numerous economic and political figures, virtually all proponents of free trade, expounded their ideas as Cable News Network dutifully recorded the proceedings.

When Clinton took office, globalization became the international bedrock of his economic policy. On January 25, 1993, only weeks after taking office, he announced the formation of the National Economic Council to assist him in forming economic policy. Although created by executive order rather than by statute, the parallel to the National Security Council was apparent, and the clear signal was that the new council would have equal billing with the NSC in the Clinton White House. To emphasize the international component of his economic emphasis, Clinton made a very public appearance at the initial meeting of the Asia-Pacific Economic Cooperation (APEC) in Seattle where, among other things, he met with Chinese leader Deng Xiao-peng and began the process of building strong economic ties between the two countries.

Despite the fact that Clinton's party contained many of the most prominent and vociferous opponents of globalization on the American political scene, free trade became the centerpiece of his international policy. Clinton completed the process of getting congressional approval of the North American Free Trade Agreement (NAFTA) in 1993 (it had been negotiated by his predecessor, George H. W. Bush), emerged as the leading force in promoting closer ties within APEC, and lent American leadership and prestige to the Free Trade Area of the Americas (FTAA) proposal. All were premised on the idea that greater economic interchange through trade was beneficial to both American and world prosperity and tranquility. In foreign policy terms, the posture was known as "engagement and enlargement," which emphasized support for countries that shared basic American political and economic values.

During most of the 1990s, there were few overt negative repercussions of the Clinton emphasis on economics. The Persian Gulf War had been decided before he came to office, and the only remaining loose end from that experience was the continued intransigence of the Saddam Hussein government, particularly in the area of international inspection of suspected production of weapons of mass destruction—an issue passed along to the current Bush administration and answered by overthrowing the Iraqi regime. Otherwise, national security problems were muted, essentially limited to questions of intervention in internal wars in the developing world.

Domestic politics did not impede this emphasis either. Clinton never attained a widespread level of support within the national security community, most of whose members held him in some private disdain, but neither was there any concerted opposition to his leadership. The fact that he did not serve in the military during Vietnam and had apparently "dodged the draft" (by means of student deferments, employed by many others during that period) raised some hackles, as did his administration's advocacy of gays in the ranks. There was also muted criticism of his inattention to such issues as military modernization and force morale, but in a generally peaceful atmosphere, these criticisms did not gain great weight.

By the end of the 1990s, things had changed. The great prosperity of the early and middle years of the decade had been dampened by a general international economic downturn, and the general prosperity that muted criticism on other fronts had given way to more general levels of criticism than before (emboldened, of course, by Clinton's personal problems). Suddenly, it became acceptable to criticize both the process and the consequences of globalization and its advocate, the United States.

Challenges to American Leadership from the 1990s

As long as the good times rolled, there was very little argument about the virtues of globalization or concern about its rules or other matters of potential disagreement. When the financial crisis in East Asia in 1997 revealed serious flaws in the structure of the emerging system and cracks appeared in the prosperity of the go-go 1990s, the result was second guessing and criticism of the United States and its stepchild, globalization.

The East Asian financial crisis was the first crack in the general prosperity of the 1990s. It began in Thailand in 1997 when the national currency, the *baht*, collapsed on local and international markets. Triggered by a currency devaluation (a policy stating that the currency would be exchanged with other currencies at a lower value), the crisis rapidly spread to other countries in the region, causing collapse and dislocation in countries such as Malaysia, Indonesia, South Korea, and even Japan.

The crisis contained both domestic and international elements. Panicked by the announcement of the devaluation, foreign and domestic investors descended on Thai banks and later on banks in other countries, demanding to withdraw their funds before their worth could erode even more. The banks had dreadfully insufficient funds to cover these demands, because their reserves had been largely depleted by bad—often corrupt—lending practices. Many had lost money entrusted to them but had hidden that fact from investors by opaque, secretive banking practices. This revelation further dampened investor confidence, leading to further devaluation and spreading the crisis to other countries that held increasingly worthless Thai currency.

International investors added to the panic. Overly optimistic estimates of the strengths of East Asian economies had resulted in foreign direct investment well in excess of the ability of East Asian economies to absorb it responsibly. The result was excess capital that could be diverted to economically unsound, often corrupt uses. Often these instances of "crony capitalism" involved collaboration among bankers, borrowers, and government officials who were nominally entrusted to protect investors' funds but instead hid behind inadequate or nonexistent accounting regulations that allowed the misuse of funds. Mesmerized by short-term profits, international investors largely overlooked these practices as cultural prices that had to be paid to do business in these countries. When the economic collapse began, these same investors extricated their funds as quickly as they could, adding to the general panic and disorder in the area.

When the crisis threatened to spread globally, the international financial community entered the situation, demanding change. In the United States, for instance, the value of stocks on the New York Stock Exchange plunged by a quarter in the Dow-Jones index before stabilizing and rebounding, and there was great demand to ensure that the experience was not repeated.

The East Asian crisis was not the first crisis the globalizing economy had undergone. The culprit in Asia was identified as a lack of accountability in financial transactions, and the cure was greater openness and visibility for the conditions of financial institutions and the business they do (what is known as *transparency*). The United States had experienced a similar situation in the middle 1980s in the so-called S&L crisis. In that case, a number of savings and loan associations (banks providing savings accounts and making loans, especially in real estate) had collapsed because they had made unsound loan decisions that had stripped away savings accounts of small investors who had traditionally found the S&Ls to be a good and safe place for their savings. Because the executives of some of the bankrupt S&Ls had made considerable financial contributions to elected officials, the crisis became a political scandal not unlike the corporate scandal of 2002 (see Amplification 12.2). The result was a series of new regulations for financial institutions, designed to ensure transparency and thus honesty and responsibility within the American banking community.

Amplification 12.2

THE S&L AND CORPORATE SCANDALS

In December 2001, Enron, the huge energy conglomerate, declared bankruptcy, leaving thousands of investors and employees whose retirement portfolios had been based in the now worthless stock issued by the company holding the bag. As investigation of the corporate collapse spread, it became clear that Enron had been a shell corporation whose apparent health was based in legal loopholes that had been found (and restrictions that were not enacted into law) as a result of deregulation of the energy industry and others in the 1990s. At the heart of the scandal were corrupt practices by accounting firms that presumably served as accounting watchdogs of corporate behavior but were incestuously related to Enron through consultant relations. In the first half of 2002, several other large corporations followed Enron into insolvency and shame.

The scandal had both domestic and international ramifications and reminded some observers structurally of the S&L scandals of the middle 1980s (discussed in Chapter 5). In the S&L case, lax regulation of financial institutions had allowed banks to engage in irresponsible and corrupt practices that were concealed from government regulators and investors. When a number of S&Ls declared bankruptcy, robbing investors of their life savings, a political reaction resulted in the adoption of new and tighter standards, the centerpiece of which was transparency in financial practices to restore confidence in financial institutions. (The government also passed legislation to reinstate savings, the first "bail-out" of its kind.) The international ramification was that the regulations adopted became the basis of demands that globalizing states adopt the American economic model, including the financial practices demanded in post-S&L regulations.

The corporate scandals of 2002 were similar in structure and impact. The piety of advocacy of the American model came under assault when it was revealed that American law allowed the precise kind of corporate corruption that the model was supposed to eliminate and for which the United States had been battering governments in places such as South Korea. The scandal also produced widespread calls for reform legislation, especially in the corporate accounting area, to assure that the problem does not recur. Whether these reforms will become part of international standards in the same way that S&L reforms did remains to be seen.

The reaction to the financial crisis in East Asia was to demand that reforms similar to those enacted in the United States after the S&L scandal be applied to East Asian economies. This demand pitted the so-called American model of economic performance against the Asian (largely Japanese) model. As a result of cultural and historical practices, the major difference between the two approaches was the degree of openness in financial activity. Based in traditions of deference to elders, different codes of ethical behavior, and the like, Asian practices were considerably more closed than those that had evolved in the West, especially in the United States. A precondition for qualifying for funds from the International Monetary Fund (IMF) and other lenders to aid in recovery from the Asian crisis was the adoption of American financial practices. These requirements created resentment, particularly because the funds made available went first to compensate foreign investors rather than to the citizens in affected countries that had lost their savings.

Resentment was also increased by the fact that East Asian countries had no real choice but to accept the restrictions meted out by the IMF. Funds for recovery were not available elsewhere, and the IMF "seal of approval" on financial practices was necessary to attract direct investments into foreign economies. Moreover, the IMF was largely—and not entirely incorrectly—seen as little more than the agent of the U.S. government when it placed demands on countries, thereby increasing the sense of American cultural imperialism.

The Asian crisis chilled some of the enthusiasm for globalization, as countries that had bought wholeheartedly into the process reassessed their situations in the wake of the crisis and the sacrifices of recovery. In places such as Indonesia (see Amplification 11.1 in Chapter 11), the experience was particularly traumatic; in addition to the political travails it entailed, it triggered a national debate over the extent and terms of its association with the globalizing economy. The crisis exposed an underlying structural economic vulnerability in places such as Japan, the strength of whose economy had not been publicly questioned nor debated previously. Suddenly, globalization seemed neither as inevitable nor as necessarily desirable as it once had.

Questions about the globalizing economy also resulted in greater scrutiny and criticism of the United States. When globalization was producing increased prosperity for all participants, there was relatively little negative expression about the paramount role of the United States and its dominance of the world economy. The implicit sanctimony of American insistence on adopting its "superior" model privately rankled many who could not openly express their reservations while the system worked.

When the global economy slowed, such inhibitions dissolved. The forums in which the free trade motor of globalization was extolled suddenly became the objects of a wide-ranging coalition of rejectionists who saw globalization as exploitive, a threat to national sovereignty, and destructive of the environment, among other things (see Amplification 5.3 in Chapter 5). Public carping at American leadership rose globally over supposed U.S. unilateralism and heavy-handed treatment of other countries. Predictions that the American decade of the 1990s would be followed by an American century became more subdued. Rejecting the Americans became an entirely more reputable position than it had previously been.

THE IMPACT OF SEPTEMBER 11, 2001

The impact on the globalizing economy of the terrorist episode of 2001 remains ambiguous. International reaction has been decidedly mixed. All of the most developed countries have roundly condemned the attacks and have joined either in the overt campaign waged in Afghanistan against the Taliban and Al Qaeda or the much quieter international effort to improve detection and suppression of terrorists. No government has publicly condoned the efforts by Usama bin Laden and his associates.

Beneath the surface of official condemnation, however, has been an expression in some quarters of feelings that the United States somehow deserved what happened to it. This sentiment has been most widely expressed in the Middle East, on the so-called "Arab street," but it is also present elsewhere. These expressions manifest themselves in ways as diverse as anti-American demonstrations and the sale of T-shirts bearing the image of bin Laden, and they carry the universal theme of an American comeuppance and satisfaction that the arrogant Americans have been brought to earth. To some extent, this sentiment reflects the kind of resentment felt toward whoever is the most powerful country; it also probably reflects a belief that it is appropriate for Americans to suffer some of the same kinds of indignities others routinely face.

Although the equation is rarely made, part of this sentiment may reflect a reaction to American economic dominance of the global economy, a kind of extension or even climax of the criticisms that have surrounded globalization since the Asian crisis and are manifested in the triumphal imposition of the American model. It is probably not coincidental that the support for anti-American terrorism comes from the Middle East, which has been the region of the world that is most resistant to globalization and whose leaders feel the most threatened by the economic and political changes entailed by membership in the globalizing economy. That the major target of the terrorist attacks was the World Trade Center towers in the heart of New York's financial district may also be less than coincidental, since they were important hubs and symbols of globalization. The fact that citizens from eighty countries were killed in the attacks is only further evidence of how broadly the globalization and the pervasiveness of the global economy had spread. That the symbolism they evoked was part of the motive for the targets chosen has not been established, and other, more mundane explanations may have provided the reasons (for instance, the towers were the tallest buildings in New York and could be attacked without having to dodge through other structures, as an attack on the Empire State Building would have required). At any rate, the coincidence is there, and it is intriguing, to say the least.

Even as time passes, we are still assessing the general and specific impacts of the attacks and the responses to them on international life. One of the more obvious policy areas in which there is the potential for conflict is the clash between responses to terrorism and the continuing globalization of the international economy.

Globalization and Terrorism

Globalization and the response to terrorism appear on the surface to pose two antithetical phenomena, arousing very different impulses. A basic, underlying theme and requisite of globalization is openness and free, unimpeded movement of people, products, services, ideas, and financial resources across national borders. Indeed, most observers agree that globalization has been made possible by advances in telecommunications and transportation, which have facilitated openness and movement. Before commodities and people could be moved rapidly around the world, globalization as it now exists was impossible. For globalization to continue and expand, boundaries and other man-made restrictions on movement must continue to be progressively reduced.

Terrorism and responses to terrorism, however, suggest closure and restriction of movement. Terrorist organizations are, by their very nature, clandestine and secretive, and it is not coincidental that they thrive in conditions of state sponsorship or sanction in the very closed societies that are outside the reaches of the globalization system. Terrorists prosper, however, when they can carry out their missions in open, unrestricted environments that they can penetrate easily with minimal danger of exposure or interference. Part of the response to terrorism is making it more difficult to penetrate target societies.

The contemporary environment places international terrorists and globalizers at direct odds theoretically as well. For the globalizers, extension of the global system is at the heart of modernization, and its spread globally represents a value to be exploited and maximized. To terrorist organizations such as bin Laden's Al Qaeda, the intrusion of modernity, of which globalization is an important symbol, is the evil to be resisted. Because the United States is clearly identified as the major symbol of globalization and its system is at least a rough model of the societal changes that come with globalization, it quite naturally becomes the object of efforts to resist change.

In the roughest terms, this incompatibility frames the relationship between terrorism and globalization. Globalization requires openness and the unfettered ability to move about, and terrorists find openness conducive to carrying out their nefarious actions. Responding to terrorism may require removing some of that openness so as to prevent the success of terrorists by intercepting or monitoring their movement. Globalization needs openness to thrive, but responses to terrorism equally dictate restriction on that openness. The values of prosperity and security thus clash in ways that were unnecessary to contemplate during the 1990s.

The emphasis on incompatibilities, however, reflects a short-term rather than a longer-term view of the relationship between response to terrorism and globalization. Short-term assessments are reactive—quite rightly concerned with responses to traumatic events and to the prevention of their recurrence. In the contemporary environment, this emphasis makes the response to terrorism the more immediate and more important problem. When the dictates of antiterrorism and counterterrorism and the promotion of globalization collide, dealing with terrorism takes precedence.

But is an emphasis on closure and restriction a wise longer-term strategy? Are the concepts of globalization and response to terrorism locked in a zero-sum game in which one value can be promoted only at the expense of the other? Or is it possible to examine the problem and conclude that responding to terrorism and promoting globalization are both necessary tools in a strategy for "draining the swamp" in which terrorism thrives and thus contributing to the ultimate goal of defeating terrorism by removing the reasons for its existence?

The answer to the last question is overwhelmingly positive and is directly parallel to the relationship between conflict suppression and state-building elaborated in Chapter 11. The war on terrorism can be viewed as a problem similar to conflict suppression—making it impossible for combatants to fight one another or to engage in acts of terrorism. Just as conflict suppression does not get at the underlying reasons for internal war, neither will tactical responses to terrorism overcome the reasons people become terrorists. Rather, the state-building exercise designed to convince formerly warring parties that peace makes more sense than a reversion to war has its parallel in state-building efforts whose purpose is to make terrorism unattractive by economically and politically uplifting formerly terrorist states and drawing them into the globalization system. In this sense, the Bush administration's dual emphasis in the campaign against Al Qaeda—suppressing and destroying the terrorist network while simultaneously engaging in state-building in Afghanistan—makes perfect sense. How well the campaign to reform and materially uplift Afghanistan works will thus be a strong indication of how well terrorism can be eliminated, just as earlier but ongoing efforts in Kosovo are a test of the ability to build states after ruinous internal wars. State-building is as much a part of the successful outcome of this war as physical fighting, as the situation in Afghanistan attests. In 1988 the Soviets withdrew from Afghanistan, as did the Americans. Neither power attempted to rebuild the ruins, and the results were disastrous. Have we learned anything?

The parallels suggested here are not yet part of conventional, orthodox national security strategy. Just as state-building writ large is a new and unproven approach whose details are still being developed, applying state-building to the problem of terrorism is even newer. If there is a lesson to be learned from earlier efforts at state-building, it is that the task will be long and arduous.

The short-term incompatibility and longer-term compatibility between responses to terrorism and globalization will occupy the remainder of this chapter, because that evolving and changing relationship may well be one of the cornerstones of future national security politics—an important part of the way in which globalization and geopolitics blend together. We will begin by looking at short-term incompatibilities and how they are likely to interact in the next few years. Following that discussion, we will speculate on the longer term, on how state-building may help transform states that were formerly hotbeds of potential terrorism into members of the globalizing economy for which terrorism is an unappealing option.

Short-Term Incompatibilities

In the immediate future, attempts to prevent or limit the recurrence of terrorist acts against the American homeland or American interests overseas will retain policy predominance. In that entirely understandable ordering of priorities, the relationship between open, nurturing globalization and restrictive responses to terrorism will almost certainly emphasize the incompatibilities between the two policy aspects. Where the two clash, the globalizers will be forced to yield, to accommodate and adapt to the dictates of dealing with the geopolitics of the new century.

A small but growing literature is beginning to appear that deals with the short-term relationship. To date, this literature has suggested two specific areas of concerns. The first reflects the vulnerability of the globalization system to disruption, a situation in which the efficiency of the globalizing system creates its own primary weakness. The second area of concern reflects the consequences of emphasizing policies that maximize responses to terrorism in terms of their dilatory impact on globalization. These analyses tend to emphasize the difficulty of reaching compromises that are favorable to both values.

Vulnerabilities.   One of the major reasons for the success of globalization during the 1990s was its ability to establish greater efficiencies in the productive cycle. In large part, these improvements occurred as part of the privatization of economic activity that is one of the signal characteristics of globalization. This efficiency, however, has come with the cost of vulnerability. Flynn describes the problem: "The competitiveness of the U.S. economy and the quality of life of the American people rest on critical infrastructure that has become increasingly more concentrated, more interconnected, and more sophisticated. Almost entirely privately owned and operated, the system has very little redundancy."

There is a certain irony in this development, because the very forces that have improved the material lives of people have also created the conditions in which the underpinning of that prosperity can be undermined more effectively than in the past. Thus we create efficiency-compromising redundancies—such as multiple accounting and record-keeping systems, maintaining both electronic and nonelectronic records—to provide safeguards against the disruption of any single source of information. As Campbell puts it, "Many of the things that have left sophisticated Western societies vulnerable to terrorist attacks are the very efficiencies that have come as a consequence of persons', companies' and countries' relentless search for efficiency and maximum productivity." He cites examples of efficiencies such as curbside check-in at airports, e-tickets, and freer immigration policies that make the system more responsive and faster.

The public, including the national security community, has not been immune to this trend. Several years ago, for instance, the U.S. Air Force announced its goal to create a "paperless Air Force," in which all paper records would be eliminated and all information would be retained electronically. Beyond the air force's well-known obsession with technological gimmickry, the purpose was to enhance efficiency and save money by eliminating the need to produce, store, and maintain the mountains of paperwork the air force bureaucracy routinely generated. The problem was that instead of having several copies of information stored at several different places (redundancy, but safety), it was all in one computerized system that, if disrupted, could cause the information to be lost—irretrievably, in some cases. At the other end of the spectrum, the disaster of the World Trade Centers destruction was partially mitigated by the fact that most of the firms located there had copies of records stored elsewhere to compensate for those lost in the attack.

A theme that recurs in discussions of globalization-related economic vulnerability is the concentration of activity that globalization has induced. Homer-Dixon summarizes this aspect of the problem: "This additional vulnerability is the product of two key social and technological developments: first, the growing complexity and interconnectedness of our modern societies; and second, the growing geographic concentration of wealth, human capital, knowledge, and communication links." Modern society, physically shaped by a globalizing economy, makes an attractive target, and the attack on the World Trade Center was an almost perfect symbol of the consequences of that vulnerability.

The very openness of the American and, increasingly, the global community creates conditions in which terrorists can operate more easily. An irony of the problem is that closed, deprived social settings produce terrorists who could not possibly carry out terrorist acts in their own societies because of the preponderance of coercive, suppressive force that helps make conditions wretched. They can flourish, however, in the very kinds of societies that represent conditions in which terrorists would not arise.

The vulnerability of open societies has been the basis of much discussion about antiterrorist efforts in the United States and the degree to which attempts to shore up those vulnerabilities lead to necessary or unwarranted infringements on civil and other rights. Openness has meant that it has been relatively easy to enter and leave the United States, for instance. When those entering and leaving are businesspeople engaged in productive commerce, we view that as a virtue and as one of the reasons for the success of globalization. When that same permeability permits terrorists to enter and leave the country without detection, that is another matter. The same is true of communications. The ability to communicate instantly across the globe has been extolled as a major reason for the success of globalization, facilitating the flow and coordination of commerce, the movement of capital and ideas and the like at speeds and in ways that were unthinkable before the telecommunications revolution. Those same instruments of communication, however, also allow terrorist organizations such as Al Qaeda to communicate with their far-flung cells and to coordinate their nefarious activities in ways heretofore impossible. As a concrete example, the uprooting of Al Qaeda would have disrupted their ability to communicate more were it not for cell phones.

The globalization age is also an information and information-sharing age, through such devices as the enormous amount of material available on the Internet. Although this aspect of the telecommunications revolution facilitates the sharing of a variety of useful information for legitimate purposes, it also allows access to information by terrorists to put to their own ends. As Homer-Dixon observes, "The September 11 bombers could have found there [the Internet] all the details they needed about the floor plans and design characteristics of the World Trade Center and about how demolition experts use progressive collapse to destroy large buildings." The same Internet that makes researching term papers easier can also help terrorists conduct *their* "research."

Consequences.   The short-term incompatibility between efforts to frustrate international terrorists and those to promote the expansion of the globalization system of economic commerce has numerous consequences, from security and vulnerability to the movement of people and goods across borders. The problem is probably greater and receiving more attention in the area of border security than in any other issue.

Because of historic reasons (friendship with Canada), practical and financial constraints (the difficulty of sealing the long border with Mexico), and policy decisions to facilitate the flow of goods and individuals into and out of the country (a direct result and purpose of globalization), the United States has extremely porous borders. This porosity has facilitated commerce and prosperity in the past. It has allowed an unimpeded flow of goods, where prices are not inflated by elaborate inspection requirements for entering and leaving the country, and it has permitted cheap (and often illegal) laborers to enter the country and produce goods at lower labor costs than would have been possible employing American citizens. Moreover, liberal immigration policies that allow large numbers of foreign students to enter the country and study at American colleges and universities, for instance, also enhance the talent pool for American private enterprise, especially in the areas of science and engineering, where American students are in short supply.

That same porosity also facilitates the activities of terrorists, however. Terrorists have been able to move fairly easily across the borders between the United States and its neighbors, and it has also been relatively easy for them to move weapons (probably including weapons of mass destruction) across those borders. As Flynn argues, the United States currently has no means to screen nefarious from legitimate entrants into the country: "The problem . . . is that the existing border-management architecture provides no credible means for denying foreign terrorists and their weapons entry into the United States."

There are two subproblems here: who and what can get into the United States. Both of these issues put terrorism suppression and globalization into direct conflict. Take the human part of the problem. As the investigation of the September 11 attacks reveals, a number of the terrorists originally entered the country on student visas, presumably to study at American universities. Surveys conducted after the terrorist attacks revealed that literally thousands of foreigners who entered the country under those pretenses were no longer enrolled in college (if they ever had been), and their whereabouts were unknown. Canvasses to find the missing were less than overwhelmingly successful, and many of these "students" remain unaccounted for.

What can we do about the problem? Hardly anyone disagrees with the proposition that real students, who may become part of the skilled American workforce (or return to their native countries and improve conditions there), should not be denied entry to the United States, and no one disagrees with the proposition that potential terrorists should be excluded. If there were some foolproof litmus test that would show which group young foreigners belonged in (most students and most terrorists are young, unmarried men in their 20s, as a recent study of suicide terrorists has concluded), there would be little problem. The difficulty, of course, is that such a test does not exist, and if it did, it would probably be only partially effective. Reconciliation between the dictates of countering terrorism and promoting globalization requires that some better form of discrimination be devised. Better screening of applicants before they leave their countries offers a partial, if expensive and time-consuming solution, but it is a start.

The problem of monitoring *who* enters the United States pales beside the problem of knowing *what* enters the country. In addition to the 489 million people who passed through American border posts in 2000, Flynn reports that 127 million passenger vehicles, 11.6 million maritime containers, 2.2 million railroad cars, 629,000 airplanes, and 211,000 vessels went through American border checkpoints in that year. Most of the freight was not inspected for the simple reason that there are not nearly enough inspectors to monitor more than a tiny percentage of what comes across the border. This is particularly true at heavy-usage entry points, such as the Ambassador Bridge between Windsor, Ontario, and Detroit, Michigan. According to Flynn, "nearly 5,000 trucks entered the United States each day in 2000. . . . U.S. Customs officers must average no more than two minutes per truck." He adds that a thorough inspection of a 40-foot eighteen-wheeler requires fifteen man-hours.

Aside from the problem of gridlock that would result if efforts to monitor goods and people were to increase enough to have reasonable assurance that contraband, including terrorist weapons, did not penetrate the country, there is also the disaster such an interruption would have on the American commercial system. Closing the bridge between Windsor and Detroit, to cite one example, would interrupt the flow of automobile parts from manufacturing to assembly plants on the other side of the border; in December 2001, such an interruption closed several American automobile assembly plants.

The permeability of America's borders both reflects the incompatibility of dealing with terrorism and globalization at the same time and highlights the difficulties associated with antiterrorism generally. In fact, most of the substantive areas in which the two forces of globalization and terrorism suppression collide will be in the area of antiterrorist operations. The transportation example shows the inherent difficulty of antiterrorist actions generally—it is essentially impossible to anticipate all forms and places where terrorism might be planned, and a strategy that relies wholly or even largely on antiterrorism will almost certainly fail some of the time. In terms of regulating boundaries, even the most draconian measures probably cannot succeed perfectly. As a result, decisions to improve the effectiveness of such measures, which may compromise the movement of goods, services, and people, have to be balanced against the limits on how effective these measures can actually be.

Reconciliation.   Efforts aimed at reducing terrorism have taken public precedence over the promotion of the global economy, an emphasis that suddenly appeared much less important than preventing a feared repeat of the awful attacks. At some point, however, it will be necessary to reconcile the contradictory interests of security and prosperity and to assess the degree to which American economic interests tied to globalization balance with interests connected to homeland security.

Those who would promote the primacy of economic interests have clearly been on the defensive and have not loudly asserted a return to emphasizing and expanding globalization. The reasons for this quiescence undoubtedly are diverse, but they include a fear of being deemed unpatriotic by declaring a false return to preattack normalcy. Arguing the case for renewed emphasis on globalization is tantamount to claiming that it is time to get back to business. The popular mood, fanned by political leaders and the media, counters that we remain "at war," which is clearly not the normal environment for commerce.

When will the political atmosphere move back toward a more balanced view of the country's priorities? The answer to that question, ironically, lies largely in the hands of those who would do the United States harm through acts of terrorism. The longer the lull between September 11 and the next serious terrorist incident, the more public attention will move away from terrorism and toward a return to preterrorist normalcy. Issuing warnings of threats that do not materialize, as the government did frequently in the months after the attacks, not only does not reinforce vigilance but probably undermines it and works to increase demand for a change back to a normal life.

A period of some calm will almost certainly produce a calmer, more even-handed analysis of American priorities, one that will restore some, if not necessarily all of the American enthusiasm for globalization. As the effort to deal comprehensively with the problem of terrorism evolves, it may also produce the realization that, in the longer run, responses to terrorism and globalization not only are not incompatible elements of American strategy, but are complimentary pillars of such a strategy.

Long-Term Compatibilities

The idea that globalization and the campaign to end terrorism are related comes from extending notions about dealing with new internal war to the problem of dealing with terrorism. Such a comparison can be made on three bases: the environments in which the two problems arise, the comparability of the two approaches to solving the problem, and a comparison of the relative differences between the two.

It is striking that most of the states on the U.S. Department of State list of terrorist sponsors or sanctioners are also on or candidates for inclusion on the list of failed states. The two lists are not synonymous—Haiti and Sierra Leone, for instance, are clearly failed states but have not produced international terrorists, although in both cases, elements—including the government—have engaged in domestic terrorism that is as reprehensible as its international counterpart. In each case where a failed state has become an international problem that the international system feels the need to remedy through something like state-building, there have been indigenous movements that have applied the same kind of fanaticism and terror against their own populations that international terrorists have applied toward foreign targets. The "fighters" of Sierra Leone's Revolutionary United Front, hacking off the limbs of innocent civilians, were certainly sending a terrorist warning to others who might consider not cooperating with them in the future. The narco-terrorists of Colombia use kidnappings and assassinations of Colombian officials and citizens to increase their power by frightening their opposition. Terrorism, whether directed domestically or internationally, is terrorism, after all, and the circumstances that produce either variety are also similar.

Without going into a detailed psychological or sociological profile of either terrorists or the fighters attracted to internal wars, there is a striking similarity in the countries in which both exist. Certainly there is a geographic distinction: Most of the known international terrorists currently come from the Islamic Middle East, whereas most of the internal wars are in Africa and Asia. A kind of hybrid, in which avowed revolutionaries engage in both civil war and terrorism, exists in places such as Sri Lanka (the Black Tigers of the Liberation Tigers of Tamil Eelam) and the Philippines.

What all these places have in common is a sense of societal hopelessness and despair. For half a century, the Palestinian refugee camps have been the recruiting grounds for a variety of terrorist organizations, including those involved in the 2002 and 2003 suicide bombings, and the dynamic of attraction is simple enough. If one's life is sufficiently miserable, then there is little to lose in joining a terrorist movement, even if one may become a *shahid* (martyr) in the process. Springzak, citing an Israeli study on suicide terrorists, describes the typical Palestinian recruit as "a male, religious, unmarried and unemployed high school graduate" who may have had a relative killed in the struggle against Israel. The Black Tigers have a similar demographic profile. Recruits for Al Qaeda from the *madrassa* system are typically young male children who have been orphaned or abandoned.

These similarities suggest that a similar approach to dealing with the problem may be advisable as well. Conflict suppression is the first step in "curing" failed states, but it is clearly not enough to produce postconflict political systems that are stable and violence free. Similarly, antiterrorist and counterterrorist methods are necessary first steps in eliminating or containing the threat posed by a particular terrorist group or groups. In and of themselves, however, such actions cannot address the broader, underlying circumstances from which terrorism arises.

If the solution to new internal wars is to produce stable societies through state-building, the same logic applies to reforming terrorist-sanctioning states, a conclusion apparently accepted by the Bush administration in its overall campaign in Afghanistan. Terrorist organizations thrived in Afghanistan because of the association of Al Qaeda and the government, but the underlying reality for the country was the human misery that served as "the swamp" from which willing terrorists (many of whom were not Afghans but foreigners from more affluent countries such as Saudi Arabia) arose while others tolerated them in their midst. If a government is to succeed in Afghanistan that opposes and successfully suppresses terrorists, it will have to have the active political and economic support of a population that grants it support and legitimacy. Politics and misery as usual will only breed the next generation of terrorists; state-building aimed at improving the human lot is necessary to "drain" the swamp. It is somewhat curious in this regard that Israel, a country with more experience with terrorists than virtually anyplace else in the world, does not see that its harsh policy of retribution and economic deprivation against the Palestinians may be effectively creating the next generation of Palestinian terrorists (see Amplification 12.3).

Just as in state-building for humanitarian purposes, terrorism-reducing state-building ultimately will focus its economic component on making the target country attractive to the globalizing economy. Before this transformation can occur, target countries need to develop sufficient political stability and economic infrastructure to become attractive to private investors. International companies, the backbone of globalization, are not going to invest in places where the government cannot provide basic protection of their assets or where the government might be swept away by opposition forces at any moment. Furthermore, a country with poor roads, ports,

Amplification 12.3

THE ISRAELI CAMPAIGN AGAINST PALESTINIAN "TERRORISM"

As described in Chapter 10, relations between Israel and the Palestinians have deteriorated markedly since the failure of Camp David II. In December 2000, fighting broke out between the two sides that continued throughout 2001, 2002, and 2003. That fighting between the Israeli army and bands of Palestinian youth (many of whom reflect the physical profile in the accompanying text) has gradually expanded and has become more bitter. Acts of violent terror (suicidal bombers) have resulted in recrimination and retaliation, followed by counter-retaliation, and so on. Both sides blame the other for the violence and the failure to stop it, and there are good arguments on both sides.

The violence has hardened the political positions on both sides. The Sharon government has insisted that this *intifada* (uprising) is proof of Palestinian perfidy, especially the intransigence and ineffectiveness of Yasser Arafat. The Palestinians counter that the Israelis are slaughtering innocent Palestinians and are intruding on territory ceded by Israel to the Palestinian Authority.

One can debate the merits of the case on either side and even sympathize with the spirit of vengeance the situation has engendered. A question increasingly asked as the violence drags on, however, is whether the policies are short-sighted or not. Particularly in the case of the Palestinians, is Israeli policy not virtually ensuring that the conditions in which terrorism arises will be present for the foreseeable future? Faced with economic desolation and physical and economic helplessness, will another generation of Palestinians emerge who are willing potential terrorists? If peace is the long-term goal of both sides, should either or both sides be nurturing the culture of continued violence—in effect assuring that the "swamp" that breeds terrorism remains fertile? Moreover, has Palestinian terrorism so alienated those Israelis who have favored accommodation that they have lost control to the hard-liners who oppose reconciliation? Has peace been made impossible by the actions on both sides?

and airfields, an unreliable power supply, and a largely unskilled labor force will not attract foreign direct investment. Much of the basic infrastructure development necessary to reverse these conditions must come from public sources, since the projects they entail will not be self-liquidating (directly producing profits that can repay loans). Public funds have to do those things, and they must be aimed at making the target country attractive to the globalizers. Globalization thus becomes the handmaiden of counterterrorism.

The international community has not wholeheartedly embraced state-building for humanitarian purposes. When he entered office, President George W. Bush was one of the major skeptics of American involvement in humanitarian peacekeeping that had state-building as an element. Yet within less than a year, he had become a vocal proponent of doing exactly in Afghanistan what he was opposed to doing elsewhere. The reason, of course, was obvious: State-building in Afghanistan was part of the broader war on terrorism and thus a matter of American vital interests. We have a more important rationale there; making life more prosperous for Kosovars does not occupy the same level of priority.

The dynamics of state-building, however, are much the same in the two situations. If anything, state-building in the kinds of states that have traditionally harbored terrorists may be more difficult, because those countries also tend to be the kinds of states that have been most resistant to the incursion of the globalizing influences that are, in turn, key to terrorist-proofing them. Fundamentalism, in this case mostly Islamic, opposes the very changes that globalization brings with it.

State-building in states that have harbored terrorists is also terribly important if terrorism is to be eliminated or reduced to international inconsequence. The Afghan experiment is enormously important in this regard. It is inherently important because the country was the host of Al Qaeda, and their elimination is a necessary first step to restoring the integrity of North American security. Beyond that, the success of state-building in Afghanistan will have enormous importance as a precedent for future American national security and foreign policy, particularly if something like state-building will have to be undertaken in other places to which displaced terrorists flee to find safe haven.

The Case of Afghanistan

Before 2001, Afghanistan was a country about which the average American knew very little. A landlocked country in the middle of central Asia, its historic importance has been that it sits astride some of the major trading routes between Asia and Europe, giving it a strategic importance that has brought legions of invaders to the land. During the nineteenth century, the British and the Russians played "the great game" for influence and control. In 1979, Soviet tanks rolled into the country, only to meet fierce resistance from the *mujahadeen* (freedom fighters), an experience from which both the Taliban and Al Qaeda claim their birth. In 1988, the Soviets limped out of Afghanistan in military disgrace; the experience helped hasten the collapse of the Soviet Union three years later. In 1996, the Taliban, advertised as reformers who would root out legendary corruption in the Afghan government, captured Kabul and began their fundamentalist reign of terror. In December 2001, after their rout, an interim government under Hamid Karzai began the task of rebuilding the country in preparation for national elections. A major emphasis of his tenure was the forceful rejection of both the Taliban and terrorism. The American embassy in Kabul, abandoned in December 1989, reopened in December 2001; the Afghan embassy in Washington, closed in 1995, reopened on January 28, 2002, with Karzai in attendance and extolling a new and perpetual solidarity between his country and the United States.

Afghanistan is also one of the poorest, most desolate countries of the world, and its physical condition has been made worse by over twenty years of warfare that has virtually destroyed Kabul and scarred the countryside. By any measure, the country's economy is a shambles. *The World Almanac and Book of Facts 2003* lists per capita gross domestic product at $800, and says that Afghanistan has three airports and sixteen miles of rails in a country the physical size of Texas with a population of nearly twenty-eight million. Life expectancy for males is 47 years; in an anomaly that demonstrates the fate of women under the Taliban, female life expectancy is 45.9 years.

By any measure, Afghanistan has been a failed state, and any efforts to raise standards to the level that the country will become attractive to outside investment are daunting at the very least. Despite a lull in intertribal political and military bickering attendant to the overthrow of the Taliban, the country remains deeply divided along ethnic lines, and ethnic disagreements have often been solved violently throughout Afghan history. Forming a government that reflects ethnic realities will be difficult, particularly since the deposed Taliban were mostly from the largest ethnic group, the Pashtun (who constitute 38 percent of the population). Building and rebuilding the economy will be a very difficult and costly process.

Overcoming these obvious physical difficulties is not the only challenge facing efforts to stabilize Afghanistan and make it part of the terrorist-opposing coalition of states. As already suggested, the kinds of actions that will make Afghanistan a modern, stable member of the international community will be opposed by some in Afghanistan and others in the region on religious and cultural grounds. While the fanatical excesses of the Taliban were greatly hated, shedding the burkas did not mean that many Afghans have lost their adherence to Islam. There remain fundamentalists in the country who find Westernization and its attendant secularization of society offensive. Fundamentalism is still part of the Afghan equation, and fundamentalists are also active in the surrounding states, most notably Tajikistan (ethnic Tajiks are the second largest ethnic group in Afghanistan) and Pakistan, where there are large numbers of Afghan refugees including supporters of bin Laden and the Taliban.

Efforts to rebuild Afghanistan—especially to try to transform it into something like a normal Westernized state that can enter the globalization system—have to be sensitive to the fact that this is exactly what many Afghans do not want to see happen. In the early relations between the United States and the post-Taliban rulers, the most prominent Afghans were also those who were most Westernized and most involved in transforming their country. Karzai, for instance, speaks fluent and highly articulate English, and members of his family are prominent restaurant owners on the East Coast of the United States. His visions for Afghanistan seem to match our own and make the job at hand seem conceptually and physically easier than it almost certainly will be. Karzai may prove to have more support in the United States than he does in his native Afghanistan.

There is also considerable anti-Americanism in the "Arab street." A prominent American presence in Afghanistan, especially the longer it lasts and the greater the transformation of Afghan society it creates, is going to be watched very closely in the region by elements that do not want to see Americanization of the Middle East succeed. In fact, it is the prospect of that Americanization that fuels much of the hatred that many feel toward the United States. We have been down this road before in neighboring Iran, with disastrous results.

If Americans have any doubts about how carefully to tread to avoid creating more antipathy than sympathy and support, we need only look toward our closest ally in the region, Saudi Arabia. Since 1990, when the United States accepted the Saudi invitation to protect the regime from Iraq, there has been a continuous American military presence on Saudi soil. That presence is unpopular enough that bin Laden has considerable support in Saudi Arabia for his stated goal to force the

Americans to leave and end the desecration of the Arabian peninsula, and Saudi millionaires are among the chief benefactors of the violently anti-American *madrassas* in Pakistan and reportedly in Indonesia. To make the American presence less offensive, Americans are stationed in remote areas and are not encouraged to interact with the natives. The Saudi royal family's support for the United States is unpopular in the country and causes them to treat the United States with less warmth than one might expect given the extent of the relationship across time. For them, embracing the United States—especially American policy in matters such as Palestine—is the potential kiss of death.

The real danger against which any state-building effort in Afghanistan must guard is the kind of experience the United States had when we supported the Shah of Iran from the end of World War II until Shah Reza Pahlevi was deposed in the Iranian Revolution of 1979 and replaced by a fanatically anti-American fundamentalist government that had Ayotollah Ruhollah Khomeini as its titular leader.

This is not the place for a detailed examination of the Iranian Revolution, but our experience there does serve as a warning to the United States as it seeks to help Afghanistan and Iraq. The Shah of Iran, after he was returned to power in 1953 with the help of the CIA (he was briefly overthrown that year), sought to transform his country into a resurgent power in the region and the world—in effect restoring the old Persian Empire. He calculated that the only way he could succeed was by embracing the ways of the West, and his White Revolution sought to transform Iran into a modern, Western power. The United States was the chief advisor in the process and helped direct the changes being instituted.

In retrospect, it is clear that Iran was possibly the worst country in the world to try to Westernize rapidly. The basis of Iranian society was a very conservative Shiite Muslim majority, led by an activist clergy (a tradition within Shiism) who were deeply offended by the effects of Westernization on traditional Islamic values; the Shah and his partners, the "Great Satans," were blamed for the dilution of Islamic values that was occurring. The movement led by Ayotollah Khomeini was, in large measure, a fundamentalist reaction to the efforts to modernize the country, and it succeeded in toppling the Shah's regime and replacing it with a fanatically anti-American alternative that still retains its position as a member of the "axis of evil," despite some moderation in its policies. In Iran, the United States attempted to aid in the Westernization of an Islamic society into the equivalent of membership in the globalizing economy, but the results were quite the opposite of what was intended.

Could the same thing happen in Afghanistan? As the Taliban's period of rule proves, Afghan society is certainly capable of producing a Sunni fundamentalist regime that is equally anti-American and arguably more fanatically antimodernist than the Iranian Revolution produced. Although there was obvious popular relief at the lifting of Taliban restrictions and a visible embrace of some Western symbols such as televisions and other symbols of Western-style modernity, some of the fundamentalist instincts undoubtedly remain.

Afghanistan is not Iran, but recent evidence suggests that the Taliban are back and operating in the Pashtun-controlled regions of the countryside. It still must be remembered that the Taliban had popular support when they came to power and only lost much of that support as they imposed a much more puritanical, draconian rule than they had suggested before they achieved power. Clearly, it is in the American interest not to induce change that could reawaken the emotions that created the original broad appeal of the Taliban.

The key factor for state-building success in Afghanistan is likely to be a political and economic program that can overcome traditional ethnic differences. Politically, this effort requires nurturing institutions that all groups feel are fair and that cannot be distorted by one ethnic group at the expense of others or twisted to allow the traditional Afghan corruption the Taliban promised to overcome. That emphasis seems obvious enough, but it requires power sharing and cooperation that has long been absent in Afghan politics. Economically, the pace and structure of building and rebuilding must also be uniform countrywide, so that regions dominated by some ethnic majorities do not prosper while others are ignored. With well over a billion dollars a year pledged to reconstruction but not physically committed in early 2003, monitoring the progress of programs will be important, as will ensuring that the development that occurs does not have the unintended and untoward consequences that occurred in Iran a quarter-century ago. Progress in Afghanistan will be a measuring stick against which to measure similar efforts in Iraq.

CONCLUSION: RECONCILING GLOBALIZATION AND TERRORISM

The tranquil, go-go 1990s have given way to the troubled, insecure 2000s. The optimism that accompanied spiraling global prosperity through much of the 1990s has been replaced by a wary anxiety in an international environment where terrorism dominates our conversations, if less obviously the actual sequence of international events. Geopolitics in the new clothing of terrorism responses has overtaken the spreading of prosperity through globalization in the center of public consciousness about the world and our place in it.

It has become commonplace, virtually a cliché, to say that *everything* has changed since terrorism visited the American homeland on September 11, 2001. Although national and international dialogues have certainly come to focus much more clearly on the terrorist threat, the assertion seems inflated. If it is true, it is largely because we have said it is true so often that we believe it. The terrorist act on that fateful day was, after all, a single—if horrific—act that has not been repeated in any equivalent way. It may well be true that the lack of repetition has been because we are more vigilant and have thus thwarted other plans that might have succeeded. At a minimum, the Afghan campaign has made it more difficult for the current terrorists to operate their deadly networks. How much harder it is for them we do not know.

Has September 11, 2001, truly changed the environment? Or has it changed the way we *look* at the environment? There was a terrorist threat before the event, and as noted earlier, there were clarions warning us of our vulnerability to that which befell us. Their warnings were generally not heeded then, but they are today. Is that a change in the environment or in how we view the environment? Has reality or our perception of reality changed the most?

The question of perspective applies as well to the more fundamental relationships explored in this chapter, notably the shifting relationship between globalization and geopolitics. Bill Clinton was clearly a globalizing president, although in the waning days of his second term, his personal and political difficulties drowned out much of the focus of his zeal. A sagging global economy added to a defocusing of the public on globalization issues. George W. Bush entered office without any known preference for geopolitics or globalization. He campaigned as a free trader but also as an adherent of stronger defenses. The events of September 11 dictated his emphasis for him.

The emphases on terrorism-driven geopolitics or expanding globalization continue to struggle for conceptual supremacy. In the early going after the terrorist attacks, geopolitics rapidly came to the ascendancy in terms of domestic priorities and international dealings. The incompatibilities of the two concepts were emphasized in areas such as border control and the permeability of those borders, immigration restrictions, and the like. Those promoting openness and the free movement of goods and people were viewed as suspect, since free-moving people could be terrorists and their cargo weapons. Globalization issues became wrapped in the general discussion of security and the sacrifices in terms of civil liberties and other freedoms that would be necessary to increase that security.

Will the advantage of geopolitics in the debate endure? As noted, the terrorists will have something to say about that question with their future activity or inactivity, but it is difficult to imagine that the fervor will continue forever. The continued reference to the state of a war that does not actually exist will almost certainly lose its magnetism unless some concrete entity emerges with which to fight. Questions of economic well-being, which is certainly part of national security, will begin to compete with questions of the physical safety of the homeland. Globalization is, after all, a part of national security strategy, not an alternative to it.

The darker side of the debate over globalization and geopolitics is its equation with the debate over internationalism and unilateralism-neoisolationism. Globalization is a quintessentially internationalist idea. Although globalization can be justified in terms of the unilateral national advantages it produces, rather than for its systemic virtues, the core and most of the rationalizations for globalization will necessarily involve its contribution to economic and political global improvement. Terrorism-driven geopolitics can be promoted as either an international or a national movement, but its virtue ultimately will be judged on the contribution of antiterrorist measures to the security of the country.

The two emphases are not mutually exclusive, of course. The elimination of terrorism can probably be most efficiently accomplished through international efforts and collaboration in tasks such as identifying terrorists and their movement. Since secret intelligence agencies will have to do the sharing and are, by their nature, interested in concealing rather than sharing what they know, there will always be limits on international cooperation, but it is clearly part of any strategy that is likely to succeed.

If the conceptual odds now favor an emphasis on geopolitics over globalization over the near term, what could cause that to change? The answer involves one or both of two trends. The first would be a deemphasis on terrorism that would return

Challenge!

Will Globalization Really Work?

An underlying assumption of those who favor the extension of globalization as a way to dampen violence and instability in the international system is that globalization will, *in fact* as well as in theory, have that desired effect. But is that assumption valid? Will globalization really work to achieve the goals its champions claim for it?

Since globalization has not occurred everywhere, we cannot observe its effects and thus provide a definitive answer to our question. Something like globalization has been advocated for a long time, and there was a theoretical strand during the Cold War period that advocated something called *complex interdependence*, the gist of which was that as economies became more intertwined globally, the ability to make war would become physically impossible. The same sentiment had proved wrong at the turn of the twentieth century, when interdependence was supposed to render war highly unlikely, if not physically impossible. At the end of World War II, the functionalists hoped that the United Nations system would so involve countries as to produce peace.

These experiences suggest that the success of globalization in producing a more tranquil environment cannot be accepted as a given. At the same time, the same experiences do not provide conclusive evidence that globalization will *not* produce peace. The international system has, after all, undergone a "long peace" for nearly sixty years. There has not been a major, systemic war since the conclusion of World War II, and the democratization and economic globalizing of the world has had something to do with that. Moreover, no reputable observers have looked at the evolving international environment and prophesied the likelihood of fundamental, system-threatening conflict.

So, does globalization work? The evidence is clearly ambiguous, and the answer is a firm and unequivocal "maybe." Realizing that uncertainty should temper advocacy and opposition, what do you think?

---

terrorism to something like its pre–September 11, 2001, place in international and national priorities. The absence of major terrorist incidents over some period of time is probably the necessary condition for that to occur. The second trend would be an upturn in the global economy from which all countries would benefit but those most heavily invested in globalization could benefit the most. Both of these things almost certainly will happen sometime. The question is when and with what effects.

SELECTED BIBLIOGRAPHY

Ajami, Fouad. "The Sentry's Solitude." *Foreign Affairs* 80, 6 (November/December 2001), 2–16.

Appleby, R. Scott, and Martin E. Marty. "Fundamentalism." *Foreign Policy*, January/February 2002, 16–22.

Bearden, Milton. "Afghanistan, Graveyard of Empires." *Foreign Affairs* 80, 6 (November/December 2001), 17–30.

Bhagwati, Jagdish. "Coping with Antiglobalization." *Foreign Affairs* 81, 1 (January/February 2002), 2–7.

Campbell, Kurt M. "Globalization's First War." *Washington Quarterly* 25, 1 (Winter 2001–02), 7–14.

Flynn, Stephen E. "America the Vulnerable." *Foreign Affairs* 81, 1 (January/February 2002), 60–74.

Homer-Dixon, Thomas. "The Rise of Complex Terrorism." *Foreign Policy*, January/February 2002, 52–63.

Lewis, Bernard. "The Roots of Muslim Rage: Why So Many Muslims Deeply Resent the West, and Why Their Bitterness Will Not Easily Be Mollified." *Atlantic Monthly*, 266, 3 (September 1990), 47–60.

Springzak, Ehud. "Rational Fanatics." *Foreign Policy*, September/October 2000), 66–72.

———. "Tinker, Tailor, Soldier, Bomber." *Foreign Policy*, September/October 2000, 70–71.

PART IV

THE FUTURE

The book will end with an attempt to bring together some of the observations about the past and present and try to extrapolate them into the future of national security for the United States. Because the future, by definition, has not occurred and thus cannot be observed and described, this process is necessarily less precise and more suggestive than other discussions.

The major purpose of Chapter 13 is to assess the relative impact of the two major themes of the book, geopolitics and globalization, on the future. This discussion is developed around two major observations about the likely future, both of which were proposed in the Introduction and represent recurrent themes. First, it argues that the events of September 11, 2001, while disastrous and horrific, may have been overly interpreted in terms of their profound effect on American national security in the future. American vulnerability to harm was demonstrated by the September 11 terrorist attacks, and dealing with terrorism will certainly be a more important concern than it was before. Nevertheless, the physical integrity and survival of the United States were not and are not fundamentally threatened by those events. The second observation is that globalization and geopolitics are not an either/or proposition. Both concerns existed before the attacks of September 11, and both have survived it. The question is which dynamic will receive greater emphasis in the future.

CHAPTER **13**

Globalization and Geopolitics

The degree of trauma caused by the second fault line and the future balance between globalization and geopolitics are the principal foci of this concluding chapter. Organizationally, we will look at the two major concepts sequentially, first raising the question of the future of geopolitics (largely through the lens of reactions to September 11) and then examining the future of globalization in light of the antiglobalization movement that emerged at the end of the 1990s. We will then reexamine where geopolitics and globalization can come together as elements of national security policy. We will conclude by repeating the age-old question: What makes us secure?

The pace of change in American national security has quickened and has become more complicated in the past fifteen years. For most of the history of the American Republic, national security was a fairly minor, not very immediate concern, because American soil was only episodically threatened—and infrequently at that—by outsiders wishing to do us harm. After the British finally abandoned the goal of recolonization at the end of the War of 1812, the United States was essentially physically invulnerable to serious attack for almost a century and a half, until the Soviet Union gained the capacity to menace the American homeland with nuclear-tipped intercontinental ballistic missiles.

The great shock of the September 11, 2001, attacks, as noted in Chapter 3, was partly the result of the shocking loss of a sense of total safety or physical security. The danger posed by the terrorists who attacked us did not threaten the basic existence of the American Republic; there could and would be no follow-up invasion that might topple the American system and enslave our citizens. American survival was not at stake, but our sense of physical immunity from harm was. Superficial comparisons were drawn between the September 11 events and Pearl Harbor in 1941, but in retrospect, the principal analogy was the limited nature of the threat and the awakening it produced. Usama bin Laden awakened the same sleeping giant that Admiral Yamamoto identified after Pearl Harbor and, like the events sixty years earlier, filled us with a "terrible resolve."

The last decade and a half have witnessed the quickening of the pace of changes in the environment in which national security questions are raised and dealt with. Before the fault lines were exposed, the preceding periods were long and, by current standards, fairly leisurely: The formative period lasted for over a century and a half, and the Cold War occupied our attention for about forty-five years. The two periods differed in intensity, however, and in how they ended. National security was a relatively unimportant concern for most of the time during the formative period ending in 1945, whereas the Cold War transformed our concerns and placed the state of national security at the center of public policy.

Did a new and similar cycle begin on September 11? Certainly, there was change for which analogies could be drawn. The Cold War historian John Lewis Gaddis, for instance, drew a dramatic comparison: "The post–cold war era . . . began with the collapse of one structure, the Berlin Wall on November 9, 1989, and ended with the collapse of another, the World Trade Center's twin towers."

Could we be repeating the earlier cycle in the events since 1989? The formative period (1789–1945) and the post–Cold War period (1989–2001) share an environment featuring the relative absence of apparent threats and thus a lesser urgency and importance accorded to national security concerns. The Cold War and the post–September 11 environment share a greater sense of national security salience, whereby dramatic threats have energized the public and policy elites.

But are emphases on the dramatic impact of change overdrawn? The factors that dominate our current concerns were also present between 1989 and 2001: Militant, fundamentalist Islam was a rising factor in the Middle East, and terrorism was a force that was widely prophesied but largely ignored. There were precursors of the September 11 attacks on Americans overseas and at home that could have served as a presage to the direct assaults on U.S. soil: the 1993 attack on the World Trade Center, the 1998 bombings of American embassies in Kenya and Tanzania, and the 2000 attack on the USS *Cole* in Yemen, for example. In fact, virtually the only things that changed after the attacks on New York and Washington were the facts of the attacks themselves and the heightened awareness of the preexisting problem of terrorism that they created. Those changed perceptions, of course, spawned new policy emphases (the so-called war on terrorism and the extension of that war to such states as Iran, Iraq, and North Korea, for instance). The war on terrorism became the umbrella under which a variety of policy initiatives and changes have been justified.

These introductory remarks provide the context for this concluding chapter. Because it reflects the current debate, we will look sequentially at the roles of geopolitics and globalization, and where they intersect, using the events of September 11, 2001, as the watershed between their past and future statuses. The first part of each discussion will focus broadly on established facts and interpretations of those facts, and the discussion after the watershed will raise and examine questions and policy options.

THE FUTURE OF GEOPOLITICS AND TRADITIONAL NATIONAL SECURITY

Those analysts and policy makers who are principally concerned with geopolitical questions defined in national security terms have been on a roller coaster ride since the fall of the Berlin Wall. Once it was clear that the crumbling of Communism was irrevocable and that the flame that had necessitated and fueled the Cold War had been extinguished, national security concerns faded into the policy background, muscled out of the way in large measure by the globalizers. In the wake of the Cold War, defense budgets shrunk globally, as did military forces virtually worldwide, although this contraction was less pronounced in the United States than elsewhere. Still, the prospects of continued peace made traditional military concerns increasingly farfetched. Warnings about threats coming from rogue states such as North Korea, Iran, and Iraq from the neo-conservative right (President Bush's "axis of evil") and looming images of the proliferation of weapons of mass destruction and terrorism in those and other rogue states and organizations appeared to be desperate cries from segments of a national security community that was trying, not very successfully, to justify its continued relevance in a progressively less threatening world. Particularly within the military itself, the 1990s were a disheartening follow-on to the glory days of the Reagan build-up of the 1980s. Even the sumptuous accolades lavished on the military's success in the Persian Gulf War could provide only fleeting sustenance to the thin gruel of attention in the 1990s.

The terrorist watershed revived the national security community. President Bush (as well as then Vice President Gore) had campaigned on a promise of renewed interest in and funding for defense, and after the election, Secretary of Defense Rumsfeld had promised a thorough review and updating of American strategy and capabilities. In the months prior to September 2001, these rhetorical promises did not translate into concrete actions, causing some disquiet in the military and even muted criticisms of the new leadership. A return to center stage for the geopoliticians required some compelling event to recapture the public, and congressional, attention. September 11 provided that impetus; the threat had returned.

President Bush noticeably widened the mission for traditional national security instruments and promised to provide the tools for that expansion in mission and capability in his 2002 State of the Union message and subsequent budget request. The expansion of mission was made most vividly with his "axis of evil" designation of Iran, Iraq, and North Korea. Though not specifying what military action might be contemplated against any of them, he did promise that there would be "consequences" if any of them planned to engage in acts of terrorism or provided the wherewithal—notably WMD or ballistic missiles—to terrorist causes. Most ominously, he did not rule out preemptive, unilateral action, presumably including the use of military force against them. "I will not wait on events while dangers gather," he said in his speech. "The United States of America will not permit the world's most dangerous regimes to threaten us with the world's most destructive weapons." The seed of the Bush Doctrine contained in his 2002 *National Security Strategy* was thus sown. In order to implement this ambitious and expanded geopolitical agenda, the president proposed an increase of $46 billion in defense spending over the previous year's projection. Some of this increase would go directly to the homeland security program, while the rest would be devoted to selective modernization of the force congruent with the administration's vision of the conflict environment (see Amplification 13.1).

Although initial criticism of the president's defense agenda was muted by the patriotic glow of September 11, various objections have been voiced as time has

---

Amplification 13.1

THE SECDEF ON FUTURE FORCE

In an article in the May/June 2002 edition of *Foreign Affairs* (see Selected Bibliography for full citation), Secretary of Defense (SECDEF) Donald Rumsfeld laid out his vision of the future of American military force, in terms of both the kinds of conflicts in which we may become involved from now on (see *Challenge!* box in this chapter) and the kinds of challenges and problems we will encounter. His arguments are largely taken from the 2001 QDR, a document mandated by Congress and published over his name. Because the problems and challenges he presents will, among other things, presumably provide guidance to efforts to modernize the American military, they are worth noting. Six challenges are quoted here, though not in the order he presented them.

1. Flexibility and adaptation: "Preparing for the future will require new ways of thinking, and the development of forces and capabilities that can adapt quickly to new challenges and unexpected circumstances."

2. Environment of surprise: "In the years ahead, we will probably be surprised again by new adversaries who may also strike in unexpected ways."

3. Asymmetrical warfare: "Rather than building up conventional armies, navies, and air forces, they [our adversaries] will likely seek to challenge us asymmetrically by looking for vulnerabilities and trying to exploit them."

4. Terrorism: "Potential adversaries know that as an open society, the United States is vulnerable to new forms of terrorism."

5. Defense against the unknown: "Our challenge in this new century is a difficult one: to defend ourselves against the unknown, the uncertain, the unseen, and the unexpected."

6. As a result of numbers 1 through 5, transformation: "The Department of Defense must focus on achieving six transformational goals: first, to protect the U.S. homeland and our bases overseas; second, to protect and sustain power in distant theaters; third, to deny our enemies sanctuary; fourth, to protect our information networks from attack; fifth, to use information technology to link up different kinds of U.S. forces so that they can fight jointly; and sixth, to maintain unhindered access to space."

passed. It has been pointed out, for instance, that the proposal has a "back to the future" air to it. After the demise of the Soviet threat, defense planners had initiated a two-war scenario for force planning purposes. In this scenario, the planning problem was how to fight simultaneous wars with Iraq (a reinvasion of Kuwait) and North Korea (a reprise of the Korean War), thereby creating a "threat-based" planning process. The scenario was ridiculed as so implausible as to provide no realistic guidance, and threat-based planning was replaced by capability-based planning (as discussed in Chapter 7). The "axis of evil" seemed to revive the 1990s scenario, except that it was now tied to the overarching concern with terrorism. This was the neo-conservative dream realized in the Iraq war.

A second objection arose from the reactions of American allies and friends, many of whom saw the assertions of these scenarios as both excessively bellicose and unilateralist. Because the Bush administration emphasized what the United States would do, with apparent disregard for the opinions of others and even over their strongly voiced objections, many American friends and allies who have otherwise supported the American effort against terrorism were given pause. Singling out North Korea and Iran as among the "world's most dangerous regimes" was particularly curious to some foreign leaders and analysts. The harsh denunciations made quiet North Korean overtures to South Korea more difficult to sustain and reinforced the anti-Americanism of Iranian clergy, who were opposed to moderating influences in that country. Nevertheless, administration officials, led by Rumsfeld, downplayed apparent North Korean compliance with demands to shut down its nuclear and missile programs and asserted that Iran was still actively pursuing nuclear capability. Critics here and abroad openly came to question this bellicose approach to what seemed to them to be a political situation with diplomatic solutions. These criticisms were particularly intense as the administration publicly lobbied for support for invading Iraq despite universal international opposition.

The equation of geopolitics with terrorism through the extension of the antiterrorism campaign to cover a wider range of potential situations and actions guarantees that national security debates and advocacies will be tied, for the foreseeable future, to what is and is not the appropriate way to combat terrorism. Certainly the president has made terrorism suppression the centerpiece of his administration in the international realm. The question that will increasingly be raised is whether it is a durable and adequate basis for the consideration of how the United States will face the world geopolitically.

Consciously or not, this adjustment of national security direction moves the military from its traditional mooring in Western-style, symmetrical warfare toward a new focus on asymmetrical warfare. This reemphasis was temporarily lost within national security circles in the general prosperity over the most sizable peacetime budget increase proposal since the administration of Ronald Reagan.

At some point, however, the hard question of what vision of future war the administration holds (a version of which is raised in this chapter's *Challenge!* box) has to come to the forefront and must be reflected in budgetary and other priorities. The traditional military role of "preparing for and fighting the nation's wars" requires an assessment of the kinds of wars those are likely to be and how (and with what) we might be prepared to fight them. Granting that any answer will encompass more than one narrow type of conflict, there inevitably has to be some sense of focus—a one-size military probably does not fit all wars.

Are asymmetrical wars the future for which the national security community can and will prepare? Fighting foes who are employing asymmetrical means is certainly nothing new for the United States, although it is a form of warfare with which the United States has not had great success. The Vietnam conflict was an asymmetrical war, and most of the other American experiences in the developing world have had asymmetrical warfare components. If most of the places where the United States will find cause to pursue opponents in the war on terrorism are in the developing world—which they are—a robust asymmetrical capability may make sense, especially since none of these potential foes will willingly confront U.S. forces on our preferred terms.

It is not at all clear that the traditional military community that has been signing up with apparent enthusiasm for the war on terrorism truly accepts the implications of such a major reorientation of its priorities. The military aspect (phase one) of the campaign in Afghanistan had the effect of shielding the need to take harsh stock of what elevating terrorism to the center stage of our concerns and preparations implies; the more restrained success of rounding up Al Qaeda (phase two) may be the real future.

If the real opponent in Afghanistan has always been Usama bin Laden and his Al Qaeda cohorts and if countering threats like those posed by bin Laden is the model of what the war on terrorism will be, then the positive lessons of imposing symmetrical solutions with some asymmetrical embroidery are highly misleading. The Taliban was swept away fairly traditionally as the prelude to hunting down and destroying Al Qaeda, but the major quarry eluded the effort. Bin Laden remains at large, and the United States has admitted since April 2002 that it had little idea where he might be; as Rumsfeld put it, the trail had gone cold. Even Bush implicitly admitted the limited success of asymmetrical counterterrorism efforts to date in his 2002 State of the Union address, when he declared: "yet tens of thousands of trained terrorists are still at large. These enemies view the entire world as a battlefield, and we must pursue them wherever they are. So long as training camps operate, so long as nations harbor terrorists, freedom is at risk, and America and our allies must not, and will not, allow it."

Is this how to focus American national security assets? Are the virtual moonscapes of parts of Afghanistan and the steamy jungles of the Philippines archipelago the battlefields where American forces will operate to track down and destroy terrorist cells? In its February 4, 2002, edition, *Newsweek* identified Somalia, Malaysia, and Indonesia as likely breeding and training grounds for religiously motivated terrorist organizations. Given the disaster of the early 1990s, does the United States really want to reenter Somalia to attack shadowy terrorist cells? How many of the 7,500 islands of the Indonesian archipelago are we willing to assault to defeat terrorism? In other words, how far are we willing to pursue an emphasis on eradicating terrorism in the world?

If the war on terrorism is indeed the focus of American national security policy, that clearly implies a reorientation of the national security structure, and it is not at all clear that the national security establishment embraces or is ever likely to embrace such a change. Traditional military force is likely to be deemphasized in such a strategy, as other assets such as intelligence and border security are enhanced to deal with different aspects of this semimilitary problem. Within the military and beyond, elements such as special forces—those "snake eaters" who have long been the pariahs of the services in which they are housed and who are now apparently augmented by CIA operatives carrying the special forces designation—suddenly become central players, while more traditional combat specialties are downgraded in importance. How many tanks, for instance, does the military need to pursue terrorists in Malaysia? How many Crusader artillery pieces (assuming they are ever built) can be meaningfully employed in the jungles of some far-flung corner of the Indonesian archipelago? Does the use of nonmilitary personnel, such as CIA agents in special forces roles, somehow further muddy the conceptual waters about war, as it appeared to when a CIA element assassinated a suspected Al Qaeda leader in Yemen in late 2002?

In the midst of the strong emotional response to the September 11 incidents, it has been easy to commit primary American assets and priorities to the war on terrorism and thereby appear to have created a focus for strategy that had been missing in the post–Cold War period. That effort creates an apparent basis, much as the Soviet threat did during the Cold War, around which to orient national security. Terrorists become the geopolitical equivalent of the Red menace. If we still lack a "peer competitor" in the shadowy world of terrorism, at least we have a compelling opponent.

But does the amorphous face of terrorism provide a firm enough grounding for national security policy, or is it, rather, a prominent part of a more comprehensive policy? In the short term, the campaign against terrorism will remain in the spotlight. But if terrorism suppression succeeds and we gradually lose our fear, so will our fervor for the effort fade back in the popular mind into the more traditional, limited role that countering terrorism has occupied in the past. There are several reasons for this likelihood.

The first is that a national strategy that has terrorism as its lynchpin will almost certainly meet growing domestic opposition if its implications are implemented with relish and enthusiasm. The most likely opponent will be the military itself, for several reasons. For one thing, a national security strategy based in countering terrorism relegates the military to a reduced stature in the national security universe. Even Secretary Rumsfeld has admitted that in the overall campaign against terrorism, military force has a limited role, since terrorists are rarely organized and seldom fight in ways for which regular armed forces are appropriate. The dispatch of several special forces A-teams to assist the Philippine armed forces in tracking down jungle-based alleged terrorist insurgents is a much more likely model than the conventional effort early in Afghanistan.

This effect on roles and missions is unlikely to be lost on the more traditional military specialties, especially when the budgetary implications of developing asymmetrical forces collide with plans to modernize traditional forces. Special forces are a lightning rod; their role has always been the stepchild of the armed forces since their conceptual formation in World War II in the form of the Marine Raiders (which the Marine command structure opposed) and in American assistance to the Greek government during the Greek Civil War. When the special forces were formed in the 1950s and became the Green Berets, they were largely shunned within the army, derided as "snake eaters," to suggest that they were little more than fringe psychopaths performing minimally useful military tasks. In Vietnam, they reached their nadir when special forces became implicated in Operation Phoenix, a program of assassination of village figures who cooperated with the Viet Cong. Yet they are the centerpiece of the war on terror.

Moreover, the nature of the military role played by the armed forces in a terrorism-based strategy is likely to breed other opposition in the longer run. One source of opposition will come from the extensive activation of the National Guard and the reserves whenever a terrorist problem arises. In the immediate wake of the terrorist attacks of September 11, reservists were activated without complaint as part of the subsequent patriotic fervor. If follow-on terrorist attacks do not occur but reservists continue to be asked to sacrifice, their willingness will almost certainly wear thin over time. Moreover, the primary use of military forces in the day-to-day campaign against terrorism is in mundane tasks such as guarding public facilities and athletic events. The question will almost certainly be raised of whether this duty overly deploys forces, committing them to less-than-vital concerns and eroding their effectiveness as combat soldiers—charges that have been levied against using soldiers as peacekeepers. It is ironic that President Bush campaigned on a pledge to end such "misuse" of armed forces, and in less than a year he created the basis for the same problem.

A terrorism-based strategy also has problems of coherence. Declaring war on a phenomenon (terrorism) provides ambiguous guidance in a way that focusing on a concrete opponent does not, and even supporters of the terrorism emphasis have admitted that one of their problems is specifying opponents. Since the military function in the campaign to suppress terrorism is not completely clear and may, in some cases, be decidedly marginal, the strategy does not provide clear guidance for those who define military roles and missions and prepare service members to conduct hostilities regarding who they are fighting and what they are meant to do. Defining force development in terms of a capability-based force (as the QDR does) simply evades the questions of against whom and for what purpose those forces exist and is bound to create confusion and exacerbate misunderstanding and controversy about the appropriate use of force in the contemporary environment.

Negative international reaction to such an emphasis is likely as well. Although the United States' closest allies expressed sincere sympathy for the terrorist attacks and the resultant action in Afghanistan, the extension of the campaign to other places and for other purposes—overthrowing Saddam Hussein, for instance—created a mounting level of dissent. In a March 2002 column, Steven Erlanger suggested the basis for allied concern about elevating terrorism to central status in American defense policy. The fear he attributes to NATO sources is that the United States is becoming so much more powerful than everyone else physically (a trend that can only be accentuated by increased spending), especially technologically, that we no longer need the assistance of our allies but can, and will, increasingly act on our own, regardless of their sentiments. The way the United States operated essentially by itself in Afghanistan and in Iraq is simultaneously a compliment to the prowess of American forces and a fear held in many foreign capitals that this ability will only reinforce the American tendency toward unilateral, imprudent action. The deeper implication could be a negative impact on alliance cohesion at a time when it is universally conceded that greater international cooperation is necessary to deal with the threat posed by terrorism.

Will the problem of terrorism provide a substitute for the Soviet threat of the Cold War, a mooring around which strategy can be developed? In the short run, the answer appears to be yes. Terrorism is a fickle problem, however, in the sense that a simple—even tactical—lull in the phenomenon by the forces of terror will almost certainly erode our resolve and cause us to defocus on terrorism and refocus on something else. The focus on terrorism works better conceptually as part of a broader problem such as developmental imbalances or poverty than it does as the central peg of strategy. In other words, a longer-term strategy is probably better served by a more concrete and durable problem.

THE FUTURE OF GLOBALIZATION

There is an old saying that anything that appears too good to be true probably is. During the early and middle 1990s, this cliché could easily have been applied to the globalizing economy. Accompanied by lavish predictions of continuing economic expansion, prosperity, and attendant political democratization, the progress of a revitalized global economy seemed inexorable. In some respectable economics publications, there was even speculation that the American-led new economy was so robust that it might have surmounted the historical business cycle of boom and bust, replacing it with an ever-expanding economic condition. All this has indeed proven too good to be true.

Any assessment of the future of globalization must begin by asking why its promise was not fulfilled to the extent predicted by its most expansive advocates. The general conclusion is that globalization was oversold as a panacea for the troubles of the world. It was advertised as the solution to the world's economic and political ills, which was almost certainly more than could be expected of it. The 1990s round of globalization foundered on overly inflated expectations. If globalization is to rebound in the current atmosphere of geopolitical dominance, its champions must learn from the past what is realistic and what is not. How great and in what form can we expect the reasonable contribution of globalization to the international condition to be?

The overinflation of expectations had both economic and political dimensions. The triumph of the philosophy of free trade in the United States and elsewhere provided much of the fuel to pull the global economy (including the United States) out of the recession of the late 1980s and early 1990s and combined with a wave of national legislation and enforced international practice in deregulation and privatization to help propel the go-go 1990s in the economic realm. Globalization was advertised as the high tide that raised all boats in the water, and the answer to any country's ills was adoption of something like Friedman's "golden straightjacket" (the applied version of the American model). Because the economy had become global and had grown to such an enormous size, it appeared to be insulated from the vicissitudes of economic downturn anywhere. Globalization was going to be a universal positive-sum game, a win-win situation for all who partook of it.

This optimism was captured in the Clinton administration's foreign policy of engagement and enlargement. As suggested earlier, that policy replaced traditional national security considerations with economic globalization as the centerpiece of foreign policy. The operative principle was free trade to promote economic growth and globalization; states engaged in the global economy could be added to the enlarged "circle of market democracies." Economics and political development were thus woven together as part of the emerging "democratic peace."

This assessment, of course, has proved overly optimistic, even romantic. Deregulation and privatization—the economic *and* political heart of Newt Gingrich's "contract with America" in 1994—coincided with and arguably aided the economic expansion, but it also created the atmosphere in which the infamous Enron Corporation could fashion and operate its financial deception until its Ponzi scheme collapsed in late 2001 and was followed by other revelations that were partly caused by overly zealous deregulation. In the midst of the great expansion, the possibility that much of the good times was the result of bubble economies that would eventually burst was swept aside as old thinking in the "new economy." The expanding list of countries whose leaders reached office through the ballot box created a rarified atmosphere that suggested the triumph of political democracy (Francis Fukuyama's "end of history"). At the same time, the possibility that economic globalization might not lead to democratization, but that, instead, globalization might have, as Joseph S. Nye Jr. called it, a "democracy deficit" was underplayed.

Unfettered optimism belied history and even the views of its champions. A wave of economic interdependence and growing trade had washed through the international system at the turn of the twentieth century, had produced the same kind of euphoric predictions, and had been given the lie in the human bloodbath of World War I. At the same time, even such ardent supporters as Friedman warned that there were countries that either would reject globalization or simply could not compete successfully.

The storm clouds were lurking only slightly below the horizon. In 1997, the first warning sign appeared in the form of the East Asian crisis, and it was followed by a series of events that culminated in the terrorist attacks of September 2001 and the corporate scandals of 2001–02. These fissures represented warning signs about the expansive optimism of the early 1990s. Although one might quibble with the selections, I have chosen five "lessons" that arise from events and occurrences, starting in 1997, that illustrate questions about the universal inevitability and desirability of globalization:

1. *The effects of globalization are not always positive.* This was the underlying message of the East Asian financial crisis. For half a decade or more, the secret to prosperity and progress for developing countries was adoption of the values of the globalizing economy and admission into its organizations, such as the APEC or the WTO. Prior to 1997, no country had ever been seriously hurt by being part of globalization. As the crisis spread through eastern Asia and resulted not in instant remuneration to minimize the effects but instead in belt-tightening demands accompanied by painful structural reform, the possibility that there could be losers as well as winners in the globalizing economy had to be weighed. The unvarnished optimism of the 1990s lost some of its luster in the process. In its most extreme impact, the crisis produced political upheaval in Indonesia, resulting in the toppling of the thirty-two-year Suharto regime (in itself not an entirely bad thing) and leaving many Indonesians wondering if they wanted to rejoin the globalization system.

2. *The business cycle still exists.* This was a lesson that was at least partially induced by the East Asian crisis as it swept through the rest of the world. Although markets in most places (notably the United States) did rebound from the impact of financial failure in Asia, the crisis did contribute to a general increase in caution about the seemingly endless expansion of the global economy. Chastened by the effects of the crisis and the subsequent slowing of the global economy, there has been a growing realization that the most effusive promotions of globalization were hyperbole; nothing as fundamental as changing the basic nature of economic life (the business cycle) has occurred. The global recession of 2001 and beyond has simply added to this sense of caution.

3. *Some people and groups do not like globalization.* During the heyday of globalization in the 1990s, there was virtually no organized dissent about whether globalization was a good idea or whether its spread should be opposed. Certainly there was discussion, largely academic in nature, about the compatibility of globalization with different people's values, but most of the criticism was isolated. H. Ross Perot's "great sucking sound" depiction of American jobs disappearing into Mexico after NAFTA was implemented came in the midst of an apparently unstinting run of global expansion. After the East Asian debacle, however, the opponents became very public, demonstrating—sometimes violently—at meetings of the various forums that promoted globalization values. These *rejectionists* have clearly put the defenders of globalization on the public relations defensive. The emergence of this opposition has further dampened the heat of advocacy. When the World Economic Forum met at New York's Waldorf-Astoria Hotel in February 2002, for instance, the event was much more subdued than when globalization burst on the public scene at the initial APEC meeting in Seattle in 1993.

4. *Some places and groups violently oppose and resist the concept and application of globalization.* One of the underlying lessons of Usama bin Laden and Al Qaeda's terrorist attacks had to do with why they launched them. Although these motives have

been widely vilified as not justifying the means, the underlying theme of bin Laden's hatred for the United States is its desecrating effect on the environment in which he wants to practice and enforce his own vision of Islam. Americans desecrate the holy lands of Arabia by making them Western, a part of the globalization culture that the Americans personify. Bin Laden's assault on the United States may indeed be a single application of Samuel P. Huntington's "clash of civilization" thesis that future conflict will occur where different cultures with diverging values come into opposition. At a minimum, however, the fundamentalist Islam that bin Laden portrays himself as representing demonstrates that the values and aspirations of globalization are not universally held. Although one can argue that the peculiar values that bin Laden and his supporters adhere to are isolated and unique, they still demonstrate that the appeal of globalization is not universal.

5. *The rules of globalization are not as well established as formerly advertised.* Since the East Asian crisis, the Western, essentially American model has been the benchmark by which economic virtue has been measured, and the basis for that ascendancy is the transparency and rectitude of American capitalism. What distinguished the American from the Asian model was the emphasis on honesty and trustworthiness that firms and governments demonstrated under the American model and that provided the transparency and openness in which investment and commerce could flourish. That assumption was at least partially laid low by the 2002 corporate scandals. Among the apparent lessons that have emerged was that transparency failed; the extensive deregulation of the accounting industry allowed collusion and misrepresentation in ways and to extents not witnessed anywhere since the S&L crisis of the 1980s. That Enron and others could get away with their misdeeds as long as they did punctured the sanctimony of American pronouncements of virtue in the management of our economy. The United States can no longer seek to impose its rules on the basis of rectitude with the same confidence it did before, because the scandals exposed another, darker side to the "new economy." The eventual resolution of the issues raised by the scandal may or may not result in useful reforms that can become part of global standards, as the S&L outcome did. In any case, blind acceptance of the American vision of globalization took a clear shot.

Most of these dampening effects were in place or in the offing when the events of September 11, 2001, occurred, and the Enron scandal only added fuel to the antiglobalization fire. Of the two events, the terrorist attacks were clearly the most dramatic and influential. The attacks certainly changed the nature and the character of the debate about the American place in the world and how to secure it. The national foreign policy agenda is now, and for the foreseeable future will remain, a national security agenda, not a globalization agenda. The attacks on the World Trade Center were directed against probably the most visible symbol of globalization in the world. People of eighty nationalities were killed in the attack and collapse of the two buildings; almost all were there doing the work of a globalizing economy in one way or another. The events threw the global economy a blow, and it was reflected on stock exchanges—the lifelines of the globalization system—for the rest of 2001 and 2002 and into 2003.

Depending on whether there are more instances like the 2002 scandals and how they play out in the public realm, the impact on globalization could be as profound as or more so than the terrorist attacks. In many ways, the scandals personified the ultimate new, globalizing economic enterprise. Enron and the others proved to be bubble enterprises—elaborate shells with no substance, built on dishonest accounting procedures that were a byproduct of the deregulation and privatization provisions of the 1980s. Revelations of insider advantage, cronyism, and corruption sound remarkably like the kinds of charges leveled against Asian companies that compliance with American-inspired rules were supposed to cure. In light of these scandals, how can the next American-inspired IMF official confront the economics ministers of developing countries and tell them that they need to root out corruption in their systems?

What do these experiences mean for the future of globalization? It is premature to assess this in detail, but two points seem apparent. One is that the next wave of globalization, when it occurs, will be structurally different from the globalization of the 1990s. One of the principal differences will be that the United States will be less morally advantaged in shaping the evolving rules. The scandals here robbed the United States of its virtue. That is bad news for Americans who believe that only we can provide global economic leadership; it is good news to foreigners who are looking for a more level intellectual and moral playing field on which to compete with the United States.

The other effect is that the next wave of globalization will have to be tied to, rather than distinct from, geopolitics and national security. Geopolitics is back and will remain important as long as two conditions hold: Americans must retain an interest in defeating terrorism, and terrorism must prove resilient, a problem worth our concentrated effort. Both conditions are likely, and the geopolitical task will center on how to stretch and ultimately break that resilience.

WHERE GLOBALIZATION AND GEOPOLITICS MEET

President George W. Bush has committed himself, and thus much of the national agenda, to the primacy of the geopolitical pursuit of international terrorism for the remainder of his term. His neo-conservative version of *realpolitik* contends that this is the most serious problem facing the United States and the world, and that as long as this menace continues, other areas of foreign and national security policy must remain subservient to the eradication of this scourge against mankind. Among the former emphases of policy that are subordinated in the determined pursuit of this foreign policy is the emphasis on expanded globalization, including the aggressive pursuit of market economics and democracy.

Given the sinister, ubiquitous nature of the terrorist problem, this emphasis is likely to be, or certainly can be construed to be, highly durable across time. Even if American and allied efforts are successful in corralling Usama bin Laden and dismantling his Al Qaeda network, doing so will not be the same as eradicating terrorism. As long as there are disaffected individuals and groups who focus the source of

Amplification 13.2

FRIEDMAN AND KAPLAN REPRISED

Thomas Friedman and Robert Kaplan, the *New York Times* foreign correspondent and the *Atlantic Monthly* correspondent first highlighted in Chapter 7, have had an ongoing dialogue regarding the future of the international system. The March/April 2002 *Foreign Affairs* featured a give-and-take session between them, and some of their comments there are excerpted here.

Kaplan agrees with Friedman about the importance of globalization, but not its consequences: "Tom wrote that globalization does not end geopolitics. That's the key. Globalization is not necessarily good news; it's just *the* news."

Friedman partially agrees, adding some nuances to his view of globalization. "The first thing to understand about globalization is that, oddly enough, it's not global. It affects different regions in different ways, and it links different countries in different ways." He also argues the basis of globalization is misunderstood: "The dirty little secret about globalization is that the way to succeed is to focus on the fundamentals. It's not about bandwidth or about modems. It's about reading, writing, and arithmetic."

Kaplan has a different set of concerns about the dynamics of change. Among those dynamics, he emphasizes two: "First, we are seeing a youth bulge in many of the most unstable countries. And as we know from television, one thing that unites political unrest everywhere is that it's carried out by young males." He cites the West Bank, Gaza, Nigeria, Zambia, and Kenya as particularly troubling examples. "Another factor is resource scarcity—the amount of potable water available throughout the Middle East."

Friedman also points out a danger of globalization introduced in Chapter 12: "We also saw the forces of globalization on September 11, 2001. Again, globalization goes both ways. It can threaten democracies as well as strengthen them. But on net, globalization will be a force for more openness, more rule of law, and more opportunities for people to enjoy personal freedoms and challenge authorities."

their misery on the United States, terrorism will be a worldwide problem, since some other states will likely be both targets and nurturers of terrorists. The question is how visible and threatening terrorism remains, and thus what priority can and should reasonably be assigned to fighting it.

The president has an interest in retaining this focus. Prior to the attacks of September 11, 2001, his administration had no clear, overriding theme in the area of foreign and national security policy. He had campaigned on revitalizing the military, but his first budget request included a smaller increase in defense spending than Democratic nominee Al Gore had promised in his campaign. To many, the early Bush foreign policy ship seemed to lack any semblance of a rudder.

Responding to terrorism brought a clarity to the Bush administration's national security policy that it had previously lacked. One can question whether the "war on terrorism" label is useful, but it certainly galvanized public opinion—including the support of the normally more critical print and electronic media—behind the effort.

The focus has the virtues of being both plausible and enduring. The president has clearly established the political high ground in the national security debate with this effort, and there seems little danger he or his neo-conservative advisers will relinquish it, unless there is a negative backlash as the Iraqi occupation lengthens.

Is there any danger of overplaying the very strong hand the president holds? In the short run, the answer has been no. One of three things could change that assessment, however. One is what we might call the "cry wolf" scenario. Since September 11, the White House, usually through homeland security secretary Ridge, has issued periodic color-coded alerts about possible impending terrorist events that have not materialized, and has engaged in highly complex, expensive efforts to insulate very public events such as the Super Bowl and the Winter Olympics in Utah. In the latter cases, it cannot be demonstrated that the efforts were responsible for preventing untoward occurrences, partly as a matter of logic (the fallacy of affirming the consequent—we did this to prevent X, X did not occur, therefore the effort was successful) and partly because revealing how a plot was foiled would probably compromise future efforts. At some point, however, warnings followed by the absence of consequences may begin to look suspicious, which may result in an erosion of support.

The second danger is in overextending the emphasis. In the months following the terrorist attacks, virtually all administration policy seemed to be justified as part of the war on terrorism. The need for budget deficits was rationalized on the basis that the war necessitated whatever efforts were necessary, including paying the country's bills with borrowed money. It was further argued that deficit spending is common during wartime. The fact that there was nothing resembling a war being fought to justify deficits after the Afghan military campaign ended in December 2001 and before the Iraq war began in 2003 did not seem troublesome to many Americans. Similarly, the proposed 2003 federal budget requested the biggest defense spending increase since the Reagan administration in the 1980s. The justification, of course, was to help prosecute the war on terrorism, including its argued extension to Iraq. The fact that most of the increases would fund weapons that could scarcely be argued as antiterrorism weaponry also did not seem worrisome.

A third possibility is that the focus will run against contradictory international conditions, as it appeared to when the administration finally involved itself publicly in the Israeli–Palestinian confrontation in spring 2003. The focus on terrorism had arguably contributed to American inattention to the growing crisis in the Holy Land. As engagement proceeded, Secretary Powell and President Bush discovered that those in the region were more interested in some form of equitable outcome than in the American terrorism campaign. When the United States appeared to tilt toward the Israeli campaign on the West Bank, angry regional leaders even came out in support of Saddam Hussein, the next designated target of the war on terrorism, declaring in an Arab League resolution that an attack on any Arab state was to be considered an attack on them all. A variant of this focus is that the emphasis on global democracy will be weakened as the United States embraces opponents of democracy who join the antiterrorist campaign, as several Central Asian former Soviet republics have done.

Where does the promotion of globalization fit into the policy equation? It has not disappeared altogether. In his 2002 State of the Union message, the president did repeat his plea to Congress to be granted trade promotion authority (it was subsequently granted). However, the growing stain of the 2002 scandals seemed likely to preoccupy relevant committees of both houses of Congress at least for the remainder of the 2002 session, although in an increasingly quiet way. Globalization will remain on the periphery as long as the emphasis on a state of war is accepted by the people.

There is a glimmer of optimism about the resurgence of a policy emphasis on globalization within the American political system. The campaign against terrorism has pushed aside the emphasis of the Clinton administration and the United Nations on peacekeeping for humanitarian purposes. Peacekeeping missions to resuscitate failed states—the victims of bloody internal wars—remain in place (in Kosovo, for instance) and continue to involve American forces where they had been committed prior to the shift in emphasis caused by the terrorist episode. The current administration has shown little interest in expanding that participation, however, and continues to deride the idea when it arises. The commitment to the war on terrorism provides political cover to avoid future entanglements under the humanitarian banner. Military action against the states designated as the "axis of evil" in Iraq and possibly beyond further justifies trying to avoid committing U.S. forces to humanitarian-based peacekeeping, but the situation in Liberia in July 2003 quickly tested that policy.

The glimmer of optimism comes in the form of state-building in the service of the campaign against terrorism rather than for purely humanitarian reasons. The prototype and test case, of course, is Afghanistan, since rebuilding the Afghan state was part of the original public American rationale for intervening and remaining in that country. The dynamics and effects of state-building in Afghanistan are likely to be essentially identical to those involved in humanitarian state-building, though obviously customized to differentiate between the political and economic conditions in Afghanistan and, say, Kosovo. The participants will be different: European organizations such as the EU or OSCE will not likely be present in Afghanistan, although much of the assistance will have to come from their members. The problems of state-building in Kosovo and Afghanistan are likewise different, there being, for instance, no direct equivalent of the tribal cleavages found in Afghanistan in Kosovo. Nevertheless, the tasks of infrastructure development and the like will be similar in concept and design; if there is a difference, the effort in Afghanistan will have to begin from a more modest developmental base.

If these efforts are successful, the outcomes should also be similar, if for different reasons. Successful state-building in Afghanistan, as in Kosovo and elsewhere, is intended to produce stable, prosperous countries that become productive, reliable members of the international system. In the case of Kosovo, the reason for producing such a state is to increase the stability of the Balkans and thus reinforce the peace in Europe—in addition, of course, to humanitarian motives to improve the lot of the Kosovars. In Afghanistan, the purpose is less altruistic: to create a state and society whose members are resistant to terrorists (draining the swamp), in addition to a humanitarian concern for the Afghan people.

Part of the strategy of state-building for either reason is to make target countries attractive to the private investors who are at the heart of the spread of globalization.

A Taliban-dominated Afghanistan that forcefully removed half its human resources (women) from the workforce, destroyed the physical and intellectual infrastructure, and ruled through a system of random violence and repression was not going to attract foreign direct investment in the form of cash or imported industry. A democratizing, progressive, economically developing Afghanistan operating under the rule of law presumably not only will be resistant to the incursions of terrorist groups but also will attract outside investors who can reinforce growing stability. Achieving this will not be easy. The limited lessons of humanitarian state-building apply, and the principal lesson may be the extreme difficulty—in some cases, the impossibility—of getting from the prior condition of instability and despair to a subsequent condition of peace and stability. In the case of state-building for humanitarian purposes, there are questions about the international will to see the difficult course through to its uncertain conclusions. Whether state-building to destroy terrorism will prove a more durable motivation for confronting the difficulties remains to be seen.

Afghanistan is, to repeat, the testing ground for similar efforts in Iraq. The plan for Afghanistan is the replica for implementing the neo-conservative dream that an imposed democracy can take root in Iraq and become a model for the region that other Islamic states will emulate (the rationale for benign hegemony). The experience in Afghanistan through summer 2003 contains some caution about American willingness to follow through and actually engage in state-building. If the same thing happens in Iraq, what becomes of the neo-conservative vision?

The idea of combining globalization and the geopolitical instinct to undermine terrorism demonstrates that the two forces are neither necessarily contradictory nor incompatible. Which force is the dominant concern at any point in time will certainly reflect international realities and subsequent policy priorities. The 1990s offered no overarching security challenges that seemed to dictate the supremacy of traditional national security concerns, although one can argue that more concern earlier on with the growing terrorist threat represented by bin Laden would have been appropriate and might have prevented the events of September 2001. The reality of terrorism similarly dictated a concentration on more traditional national considerations. Although our preferences will influence the environment to some extent, events beyond our control will also help set the agenda. There is nothing profoundly new in that situation.

CONCLUSION: WHAT MAKES US SECURE?
WHAT MAKES US PROSPEROUS?

The interests of states and their citizens are various and hierarchical. The most basic purpose of the state is to maintain its own survival and to protect its citizens from harm or death. A state that cannot perform that basic function has very little utility to anyone and clearly cannot pursue other, more mundane priorities. First things always come first.

The physical survival of the United States and the protection of its citizens from harm has hardly ever been a lively concern for the U.S. government. For almost all of its existence, the United States has been invulnerable to threats that imperil our existence and our safety. The greatest reason for the trauma of the terrorist attacks was that they exposed to us that our sense of invulnerability to harm was mistaken; American soil *could* be attacked and American lives taken without the apparent American ability to prevent it. We quickly experienced what most the citizens of other states had known for a long time: There is no such thing as absolute security in this world.

Security has both a physical and a psychological dimension, of course. The physical sense has to do with the absolute physical ability to provide safety from harm and destruction. For most of American history, broad oceans and friendly or weak neighbors meant that there was little, if any, physical peril for the United States except when the country extended itself and thus placed itself at risk (the acquisition of Hawaii and the Philippines in the 1890s are primary examples). Physical security is, of course, the most basic, fundamental form of security. Technically, the U.S. ability to guarantee our physical existence has been at risk since the then Soviet Union fielded nuclear-armed ballistic missiles capable of reaching our country with no means to intercept them. That prospect has become abstract for most Americans and has faded with the demise of the Soviet Union and the absence of plausible enmity between America and Russia. Usama bin Laden demonstrated that our absolute security could be breached and that Americans could be subject to harm on our own soil.

Knowing that one is vulnerable changes the way one looks at the world, and we have just recently come to that realization. If Americans seem more obsessed with the consequences of the terrorist attacks than other peoples, it is largely because we have recently lost part of our national innocence. Afghans, to cite our current focus, learned a long time ago what the consequences of geography (occupying a major trade route) can be. The shocking loss of invulnerability to harm may have caused us to overreact about the extent of our vulnerability, making us equate vulnerability to harm to more fundamental survival dangers.

The other form of security is psychological—what makes us *feel* secure or safe. In the absence of direct physical threats to security, the American debate over national security historically has concentrated, by and large, on the conditions that make us feel safe and allow us to prosper. The fact that the United States has done almost all of its fighting since its establishment overseas somewhere (the major exception being the Civil War, when we fought one another) is not a coincidence. Certainly there were important American interests involved, for instance, in American participation in the world wars, but it stretches credulity to maintain that the physical survival of the United States was one of them. Life would have certainly been more difficult for American commerce and security with a German-dominated Europe in 1918 or 1945 or a Japanese-ruled East Asia and the Pacific in the 1940s, but the country would have survived.

Most of our other uses of armed force have been deployments of choice rather than necessity, reflecting the distinction between the physical and psychological dimensions of security. The bulk of the national security debate since the end of World War II has revolved around questions about what makes us feel secure—once the necessity of dealing with the Soviet nuclear threat was removed by the establishment of the condition of mutual nuclear deterrence. In the post–Cold War world, the nuclear threat faded in plausibility and (partially) in capability, and major threats to other U.S. interests did not emerge to dominate the agenda. In that atmosphere, the emphasis could move to those conditions that make for a better *quality* of life and to economic well-being through globalization as our major focus of concern. It was during the 1990s that notions such as economic and environmental *security* entered the public discourse, and we made war on drugs, not on Communism or some other more traditional national security problem. The concern was clearly on the psychological dimension of security.

In intellectual terms, the great impact of the 2001 terrorist attacks was to move the center of the debate back in the direction of the physical realm of security. In our collective shock, the extent of the threat was probably overdrawn: Usama bin Laden and his cohorts could not destroy the United States or topple our government, terrorist threats that would be far beyond the capabilities and aspirations of any terrorist organization. Rather, the attacks demonstrated that our physical security was not absolute and that steps to minimize future breaches of our physical security were necessary and occupied the highest priority within the security realm.

As time and recent experience have demonstrated, the national security debate is now defined in terms of homeland security, a term almost entirely missing from the dialogue on security prior to the terrorist events. Other security concerns have slowly returned as well. The Bush administration has led this trend, trying to maintain the focus on terrorism by progressively widening the range of concerns that fall under the rubric of homeland security to encompass more conventional national security concerns such as force modernization.

So what makes us secure? In 1989, before the Poles elected a non-Communist government and the Berlin Wall fell, the answer was the deterrence of the Soviet Union and the avoidance of World War III—keeping the Cold War cold. For the next dozen or so years, the absence of a peer competitor allowed us to relax our focus on military threats (except, of course, during the Persian Gulf War) and to turn our attentions to making ourselves prosperous—the ascendancy of the globalization system. The post–Cold War world allowed us to extend the "long peace" of the Cold War; there has been no major war involving the largest powers fighting one another since World War II.

Did the terrorist attacks of September 11 end the long peace and usher in a fundamentally different set of concerns? Clearly, the tectonic shift of 2001 has moved the debate about safety and prosperity from the clearly dominant role of prosperity to much more of an emphasis on the physical dimension of security. That is novel for Americans because it is a perspective with which we have not had to grapple very often in the past. What makes us secure now includes vigorously backed assurances that our physical safety against terrorists can be reasonably ensured and that our vulnerability to harm can be contained, if not eliminated altogether. Until that issue is resolved to the satisfaction of most Americans, we are reluctant to move back completely to an emphasis on what makes us feel prosperous.

The Cold War lasted roughly forty-five years. It took us seventeen years until the Cuban missile crisis of 1962 to understand that the principal objective of that competition had to be to avoid a system-threatening nuclear World War III that might destroy us all. It took another twenty-eight years to complete the job of defusing that

Challenge!

Visions of the Violent Future

In his *Foreign Affairs* article, Secretary of Defense Donald H. Rumsfeld also lists eight "lessons from recent experiences that apply to the future":

First, wars in the twenty-first century will increasingly require all elements of national power: economic, diplomatic, financial, law enforcement, intelligence, and both overt and covert military operations.

Second, the ability of forces to communicate and operate seamlessly on the battlefield will be critical to success.

Third, our policy of accepting help from any country . . . is enabling us to maximize both other countries' cooperation and our effectiveness against the enemy.

Fourth, wars can benefit from coalitions of the willing, to be sure, but they should not be fought by committee.

Fifth, defending the United States requires prevention and sometimes preemption.

Sixth, rule nothing out—including ground forces.

Seventh, getting U.S. special forces on the ground early dramatically increases the effectiveness of an air campaign.

And finally, be straight with the American people.

What do you think of the SECDEF's list? How is it different from past formulations of the American posture? Is it more aggressive, more unilateralist? What are the implications for the kinds of forces the United States should develop for the future (in other words, what are its implications for force modernization)? How many of these lessons applied in Iraq? Finally, based on your knowledge, do you agree with this vision of the future?

problem. The post–Cold War world did not last as long, and the fact that we never found any name for it other than what it was not (it was *not* the Cold War) may suggest that we never entirely comprehended or adjusted to it.

And now the ground has shifted again. The shift has been dramatic, even traumatic, and it has caused us to react strongly. Like the end of World War II and the end of the Cold War, there will be a period of adjustment to new realities. The perspective of 2002 is probably too close to the fault line to see what has profoundly and fundamentally changed and what has not. The first answer to what will make us secure in the future is dealing with terrorism, but that is almost certainly not the total answer. The pendulum of central concern with physical and psychological security will continue to swing. We have not seen the last of geopolitics or of globalization.

SELECTED BIBLIOGRAPHY

Bhagwati, Jagdish. "Coping with Antiglobalization." *Foreign Affairs* 81, 1 (January/February 2002), 2–7.

Erlanger, Steven. "Europe's Military Gap." *New York Times* (national edition), March 16, 2002, A1, A4.

Friedman, Thomas L. "The End of NATO?" *New York Times*, February 3, 2002, A27.

———. *The Lexus and the Olive Tree: Understanding Globalization*. New York: Farrar, Straus & Giroux, 1999.

———, and Robert D. Kaplan. "A Debate between Thomas Friedman and Robert Kaplan." *Foreign Policy* (electronic edition), March/April 2002.

Fukuyama, Francis. *The End of History and the Last Man*. New York: Free Press, 1992.

Gaddis, John Lewis. "Setting Right a Dangerous World." *The Chronicle Review* (electronic edition) 48, 18 (January 11, 2002).

Hirsh, Michael. "Bush and the World." *Foreign Affairs* 81, 5 (September/October 2002), 18–43.

Huntington, Samuel P. *Clash of Civilizations: The Debate*. New York: Council on Foreign Relations Press, 1993.

———. *The Third Wave: Democratization in the Late Twentieth Century*. Norman: University of Oklahoma Press, 1991.

"Is Globalisation Doomed?" *Economist* 360, 8241 (September 29, 2001), 14–15.

Mandelbaum, Michael. "The Inadequacy of American Power." *Foreign Affairs* 81, 5 (September/October 2002), 61–73.

Nye, Joseph S., Jr. "Globalization's Democracy Deficit." *Foreign Affairs* 80, 4 (July/August 2001), 2–6.

Quadrennial Defense Review. Washington, DC: United States Department of Defense, September 30, 2002.

Rumsfeld, Donald H. "Transforming the Military." *Foreign Affairs* 81, 3 (May/June 2002), 20–32.

Snow, Donald M. *September 11, 2001: The New Face of War?* New York: Longman, 2002.

Index